It is with great pleasure that I re
mentioned in this biography hav
tions about the issues that I have had over the years. I suspect that a number
of others will welcome those clarifications. The book is comprehensive, but
while giving a clear and complete outline of his ministry in various venues,
nevertheless focuses upon Clark's views and the responses of various persons to them over the years. The issues over the knowledge of God are thoroughly and fairly discussed, and the reader is left to decide whether or not
Clark's view of human and divine attributes is "cold" as has been charged.
The author seems not to think so, yet on this as on other issues, allows you
determine your own opinion from the information that he presents rather
objectively. For those who want to know more about the history and work
of Gordon Clark, I can confidently recommend this book.

—**Jay Adams**, Founder of The Institute for Nouthetic Studies

Dr. Cornelius Van Til was absolutely correct when he stated that " . . . Clark"
was an " . . . outstanding Christian Philosophers of our time." How can
anyone disagree with Dr. Van Til's assessment of Dr. Gordon H. Clark? In
this book on the life of Gordon H. Clark, you have the factual events that
drove a wedge between Clark and Van Til. Even today the heart of the issue
is hidden beneath years of misunderstanding. This is the definitive book
on Clark's life, researched and documented by Doug Douma. A must read
by laymen, students, pastors, and professors who love Reformed Christian
Philosophy and Apologetics.

—**Dr. Kenneth Gary Talbot**, President, Whitefield Theological Seminary and College

To understand Gordon H. Clark is to understand the New Evangelicalism.
As professor of philosophy at Wheaton College in the 1930s he influenced
beyond measure their emerging leaders: Carl Henry, Ed Carnell, Paul
Jewett, and Ed Clowney. His bigger-picture understanding of culture and
Christianity and trenchant way of critiquing Liberalism went far beyond the
good-intentioned but shallow Fundamentalism that had gone before. His
evaluation of Barth and Bultmann was searchingly critical while recognizing their rejection of the old Liberalism. Cornelius Van Til had also been
critical of previous Christian thinking, but his approach had led to a new
Reformed narrowness while Clark's own scholarly way provided a more balanced response for our way ahead. I appreciate Douglas Douma's thorough
and sympathetic treatment of GHC's work, and I am confident he will show
us from Clark where we may find new hope and vigor to focus the Christian
gospel against humanistic culture.

—**Dr. D. Clair Davis**, Professor of Church History Emeritus, Westminster Theological
Seminary

This fascinating account of the life and work of controversial Presbyterian theologian Gordon H. Clark is not only of interest to every Reformed believer, especially every Reformed minister of the gospel. But it is also of urgent importance. Again at the beginning of the 21st century, the fundamental doctrines for which Clark contended, and suffered, are lively, urgent issues in the Reformed and Presbyterian churches. Indeed, they are at issue also in the more broadly evangelical communities. These doctrines include Scripture as the infallible source and standard of the knowledge of God; the logical and, therefore, comprehensible (understandable, knowable) nature of divine revelation in the Bible; the real and binding authority of the Reformed, in Clark's case Presbyterian, creeds; the particularity and sovereignty of the gracious, saving call of the gospel, in opposition to the popular theory of an inefficacious "well-meant offer" to all alike; and more. Presbyterians neglect or dismiss Clark to their peril.

—**David J. Engelsma**, Professor of Theology Emeritus, Protestant Reformed Theological Seminary

Gordon H. Clark was one of the most significant Christian thinkers of the 20th century. Through numerous books and effective classroom teaching at more than four institutions of higher education he influenced several generations of scholars, especially in Presbyterian and Evangelical circles. Biographer Douglas Douma has skillfully woven distinctive elements of Clark's philosophical and theological thought through this thoroughly researched account of his life, including his activity as a churchman, revealing much about American Presbyterian history. His narrative also interestingly captures much of the humanness of Gordon Clark the man.

—**Dr. William S. Barker**, Professor of Church History Emeritus, Westminster Theological Seminary

Dr. Clark had a significant influence on my desire to study philosophy. I studied with him during the summer of 1969. His emphasis on logic aroused my philosophic mind to think through certain issues from a rational standpoint. He also increased my understanding of Calvinism and solidified many doctrines that I had already come to accept.

—**Dr. Erwin W. Lutzer**, Senior Pastor, The Moody Church, Chicago

A biography of Gordon Clark, which he did not think necessary, is long overdue. Douma has admirably corrected this oversight. His work is well researched, accurate, and interesting. Most importantly, it gives the historical context in which Clark's contributions to Christian thought arose.

—**Dr. Frank Walker**, Professor of Historical Theology, City Seminary Sacramento

Gordon Clark had a small but loyal following of those who learned and gained much from his philosophical approach and thought. One said that Clark was "one of the profoundest evangelical Protestant philosophers of our time." Another celebrated him as "one of the greatest Christian thinkers of our century." Yet, for all of his many books, more than 40 during his academic career, and his scholarly articles, Clark is not well known in the Evangelical church. This biography of Gordon Clark's life and thought was written with the desire to reintroduce us to a man who, though not well known, had an impact in his generation, and through his writings continues this influence. Readers will be reminded and challenged by Clark's indefatigable commitment to and defense of propositional revelation against all other philosophical thoughts. In fact, Clark's commitment to Scripture as the revealed Word of the sovereign God is so foundational to his thought that his view is usually called scripturalism. This biography casts new light on a leading scholar and thinker of the 20th century, who yet dead continues to speak and influence.

—**Dr. Dominic A. Aquila**, President, New Geneva Theological Seminary, The Aquila Report

Doug Douma is to be commended for this biography; it is fascinating and thoroughly researched. Gordon Clark's passion was Biblical truth and his gift was logical consistency. He also had the fortitude to confront anyone whose views were not Biblical or consistent. This of course frustrated and even angered many. While living in his home during my college years, I particularly observed and learned that he, my grandfather, was more gracious, patient and brilliant than most of his students and opponents would ever understand.

—**Andrew S. Zeller**, President, Sangre de Cristo Seminary, D.Min.; Th.M.; M.Div.; Chap. COL (Ret.).

I got hooked on reading this book! It was a great experience walking down those trails again. Doug Douma has really done an incredibly good job at documenting everything and putting together an accurate and sober narrative. He has done a wonderful job at putting together the history of Gordon Clark to present him both as a thinker and as a Christian man. I was delighted to learn so many things about the history and views of this truly great Christian philosopher.

—**Dr. John Frame**, Professor of Systematic Theology & Philosophy, Reformed Theological Seminary

The Presbyterian Philosopher

The Presbyterian Philosopher

The Authorized Biography of Gordon H. Clark

DOUGLAS J. DOUMA

Foreword by Lois Zeller and Betsy Clark George

WIPF & STOCK · Eugene, Oregon

THE PRESBYTERIAN PHILOSOPHER
The Authorized Biography of Gordon H. Clark

Wipf & Stock
An Imprint of Wipf and Stock Publishers
199 W. 8th Ave., Suite 3
Eugene, OR 97401

www.wipfandstock.com

PAPERBACK ISBN: 978-1-5326-0724-0
HARDCOVER ISBN: 978-1-5326-0724-4
EBOOK ISBN: 978-1-5326-0723-7

Manufactured in the U.S.A.   JANUARY 3, 2017

To Henry.

Contents

Foreword

THIS BIOGRAPHY IS THE result of the tireless efforts of the author in researching the life of Gordon Haddon Clark. So many facts, both trivial and momentous, have been uncovered in Clark's books and correspondence, that we, his children, have been surprised at learning new details about our father, whom we thought we knew so well!

To many, he was a philosopher, since philosophy is what he taught full-time in four colleges and universities and part-time in at least four other institutions during his sixty-year career. To others, he was a theologian who was faithful to Jesus Christ and relentless in attempting to clarify perplexing passages from the Bible, so that Christians could be consistently "sure of what we hope for and certain of what we do not see" (Heb. 11:1). To a small flock, he was a kind shepherd with a gentle heart. And to a few, he was a driven chess devotee.

To us, his two daughters, he was a patient father who taught us Scripture and Catechism, encouraged us to expand academic pursuits, develop musical talents, or follow whatever interests we had. His emphasis on learning foreign languages has been useful, and a source of joy, throughout our lives. He and our mother established the routine of a quiet home, but the calendar always included summer vacations that took us to fascinating places from Maine to California, with the high point of our teenage years being a marvelous and unforgettable four-month trip to Europe.

To you, the readers of the volume, may this man become a guide to wider experience and deeper thought. But primarily, may he become to you a true brother in Christ, our Lord.

We are thankful to Doug Douma for the years of work he has spent collecting and organizing material from various sources to show what an unusual man Gordon Clark was, and what an impact his writing has had on countless numbers of serious students of philosophy and Christianity. We appreciate this labor of love so very much.

To God be all the glory!

Lois Zeller
Betsy Clark George

Acknowledgments

THIS BOOK WOULD NOT have been possible without the assistance of the Clark family—including Dwight and Lois Zeller, Wyatt and Betsy George, Andrew Zeller, and Nathan Clark George. Their willingness to provide documents, photos, and interviews brought out a greater depth of understanding of "Dad" and "Grandpa" Clark as a man. My thanks are also due to Kenneth Talbot, Clair Davis, and Wayne Sparkman for their considerable support in my research. Excellent contributions improving the biography were also made by Patrick McWilliams, Erick Nieves, David Engelsma, and Felipe Sabino, among others. My editor Lydia Ingram also deserves recognition for her great work.

Abbreviations

Frequent correspondence is designated with the following acronyms:

GHC   Gordon H. Clark
CFHH   Carl F. H. Henry
CVT   Cornelius Van Til
EJC   Edward J. Carnell
JGM   J. Gresham Machen
JOB   J. Oliver Buswell
VRE   V. Raymond Edman

Presbyterian and Reformed Church and Institution Acronyms:

BPC   Bible Presbyterian Church (1937–present day)
CRC   Christian Reformed Church (1857–present day)
OPC   Orthodox Presbyterian Church (1936–present day)
PCA   Presbyterian Church in America (1973–present day)
PCUSA Presbyterian Church in the United States of America (1789–1958)
PC(USA) Presbyterian Church (U.S.A.) (1983–present day)
PCUS   Presbyterian Church in the United States (1861–1983)
PRC   Protestant Reformed Churches (1924–present day)
PTS   Princeton Theological Seminary (1812–present day)
RES   Reformed Episcopal Seminary (1887–present day)
RPCES Reformed Presbyterian Church, Evangelical Synod (1965–1982)
RPC,GS Reformed Presbyterian Church, General Synod (1833–1965)

UPCNA	United Presbyterian Church of North America (1858–1958)
UPCUSA	United Presbyterian Church in The United States of America (1958–1983)
WTS	Westminster Theological Seminary (Philadelphia) (1919-present day)

Archives Referenced:

Wheaton Archives: Office of the President Records (J. Oliver Buswell), 1917–1980, Wheaton College Archives and Special Collections.
BGC Archives: Billy Graham Center Archives, Wheaton College.
PCA Archives: Presbyterian Church in America Archives, St. Louis.
WTS Archives: Westminster Theological Seminary Archives, Philadelphia.
SDCS: Clark Collection, Clark Library at the Sangre de Cristo Seminary, Westcliffe, CO.

Where possible, all books referenced in footnotes are the editions which Dr. Clark owned and are housed in the Clark Collection at the Sangre de Cristo Seminary Clark Library.

Introduction

THESE PAGES TELL THE story of Gordon Haddon Clark (1902–1985), a great thinker who held that Christianity, as a logically coherent system, is superior to all other philosophies. In propounding this view, he encountered frequent and fervent opposition. This opposition came, in fact, most often not from the secular world but from within the very denominations of which he was an active member. This biography seeks to explain why his thought was so profound, why resistance mounted against him, and how the results of his struggles significantly impacted American Presbyterianism and American Christianity at large. Additionally, this book calls for a re-appraisal of Clark's views, which have been maligned by the controversies in which he figured. Understanding and applying these views would significantly fortify Christians combating the various irrationalistic, non-systematic, and non-Reformed views prevalent in today's churches.

Gordon Clark was a respected Christian philosopher who wrote extensively in defense of the Christian faith. Although Clark remains relatively unknown to most Christians today, he has received praise from a range of powerful voices in American theological circles. When asked which twentieth-century theologians will still be read 500 years hence, the well-known American pastor and theologian R.C. Sproul answered, "Gordon Clark." Indeed, Clark's literary works contained such breadth of material and depth of insight that Carl F.H. Henry, the first editor of *Christianity Today*,[1] wrote of him, "Among articulate Christian philosophers on the American scene,

---

1. *Christianity Today* (1956-present day) is an evangelical Christian magazine founded by Billy Graham.

xix

none has addressed the broad sweep of contemporary concerns from an evangelical Protestant view more comprehensively than Gordon Clark."[2]

What then, did Clark believe? Why should Christians, particularly Christian theologians, wrestle with his philosophy and apply his insights? Clark provides perhaps the best philosophical understanding of Protestant Christianity. For its breadth and depth, his work can be difficult at times. He challenges us to question basic assumptions of the world, and of our faith, and he forces us to think in a rigorous, logical fashion. This study then is intended to serve as introduction to his thought, to explain them as clearly and as simply as possible given their often complex nature, and to show how these thoughts developed within the general course of his life.

The contours of Clark's philosophy are as follows: He argued that any valid system of thought needed to be grounded in foundational first principles. From such principles, known as axioms, one could deduce further truths about the world. Most of the philosophies of his day, Clark felt, were hopelessly adrift because they were based on sensory experience. At the root of much of the problem was the philosophy of the empiricists, those who argued that ultimate truth could be derived solely or primarily from observation. Empiricism today is most visible in the sciences, where broadcasted discoveries based on observation can sometimes appear to contradict Biblical truths. Christians then find themselves on the defensive, and giving their own theories based also on observations to derive more palpable results. But Clark felt such competition for interpreting data was useless, since one could never derive absolute truths from observation. Turning to both sides, Christian and secular, Clark declared that one could, through empirical testing alone, neither confirm nor deny the validity of the theory of human evolution, the validity of miracles, nor even the existence of God. Clark's arguments against empiricism were extensive because he believed it was necessary for Christians to reject empiricism and seek higher ground to understand God and His will.

If however, science could neither prove nor disprove God, how can one come to know the world? Rationalist philosophers like Plato, Descartes, and Spinoza had argued that one could derive a theory of the world, or even a proof of God, through logical reasoning alone. Clark agreed that a correct theory needed to be logical, and much of his writings were focused on finding logical contradictions in competing philosophies. A good Christian theology, he argued as well, needs to be logical and recognize that logic is the very way in which God thinks. But Clark took exception to theories that used logic as a starting point. From logic alone he saw that the Rationalist

2. Henry, "A Wide and Deep Swath." 11.

philosophers were unable to advance their philosophy beyond a few basic contentions.

In recognizing the insufficiency of empiricism, and indeed all secular philosophies to provide for any knowledge, Clark arrived at the thought that knowledge can only come through a third method, relying neither on experiential data nor derived from logic alone. This knowledge, he claimed, was only possible through revelation, as provided through the Bible. The essence of Clark's philosophy then is to show why all other axioms end in failure and how Biblical revelation as a given axiom provides man with a coherent and beneficial worldview.

The philosophy of Gordon Clark has been called Scripturalism because of his reliance on the truth of Scripture as his fundamental axiom or presupposition. Stated simply, his axiom is "The Bible is the Word of God." Scripturalism teaches that the Bible is a revelation of truth from God, who Himself determines truth and is the source of all truth. In this theory, the propositions of Scripture are true because they are given by inspiration of God, who cannot lie. For Clark, the Bible, the sixty-six books accepted by most Protestant churches, is a set of true propositions. All knowledge currently available to man are these propositions along with any additional propositions that can be logically deduced from them.

Clark believed his philosophy to be aligned with, or even derived from, the Presbyterian Church's *Westminster Confession of Faith*. In his writings, he wasn't usually saying anything new—rather, he was repeating the teachings of Augustine, John Calvin, and of the divines who framed the *Westminster Confession*. In his dedication to the *Confession*, his very ordination vow, he could be considered the most strict, rigorous philosopher in the Presbyterian tradition. As per his academic background, having earned his Ph.D. at the University of Pennsylvania, he often employed philosophical terms in his writings, not always the biblical language which may be of greater familiarity to Christians.

He also employed the insights of presuppositionalism, a philosophical approach to which he helped formulate. Along with James Orr, Abraham Kuyper, and Cornelius Van Til, Gordon Clark was a pioneer in the field of presuppositionalism or presuppositional apologetics, which seeks to understand the underlying commitments of one's worldview, commitments recognized or not. Presuppositionalism asks: What are the preconditions of knowledge? What must reality be like if we are to be capable of knowing reality? Must not the ground on which we stand be sufficiently solid to support our weight?

Clark employed the tests of consistency and of explanatory power to show why biblical Christianity should be preferred over other philosophies. He wrote,

> "If a philosopher ponders the basic principles of Aristotle, Kant, or even Sartre, he will do so by considering how well the author succeeds in solving his problems. So too it should be with Christian revelation as an axiom. Does revelation make knowledge possible? Does revelation establish values and ethical norms? Does revelation give a theory of politics? And are the results consistent with one another? We can judge the acceptability of an axiom only by its success in producing a system."[3]

Let us judge Clark by his own standards.

Why would one write a biography of a philosopher? Gordon Clark questioned this very thought late in his life when his publisher John Robbins had mentioned his own intentions of writing such a book on Clark. Clark insisted that no one would be interested in his life; he had done nothing exciting, he had neither led armies nor conquered kingdoms, nor discovered a cure for cancer.[4] In fact, in large measure I felt the same at the beginning of this project, for this project did not begin as a biography, but as a summary of Clark's philosophical thought. Quickly, however, I realized that Clark's theology and philosophy were not restricted to the confines of the academy, but had significant ramifications for Church history. An unimposing 5' 7", Clark fought no wars and conquered no kingdoms. Yet he was a leading figure in many theological wars fought for the Kingdom of God. And these wars for the minds and souls of men were every bit as crucial as physical wars between nations.

Clark's life intertwined with the history of twentieth-century Presbyterianism in America. From the Fundamentalist-Modernist controversy[5] in the Presbyterian Church in the United States of America during the 1920s and '30s, to the growth by acquisition of the Presbyterian Church in America in the 1980s, he was directly involved in most of the major American Presbyterian denominational separations and mergers of his era.[6] Neverthe-

3. Clark, *Introduction to Christian Philosophy*, 59–60.

4. Robbins, *Gordon H. Clark, Personal Recollections*, 1.

5. The Fundamentalist-Modernist Controversy was a religious controversy in the 1920s and 1930s that led to divisions in many American Christian denominations.

6. The Presbyterian Church in the United States of America (PCUSA) existed from 1789–1958 until its merger with the United Presbyterian Church in North America. The Presbyterian Church in America (PCA) was formed in 1973 and is presently the largest conservative Presbyterian church in the United States.

less, second only to his voluminous writings, Clark is largely known today for the controversy regarding some of his theological views surrounding his 1944 ordination in the Orthodox Presbyterian Church. This controversy, called the Clark-Van Til Controversy after its leading adversaries, has brought continued debate over the doctrines involved and has engendered some lasting animosity between the theological parties it helped to define.

As much as the story of Gordon Clark connects with American Presbyterian history, the philosophy of Gordon Clark engages the most important Presbyterian confession, the *Westminster Confession of Faith*. Time and again in Clark's life and works, his commitment to the system of belief described in this historic document is revealed. To evidence this point, the teaching of the *Confession* that "the Bible is given by inspiration of God to be the rule of faith and life" prompted him to fight against the theology of the Auburn Affirmation[7] in the Presbyterian Church in the United States of America and to join a reforming movement that later founded the Orthodox Presbyterian Church. The *Confession* set the boundaries for Clark's philosophy beyond which he would strive not to venture. But Clark's strict adherence to the *Confession* proved to be the cause of repeated controversies. His adherence to its Calvinist foundations led to conflict with the administration at Wheaton College, and his reading of the *Confession* that "God has neither parts nor passions" supported his sometimes controversial view that God has no emotions.[8] Notwithstanding the controversies his adherence to it engendered, Clark remained convinced of the truth of the system of doctrine contained in the *Westminster Confession of Faith*, a truth centered in biblical revelation alone.

Uncompromising in his thoughts, and unwilling to back down from philosophical challenges, Clark made few friends in higher circles of American theologians. He was not a self-promoter; nor did he actively seek a popular audience. In fact, he once admitted to a fellow church minister to being the world's worst diplomat.[9] Instead, Clark was content to develop his thoughts quietly and in the relative isolation of his academic posi-

---

7. The Auburn Affirmation was written in 1924 by a Modernist movement in the PCUSA that sought to prevent five fundamental doctrines from becoming requirements for ordination in the church.

8. Clark's position, known as theological anthropopathism, is the standard position of Reformed orthodoxy and argues that just as the physical features attributed to God in the Bible (hands, wings, etc.) are anthropomorphisms (attribution of human form or other characteristics to anything other than a human being) given to allow man to understand, so also God's emotions in the Bible are anthropopathisms (the ascription of human feelings to something not human); likewise, not attributes God has, but figures of speech.

9. GHC to Robert Strong, May 9, 1942. PCA Archives, 309/56.

tions – thoughts which he published in an extensive set of books. Clark's participation in theological controversies earned him some press, alternately some notoriety and fame; but he was ultimately viewed as being on the losing side of these controversies because many of his views remained in the minority within the institutions where he labored. Clark's students often carried on his views, but few could completely understand them as few had the academic training to understand their philosophical complexity. At Westminster Theological Seminary, Clark's views were pushed aside in the wake of the Clark-Van Til Controversy, and the views of his rival, Cornelius Van Til, were promoted instead. That American religious historians have neglected Clark speaks more to circumstance (to his place in the practical power structure of the church, and to the myopia of fast-paced American religious life) than it does to the strength or weakness of his arguments.

In many ways, Clark's personality matched his philosophy. He insisted on proper logic in the classroom, and the very idea of being logical became his most well-known attribute. His rigorous insistence on correct logic made his writings eminently clear, but often frustrated those whom he knew personally. At times students were afraid to ask him questions as they suspected he would respond with a critique of their logic. Additionally, Clark's dedication to his logical philosophy alienated the administration of Wheaton College where he was teaching and brought a complaint against his ordination in the Orthodox Presbyterian Church. Yet despite the frequent attribution to him of a personal "coldness" to match his "cold" logic, he was known also as an incredibly kind man and even a jokester. His kindness was perhaps best shown in his willingness to teach students after class in his home and in his dedication to his family and church. His extant audio lectures are replete with jokes. For many who shared remembrances of him for this biography the first thing they often recalled was his comedy.

Clark's true import, however, is that, in an age of increasing secularization and rising atheism, he put up an intellectual defense of the Christian faith. This faith, he believed, was a system. All of its parts link together, a luxury of no other philosophy. The Scriptures exhort us to "Be prepared to give an answer to everyone who asks you to give the reason for the hope that you have" (1 Peter 3:15). This requires that we love God fully with our minds and study His Word. Only from God's revelation can we be assured of the truth of our reasons.

The supporters of Clark at present are few in number and lacking in high-profile academic posts, but those who comprehend his life's work recognize the power of his arguments. His theology has something to teach us, as does his life itself. If we ultimately reject Clark's views, we should do so only after thoroughly grappling with them. And if we are honest with ourselves, we will discover much in his works that challenge fundamental beliefs, whether they be beliefs in science, philosophy, or mainstream Christianity.

To address the entirety of Clark's philosophical writings would require a volume far larger than the present one. I have endeavored therefore to discuss only those topics which I have deemed to be integral to Clark's life and philosophy. Certainly, zealous "Clarkians" will find fault in that I have insufficiently addressed Clark's views on philosophical topics such as "common ground," traducianism, or the noetic effects of sin (among countless others he addressed). I must therefore beg the reader to find fault not in what I haven't written, but in what I have.

I am proud to say that Gordon Clark's writings helped keep me solidly grounded in the Christian faith when I was looking for a defense of it. Clark was not a compromiser, and this is perhaps why I have gravitated so much to him. His uncompromising stance shows a Christianity which is in fact intellectual, not relying simply on appeals to emotion or experience. It is my hope that the readers of this biography are strengthened in their confidence of the truth of the Christian faith through the arguments made by Gordon Clark and life he lived out.

Chapter 1

The Presbyterian Heritage of Gordon Clark

Clark—an English surname ultimately derived from the Latin *clericus* meaning "scribe," "secretary," or a scholar within a religious order, referring to someone educated.

GORDON HADDON CLARK (1902–1985) was born into the Christian tradition of Old School Presbyterianism. Known for requiring ministers to subscribe to the system of Protestant Christian doctrine contained in the *Westminster Confession of Faith* (1646), Old School Presbyterianism shaped Clark's understanding of the world. In his career as a theologian and a Christian philosopher, Clark defended the Confession and sought to keep his own philosophical views in line with its teachings. In fact, it could be said that he was a philosopher of the *Westminster Confession*, truly a Presbyterian philosopher.[1]

Historical circumstances initially set Clark on this course. In fact, he was the son of a Presbyterian minister who, in turn, was the son of a Presbyterian minister. For two generations then, starting with his paternal grandfather, James Armstrong Clark (1831–1894), Presbyterian ministry

---

1. The term "Presbyterian" is derived from the Greek word *presbuteros*, meaning elder or pastor. Churches in Scotland and England took the name "Presbyterian" to distinguish their style of elder-led church governance from the hierarchical Church of England. Presbyterian denominations also adhere to Reformed theology, exemplified by John Calvin's teachings.

was of central importance to the family. While Gordon Clark never met his grandfather, who died before Gordon was born, he did travel as a child with his parents to visit relatives in western Pennsylvania where the family had lived since shortly after James arrived from Scotland in 1854.[2]

Digging into the Clark family line, we can see how he inherited the Christian doctrines that shaped the core of his thought. Basic knowledge of his grandfather, James Clark, survives in a fifteen-page handwritten autobiography written sometime in the late nineteenth century.[3] Because the content of the autobiography ends abruptly in 1858, and other sources on his life are scant, we can only piece together the basic contours of James' life.[4] What we do know shows that he was deeply committed to the Presbyterian faith. James was born December 4, 1831, to William Baldwin Clark[5] (1791–1858) and Jean Armstrong (1796–18??) in Hawick, Scotland, and baptized at Hawick's East Bank Associate Church.[6] As a child, he was affected by the Disruption of 1843, which fractured the established Church of Scotland. In this seminal event in Presbyterian history, some 450 ministers of the church's total of 1,200 ministers broke away and formed the Free Church

2. In the possession of the Clark family, Gordon Clark's baby book relates that as a child, Gordon traveled with his parents to visit relatives living in western Pennsylvania, where some of the family had lived since shortly after James Armstrong Clark arrived from Scotland in 1854.

3. Clark, "An Account of Life of Rev Jas. A. Clark."

4. A notable reference in James Clark's autobiography is to one of his mother's ancestors: "My great-great-grandfather was John Armstrong of Glenlacky Hall, famous in the history of the border warfare." This John Armstrong, known as Johnnie of Gilnockie, was a well-known border reiver, or raider, on the borderlands of Scotland and England in the early sixteenth century. Operating from lands scarred by centuries of war, Johnnie and Clan Armstrong disdained to take orders from either the King of England or the King of Scotland. To keep the region in fear and his income flowing, Johnnie pursued the centuries-old *modus operandi* of late-night horseback raids and blackmailing towns with threats of burning them down. His wealth and reputation, however, roused the jealous ire of seventeen-year-old King James V of Scotland who deemed the reivers' forays a threat to peace with neighboring England. In the summer of 1530, James V issued a royal writ of safe passage to Johnnie Armstrong and his followers to attend peace talks over a hunting expedition. However, upon their arrival, they found they had been tricked. Thirty-seven men, including Johnnie Armstrong, were captured and hanged at the chapel of Caerlanrig, a few miles south of Hawick, Scotland. The "Ballad of Johnnie Armstrong," commemorates the infamous reiver. See: Fraser, *Steel Bonnets*, 225–236.

5. Two books in the Gordon H. Clark Collection at the Sangre de Cristo Seminary library contain the signature of William Baldwin Clark. These books are *The Intuitions of the Mind* and *Defence of Fundamental Truth* both authored by the prominent Scottish philosopher James McCosh.

6. The Associate Church (the "Seceders") was formed from the "First Secession" out of the Church of Scotland in 1733.

of Scotland. The secession came as a response to the state's encroachment upon the spiritual affairs of the church. Although James was only twelve years of age at the time of the Disruption, he recalled in his autobiography that at that time he had "religious impressions & dispositions" and "took sides against the establishment." By the time he was fourteen years of age he had "taken sides with the Calvinist docs" and "made a fair offer in argument on the five points [of Calvinism]." Soon after the Disruption, James's parents chose to join a Free Church congregation and James's father, William, was elected as an elder. A few years later, James left home to attend the Free Church Normal College in Edinburgh.[7] Following his graduation, he became a teacher at the Free Church Normal School in Yarrow, Scotland (1851–1854).

Historical knowledge of Presbyterianism came to Gordon Clark through family stories of the church in Scotland and in the United States. In fact, for generations, Clark family history was largely tied up with the history of the church. Although Gordon Clark's grandfather James arrived on American shores in 1854, James's brother Will had preceded him by a few years. Will found in the United States a "very large field of usefulness" for the ministry. Inspired by the potential for ministry in the U.S., James resigned his teaching position in Scotland and followed his brother's path across the ocean.[8] On April 24, 1854, just weeks prior to leaving Scotland, James married Margaret Scott (1835–1881), satisfying his mother's wish that he would not emigrate alone. Once in the United States, he taught bookkeeping and was the principal of a business college which he owned and operated in Philadelphia for a year before selling its assets and returning to college as a student. He enrolled first at Franklin College in Ohio, but left in 1855 to attend Allegheny Seminary where he studied theology, graduating in 1858. Upon his arrival in the U.S., James joined the Associate Presbyterian Church, an ethnically Scottish denomination with roots reaching back over a century in the United States.[9] When, in 1858, this church merged with other Scottish Seceder and Covenanter churches in America to form the United Presbyterian Church of North America (UPCNA), James, who had been licensed to preach in the Associate Presbyterian Church in 1857, joined the new body in short order and was ordained in 1859. He preached for the remainder of his life in the UPCNA at a number of churches in Butler County, Pennsylvania. After the death of his first wife, Margaret Scott,

7. The Free Church Normal College was founded in 1845 to train teachers in the Free Church of Scotland.

8. Clark, "An Account of Life of Rev Jas. A. Clark."

9. The Associate Presbytery of Philadelphia was constituted on November 2, 1753. McBee and Stewart, *History of the Associate Presbyterian Church of North America*, 17.

in 1881, James married Frances N. Wilson in 1884. In total, he had two daughters and seven sons.[10]

Among the children born to James Armstrong Clark and his first wife Margaret Scott was the father of Gordon Clark, David Scott Clark (1859–1939). Although few records remain providing details of David's early life, it is possible to provide a basic outline of his academic track.[11] According to United Presbyterian Church records, David graduated in 1884 from Mount Union College in Ohio, received an M.A. from the same college in 1886, and was awarded an honorary DD in 1908.[12] He also studied at Princeton Theological Seminary (1883–1885), as well as at the Free Church College in Edinburgh (1885–1886), before returning to Princeton where he graduated in 1887 with a Master of Divinity degree.

David's learning would prove influential in Gordon Clark's upbringing. David equipped his son with a set of competencies that other young students would not learn until seminary, including knowledge of Presbyterian history, church doctrine, and the nature of recent events in the church. From his father, Gordon learned about the influence of Princeton Theological Seminary on the American religious scene. David based his views on first-hand experience. As a student at Princeton in the 1880s, he witnessed the institution at the peak of its historical influence. In the first one hundred years of the seminary (1812–1912), it had graduated nearly 6,000 ministers, 1,000 more than any other seminary in America, and these students spread Princetonian ideas far and wide.[13] Leading the seminary at the time of David's attendance were the prominent theologians A. A. Hodge (1823–1886) and B. B. Warfield (1851–1921). These two improbably-named men stood firm on the doctrine of the Bible's inspiration and authority, an essential element of the seminary's conservative theology that came to be known as "Princeton Theology."

Alongside Princeton Theology, the seminary was also a stronghold for Old School Presbyterianism. The term *Old School Presbyterianism* is traced back to 1837 when a schism tore the Presbyterian Church in the United

10. *Minutes of the Thirty-Seventh General Assembly of the United Presbyterian Church of North America*, 786–787.

11. A single extant letter from David's early years, dated July 18, 1880, is a letter of recommendation from James A. Brush, David's professor at Mount Union College, Ohio. In the letter, Brush writes to a prospective employer that David is a student in good standing who is "industrious, faithful, and thorough" and is seeking a teaching position. The letter is in the Clark Collection at the Sangre de Cristo Seminary Library, 1/53.

12. DD is a Doctor of Divinity, traditionally an honorary degree used to recognize the ministerial accomplishments of the recipient.

13. Noll, "The Princeton Theology," 24.

States of America into two camps. Known as the Old School-New School controversy, the resulting schism separated the two "schools of thought" from 1837 to 1865. In this episode, as throughout much of Presbyterian history, the church faced a difficult question regarding the extent to which subscription to the *Westminster Confession of Faith,* that is, a profession of belief in and promise to teach and defend its doctrines, should be required of ministers. The theologians of the New School embraced revivalism and modified a number of the historical Calvinistic doctrines.[14] The Old School theologians, on the other hand, were largely suspicious of the New School's views and advocated subscription to the *Westminster Confession of Faith* as a check on their perceived deleterious effects. The two schools officially merged in 1865, but factions within the church were still visible decades later.[15]

David S. Clark found his pastorates in Philadelphia and so Gordon Clark grew up in a city which had long been a hub of Presbyterianism in America. In fact, the very first presbytery (or session of church elders) in the American colonies was formed there in 1706, and the Presbyterian Church in the USA chose to hold its first General Assembly in Philadelphia in 1789. One hundred years later, in 1889, David accepted a call to Wissinoming Presbyterian Church, just outside of Philadelphia, for his first position as a minister.[16] It was at this church that David Clark met Miss Elizabeth Yates Haddon (1878–1931). In retelling his father's story, Gordon Clark wrote, "One day a girl appeared in church wearing a red hat and apparently the attraction was so obvious that she never wore it again. They were married in 1895 and I was born in 1902."[17] In 1894, David took charge of the Memorial

14. *Revival,* as Protestant theology has used the word for 250 years, means God's quickening visitation of his people, touching their hearts and deepening his work of grace in their lives. It is essentially a corporate occurrence, an enlivening of individuals not in isolation but together. See: Ferguson and Packer, *New Dictionary of Theology,* 588.

15. The *Westminster Confession of Faith,* formulated in 1646 as part of the *Westminster Standards* (including also the Shorter and Longer Catechisms), provides a systematic summary of the teachings of the Bible according to traditional Reformed Presbyterian theology. Although subscription to the *Westminster Confession of Faith* places a number of requirements for belief on those seeking ordination in a Presbyterian church, it also serves as an upper limit on these requirements. These requirements apply to officers of the church only (pastors, elders, and deacons) and not to the laity. Under this arrangement, standards of belief are set which give unity to the leadership, while preserving freedom for the laity to attend and become members of the church without necessarily agreeing to the WCF *in toto.*

16. David S. Clark was officially ordained and installed as pastor at Wissinoming, Pennsylvania, on May 10, 1889.

17. Clark, "Gordon Clark Remembrances." 6.

Collegiate Chapel and, in 1899, organized a church at the same site on the corner of Nineteenth and York streets. The congregation, which changed its name to Bethel Presbyterian Church, flourished under David's tenure, so that by 1912 it counted 340 members.[18]

Shortly after the founding of Bethel Presbyterian Church, Gordon Haddon Clark was born to the Rev. David Scott Clark and his wife, Elizabeth Haddon Clark, on August 31, 1902.[19] He was their only child. Growing up in the shadow of Bethel Presbyterian Church, Gordon gained from his father the wisdom of years of practical experience as a Presbyterian minister as well as insight into writing for publication and inspiration for academic work. The elder Clark wrote three theological books, including a commentary on the book of Revelation titled *The Message From Patmos*.[20] He also penned multiple position pieces for Presbyterian journals.[21] As an instructor in doctrine at the Presbyterian School for Christian Workers (Tennent College) in Philadelphia from 1917–1929, and later as an instructor in philosophy at Eastern University,[22] also in Philadelphia, David Clark kept one foot in the academic world. By all indication, Gordon's respect and

18. *Directory of Bethel Presbyterian Church.* See also: Hallock, "Among the Churches," 113.

19. He was given the name Gordon after the popular British Army Major-General and Christian evangelist Charles George Gordon (1833–1885), known for a number of military campaigns, including training and leading a Chinese army to victory in the Taiping Rebellion in the 1860s. Lois (née Clark) Zeller and Dr. Dwight Zeller, interview by Douglas Douma, Sangre de Cristo Seminary, 29 May 2014.

20. David S. Clark, *The Message From Patmos* (Reading, PA: Christian Faith and Life, 1921); ——*A Syllabus of Systematic Theology* (Reading, PA: Christian Faith and Life, 1921); ——*Protestant Unbelief, or Rationalism Past and Present* (Reading, PA: Christian Faith and Life, 1937).

21. David S. Clark, "Christianity in Its Modern Expression," *The Presbyterian*, 21 September 1921.; ——"Dr. McCosh and Evolution," *The Presbyterian*, 12 January 1922.; ——"The Philosophical Basis of Christianity," *The Presbyterian*, 11 December 1924.; ——"The Modernist's Creed," *The Presbyterian*, 13 March 1924.; ——"Bodily Resurrection Scientifically Sound," *The Presbyterian*, 5 June 1924.; ——"Modernism and the Higher Criticism," *The Presbyterian*, 1 January 1925.; ——"The Reality of Me," *The Presbyterian*, 25 June 1925.; ——"Theology and Evolution," *The Princeton Theological Review* 23, no. 2 (1925): 193–212.; ——"Paul a Modernist!" *The Presbyterian*, 24 June 1925.; ——"Pantheistic Modernism," *The Presbyterian*, 5 September 1929.; ——"Super-Behaviorism," *The Presbyterian*, 6 March 1930.; ——"The Independent Board and Its Critics," *Christianity Today* 5, no. 7 (1934): 159–160, 167.; ——"Disgraceful Doings," *The Presbyterian Guardian* 6, no 3 (1935).; ——"Relativity and the Absolute," *Christianity Today* 7, no. 1 (1936).; ——"Barthian Fog," *The Presbyterian*, 2 December 1937.

22. Eastern University existed c. 1927–1935. It should not be confused with the Eastern University located in St. Davids, Pennsylvania, which was then called Eastern Baptist Theological Seminary.

admiration for his father was deep, and the ultimate inspiration he gleaned from his father as role model cannot be overestimated.[23]

Presbyterianism also ran deep in the Haddon family, Gordon Clark's maternal line. The Haddons came from English Presbyterian stock in the county of Devon, England. Gordon's maternal grandfather, Thomas Deacon Haddon (1834–1914), was not a minister, but had mastered biblical Greek in his free time apart from his work as a wool carder.[24][25] Gordon's uncle, Charles K. Haddon (1867–1935), was also a churchgoing man, a supporter of prohibition, and, for fifteen years (1906–1921), the vice president of the Victor Talking Machine Company, a leading manufacturer of phonographs and phonograph records.[26] The company was founded by Charles's close friend Eldridge Johnson and later successfully defended itself in a court case on patent infringement raised by Thomas Edison. Shortly after Charles retired, he traveled around the world twice, first on the R.M.S. *Samaria* in 1923, then on the R.M.S. *Franconia* in 1927. After each voyage, Charles published the letters he had written and received while abroad.[27] Charles's wealth not only afforded his world travels but also made it possible for his father (Gordon Clark's maternal grandfather), Thomas Deacon Haddon, to retire at sixty years of age and devote much of his remaining years to studying the Bible.[28]

Gordon Clark embraced his Presbyterian heritage. When he was a child his father taught him the *Westminster Shorter Catechism*—a question and answer summary of the basic beliefs of the Presbyterian church. He also followed his father's interest in theology by reading from the many books in their home library.[29] Local neighborhood children associated Clark so strongly with the church, that they gave him the nickname "Clerg," a

23. The effect of this bond can be gauged by Clark's attempt to have his father's sermons published following his father's death. See: Peter de Visser of Eerdmans Publishing to GHC, 10 July 1939, PCA Archives, 309/59. See also: B. D. Zondervan to GHC, n.d. circa 1939, in the original papers of Gordon Clark, A.E. 0.4, 1/128.

24. Elizabeth Clark George, "Life with Father," *Gordon H. Clark, Personal Recollections,* ed. John W. Robbins (Jefferson, MD: The Trinity Foundation, 1989), 17.

25. Carding is a manufacturing process which disentangles and cleans wool to produce long continuous fibers. Though the Haddon's had Presbyterian roots, Thomas Deacon Haddon himself was a member of the Plymouth Brethren. Clark, "Gordon Clark Remembrances."

26. "I am unqualifiedly in favor of National Prohibition."—Haddon, *The Mixer and Server,* 35. See also: Aldridge, "Confidential History of the Victor Talking Machine Co."

27. Haddon, *Memoirs of a Trip Around The World* (privately printed book, 1923).; ——*Around the World in the Southern Hemisphere* (privately printed book, 1927).

28. Clark, *Lord God of Truth,* 46.

29. Henry, "A Wide and Deep Swath," 49.

dig at his father's status as a member of the clergy.[30] Looking back on his Presbyterian heritage later in life, Clark recalled:

> Well, I've known about Scottish Presbyterianism from both sides of my family; I guess you call it heritage. So many of us are blindly proud of our heritage without knowing what it is. But in my experience I think heritage is like a bedtime story of grandpa's reminiscence. It's really kind of a naive thing like the Jews remembering the wilderness and the walls of Jericho. It's to give you a respect for courage as well as a feeling of worth as a descendant of Abraham."[31]

With the family's income dependent on David's job as a pastor, Clark grew up fairly poor. He noted in a handwritten document of his recollections that there was one time when the church was nine months in arrears paying his father's salary. He also noted that they did not have electricity in their house until about 1914. It was only after Clark was in college that the family received a great boon when Gordon's wealthy uncle Charles (Elizabeth Haddon Clark's brother) gave them checks at Christmas. Each Christmas in the late 1920s and early 1930s Charles gave Clark and his cousins $100 checks. To Clark's mother he gave checks of $1000.[32] Charles was also the financial source of Clark's cherished childhood dog Victor, named for the phonograph company.[33]

As Clark grew to adulthood, he deepened his involvement in his father's church by teaching Sunday school lessons and later was appointed the Sunday school superintendent, a post he held for ten years.[34]

Clark also benefitted from the cultural opportunities abounding in the city of Philadelphia. He first professed to be a Christian at a campaign of the popular Presbyterian evangelist-preacher and former professional baseball player Billy Sunday, when his tour came through Philadelphia in early 1915.[35] This revelation may come as a surprise to many who knew Clark later in his life, as Clark's own methods of evangelism diverged greatly from

30. Clark, "The Life of a Minister's Son," 3.

31. *Tartan 1971 Yearbook.*

32. Clark, "Gordon Clark Remembrances."

33. Clark, "Gordon Clark Remembrances." 4.

34. Form letter to prospective Sunday school attendees from Gordon H. Clark, Superintendent, 16 September 1931, PCA Archives. See also: Gordon H. Clark to J. Oliver Buswell, 17 June 1933, PCA Archives. See also: Application to teach in the philosophy department, Wheaton College, signed by Gordon H. Clark, 3 March 1937.

35. Application for appointment as professor of philosophy, Wheaton College, signed by Gordon H. Clark, 5 March 1936.

those of Billy Sunday; Clark emphasized the intellect, whereas Sunday, following the methods of the Second Great Awakening revivalists, appealed to his audience's emotions. Also in Philadelphia, Clark was fortunate to see a performance of the famed composer, John Philip Sousa. Clark himself had an interest in music, for a time taking up the cornet.[36]

Clark's public school education was fairly standard, but it also provided him some advantages. He attended the all-boys Northeast High School of Philadelphia. The school, founded in 1890, was originally known as the Northeast Manual Training School; but by the time Clark attended (1917–1920) it had changed its name, removing the "Manual Training." Although the school retained some hands-on courses after the name change, its main focus became the liberal arts and college preparation.[37] In keeping with that focus, Clark studied a number of languages, including French, Latin, and Greek (not biblical or Koine, but Attic Greek, which was commonly taught at secular high schools in that period). With just two exceptions—a "deficient" in both Latin and Freehand Drawing in his senior year—his report cards show that he received a fairly even mixture of good, fair, and excellent marks.[38]

Given the influence of his family, church, and school, Clark developed into a young man knowledgeable in the Scriptures and the Presbyterian tradition. By the time he left for college at the University of Pennsylvania (Penn), he had a strong Christian faith, was well read, and was conscious of his Presbyterian identity. In many ways, this made him a prime candidate to be an uncompromising scholar and elicited opportunities to delve deeper into philosophy, a subject that required the language and logic skills he had already acquired as a youth. At Penn, Clark improved his knowledge of foreign languages, and as a top student in French language he received the Alliance Française medal from the French language honorary society. He also studied Hebrew under James Alan Montgomery (1866–1949), whom Clark thought was one of the best living scholars then working against biblical criticism.[39] About Professor Montgomery, Clark once wrote, "[He was one] to whose very slender six-feet-five we students all looked up."[40] During his

36. His cornet was a Christmas gift from his uncle Charles. Clark, "Gordon Clark Remembrances."

37. Michener, "A History of the Northeast High School, Philadelphia."

38. Report cards of Gordon H. Clark, 1917–1920, Northeast High School, Philadelphia, PCA Archives, 309/24.

39. Biblical criticism is the discipline of investigating the nature of Scripture from the viewpoint of the Bible having fully human origins. In other words, it is the naturalistic treatment of the Bible as a historic document.

40. Clark, *Johannine Logos*, 8.

undergraduate years, Clark was elected a member of the prestigious honor society, Phi Beta Kappa, but later admitted in a job application to Wheaton College, a college which frowned upon anything even resembling a secret society, to having attended only one meeting and even then just to accept an award.[41]

In 1924, at the age of twenty-two, he received a bachelor's degree in French and proceeded to the graduate school at the University of Pennsylvania, where he studied philosophy. Although he was interested in attending Princeton Theological Seminary, like his father before him, Clark believed modernizing trends at the seminary made it an uncongenial place for true Christian study.[42]

Clark thrived during his graduate years under the impressive philosophy faculty at the University of Pennsylvania. There were four main professors under whom he studied: Edgar A. Singer Jr. (1873–1955), Isaac Husik (1876–1939), Henry Bradford Smith (1882–1938), and William Romaine Newbold (1865–1926).[43] All four of these men had received their doctorates in philosophy from Penn and had taken faculty positions at the university, a path Clark would soon follow. Professor Singer was a philosopher of pragmatism and former student at Harvard of the influential American philosopher and psychologist William James (1842–1910).[44] For years after leaving Penn, Clark remained in correspondence with Singer, likely distilling some of these conversations into his own monograph critiquing William James's philosophy.[45] It was also at Penn that Isaac Husik, a noted historian of Jewish philosophers, introduced Clark to Aristotle's *De Anima*, about which Clark chose to write his dissertation. Clark studied logic at Penn under Henry Bradford Smith, the author of several logic textbooks.[46]

---

41. "In 1926 a fraternity here elected me an honorary member. I accepted the honor and have not attended since."—Application for appointment as professor of philosophy, Wheaton College, signed by Gordon H. Clark, 5 March 1936.

42. "It was my purpose, when I chose to teach philosophy at the University of Pennsylvania rather than study theology at your Seminary, to defend and promulgate an Evangelical faith in Christ. The door has indeed been opened. I do not regret my choice."—GHC to JGM, 25 October 1928, WTS Archives.

43. Newbold, PhD., 1891; Singer, PhD., 1894; Huzik, PhD., 1906; Smith, PhD., 1909.

44. Clark and Nahm. *Philosophical Essays*, vi.

45. Clark, *William James*.

46. Books written by Henry Bradford Smith include: *A Primer of Logic* (Pulaski, VA: B. D. Smith & Bros., 1917); *Non-Aristotelian Logic* (Philadelphia: The College Bookstore, 1919); *A First Book in Logic* (New York: Harper & Brothers Publishers, 1922); and *Foundations of Formal Logic* (Philadelphia: Press of the University of Pennsylvania, 1922).

Clark was impressed by Smith. He wrote, "I find H. B. Smith's *First Book in Logic* very satisfactory."[47]

It was, however, William Romaine Newbold, Clark's advisor for his first two years, of whom he was most fond. This attraction was likely due in part to their shared Christian convictions within the mostly secular philosophy department and university. In addition to being a talented academic, Newbold had eccentric study interests including Gnosticism, hypnosis, telepathy, and cryptography—even attempting to decipher the famed, and still to this day undeciphered, Voynich Manuscript.[48] Newbold demonstrated his affection for Clark in giving him a book inscribed: "To Gordon Haddon Clark, in whose mind the mind of William Romaine Newbold took much delight."[49]

Newbold's premature death in 1926 affected Clark deeply, both personally and professionally. Clark spoke at Newbold's memorial service; he was the only student given that honor.[50] He later recalled the circumstances in which he was offered a teaching position "upon the death of my beloved superior."[51] In Clark's 1929 doctoral dissertation, *Empedocles and Anaxagoras in Aristotle's De Anima*, he praised Newbold for being a "fountain of inestimable value during my first two years of study in Greek philosophy."[52]

With all of the new intellectual thoughts and challenges at Penn, it was appropriate that Clark begin to test himself also as a teacher. In 1924, as a graduate student, he began teaching undergraduate philosophy courses. In 1926 he inherited a course on the history of the philosophy of Christianity

47. GHC to C. Gregg Singer, 6 August 1941, PCA Archives, 309/53.

48. The Voynich Manuscript is an illustrated codex, or book, hand-written in an unknown language and including numerous strange drawings. Though its provenance before 1912—when it was purchased by the Polish book dealer Wilfried Voynich—is mostly unknown, it is generally thought to date from the fifteenth century and to have originated in Italy. With the trust of Wilfried Voynich, Newbold began study of the manuscript in 1919 and made news in 1921 when he made a number of fantastic claims including that he had deciphered parts of the manuscript. Agreeing with Voynich's supposition, Newbold claimed that the manuscript was written by Roger Bacon (1214–1294) and that Bacon had invented the telescope and drawn the arms of the Andromeda galaxy. The entire theory was discredited by their colleague, John Manly, in 1931, after both Newbold's and Voynich's deaths. See: Newbold and Kent, *The Cipher of Roger Bacon*, xi–xxxii. See also: Kennedy Churchill, *The Voynich Manuscript*.

49. Rudolph, "A Truly Great and Brilliant Friend," 100.

50. Program for the Memorial Meeting in Honor of William Romaine Newbold PhD., LLD. (1 December 1926), found stuffed inside the front cover of a Bible belonging to GHC, Sangre de Cristo Seminary Library.

51. GHC to Ned Stonehouse, 8 August 1929, WTS Archives.

52. Clark, "Empedocles and Anaxagoras," preface.

from Dr. Newbold.[53] Clark continued teaching throughout graduate school with just one break to study in Heidelberg, Germany, in the summer of 1927. After the University of Pennsylvania accepted his dissertation, Clark attended the University of Paris (commonly known as the Sorbonne) during the spring and summer of 1930.[54] His knowledge of modern and ancient languages allowed him to effectively study in both Germany and France, as he was able to read each country's philosophers in their own languages. He continued to stay conversant in French and German throughout his life, later corresponding with a pen pal in Germany to help retain his German language skills, and also ensuring that his two daughters learn French. He returned to Penn in the fall of 1930 to continue teaching.

The philosophy department at Penn inspired Clark to think critically and form his own defense of the Presbyterian faith, but his time there also shaped his life in other lasting ways. During his graduate years at Penn, he met his future wife, Ruth Schmidt, who was also studying at the university. They found they had much in common. They were both native Philadelphians, had both attended public high schools (Clark at the all-boys', and Ruth at the all-girls'), and were both conversant in French. Remarkably, Gordon's father had baptized Ruth when she was a child.[55] This baptism took place despite Ruth's family's membership at a Methodist church. It is unclear why her baptism occurred in the Presbyterian Church other than the family's speculation that it might have been because of David Clark's popularity as a pastor. Two books Gordon gave to Ruth, which are now in the Clark Collection in the Clark Library at the Sangre de Cristo Seminary, indicate the blossoming of Gordon and Ruth's relationship. One, dated 1925, was simply given "to Ruth," while a second inscription, dated 1927, is much more warmly inscribed to "My darling Ruthie." While at Penn, Ruth earned both a bachelor's (1928) and a master's degree (1932) in botany. Gordon and Ruth married in March of 1929 and remained together for forty-eight years until Ruth's death in 1977. The couple had two children, Lois Antoinette (b. 1936) and Nancy Elizabeth (b. 1941).

53. Rudolph, "A Truly Great and Brilliant Friend," 100. See Also: GHC to JGM, 25 October 1928, WTS Archives.

54. Very little information could be found regarding Clark's time at the Sorbonne. It seems likely that at least one reason for his attendance was to study Plotinus under the French philosopher, Émile Bréhier. A copy of Bréhier's *La Philosophie Plotin* noted as purchased by Clark in March 1930 is extant in the Clark collection, Sangre de Cristo Seminary library.

55. Certificate of Baptism for Ruth Schmidt, Bethel Presbyterian Church in Philadelphia, signed by Pastor David. S. Clark, 14 October 1907, in the possession of the Clark family.

Following their wedding, the Clarks went on a honeymoon at a chalet in Dorset, Vermont, owned by Bishop Robert Livingston Rudolph (1865–1930), a professor at the Reformed Episcopal Seminary in Philadelphia and Bishop in the Reformed Episcopal Church.

Clark was very close to Bishop Rudolph and his son Robert Knight Rudolph (1906–1986), both of whom spent their careers teaching at Reformed Episcopal Seminary. Clark first came to know of Bishop Rudolph when Rudolph bought up nearly the entire stock of Clark's father's theology textbooks.[56] Clark came across the elder Rudolph again at the Philadelphia Philosophical Society and persuaded the bishop, thirty-seven years his senior, to agree to his position as a "five-point" Calvinist.[57] Robert K. Rudolph, the bishop's son, enrolled in Clark's undergraduate philosophy courses at Pennsylvania, and, as the younger Rudolph was far closer in age to Clark, became and remained a close lifelong friend. When the University of Pennsylvania reduced Clark's pay as a result of the Great Depression, he utilized his connection to the Rudolphs and taught a few additional courses at the nearby Reformed Episcopal Seminary.

While teaching at the University of Pennsylvania, where he remained until 1936, Clark was the founder, and then adviser, of the university's chapter of the League of Evangelical Students, an early forerunner to institutions like Campus Crusade for Christ, InterVarsity Christian Fellowship, and Reformed University Fellowship. He wrote articles for their magazine, *The Evangelical Student*, helped to organize chapters at other colleges, and once was the toastmaster at an evening banquet for the League's Eastern Regional Conference.[58] But it was not only at the university that Clark was active in his Christian mission. He also was a ruling elder at his father's church, and preached on occasion when his father was absent from the pulpit.[59] In addition, from 1935 to 1938, Clark was a guest at least six times on the "Mid-Week Forum Hour" with host Erling C. Olsen on radio station WMCA, a program broadcast from New York City and carried on stations throughout the Northeast. On this forum, he defended Christianity on topics such as the historicity of "The Resurrection" and "Is Faith in the Bible Reasonable?"[60] His involvement in Christianity-promoting activities engrossed his life.

56. Rudolph, "A Truly Great and Brilliant Friend," 100.

57. Dr. Dwight Zeller, son-in-law of Gordon Clark and personal friend of Robert K. Rudolph, interview by Douglas Douma, Sangre de Cristo Seminary, 2014.

58. Jones, *The Evangelical Student*. See also: "Dr. Clark to Address League Next Monday," *The Wheaton Record*, 5 March 1937.

59. Extant sermons of Gordon Clark for Bethel Presbyterian Church range in date from 1922 to 1939, PCA Archives.

60. *Mid-Week Forum Hour* with host Erling C. Olsen, WMCA New York (six radio

Clark's family background and education set the stage for his involvement in Presbyterian church politics as an Old School defender of the *Westminster Confession of Faith* in a controversy then enveloping the church. However, before addressing the church issues in which Clark became involved, the next chapter will address the intellectual influences on Clark beyond his Presbyterian heritage.

transcripts, various dates from 1935–1938), PCA Archives, 309/92.

Chapter 2

Gordon Clark's Intellectual Influences

"If one goes back to the Westminster divines, to Calvin, even to Aquinas, and especially to Augustine, he will find that human nature is regularly divided into intellect and will. The point is important because faith in Christ is not an emotion but a volition. One does not feel for Christ, he decides for Christ."

—GORDON H. CLARK, LECTURE ON LOGOS[1]

GORDON CLARK WAS INFLUENCED not only by the Presbyterian tradition in which he was raised, but also by the philosophers whom he read and studied at the University of Pennsylvania. Though many philosophers avoid reading the Bible, and many Christians eschew "worldly" philosophy, Clark read from both traditions; he was both a Christian and a philosopher.[2] He read widely in both Christianity and philosophy to the effect that he learned to defend Christianity with a clear understanding of the alternatives. In his approach to his writings, he sought to demonstrate the logical consistency of Christianity while exposing the logical inconsistencies of other philosophies.[3]

1. Clark, "Lecture on Logos."

2. As a disciple of Clark's later argued, the Christian position was not that philosophy in general should be opposed, but rather that one should oppose false, worldly philosophy. "Paul is warning us, not about all philosophy, but about non-Christian philosophy."—Robbins, foreword to *Three Types of Religious Philosophy*, vii–viii.

3. Clark's early interest in the relationship between Christianity and philosophy is evidenced in a 1932 letter he wrote to J. Gresham Machen in which he inquired, "Do you know of a subject of investigation which combines interest in Greek Philosophy

Clark wrote on both Greek philosophy and Christian thought, often addressing their intersection. He was a prolific writer, producing at least forty published books and more than 200 articles during his career. His writings can be placed conveniently into four categories:

1. Writings on ancient Greek philosophy 1929–1941

2. Christian philosophical constructions (middle) 1946–1972 and (later) 1980–1987

3. Critiques of non-Christian philosophies 1960–1964

4. Biblical commentaries 1967–1985[4]

Clark's first publications appeared shortly after he earned his PhD. These writings concerned topics he had studied in philosophy classes in graduate school. Prior to the early 1940s, most of Clark's writings concerned philosophy, not Christianity directly. In addition to his dissertation, *Empedocles and Anaxagoras in Aristotle's De Anima* (1929), he was involved in the writing of four books on philosophy—two as author and two as contributor: *Readings in Ethics* (1931), *Selections from Early Greek Philosophy* (1934), *Selections from Hellenistic Philosophy* (1940), and *A History of Philosophy* (1941). Later Clark produced a fairly popular textbook, *Thales to Dewey*, a general overview of the history of philosophy.[5]

In thinking about philosophical matters, Clark looked not to the latest trends but to the classic writers. He critiqued the spirit of college students who preferred to study only the latest theories to be "in the know," rather than studying the theories of history's greatest thinkers. He wrote, "There is a tendency to regard college as a young gentleman's finishing school with consequent superficiality. . . . This view in my opinion leads to the acceptance of every new idea simply because it is up to date."[6]

It was the ancient Greeks, particularly the philosopher Plato and his students, that most caught Clark's attention. Fundamentally, Plato argued that there was more to the world than what could be ascertained from the

---

and Christianity?"—GHC to JGM, 10 March 1932, WTS Archives.

4. Although Clark died in 1985, the Trinity Foundation continued to print and release previously unpublished writings by Clark up through 1993. The Trinity Foundation has also printed several compilations of previously published material by Clark.

5. One book reviewer commented that Clark's philosophical scholarship was well respected even in non-Christian circles, saying, "Gordon H. Clark is recognized as a scholar not only among believers, but he has won the acclaim of the pagan world in the field of philosophy. Though they do not agree with him, they admire him for his point of view. It has been my pleasure to hear his name extolled in university circles by men who are not Christians."—Keiper, review of *Thales to Dewey*, 34.

6. GHC to JOB, 5 March 1936, PCA Archives.

senses. He posited a supra-sensible world, a plane of existence where the true forms behind sensory objects lie. In Plato's realm of forms, ideas exist independently of physical nature.[7] This view appealed to Clark because he could agree that true forms of a sort existed, not in some other realm, but in a similar way in (or as) the very mind of the God of the Bible.

CLARK, PLOTINUS, AND DIVINE SIMPLICITY

In his earliest writings, Clark focused his work on the philosophy of Plotinus (AD 205–270), a prominent philosopher in the tradition of Plato.[8] Clark aggressively studied Plotinus, reading his entire works (the Enneads) in the original Greek, and described the school of Plotinus as the "flower and culmination of all Greek philosophy."[9]

Nevertheless, Clark rejected a key aspect of Plotinus's philosophy: his doctrine of God, or what Plotinus called "the One." For Plotinus, the One was not only supreme, totally transcendent, and indivisible, but was also without distinctions and beyond all categories of being and non-being. Clark believed that the biblical view of God was at variance with such a frozen picture of the divine. Rather, he held that the God of the Bible is a living, willing being. Clark wrote, "God is a living God, not a Plotinic One."[10] And similarly, "Plotinus explicitly denied will to his One; but will is one of the most prominent aspects of the biblical Deity."[11] Furthermore, Clark believed the biblical view of God included distinctions (these distinctions being the persons of the Father, Son, and Holy Spirit). He wrote, "For Christians . . . the doctrine of the Trinity precludes a simplicity that would reduce God to a

---

7. Suprasensible (adj.): not perceptible by the senses; beyond the experience of the material world. In many of his dialogues, Plato refers to supra-sensible unchanging entities he calls *forms* (or *ideas*) in which man participates to be able to understand the sensible particulars of the world that are in constant flux.

8. These writings include: Gordon H. Clark, "Two Translations of Plotinus," *The New Scholasticism* 13, no. 1 (1938).; ——"Plotinus' Theory of Sensation," *The Philosophical Review* 51, no. 4 (1942): 357–382.; ——"ΦΑΝΤΑΣΙΑ in Plotinus," *Philosophical Essays in Honor of Edgar A. Singer, Jr.,* eds. F. P. Clarke and M. L. Nahm (Philadelphia: University of Pennsylvania Press, 1942).; ——"Plotinus' Theory of Empirical Responsibility," *The New Scholasticism* 17, no. 1 (1943).; ——"The Theory of Time in Plotinus," *The Philosophical Review* 50, no. 4 (1944).; and ——"Plotinus on the Eternity of the World," *Philosophical Review* 7, no. 2 (1949). Note: Although today Plotinus's philosophy is called neo-Platonism, Plotinus considered himself merely a Platonist.

9. Clark, "Augustine's City of God."

10. GHC to J. Oliver Buswell, note on Nature and Will, 3 April 1937, Wheaton Archives.

11. Clark, *Thales to Dewey,* 231.

... Neoplatonic One."[12] Thus it was clear to Clark that one must not confuse the Christian concept of God with pagan Greek philosophical concepts of God like that of Plotinus.

In Clark's view, the God of the Bible is not simple in the Plotinian sense of lack of distinctions, because distinctions are necessary to differentiate the three persons of the Trinity. Yet Clark did believe that God is simple in the sense that His attributes are identical—what theologians call the doctrine of "divine simplicity." Especially in his later works, Clark argued in favor of divine simplicity. In Clark's *The Incarnation* (1988), he called "honorable" the view that "all attributes are identical in God."[13][14] In *The Johannine Logos* (1972), commenting on 1 Corinthians 1:24 where Christ is called the power of God as well as the wisdom of God, Clark wrote, "Power, wisdom, and word are identical, for in the simplicity of the divine essence all attributes merge."[15] Clark also argued for divine simplicity in his unpublished systematic theology (c. 1977)[16] where, concluding a chapter on "God," he wrote, "God therefore is his substance; his substance is his attributes; all his attributes are one; and this One is God."[17]

Though Clark accepted the doctrine of divine simplicity, it is challenging to understand how he reconciled it with his epistemology.[18] If it is

12. Ibid., 209.

13. Clark, *Incarnation*, 64.

14. It should not be discounted that Clark held to the doctrine of divine simplicity early in his career as well. In 1937 he approved of the doctrine in passing in a letter to J. Oliver Buswell, in which he wrote, " In the case of God, *the simplicity of his reality* [emphasis added] should favor still more such an identification [of attributes], rather than a development of divine faculty psychology."—GHC to J. Oliver Buswell, 3 April 1937, Wheaton Archives.

15. Clark, *Johannine Logos*, 64.

16. "A few pages back comments were made on a list of verses, relating to the eternity of God, with the exception of one. That verse was, 'I AM THAT I AM.' It is hard to say how much can be drawn from this name, or how much can be read into it. Probably one cannot validly infer from this verse alone that God is pure simple being, and that his essence and attributes are all one reality; but it would be harder to show that this verse ruled out Charnock's position. It rather supports it."—Clark, *Introduction to Theology*, 173.

17. Ibid., 226. Further support for Clark's acceptance of divine simplicity occurs in an encyclopedia article he wrote on "The Divine Attributes," in which he concluded, "The short account above might suggest that the attributes are not only the same in God, but with a little thought they appear to be the same to us too."—Harrison, *Baker's Dictionary of Theology*, 78–79.

18. David Engelsma has taken the position that Clark's view on the Trinity seems to deny divine simplicity. Engelsma wrote, "Clark's definition [of Person] seems to carry with it a challenge to the doctrine of the simplicity of God (the teaching that God's Being is not made up of parts)."—Engelsma, review of *The Incarnation*.

not too much to anticipate the controversy detailed in later chapters of this biography, Clark took the position that for man to know anything at all, he must know at least some of the same objects, the same propositions, that God knows. At first glance, the doctrine of divine simplicity might seem to indicate that man, unless he becomes divine, cannot know that which God knows. The challenge arises: either man knows what God knows, thus sharing at least one of the attributes of God, and therefore, by divine simplicity, *is* God; or man does not know what God knows and therefore knows nothing at all, i.e. skepticism.

Clark, however, held that it was possible for man to know the same propositions as God knows without sharing identically the attributes of God. For Clark, while the object of knowledge of both man and God is identical, the mode of man's knowledge differs from the mode of God's knowledge. The mode of man's knowledge, Clark maintained, is discursive, whereas the mode of God's knowledge is intuitive. In other words, man learns one item at a time, but God knows all things and always has. Though this mode distinction may not provide an exhaustive solution to the challenge mentioned above, it must be seen an integral part of Clark's answer.

The importance of the doctrine of divine simplicity as it applied to Clark's own life and career should become evident in the chapters in this volume (Chapters 6–8) on the controversy which bears Clark's name. Though the term "divine simplicity" itself was not mentioned in the controversy, Clark's opposition held that his epistemology violated the Creator-creature distinction, a distinction intimately related to God's simple nature.

AUGUSTINE, CALVIN, AND THE WESTMINSTER CONFESSION

Far above Plato or Plotinus, it was thinkers in the tradition of Reformed Christianity that influenced Clark's life and thought. Like many theologians of the Reformation, Clark was in large part an Augustinian—a follower of St. Augustine (AD 354–430)—and as such, took many of his ideas directly from the ancient church father.[19] Clark was reading Augustine in depth soon after he graduated from the University of Pennsylvania. In 1932, he sought the advice of Ned Stonehouse, professor of New Testament at Westminster

---

19. Robbins, "America's Augustine." Note also that John Robbins wrote that Clark did not accept *all* of Augustine's thought. "While Clark vehemently disagreed with much of what Augustine taught, he was indebted to Augustine for some central insights in theology and philosophy."—John Robbins, foreword to *Lord God of Truth*, ???.

Theological Seminary, on a question regarding Augustine,[20] and in 1934, he wrote again to Stonehouse mentioning that he was "slowly ploughing through 511 pages of double columns" of Augustine's *City of God*.[21] According to Clark's former student Dr. Kenneth Talbot, "Dr. Clark always spoke to me about his earliest influences of St. Augustine. He believed any theological or philosophical student needed to read Augustine's writings."[22]

The influence of Augustine on Clark can be seen in the many elements he adopted from Augustine's writings including a type of idealism, his divine illumination theory, and a rejection of empiricism. Augustine was the first Christian thinker to integrate Plato's idealism with Christianity. Whereas Plato held that there was another realm in which the forms or ideas resided, Augustine, like the pre-Christian Jewish philosopher Philo before him, identified the location of this realm as the mind of God.[23] Augustine took the theory a step further in arguing that the basic items in God's mind were not ideas, but propositions. Unlike Platonic ideas, propositions have a truth value; that is, they can be either true or false. Clark accepted Augustine's theory wholeheartedly.[24]

In Clark's *Lord God of Truth* (with Augustine's *De Magistro* or *Concerning the Teacher* printed alongside), Clark's reliance on Augustine's epistemological theory of "Divine Illumination" is evident. In his theory, Augustine argued that truth comes only from the *Logos*, our divine teacher, and not from our own independent efforts.[25] Clark in like manner wrote, "Ideas are in God, and the mind can perceive them only there."[26] In a lecture later in his life Clark explained Augustine on this topic:

> I would recommend that you read Augustine's treatise called *De Magistro*. This is the original refutation of logical positivism and the language philosophies that are common today . . . By the time you get through you will see that ink marks on a paper, or sounds in the air, the noise I'm making, never teach anybody anything. This is good Augustinianism. And Protestantism is

20. GHC to Ned Stonehouse, 6 October 1932, WTS Archives.

21. GHC to Ned Stonehouse, 21 February 1934, WTS Archives.

22. Former Clark student Dr. Kenneth Talbot, telephone interview by Douglas Douma, 2014.

23. Augustine, *Eighty-three Different Questions*, question 46.

24. "Is all this any more than the assertion that there is an eternal, immutable Mind, a Supreme Reason, a personal, living, God? The truths or propositions that may be known are the thoughts of God, the eternal thought of God."—Clark, *Christian View of Men and Things*, 321.

25. Clark, *Lord God of Truth*, 89.

26. Ibid, 16.

supposed to be Augustinian, at least it was in its initiation. And it was the most unfortunate event that Thomas Aquinas came in and replaced Augustinianism with Aristotelianism and empiricism which has been an affliction ever since. But the point is that ink marks on a paper, and the sound of a voice, this sort of thing never generates any idea at all. And Augustine's solution of it is that the Magister is Christ. Christ is the light that lighteth every man that comes into the world. This is not a matter of regeneration. This is a matter of knowledge. And Christ enlightens the unregenerate in this sense just as well as the regenerate. If an unregenerate man learns anything at all, he learns it from Jesus Christ and not from ink marks on a paper."[27]

Augustine's theory of divine illumination, depending on God's involvement in knowledge acquisition, is at odds with the theory of empiricism which holds that man learns on his own through his senses. One modern introduction to Augustine's *On Faith in Things Unseen* explains, "[The purpose of Augustine's writing] is to refute that crass empiricism which would admit no faith in the truths of revelation because they cannot be 'seen,' that is, perceived by our sensory experience."[28] Though Clark referred to Augustine as an anti-empiricist, he also noted that Augustine had not "purged his thought of all empirical elements."[29]

Augustine's thought permeated the Reformation through reformers like Martin Luther (1483–1546), who was himself an Augustinian monk. It was in part due to Augustine's insights that Luther began to diverge from the accepted Roman Catholic teachings. Yet among Reformation thinkers, it was not Martin Luther but John Calvin (1509–1564) who most influenced Clark. Clark praised Calvin as "Paul's best interpreter."[30] In Calvin, as exemplified in *The Institutes*, Clark found a thoroughly systematic and consistent Christianity which he embraced. Furthermore, Clark saw Calvin's epistemology as akin to his own in that Calvin looked to the Scriptures as the sole source of knowledge.[31] Clark argued that Calvin rejected sensation

---

27. Clark, "A Contemporary Defense of the Bible," minute 111–12.

28. Deferrari and McDonald, *Writings of Saint Augustine*, 446.

29. Clark, *Lord God of Truth*, 13.

30. Clark, "Determinism and Responsibility," 23.

31. Referring to a commentary of Calvin's, Clark wrote, "Calvin seems here to limit knowledge, or right knowledge, to what may be deduced from the assertions of Scripture. Scripture is the only rule of right knowledge. Calvin is not willing to designate the changing theories of science as knowledge. Calvin may indeed be right."—Clark, *Colossians*, 23.

as the basis of knowledge[32] and was fond of quoting Calvin's definition of knowledge: "I call that knowledge, not what is innate in man, nor what is by diligence acquired, but that which is delivered to us by The Law and The Prophets."[33]

The system which Clark admired in Calvin was most thoroughly and fully developed in the 1640s with *The Westminster Confession of Faith*. The influence of *The Westminster Confession of Faith* on Clark led him to write *What Presbyterians Believe* (1956) in which he walked through the Confession point by point. As a Presbyterian minister, Clark took seriously his ordination vow to the system of doctrine contained in the Confession. The nature of the confession, having been formulated and signed by hundreds of theologians, meant that its teachings were of no one's private interpretation of Scripture. The Confession also was written at a time when the biblical thought of the Reformation had reached its apex and maturity.

The Calvinistic and confessional tradition of the *Westminster Confession of Faith* was continued in the Old School Presbyterianism of Princeton Seminary. Clark was influenced greatly by the theologians of Princeton. Among these was Charles Hodge about whom Clark wrote, "Charles Hodge, I think I may say, is the greatest theologian America has so far produced."[34] Also among the Princeton theologians who influenced Clark were Charles Hodge's son A. A. Hodge, B. B. Warfield, and professors less well known today, Francis Landey Patton and William Benton Green.[35]

Thus, labels befitting Clark include Christian, Augustinian, Calvinist, and Presbyterian. But in addition to these labels Clark was a Machenite, a follower and supporter of J. Gresham Machen (1881–1937), the leader of the continued Princeton tradition in the 1920s and 1930s. Machen was a

32. "The disciples *heard* a message, and *saw* Jesus. Calvin saw the difficulty, though perhaps not so clearly as contemporary factors force it on us today. At any rate, Calvin considers an opponent who insinuates that the passage is nonsense because 'the evidence of the senses little availed the present subject, for the power of Christ cannot be perceived by the eyes.' Calvin does not reply with a defense of sensation but rather refers to John's Gospel 1:14, 'We have seen his glory.' For says Calvin, 'He was not known as the Son of God by the external forms of his body, but because he gave illustrious proofs of his Divine power' . . . Calvin does not instantiate these proofs, but he clearly rejects the idea that 'seeing with the eyes' is literal sensation."—Clark, *First John*, 10.

33. Clark, "Reply to Ronald H. Nash," 148.

34. Clark, *The Trinity*, 68.

35. Individual published copies of nine sermons of Francis Landey Patton are in the Clark collection at the Sangre de Cristo Seminary, Clark Library. Given the early date of these sermons (all from 1879), they were quite possibly passed down from David S. Clark ("The Person of Christ," "The Doctrine of Sin," "Retribution," "The Objective Side of Salvation," "The Subjective Side of Salvation," "The Means of Grace," "The Divine Purpose," "Faith," and "The Kingdom of Grace").

personal friend of Clark. In addition to twenty-two extant letters between Clark and Machen, there are a number of Machen's books in Clark's personal collection.[36] Clark became involved in the Machen-led struggle for a new reformation in the Presbyterian Church U.S.A. His role in this struggle is the topic of the next chapter.

36. These items are presently in the Gordon H. Clark collection at Sangre de Cristo Seminary's Clark Library. Some are personally inscribed by Machen. Titles include the following: J. Gresham Machen, *History and Faith* (1915); ——*The Origin of Paul's Religion* (1921); ——*Christianity and Liberalism* (1923);——*What is Faith?* (1925); ——*The Virgin Birth of Christ* (1932); ——*Christian Faith in the Modern World* (1936); ——*The Christian View of Man* (1937); ——*God Transcendent and Other Sermons* (1949); —— *What is Christianity?* (1951); and ——*Machen's Notes on Galatians* (1972).

Chapter 3

Gordon Clark and the Formation of the Orthodox Presbyterian Church

"For reasons which will appear as you read the document, I am enclosing a copy of a very delightful letter which I have just received from the Rev. Professor G. Engel, D.D., of the Presbyterian Theological Seminary, Pyongyang, Korea. What he says about your nominating speech in the election of moderator is certainly well deserved, so far as the speech is concerned. I know I am not worthy of that speech, and yet every time I think of it it gives me new joy and courage."[1]

—J. Gresham Machen to Gordon H. Clark, 20 August 1936

THE AUBURN AFFIRMATION

During the years he was a student and then a teacher at the University of Pennsylvania, Gordon Clark participated in contemporary doctrinal and organizational struggles within the Presbyterian church. In these struggles, Clark always sided with the conservative group of his denomination and endeavored to keep the denomination true to the *Westminster Confession*.

Like other American churches in the 1920s and 1930s, the Presbyterian Church in the United States of America (PCUSA) was embroiled in the Fundamentalist-Modernist Controversy. This controversy, as the name

---

1. JGM to GHC, 20 August 1936, WTS archives.

implies, was fought by men of two distinct theological persuasions, the fundamentalists and the modernists, each of whom were seeking control of the denomination. The modernist faction generally accepted Darwin's theory of evolution. They believed in the supposed progress of science to solve all social problems. In matters of religion, they were attracted to the so-called "higher" methods of biblical criticism, which denied that the Bible was free of error and placed human experience above biblical revelation as man's ultimate authority. Modernism, then, threatened the unity and fidelity of the church because it provided an alternative set of explanations of the world that contradicted traditional Christian beliefs.

Although modernism grew in support substantially in the late nineteenth and early twentieth centuries, its ascendance was not without resistance. The fundamentalist movement arose to combat modernism's influence in the church. The fundamentalists first appeared as a named group in 1909. In that year were published the first volumes of *The Fundamentals*, a series of booklets written by conservative biblical scholars to address crucial biblical topics. Fundamentalists generally held to the doctrine of biblical inerrancy—the teaching that the Bible, in its original manuscripts, is free from error. Though members of the fundamentalists came from a number of denominations, perhaps the most prominent among them was Princeton professor B. B. Warfield, under whom Clark's father had studied. Warfield was a strong proponent of biblical inerrancy. The Clarks (David and Gordon alike) followed in Warfield's footsteps on this doctrine.

Although there were events foreshadowing the Fundamentalist-Modernist controversy at the turn of the twentieth century,[2] the controversy truly erupted in 1923, when, in response to the pressures of modernism's growing influence, a fundamentalist group within the PCUSA adopted a motion at the general assembly calling for stricter requirements on the ordination of pastors. These requirements, known as the Five Fundamentals, called for pastors to faithfully uphold the doctrines of the inerrancy of Scripture, Christ's substitutionary atonement for man, the historicity of the virgin birth, the bodily resurrection of Christ, and the authenticity of Christ's miracles.[3] The fundamentalists knew that if the church were to limit ordination to only those who believed these central tenets, modernism would face an uphill struggle in the church. It would be incorrect to say, however, that the fundamentalists created the divide in the church with this stance. Rather, they recognized that the divide already existed and dug

2. Examples of this foreshadowing include the 1903 revisions to the *Westminster Confession of Faith* and the 1906 merger of the PCUSA and the Cumberland Presbyterian Church.

3. Rian, *Presbyterian Conflict*, 34.

a trench to defend their historic position while clearly identifying their opponents.

Though Clark was only twenty-one years of age in 1923, *The Presbyterian* published two articles by him that show his position on the controversy. In the first article, "What Shall We do?" he wrote, "If the church's adherence to Christ is going to discourage young men from entering the ministry, fine! Tell [prominent modernist leaders] Drs. Fosdick and MacColl that we want to discourage that type of young men."[4] And in the second article, "How Long?" Clark wrote, "When a presbytery ordains men who deny the virgin birth; when the church with schisms is split asunder, with heresies distressed the cry naturally goes up, How long, O Lord, how long?"[5] Clark, without any doubt, sided with the fundamentalists.

In 1924, the modernist faction within the PCUSA responded to the Five Fundamentals with their own statement, the *Auburn Affirmation*. The name for this document came from its association with Auburn Theological Seminary in Auburn, New York, where it was composed. The *Auburn Affirmation* rejected the new requirements for ordination in the PCUSA. From an initial group of thirty-two signatories, it grew to receive the support of over 1,300 (out of approximately 10,000) PCUSA pastors nationwide. Its central message was that:

> There is no assertion in the Scriptures that their writers were kept "from error." The Confession of Faith does not make this assertion; and it is significant that this assertion is not to be found in the Apostles' Creed or the Nicene Creed or in any of the great Reformation confessions. The doctrine of inerrancy, intended to enhance the authority of the Scriptures, in fact impairs their supreme authority for faith and life, and weakens the testimony of the church to the power of God unto salvation through Jesus Christ.[6]

When the *Auburn Affirmation* first appeared in print, Clark was an undergraduate senior at the University of Pennsylvania and a ruling elder in the PCUSA. Though Clark opposed the *Affirmation* from the moment he read it, he only attacked it in print ten years later in an article that redubbed it the "Auburn Heresy" and described it as a "vicious attack on the Word of God." Clark knew the *Auburn Affirmation* challenged a critical doctrine of Christianity: the inerrancy of Scripture. In his view, it was absurd to argue that the doctrine of inerrancy impaired or weakened the biblical message. In

4. Clark, "What Shall We Do?" 10–11.

5. Clark, "How Long?" 9.

6. *The Auburn Affirmation* (Auburn, NY: The Jacobs Press, 5 May 1924).

fact, it was a contradiction, he thought, to say that something truly inspired by God also contained error. On this point Clark wrote, "If [the signers of the Affirmation] say that they believe the Bible is the Word of God, and at the same time claim that the Bible contains error, it follows, does it not, that they call God a liar, since He has spoken falsely?" Ultimately for Clark, the *Auburn Affirmation* was a sign that the modernists had "excommunicated the orthodox." This, he felt, necessitated action on the part of the fundamentalists to recover the orthodoxy of the church.[7]

In 1932, Clark added his name to the counteroffensive against modernism in the PCUSA when he joined the new Reformation Fellowship, a national organization to reform the church according to the *Westminster Confession of Faith* and other historical standards of the Reformed faith.[8] Clark's father also supported the reform movement and welcomed the Reformation Fellowship in 1934 when they held their annual meeting at his church.[9] Soon the younger Clark was made a member of the Reformation Fellowship's executive committee. In one document he sent out to members of the Fellowship, he called out by name those who were in positions of responsibility and trust in the denomination who had signed the *Auburn Affirmation*.[10] In October of 1934, Clark joined fellow Reformation Fellowship members Rev. H. McAllister Griffiths (1900–1957) and Murray Forst Thompson (1906–1988) in filing six charges against eleven ministers at the Presbytery of Philadelphia who had signed the *Auburn Affirmation*.[11] The charges, written by Griffiths, declared the *Auburn Affirmation* to be in direct contradiction to the *Westminster Confession of Faith*. Since the ministers had subscribed to this confession at ordination, they were alleged to be in contempt of their vows. For this reason, Clark, Griffiths, and Thompson argued that the offenders ought to be defrocked. When the charges were dismissed at their presbytery a month later, Clark protested the decision. He argued that the charges had been illegally dismissed as the protest vote had first passed, and only later failed on an illegal second vote when some members of the presbytery had left the meeting thinking the matter was settled.

7. Clark, "The Auburn Heresy," 7–8.

8. Mass mailing from the Reformation Fellowship (J. C. Monsma) to J. Oliver Buswell and others, 24 June 1932, records of the Office of the President, 1917–1980, Wheaton College Archives and Special Collections. See also: Craig, "Reformation Fellowship Incorporated," 15.

9. "This letter announces our annual meeting to be held 8:00 P.M., October 30, 1934, at Bethel Church, 19th and York sts."—Trustees to members of the Reformation Fellowship, 25 September 1934, PCA Archives.

10. Clark, "Who Controls our Church?"

11. Rian, *Presbyterian Conflict*, 58.

Clark also objected to the practice of allowing the ministers under question to vote on their own cases.[12] Ultimately Clark's appeal failed, but he had stood on principle and displayed dedication to opposing modernism.

Neither Clark, Griffiths, nor Thompson at this point were particularly powerful figures in the church. Had more prominent leaders stepped forward with similar charges, they might have stood a better chance of success. In involving himself in this case, Clark not only demonstrated his support for the fundamentalist position but also showed he was willing to take action for the fundamentalist cause. This case was Clark's first foray into controversy. He summarized his views at the time by writing for the Reformation Fellowship, "If our opponents say we are dividing the Church, I can point to the widespread knowledge that our Church is now divided; we are trying to unite it on the only enduring basis of union: Jesus Christ as revealed in the Holy Scriptures."[13]

GORDON CLARK, J. GRESHAM MACHEN, AND NEW INSTITUTIONS

As a young church elder, Clark sought role models to guide his actions in the church. More than any other, he admired J. Gresham Machen (1881–1937), then Professor of New Testament at Princeton Theological Seminary and the leading figure on the side of the fundamentalists. Machen was one of a few men, along with University of Pennsylvania professor William Romaine Newbold, who truly inspired Clark. Clark found Machen inspiring because Machen was a learned Christian scholar who frequently published significant books and was also willing to stand on principle for the cause of the fundamentalists. In the earliest extant letter from Clark to Machen (October 25, 1928), Clark writes, "I regarded you, and still do, as the greatest figure and one of the greatest intellects among Evangelicals today."[14]

Machen had long led the resistance against modernism within the PCUSA. His 1923 book *Christianity and Liberalism* argued forcefully that Christianity (by which he meant the views of the fundamentalists) and liberalism (essentially identical with modernism) are not just competing factions within Christianity, but diametrically opposed religions. To combat liberalism and strengthen support for the traditional Christian interpretation, Machen contributed to the founding of Westminster Theological

12. Clark, "Heresy Decision Declared Illegal." See also: Clark, "Heresy Vote Assailed."

13. GHC to Rev. W. B. McIlwaine, 31 October 1934, PCA Archives.

14. GHC to JGM, 25 October 1928, WTS Archives.

Seminary in 1929, the Independent Board for Presbyterian Foreign Missions in 1933, and eventually, in 1936, the church that became the Orthodox Presbyterian Church.

Machen's first major stand against modernism was at Princeton Theological Seminary in the 1920s. The various Presbyterian churches in America had for many years relied significantly on Princeton for the training of its pastors. The seminary had even been known to some as a "citadel of historic Christianity."[15] However, when in 1929 Princeton was reorganized such that the conservatives on the board of directors lost their majority, Machen responded by founding a separate school, Westminster Theological Seminary, which ran independently on a separate site and was not connected to a denomination.[16] Shortly thereafter, Princeton professors John Murray (1898–1975), Robert Dick Wilson (1856–1930), and Oswald T. Allis (1880–1973) all resigned their posts and joined Machen at Westminster where they could train ministers apart from modernist influences.

Machen felt that modernism had even spread into the PCUSA's overseas missions so thoroughly that it had curtailed many missionaries' ability to preach the gospel. So in 1933, Machen organized the Independent Board for Presbyterian Foreign Missions (IBPFM) with the intent of sponsoring missionaries untainted by modernism.

Led by Machen, the Presbyterian Constitutional Covenant Union (PCCU) was launched on June 27, 1935, following that year's general assembly of the PCUSA. The PCCU, more commonly called the Covenant Union for short, succeeded the Reformation Fellowship and was formed, according to Machen, for the purpose of "attempting to reform the ecclesiastical organization of the Presbyterian Church in the USA and to carry on the true witness of that Church if reform proves impossible."[17] Basically, the Covenant Union was the final stand for the fundamentalists in the PCUSA before separating to form their own church. Both Machen and Clark enthusiastically joined the organization, and Clark was elected treasurer. Clark spoke at rallies of the Covenant Union in Philadelphia and once traveled to speak for the organization in North Dakota.[18]

The lasting impact of the Covenant Union was in the newspaper it sponsored, *The Presbyterian Guardian*. Prior to the formation of *The Presbyterian Guardian*, which Machen funded, Machen was publishing his own

15. Rian, *Presbyterian Conflict*, 60.

16. Ibid., 85.

17. JGM for the Executive Committee of the PCCU to Peter Stam, 4 December 1935, PCA Archives.

18. GHC to George Marsden, 1 September 1980, provided by John Muether with permission of George Marsden.

articles on the controversy in *Christianity Today*, a magazine run by Samuel Craig (1874–1960) and edited by H. McAllister Griffiths. Craig, however, came to a disagreement with Machen and Griffiths over the creation of the IBPFM. Craig felt that donors who wanted to support foreign missions should still do so through the PCUSA Board of Foreign Missions, since it was possible to earmark funds for specific non-modernist missionaries. Over this matter, Griffiths left *Christianity Today* and became editor of *The Presbyterian Guardian* in addition to his post as general secretary of the Covenant Union. Without *Christianity Today* as its mouthpiece, the PCCU needed a new press outlet, and *The Presbyterian Guardian* was born.

The PCUSA leadership, threatened by the competition for mission funds, brought Machen and the members of the IBPFM to trial on charges of disloyalty and disobedience, resulting in their suspension from ministry. With the development of the IBPFM and the PCCU, the pieces were in place for this growing network of conservatives to prepare for and eventually split from the PCUSA. For almost a decade they had tried for reform within the denomination, but their efforts were not generating the results they desired, and so, regardless of the fact that they were still a relatively small group, the PCCU met in June of 1936 for its first annual convention. Believing that the PCUSA had abandoned its heritage, the PCCU sought to be the true spiritual succession of the church. Machen encouraged a small group of conservatives in the PCCU, including Gordon Clark, to leave the PCUSA and to form the Presbyterian Church of America (PCA).[19] The new church took with it the IBPFM and *The Presbyterian Guardian*. The PCCU dissolved upon the founding of the new denomination. The leaders of the PCA emphasized the new church's commitment to *Westminster Confession of Faith*, even rejecting the 1903 modifications to the Confession of the PCUSA and returning to the original formulation.

Finding the new denomination to his liking, Clark became heavily involved in the PCA in its early years. At the First General Assembly in June of 1936, after giving a short speech, Clark nominated J. Gresham Machen as moderator of the assembly.[20] As Machen was the leading figure in the church, no other candidates were put forward and Machen's election was unopposed and successful. Clark also served as a member of the Christian Education Committee and secretary of the Home Missions and Church

---

19. The Presbyterian Church *of* America should not be confused with the later Presbyterian Church *in* America formed in 1973.

20. Strong, "The Gordon Clark Case."

Extension Committee, where he worked with Machen to secure legal counsel for the many congregations in property disputes with the PCUSA.[21]

Both Gordon and his father were well-acquainted with Machen. Clark's father had personally known Machen since at least 1921, as evidenced by a letter he received from Machen that year.[22] In the letter, Machen praised David for writing an "exceedingly able" review of a modernist's book in *The Presbyterian*. Displaying his approval, Machen concluded his letter saying, "I feel greatly heartened by the presence of such a true defender of the faith in the pastorate in Philadelphia." Gordon Clark was himself in correspondence with Machen by 1926, and in 1928 invited Machen to give a speech to the chapter of the League of Evangelical Students at the University of Pennsylvania.[23] When Machen was planning the new seminary, Clark suggested to Machen that his father, David, could be hired as he had made systematic theology his lifelong hobby and would be honored to teach the subject. Although David never would teach at Machen's seminary, he did join the seminary's board of trustees. Gordon Clark also recommended in the same letter to Machen that Bishop Rudolph might allow Machen's ex-Princeton group, which was then seeking property, to use the facilities at Reformed Episcopal Seminary. Clark sought to help Machen's cause in every way possible. Along with his suggestions, Clark sent Machen a $25 donation for the new seminary.[24]

Machen, for his part, saw Clark as an ally. He wrote to Clark, "We can certainly be thankful for a man like you, who is not a minister and is even a university professor and yet is not ashamed to be called a Christian!"[25] He praised Clark saying, "It does seem to me that God is raising up real defenders of the faith in these days. I feel mighty happy when I think of your testimony."[26]

Machen's presence in Philadelphia was one reason Clark continued to teach at the University of Pennsylvania for as many years as he did. Clark wrote, "I am very fond of being near Machen, Griffiths, et. al."[27] Clark also

21. JGM to JOB, 19 August 1938, PCA Archives, 309/24.

22. JGM to David S. Clark, 2 October 1921, in the possession of the Clark family.

23. GHC to JGM, 25 October 1928, WTS Archives.; JGM to GHC, 30 October 1928, WTS Archives.

24. In a somewhat comical episode, Machen misplaced Clark's check and then sent Clark an apologetic letter requesting that he issue a replacement check. GHC to JGM, 4 June 1929, WTS Archives.; JGM to GHC, 14 July 1929, WTS Archives.; GHC to JGM, 16 July 1929, WTS Archives.

25. JGM to GHC, 4 September 1934, WTS Archives.

26. JGM to GHC, 6 June 1935, WTS Archives.

27. GHC to JOB, 5 March 1936, Wheaton Archives.

knew the positive impact he could make for Machen's causes, as Machen had pointed out to him that "the University provides a powerful sounding board whenever I [Clark] speak or write for the public."[28]

Clark hoped that the new denomination would grow in numbers and gain influence. He wrote, "No doubt the start will be small, but there are rumors that before two years shall have elapsed, there will be an influx of congregations from an at present unexpected source."[29]

Shortly after the PCA was founded, the PCUSA filed a lawsuit which, among other items, argued:

> The name, "Presbyterian Church of America," which has been appropriated and assumed by the defendant church, is identical in content with that of the plaintiff church, except for the words "of the United States," which have been deleted . . . The similarity of the name of the defendant church to that of the plaintiff church will cause, and is intended to cause, irreparable injury and loss to the plaintiff church . . .

Clark was listed on the lawsuit as one of the fourteen defendants along with Machen and other prominent leaders of the new church.[30] The PCA lost the lawsuit and changed its name to the Orthodox Presbyterian Church (OPC).[31]

The separation of the OPC from the PCUSA was permanent and total, but it did not always produce enmity between members of the opposing bodies. Gordon Clark's father decided not to join the new church body and remained with Bethel Presbyterian Church and the PCUSA.[32] The decision to stay within the PCUSA was especially common amongst older pastors who risked losing pensions should they leave the churches and denominations to which they had dedicated their entire careers. Although David Clark remained in the PCUSA, he was nevertheless opposed to modernism and therefore became both an ally of the movement that formed the OPC as well as a charter member of the board of trustees of Westminster Theological Seminary. David's opposition to modernism is shown in the last of his three published books, *Protestant Unbelief, or, Rationalism Past and Present*, in which he declared, "The most virulent outbreak of modernism in the

---

28. GHC to JOB, 5 March 1936, Wheaton Archives.

29. GHC to JOB, 11 May 1936, PCA Archives, 309/23.

30. Machen and Stonehouse, "*The Presbyterian Church*," 232–237.

31. Birch, "What's In a Name?" 49.

32. Rudolph, "A Truly Great and Brilliant Friend," 101.

present century was the making and signing of the *Auburn Affirmation*."[33]
He further argued a logical defense of the fundamentalist position:

> The Affirmation declares unessential the Virgin Birth, Miracles,
> the truthfulness of the Bible, the Substitutionary Atonement,
> and the Resurrection of Christ. These doctrines are the heart of
> the Christian system, and the signers of the *Auburn Affirmation*
> have put their names to a virtual denial of the essential features
> of Christianity. The *Auburn Affirmation* further declares: "We
> are opposed to any attempt to elevate these five doctrinal state-
> ments, or any one of them, to the position of tests for ordination
> or for good standing in our church." But these doctrines were
> already tests for ordination since they are in the Scriptures, and
> the Scriptures are included in the ordination vows, viz: "Do you
> believe in the Scriptures of the Old and New Testaments to be
> the Word of God, the only infallible rule of faith and practice?"[34]

Following a long battle with cancer, David Clark passed away on February 28, 1939. He left a powerful legacy in both the church and in academia
for Gordon to live up to.[35] Gordon had taken a week's leave of absence to
return to Philadelphia to be at his father's bedside.[36] A letter of condolence
sent by the session of elders of Bethel Presbyterian Church to David Clark's
family demonstrates the church's profound grief over the loss of their long-
time pastor. Since David had been with the church for four decades, the
elders were able to write:

> Bethel and Dr. Clark had come to be associated in our minds
> [as] the singular rather than the plural. Now the silver cord is
> broken, and what remains for our own consolation and en-
> couragement is the memory of a great soul, maybe not too well
> understood, who gave a lowly life for the lofty aim of knitting
> together a Church and People in plain, ordinary surroundings,
> when his mental and spiritual capacity might readily have led
> him to seek a more prominent position.[37]

33. Clark, *Protestant Unbelief, or, Rationalism Past and Present*, 19.

34. Ibid.

35. Birch, "David S. Clark," 72.

36. "Prof. Clark Returns After Family Death," *The Wheaton Record*, 28 February
1939.

37. The members of Bethel Presbyterian Church Session to Mrs. Helen Clark, Dr.
Gordon Clark, and family in their bereavement, 4 May 1939, SDCS, Clark Library,
1/48. Note: Mrs. Helen Clark was David Clark's second wife. His first wife, Elizabeth
Clark (Gordon's mother), died February 11, 1931.

Shortly thereafter, and in his father's honor, Gordon Clark donated 150 of his father's books to Reformed Episcopal Seminary.[38] He also investigated the possibility of having a collection of his father's sermons published, but it seems ultimately not to have been profitable enough for any of the publishers contacted to undertake the project.[39]

LEADERSHIP CHANGE FROM MACHEN TO VAN TIL

On January 1, 1937, two years prior to the death of Clark's father, Clark's ecclesiastical hero, J. Gresham Machen, died unexpectedly of pneumonia, leaving the OPC without its leader. The reins of leadership on matters of theology within the denomination then went largely, by virtue of his influence, to Cornelius Van Til (1895–1987), Professor of Apologetics at Westminster Theological Seminary. Van Til was born in the Netherlands, migrated to the American Midwest when he was ten, and grew up in the Christian Reformed Church. After graduating from Calvin College, he attended Princeton Theological Seminary and later received a PhD from Princeton University. Following graduation he taught at Princeton Theological Seminary and then pastored a church in Spring Lake, Michigan. With considerable effort on Machen's part in convincing him, Van Til joined the faculty of Westminster Theological Seminary soon after it was founded. This was a great victory for Machen, who desired to have more than half of his faculty come from Princeton Seminary in order to legitimately claim its lineage. When the OPC was formed, Van Til transferred his ministerial credentials from the CRC to the OPC to show his support.

At the time of Machen's death, Clark and Van Til were already acquaintances. The date of their first meeting is unclear, but in 1932 Machen encouraged Clark to seek Van Til for advice on Clark's request of a suitable writing topic that would combine Christianity and Greek Philosophy.[40] That Machen in this letter referred to Van Til as "Dr. Cornelius Van Til of our seminary" may indicate that at that time Van Til was not well known to Clark. Within the next few years, however, Van Til and Clark must have become well acquainted. A letter of Clark's written in 1935 on Reformation Fellowship letterhead shows that both Clark and Van Til were members of

38. Acker, *History of The Reformed Episcopal Seminary*, 47.

39. Peter de Visser of Eerdmans Publishing to GHC, 10 July 1939, PCA Archives, 309/59.; and B. D. Zondervan of Zondervan Publishing House to GHC, n.d. circa 1939, Gordon Clark's personal papers, AE 0.4, 1/128, in the possession of Betsy (née Clark) George.

40. JGM to GHC, 17 March 1932, WTS Archives.

the group.[41] At the formation of the OPC in 1936, both Clark and Van Til were present at the First General Assembly. At the Second General Assembly, also in 1936, Clark and Van Til were elected to serve together on the Christian Education Committee. And in 1937, his first year at Wheaton College, Clark even taught from Van Til's syllabi notes. He noted that his students were "acutely interested" in Van Til's system of apologetics and Clark himself was "anxious to clarify" his own understanding of Van Til's argument.[42] Van Til, for his part, "rejoiced in serious discussion of the questions" that Clark touched on in his notes and "appreciate[d] [Clark's] effort to understand first and then criticize" what he had to say.[43] Van Til was also in correspondence with Clark's father right up to the latter's death, reviewing the elder Clark's latest book.[44]

As the early OPC developed without Machen then, there was an opportunity for Clark and Van Til to take the reigns together and form a constructive team in philosophical matters, if not ecclesiastical. The two men looked to be on the same page regarding fundamentals at least. Yet the differences in philosophical views between them would eventually lead to a major controversy in the church. It was this resulting Clark-Van Til controversy which brought Clark, Van Til, and their supporters into a lengthy and heated battle. Perhaps second only to the books he wrote, it is Clark's theological and philosophical stance maintained in the controversy for which he is best known today.

Signs of the future discord between Clark and Van Til can be seen in four letters from 1937 and 1938. For example, in one letter which Clark wrote to Van Til asking for clarification regarding the definition of "knowledge" as used in one of Van Til's syllabi (the term Van Til used to refer to his own books),[45] Clark asked, "When you say 'knowledge is knowledge and love,' what does this second knowledge mean? Naturally, the definiendum[46] cannot occur in the definition."[47] On the response letter from Van Til, Clark penned a note in the margin which reads, "I requested a distinction between

---

41. GHC to JOB, 13 April 1935, Wheaton Archives.

42. GHC to CVT, 28 August 1937, WTS Archives.

43. CVT to GHC, 24 September 1937, WTS Archives.

44. CVT to GHC, 5 December 1938, PCA Archives, 309/58.

45. A similar statement by Van Til: "The question of knowledge is an ethical question at the root. It is indeed possible to have theoretically correct knowledge about God without loving God. The devil illustrates this point. Yet what is meant by knowing God in Scripture is *knowing and loving* God: this is true knowledge of God, the other is false."—Van Til, *Christian Apologetics*, 10.

46. Definiendum: the word being defined.

47. GHC to CVT, 28 August 1937, WTS Archives.

'knowledge' and 'knowledge plus love' in the interest of epistemology. Van Til admitted no distinction."[48] Clark's logical nature showed in his desire for clear definitions, but his frustration emerged from what he perceived to be Van Til's lack thereof.

THE BIBLE PRESBYTERIAN CHURCH SCHISM OF 1937 & THE GROWTH OF THE WTS FACTION

The OPC was formed by a group opposed to modernism within the PCUSA. However, the conservatives who formed the OPC had substantial disagreements among themselves on many other theological topics. In the rapid formation of the new church, little emphasis was placed on these disagreements. Modernism was the first and common enemy. Yet once members of the OPC had successfully distanced themselves from that common enemy, the discrepancies in their beliefs became readily apparent. In 1937, the disagreements in theology among members of the new church came to a head at the Third General Assembly of the Orthodox Presbyterian Church. R. B. Kuiper (1886–1966) of Westminster Theological Seminary had written an article the previous year opposing the theology of dispensationalism. Some, including Carl McIntire (1906–2002), minister of Collingswood Presbyterian Church, saw the article as a critique not only of dispensationalism (to which neither he nor any others in the OPC held) but also of premillennialism in general (to which McIntire did hold). Many in this same group who held to premillennialism also desired that the church take a stand against alcohol. When motions on both of these topics failed at the Third General Assembly, the group led by McIntire, along with Wheaton College President J. Oliver Buswell (1895–1977) and Professor Allan MacRae (1902–1977) of Westminster Theological Seminary, separated from the OPC and formed the Bible Presbyterian Church (BPC). Clark was not present at the Third General Assembly, but both of these issues, premillennialism and alcohol abstinence, would greatly impact Clark's life in the coming years.

At the time of the BPC's founding, Clark was teaching at Wheaton College; yet despite President Buswell's departure to the BPC, Clark remained in the OPC. Clark did, however, have some sympathy for the views of Buswell and the BPC. Although it is not exactly clear what his eschatological views were at the time, Clark later supported premillennialism, though never of the dispensationalist variety. He also had sympathy with the movement to curtail the use of alcohol. Yet sympathy was not enough to motivate Clark to transfer his denominational allegiance. When the OPC broke from the

48. CVT to GHC, 5 December 1938, PCA Archives, 309/58.

PCUSA, it claimed to be the spiritual successor of the PCUSA and held to the *Westminster Confession of Faith*. The BPC, however, was truly a separatist movement, having broken away over far less fundamental issues. As a member of the OPC, a church which adhered to the *Westminster Confession of Faith* (his preferred creed), Clark saw no need to join the separatist BPC. Further, he had pressing challenges of his own at Wheaton College toward which to direct his energies.

Chapter 4

Gordon Clark at Wheaton College

"One of the best witnesses of what the Reformation taught is the Westminster Confession of 1645–49. Its reliability is such that thousands of ministers from that day to this have subscribed to it. The men who framed it were the most devout ministers of their day, the most competent, and the best informed on the theology of the previous century."[1]

—Gordon H. Clark

Gordon Clark served as a professor of philosophy at Wheaton College for only seven years (1936–1943). His resignation in 1943 resulted from his unbending adherence to the teachings of the *Westminster Confession of Faith*. At Wheaton, Clark expounded theological views that irritated the college's inter-denominational establishment, but despite conflicts with the administration and board of trustees, his years at Wheaton were some of his most productive. In the classroom, he exercised a profound influence on a number of future evangelical leaders. As a scholar, he wrote prolifically and sowed the seeds of many future book projects.

To understand the events that unfolded during Clark's tenure at Wheaton, it is important first to understand some of the background and history of the college. Wheaton was founded in 1860 as a private Christian liberal arts college located twenty-five miles west of Chicago. For the first sixty-five years of its history, the college was blessed with the stable leadership of just two presidents—the founder of the school, Jonathan Blanchard (1811–1892),

1. Clark, "Order of Justification and Regeneration."

and his son, Charles A. Blanchard (1848–1925). The Blanchard era can be characterized as a time of moderate growth for the school during which it was principally dedicated to opposing worldly evils, most notably slavery and intemperance. The death of the younger Blanchard in 1925 signaled the end of an era of two generations of family leadership. Around the time of Charles Blanchard's death, a visiting preacher named J. Oliver Buswell (then a pastor in New York, but originally from the Midwest) gained popularity among the Wheaton students through a series of sermons preached at the college chapel. Admiration for Buswell led the students to petition for his return to the chapel to preach additional sermons. Recognizing the popularity of Buswell, the college offered him the job as president of the college, which he gladly accepted.

Clark arrived at Wheaton as Buswell was busy reshaping the college. Buswell aimed to improve the school's academic standing by hiring scholars with doctorate degrees in their respective fields, a rare commodity at that time. In early 1936, when a position in the philosophy department opened up for the following school year, Buswell inquired of Clark if he would be interested in the job.[2] Buswell knew Clark from their mutual membership and involvement in the reform-seeking Presbyterian Constitutional Covenant Union (PCCU). The two men agreed on the need to reform the PCUSA and both supported J. Gresham Machen, the leading voice for reform in the church. It appears, in fact, that they found commonality on many topics. They first met in person in 1935 at a gathering of church leaders where, according to Clark, they had engaged in "a stimulating discussion."[3] With a PhD, teaching experience, and an extensive publication record, Clark was a strong candidate. Within a week of hearing from Buswell, Clark filled out an application and returned it.[4] Meanwhile, Wheaton paid for Clark to make a guest visit to the college. During his visit, Clark gave a speech in Buswell's theism class and a devotional talk at the college chapel.[5]

Although Buswell and Clark had already begun to establish a relationship through the reform movement in the PCUSA, Clark was an unknown to others at Wheaton. After Buswell offered Clark the position at Wheaton, he questioned whether Clark would fit in at the interdenominational college. Both men wondered if Clark's theological views might create a potential impasse to his hire. Buswell was expressly concerned with Clark's

2. JOB to GHC, 28 February 1936, Wheaton Archives.

3. GHC to JOB, 13 April 1935, Wheaton Archives.; JOB to GHC, 17 April 1935, Wheaton Archives.

4. GHC to JOB, 5 March 1936, Wheaton Archives.

5. JOB to GHC, 7 March 1936, Wheaton Archives.; JOB to GHC, 14 March 1936, Wheaton Archives.

unwillingness to accept the premillennial position contained in Wheaton College's "Standards of Faith and Doctrinal Platform." At Buswell's suggestion, Clark took a one-year leave of absence from his lecturer position at the University of Pennsylvania, with the assurance that he could maintain his position at Penn if things did not work out at Wheaton.[6] With the agreement in place, Clark was hired as a visiting professor at Wheaton for the 1936–1937 school year. For Buswell, this one-year trial period was designed to monitor Clark with the hope that he would come to agree with Wheaton's standard premillennial position as outlined in their official statement of beliefs. The temporary nature of Clark's appointment allowed both Buswell and Clark to weigh their options with minimal risk.

On March 5, 1937, near the end of his trial year of teaching, and after much discussion, Clark and the Wheaton administration, including President J. Oliver Buswell, Vice President Enock C. Dyrness (1902–1986), Dean Dr. Wallace L. Emerson (1886–1987), and Professor Dr. Henry C. Thiessen (1884–1947), came to a "satisfactory working understanding"[7] regarding the "Calvinistic problem" of "how the doctrine of blameworthy responsibility is safe-guarded" in Clark's theology.[8] In other words, the college accepted Clark despite his theological views which diverged from the majority at the college. Dr. Thiessen wanted Clark to be blocked from teaching the doctrines of Calvinism, but Thiessen's attempt to regulate Clark's teaching failed and the official agreement for Clark's hire was that "nothing beyond the platform was to be required."[9]

Around this same time, Clark and the Wheaton administration must have also reached an agreement on the topic of millennialism. Though the precise nature of this agreement is unclear, it probably was concerned with a particular distinction between the two common types of premillennialism. One form of premillennialism, a form taught by some of the ancient church fathers, was an acceptable position in some Presbyterian churches. This "historic premillennialism" taught, among other things, that Jesus Christ would return to earth prior to a literal 1,000-year reign of the saints. "Dispensational" premillennialism, on the other hand, was a more recent interpretation which originated in the nineteenth century and which claimed that God has two distinct peoples, Israel and the Church, and that God's promises of land, descendants, and blessings to Israel will be fulfilled

6. Telegram from JOB to GHC, 16 April 1936, Wheaton Archives.; Telegram from GHC to Enock Dyrness, 20 April 1936, Wheaton Archives.; GHC to JOB, 20 April 1936, Wheaton Archives.

7. JOB to GHC, 6 March 1937, PCA Archives, 309/24.

8. JOB to GHC, 4 March 1937, PCA Archives, 309/24.

9. JOB to Richard Willer Gray, 14 July 1943, PCA Archives.

during the future millennium of Christ's reign on earth. Most Presbyterian churches strictly opposed dispensational premillennialism. Although Clark never embraced the dispensationalist position, his acceptance of historic premillennialism appears to have been sufficient to quell the concerns of the Wheaton College administration.[10] After an agreement was reached on this issue, Clark formally resigned his position at the University of Pennsylvania on July 1, 1937, and was appointed to a permanent position as Associate Professor of Philosophy at Wheaton College.[11]

Clark's motives for relocating to Wheaton College included his promotion to associate professor and the chance to work under a supportive president in Buswell. He was also eager to escape the secular environment of the University of Pennsylvania where he felt isolated as a conservative Christian.[12] In a letter to President Buswell in 1933 (apparently a separate attempt to be considered for a position, three years prior to Buswell's overtures to hire Clark in 1936), Clark stated, "To be quite honest it was the financial conditions at this university [Penn] which prompted this letter of application to a position at Wheaton, but further reflection adds that my religious convictions would make Wheaton more agreeable than secular institutions."[13] When first contemplating a move to Wheaton, Clark expressed to Buswell that at Penn he felt like a "lone missionary, in the middle of China" and wondered if he was "perhaps sowing on stony ground"—a reference to Jesus's parable of the sower.[14]

Financial considerations also played an important part in Clark's decision to take the position at Wheaton.[15] He began his teaching career at Penn with an annual salary of $2,400. Unfortunately, tightening its belt during the Great Depression, the university slashed salaries. Clark saw his annual earnings reduced to $1,600. He was able to find extra work as a visiting

10. "Early in the Spring of 1937 he came to the premillennial position."—JOB to VRE, 18 March 1943. Also, a later chapter on eschatology in an unpublished manuscript clarifies his position: "The present volume advocates premillennialism, though in a manner that many premillennarians will not like. For it is to be feared that premillennarians are their own worst enemies. Why, may become somewhat clear as the end approaches. At any rate, the argument of the present volume is not so much that the Bible teaches it unmistakably, as that postmillennialism and amillennialism can in no way be fitted into the biblical data, and hence only premillennialism is left."—Clark, "Chapter IX: Eschatology" in *Introduction to Theology*. 80.

11. Record of employment at the University of Pennsylvania (n.d.), alumni folder of Gordon Haddon Clark, University of Pennsylvania Archives.

12. Hamilton, "Fundamentalist Harvard," 146.

13. GHC to JOB, 17 June 1933, PCA Archives, 279/235.

14. GHC to JOB, 5 March 1936, Wheaton Archives, 309/24.

15. GHC to JOB, 17 June 1933, PCA Archives, 279/235.

lecturer at the Reformed Episcopal Seminary in Philadelphia for another $100–200 per year, but this hardly made up for the shortfall. Although his salary at Penn was later raised to $1,900, in transferring to Wheaton, Clark felt justified in requesting an annual salary of $3,000. After negotiations, he accepted a salary of $2,750 a year[16]—an increase surely welcome to Gordon and his wife, who by that point had a baby to care for.

The new position at Wheaton brought Clark some much-desired recognition and respect. He had served as an instructor at Penn since 1924 while a graduate student, but despite graduating in 1929 and continuing to teach for a total of twelve years, he never received a promotion to "assistant professor." He thought this lack of a promotion was a disgrace, and decided in 1937 that he would never again return to his alma mater unless it was accompanied by a promotion in rank.[17] Clark felt that his teaching, service, and publication record merited a promotion, but some administrators at Penn actively worked to block his promotion because they saw him as a troublemaker on account of his membership in the reforming movement within the PCUSA.[18] Of his detractors, Clark wrote, "There are two persons who dislike [Dr. Henry Bradford Smith, a philosophy professor at Penn] . . . The same two love me no more and church affiliations lead one of them to wish for and work for, both in civil courts and in private, my embarrassment, whether financial, professional, or personal."[19] When Clark asked his Penn philosophy professor colleague Edgar A. Singer Jr. about his chances of getting a promotion if he returned, Singer relayed to Clark that their fellow colleague, Dr. Henry Bradford Smith, took up Clark's case with the dean and vice provost, but that Smith's efforts had ended in failure. Dr. Singer wrote to Clark, "The attitude of the administration remained absolutely unchanged." Also through Dr. Singer, Dr. Smith was obliged to relay a message from the administration: "Advise Dr. Clark to remain where he is."[20]

Ultimately, it was Clark's dedication to opposing the modernists in the PCUSA that was his undoing at Penn. Dr. Singer alluded to this in a letter to Clark: "I suspect that if the reasons [for not promoting or re-hiring Clark] were known to you, you would take the deepest of them to be an honor to you."[21] In an earlier letter Singer had lamented the future of Penn's philosophy department should Clark decide to leave. He wrote, "If you were

16. GHC to George V. Kirk, 20 May 1936, PCA Archives, 309/42.

17. GHC to Edgar A. Singer Jr., 23 January 1937, PCA Archives, 309/53.

18. Rudolph, "A Truly Great and Brilliant Friend," 100.

19. GHC to Edgar A. Singer Jr., 23 January 1937, PCA Archives, 309/53.

20. Edgar A. Singer Jr. to GHC, 15 February 1937, PCA Archives, 309/53.

21. Ibid.

not to come back, we should be utterly up a stump in the matter of finding any successor even halfway acceptable to the department, as continuing a tradition of sound scholarship in the field you cultivate."[22]

Looking back, we can see 1936 and 1937 as crucial years for Clark. Soon after Clark was hired at Wheaton, the reform efforts in the PCUSA hit their terminus. Machen and Buswell, along with other members of the Independent Board of Presbyterian Foreign Missions, were suspended from ministry. Clark followed these men out of the PCUSA and became a founding member of the Presbyterian Church of America.

Buswell became Clark's closest confidant at Wheaton. With a shared background in Presbyterian and Calvinist theology, the two were in a minority on a campus dominated by an interdenominational evangelical Christianity. For part of Clark's first year at Wheaton he and Buswell were both members of the Presbyterian Church of America. Buswell, however, left the denomination after the Third General Assembly (of June 1, 1937), which voted against his demand that the entire denomination officially renounce the use of alcohol. Buswell soon thereafter joined the group of ministers which formed the Bible Presbyterian Church (BPC). However, since the split was not over fundamental doctrines such as the inerrancy of Scripture—the issue that caused the PCA to break away from the PCUSA— it did not produce an impassable divide between Clark and Buswell who remained united on much of their Calvinist and Presbyterian theology.

THE INTELLECTUAL HONOR ROLL

When Clark joined the faculty, Wheaton College was experiencing a period of rapid growth. In this era, Wheaton had a strong reputation for both its Christian environment and its academic prowess, later even being referred to as a "Fundamentalist Harvard."[23] During Clark's years at the college, Wheaton was a fountainhead for many noteworthy future church leaders. Indeed, a list of Clark's students reads like an honor roll of twentieth-century Christian intellectuals. His students included Edward Carnell (1919–1967), Edmund Clowney (1917–2005), Lars Granberg (1919–2011), Carl F. H. Henry (1913–2003), Paul Jewett (1920–1991), and Harold Lindsell (1913–1998).[24] Even Billy Graham (b. 1918) studied at Wheaton and enrolled in Clark's Medieval Philosophy course.

22. Edgar A. Singer Jr. to GHC, 11 January 1937, PCA Archives, 309/53.

23. Hamilton, "Fundamentalist Harvard."

24. Edward Carnell later wrote a number of books on Christian apologetics and became president of Fuller Theological Seminary. Edmund Clowney became president

Believing that formal logic was essential for understanding Christian faith, Clark spent much time teaching the subject. Yet some of his students saw his emphasis on logic to be detrimental to their desired "warm" evangelism. In other words, many students were looking for an emotional, not an intellectual, appeal to faith. Samuel D. Faircloth witnessed this struggle between Clark and his students firsthand. Faircloth was a student in Clark's Medieval Philosophy class alongside a young Billy Graham. According to Faircloth, Graham objected to Clark's strictly logical and rational approach to Christianity. In an interview in 2010, Faircloth recalled,

> I was trying to catch up historically and every other way with the prof. He knew what he was talking about. He was a top-drawer teacher. Billy (Graham) was back in the background. He stood up one day and he looked Clark right in the eye. I'll never forget this because I thought he had a lot of nerve. He stood up and pointed his finger at Clark, "Doc, you're cold." And Clark looked right back, "I prefer to remain cold." Clark was a good philosophy professor and Graham was not operating on that level. He was operating on a warm evangelistic level and Clark was talking about Augustine's *City of God*.[25]

In short, Clark was not Billy Graham, an evangelist of broad popular appeal.[26]

While students like Graham may have objected to this approach, Clark's "cold" logic was a corollary principle of his main axiom or first principle: the truth of the Bible. As Clark was fond of pointing out, if one is to think or speak at all, he must abide by the laws of logic. Clark's detractors often called him a rationalist—one who presupposes bare logic itself as his main principle. Yet logic was not the starting point for Clark; rather, it was

---

of Westminster Theological Seminary. Lars Granberg joined the faculty at Fuller for a time and later held other academic posts including President of Northwestern College in Iowa and Dean of Social Science at Hope College in Michigan. Carl F. H. Henry also taught at Fuller and was later the first editor of the magazine *Christianity Today*. Paul Jewett taught systematic theology at Fuller, and Harold Lindsell taught at three theological seminaries prior to working as an editor at *Christianity Today*.

25. Samuel Douglas Faircloth, interview by Robert Shuster, 1 June 2010, BGC Archives, Wheaton College, CN 658, T1, mp3: minute 106–107, http://espace.wheaton.edu/bgc/audio/cn658t001.mp3.

26. Note also that while at Wheaton College, the Clark family attended the Wheaton Tabernacle, a non-denominational church in the city. Occasionally Clark would even preach there as evidenced by notes to that effect on his sermons extant in the PCA archives and from recollections of Clark's daughter Lois. Billy Graham also preached at the chapel and in his autobiography listed Clark as one of a group of "intimidating" persons to preach in front of.—Graham, *Just as I Am*, 66.

to him a tool of the trade, supported within Scripture itself by the "logos doctrine" of John's gospel. Clark elaborated upon this doctrine in his 1972 book, *The Johannine Logos*, in which he explained how the Greek word *logos* in the Bible often signifies the logical or rational principle of thought which enlightens all men.

Clark's approach to grading was equally "cold," with the intention of instilling in his students the habits of scholars. He believed the overriding purpose of college was study, and studying was necessary even for the top students who took his courses. The difficulty of his quizzes (he refused to call them tests) was recalled by one of his former students, Dr. Carl F. H. Henry: "Clark gave us periodic true-false or completion tests of twenty questions and never scaled the grades on the basis of 100. It was a routine comment that not even the Pope could fare better than 20 points on Clark's exams, and he would be lucky to get that."[27]

Though Clark's approach was unattractive to some students, there were others at Wheaton who appreciated his "coldness." Ironically, one such student was Ruth Bell, who later married the "warm" evangelist Billy Graham. In her book *It's My Turn*, she recounted a time when she was experiencing doubt of her Christian faith. A fellow student suggested she see a particular professor who was known to be spiritual, but Ruth objected, saying, "He will talk with me, and pray with me, and it could even get a little emotional. I don't want that. All I want are cold, hard facts." She continued, "I wanted to go see Dr. Gordon Clark, known for his logic, his unemotional brilliance. I felt he would give me nothing but the cold, hard facts."[28]

Although Clark certainly hoped his students would ultimately come to adopt the Christian and Reformed positions he embraced, he did not teach his Christian beliefs alone to the exclusion of all other thought. In fact, he was known to employ the Socratic Method; that is, he repeatedly questioned his students, forcing them to think through the logical steps of their own beliefs. Carl F. H. Henry later wrote about Clark's teaching, "When he taught Augustine, or Aquinas, or Spinoza, he was for a time the living incarnation of each thinker, defending a given philosopher's affirmations against all counterattack, and driving us to formulate our criticisms ever more lucidly and logically."[29] This teaching style of Clark shows that he was not solely a zealous Christian, but truly an academic.

---

27. Henry, *Confessions of a Theologian*, 71.

28. Graham, *It's My Turn*, 47.

29. Henry, *Confessions of a Theologian*, 71.

Clark's work at Wheaton went beyond the classroom. He formed and led a college chess club.[30] He gave a number of speeches, including at least one to the French club about his time studying at the Sorbonne.[31] In many cases, the relationships he had with his students became lasting friendships. In at least three cases, Clark attended weddings of Wheaton students. The first of these, in the summer of 1940, was the wedding of John and Miriam Lee in California where Clark's daughter Lois, then four years of age, was the flower girl. Prior to this occasion, in fact, Clark had never owned a car. He asked his students to locate a car for him which he then purchased for the trip.[32] Another wedding Clark attended was that of Edward Carnell in 1944.[33] In 1945, it appears that he officiated the wedding of James Tompkins and Charlotte Boggs.[34] Other students, including Howard Long, and Warren and Norma Davis, visited the Clark household in later years, and Clark in turn visited the Davises in Arizona (where they worked as missionaries translating the Bible into Navajo) when he was on road trips out west in later years.[35]

A NEW PRESIDENT

Clark lost his main ally at Wheaton when Buswell was fired in January of 1940 after Buswell refused the request of the board of trustees for him to resign. Though this was denied by at least one board member, Buswell had likely upset them through his advocacy of the separationist movements in the Presbyterian church. The board may have felt Buswell's stand brought too much negative attention to Wheaton and highlighted dissension in the Christian world. While Buswell's outspoken support of separationism likely contributed to his dismissal, this was not the only issue. One member of the board of trustees wrote that the reason for the difficulty with Buswell

30. "Chess Enthusiasts Elect Mackenzie in Meet at Clark's," *The Wheaton Record*, 12 October 1937.; "Clark Mentors Pawns, Pupils in Chess Club," *The Wheaton Record*, 12 October 1937.; "Chess Players Must Conquer Dr. Clark," *The Wheaton Record*, 12 November 1937.; "Chessmen Philosophize Future University Meets Possible," *The Wheaton Record*, 18 October 1938.

31. "French Club Hears Clark on Sorbonne," *The Wheaton Record*, 18 March 1938.

32. Lois (née Clark) Zeller, interview by Douglas Douma, Sangre de Cristo Seminary, 18 May 2014.

33. Nelson, *The Making and Unmaking of an Evangelical Mind*, 51.

34. A list of weddings Clark officiated, written in his own handwriting, is included in the back of a copy of *The Book of Common Prayer* in the Clark Collection at Sangre de Cristo Seminary's Clark Library.

35. Norma Davis, letter to the author, 10 February 2014.

was due to "repeated instances of friction" with those in the administration immediately under him and that he lacked the "gift of reconciling himself to the disagreements which others may have with him."[36] At the same time there were complaints to the fact that Buswell had hired a Wheaton outsider to coach the college's football team.[37] Whatever the exact cause of Buswell's dismissal, Clark lost not only a fellow proponent of Calvinism on the campus, but also a defender of his teaching and the proximity of a good friend. Buswell had defended Clark not only on the Wheaton campus but also within the Bible Presbyterian Church.[38] Despite Buswell's departure, he and Clark remained in contact for many years. Buswell continued to be proud of his own actions at Wheaton, even writing "ex-president" in the salutation of his letters from his new job as a professor at Faith Seminary.[39]

With Buswell's departure, Clark lost a defender of his Calvinist views. Swiftly enough, his dedication to a logical, intellectual, and Calvinist Christianity brought conflict with the new administration, despite his influence and generally favorable reputation among the students. The main conflict between Clark and the college arose when the New Testament professor and head of the Bible and Philosophy Department, Dr. Henry C. Thiessen, expressed displeasure with some of Clark's views. Thiessen had been opposed to Clark's presence at the college from the start, but his complaints fell on deaf ears during the Buswell administration. The new president, V. Raymond Edman (1900–1967), was more sympathetic to Thiessen's grievances. This was to be expected, since Edman, who was an inside candidate for the presidency at Wheaton, had, like Thiessen, strong connections to the college's core theological values. Prior to his presidency, Edman had been a missionary to the Quechua people in Ecuador (1923–1928), and after finishing his doctoral degree, was a history professor at Wheaton from 1936–1940. Edman was well loved at the college and popular among the students, but he was no intellectual equal to Buswell or Clark. Edman, as a former missionary, took Thiessen's concerns seriously. If Clark's Calvinism was harming evangelistic zeal, Edman would certainly want to get to the bottom of it.

Clark was never one for toeing a moderate line or hiding his views. So when Thiessen wanted him removed, Clark's actions provided plenty of

36. Herman A. Fischer (Chairman of the Board of Trustees) to William A. Gere, 21 February 1940, Wheaton Archives.

37. "What Happened to Buswell?" *The Wheaton Record*, 30 April 1982, 8.

38. "And I know too how [Buswell] defended me when some of the Bible Synod protested to him about keeping me at Wheaton."—GHC to Robert Strong, 9 May 1942, PCA Archives, 309/56.

39. JOB to Francis Schaeffer, 26 February 1940, PCA Archives, 286/73.

reasons for Edman to follow up on Thiessen's concerns. For example, Clark taught his students of the novelty, or recentness, of the dispensationalist view popular at Wheaton; that it originated in just the previous century and was unknown amongst the leaders of the Reformation. Clark also visibly promoted Reformed theology on the campus. For example, to spur students to think about Reformed doctrine, he instituted a $50 prize for the student who could write the best historical short story on the Reformation or the Reformed Faith. In addition, he formed a "Creed Club," which met on Sunday afternoons to study the *Westminster Confession of Faith*, the historic confession of most Presbyterian churches. Through this club (which at least once had an attendance of twenty-four students)[40] and his classes, Clark's influence led many students to attend Westminster Theological Seminary after graduating from Wheaton College. In fact, Clark was so effective at directing students to Westminster Seminary that a Faith Seminary student, Francis Schaeffer, (who later became a popular author and apologist) complained in a letter dated April 21, 1938, to Wheaton President J. Oliver Buswell that students were choosing the OPC-favored Westminster Theological Seminary due to Clark's influence, rather than the BPC's Faith Seminary as Schaeffer preferred.[41] Clark, therefore, influenced not only the many students who took his classes, but also a great part of the intellectual structure of the Presbyterian church across denominational lines.

CONFLICT WITH THE ADMINISTRATION

As Clark's popularity and influence grew, he became an increasing threat to the status quo and to the administration at Wheaton. Complaints arose that Clark's teaching was causing students to abandon evangelism and that his strong Calvinism constituted fatalism. Wheaton was officially non-denominational, but many of its administrators and professors were decidedly Arminian in theology; that is, they consciously followed the views of the Dutch theologian Jacobus Arminius (1560–1609) in their soteriology, believing man has free will sufficient to choose or reject God for salvation. Clark, in contrast, was Calvinist in his soteriology, holding that God is in sovereign control over all things, including man's will and eternal state.

In some ways, President Edman inherited a problem not of his own making. Clark had made his views known when Wheaton College was in the process of hiring him in 1937. In fact, Buswell even knew of Clark's views a year prior to Clark's hire, as indicated in a number of letters between

---

40. GHC to Edwin Rian, 1 March 1943, PCA Archives, 309/48.

41. Francis Schaeffer to JOB, 21 April 1938, Wheaton Archives.

the two men. In the hiring process itself, Clark's statement of faith specified the differences between his positions and the Wheaton College "Statements of Faith and Doctrinal Platform." Specifically, Clark affirmed that he was a Calvinist of the "supralapsarian[42] type" and said, "I realize this is not the most popular position, but I find it most consistent and most in accord with the Word of God." In addition, in his statement of faith, Clark would not commit initially to the premillennial position of the college, affirming instead "the traditional Calvinist position" and adding that he was not sure if he was "post-millenarian or a-millenarian."[43]

An official complaint against Clark was lodged on January 11, 1942, when Professor Thiessen wrote to the Board of Trustees of Wheaton College, urging them to condemn his colleague: "In view of Dr. Clark's extreme theological position and its harmful effects on students as evidenced over the years, and his insistence on the figurative interpretation of Joshua's long day, I, therefore, as Chairman of the Department of Bible, Theology, and Philosophy, do hereby request that Dr. Clark be no longer retained on the faculty of Wheaton College." Throughout the ordeal that ensued, Clark looked to the teachings of the *Westminster Confession of Faith* both for guidance and as a shield of defense against the accusation that something was fundamentally flawed with his views. Clark wrote to Edwin Rian (1900–1995), president of the board of trustees at Westminster Theological Seminary, saying, "I have tried to limit myself to the Westminster Confession, and the result is that I am considered 'extreme.'"[44]

That Thiessen's complaint did not lead to Clark's immediate dismissal reflects perhaps on the considerate, cautious, or even sympathetic views of Edman; but resistance to Clark was mounting. Thiessen, as the head of the Bible and Philosophy Department, eliminated the college's philosophy major in an attempt to force Clark to leave the college on his own accord.[45] Clark believed the elimination of the philosophy major was a terrible insult to him, committed, in his words, "without departmental recommendation, committee action, or faculty approval."[46] Edman followed suit of Theissen,

---

42. Supralapsarianism is the doctrine that in the logical order of the God's decrees, the decree to save some and condemn others precedes the decree of the fall of man. This is a minority position within Calvinism. The majority holds to infralapsarianism, which puts the logical order of the decree of the fall of man prior to the decree of election.

43. GHC to the President and Trustees of Wheaton College, 3 March 1936, Wheaton archives.

44. GHC to Edwin Rian, 27 June 1942, PCA Archives, 309/48.

45. Marsden, *Reforming Fundamentalism*, 45.

46. GHC to Robert Rudolph, 1 July 1942, PCA Archives, 309/49. See also: GHC to JOB, 1 July 1942, Wheaton Archives.

prohibiting Clark from teaching Reformed (Calvinist) theology altogeth-er.[47] In short, to avoid drawing more attention to Clark and his threatening views, Thiessen and Edman hoped to muzzle him in the areas he could have the most influence.

At the same time that the philosophy major was dropped from the catalog, the college also dropped the Greek and Latin majors, claiming that the decision in all three cases was due to financial considerations stemming from declining enrollment in these majors. With the removal of multiple majors, the administration contended that the loss of the philosophy major was not an attack aimed at Clark. For a time, with fewer Greek professors,[48] Clark taught an elementary Greek course, arguing all the while that he could handle the course in addition to the full curriculum necessary to retain the philosophy major.[49] With Thiessen's complaint lodged and rumors of de-clining enrollment in the philosophy major (the validity of which Clark dis-puted inasmuch as there were twenty students majoring in philosophy, but only two or three students in some other majors which were not dropped from the catalog[50]), President Edman was placed in a difficult position. Clark was not wholly innocent of the charges of negatively affecting the evangelistic zeal of students; Clark was known for having his students cri-tique chapel sermons by finding logical fallacies, which did not sit well with the administration nor contribute to the general peace of the campus.

With his hands effectively tied by the Wheaton leadership, Clark be-gan to seek other options for employment. On May 1, 1942, he wrote to his old friend Buswell saying that he was considering resigning from Wheaton. In Clark's opinion, he could not teach if he had to stay silent on matters regarding his specific theological views. He confided to Buswell, "One can-not submit to such an underhanded procedure and retain self-respect."[51] Also on May 1, 1942, Clark wrote to an OPC colleague, Burt Goddard (1910–2007), and expressed similar frustrations: "To be brief I am consid-ering resigning, though one or two of the faculty who know me a little more intimately than the rest say not to. But it seems that my days are numbered no matter what."[52]

---

47. GHC to JOB, 1 July 1942, Wheaton Archives.

48. "With one of the young faculty men called into the army, I was asked to teach four hours of Greek."—GHC to Allen C. Emery Jr., 19 May 1942, PCA Archives, 309/32. Also: "I was already helping out in Greek because one of the young men had been taken by the army."—GHC to William McCarrell, 5 June 1942, PCA Archives.

49. GHC to VRE, 14 March 1942, PCA Archives, 309/32.

50. GHC to Richard Willer Gray, 14 July 1943, PCA Archives, 309/35.

51. GHC to JOB, 1 May 1942, Wheaton Archives.

52. GHC to Burt Goddard, 1 May 1942, PCA Archives, 309/34.

As the controversy over Clark's teaching spread, supporters of Clark came to his defense. Many observers thought the actions of the board were aimed specifically at Clark's theological views, rather than being for the good of the students as the board professed. On June 1, 1942, President Edman received a letter from Gloria Grove, a recent alumna of the class of 1941. She wrote, "I've learned that the reason for the omission of a philosophy major and the reduction in the number of courses offered in philosophy is Dr. Thiessen's objections to Dr. Clark's theology. This was not altogether a surprise to me since I have a vivid memory of the insults heaped upon Calvinism and Calvinists by Dr. Thiessen in his systematic theology lectures." In fact, Clark was not the first Wheaton professor to run into conflict with Thiessen. In response to Thiessen's attack, Clark reminded one of the trustees that "last year Dr. Hoffman was dismissed from the college. I gather that the chief cause of his dismissal was theological disagreement with Dr. Thiessen."[53] This "Dr. Hoffman" was Dr. Jacob Hoffman, a conservative Methodist minister whom J. Oliver Buswell knew from his days studying at the University of Chicago, and who had been brought out of retirement to teach Hebrew and Old Testament at Wheaton.[54] Whereas Hoffman was an Arminian in theology, Theissen held to a mediating view between Arminianism and Calvinism. Thus, Theissen had disagreements with both ends of the spectrum. Clark wrote of the situation, "Now Dr. Hoffman was an Arminian, I am a Calvinist. Dr. Thiessen is neither. He has a system of his own never adopted by any denomination as far as I know,"[55] and further argued, "Dr. Thiessen's theology has never been adopted by any denomination and is only his personal production."[56] Thus, with Thiessen at odds with both opposing soteriological systems, Clark argued that, "If the trustees wish to enforce the views of Dr. Thiessen, that will settle the matter; but it will result in a Wheaton purged of Calvinists and Arminians alike."[57]

Meanwhile, repeated requests from Clark to Edman led to a faculty vote on the restoration of the philosophy major at the last faculty meeting of the year in June 1942. The vote passed and the philosophy major was back in the catalog for the following year.[58]

Suspicious of Clark's theology, President Edman launched an inquiry into the effect of Clark's teaching. Edman wrote to Carl F. H. Henry, a

53. GHC to William R. McCarrel, 5 June 1942, PCA Archives, 309/45.

54. Henry, Confessions of a Theologian, 73–74.

55. GHC to William R. McCarrel, 5 June 1942, PCA Archives, 309/45.

56. GHC to Allen Emery, 19 June 1942, PCA Archives, 309/32.

57. GHC to William R. McCarrel, 5 June 1942, PCA Archives, 309/45.

58. GHC to Richard Willer Gray, 14 July 1943, PCA Archives, 309/35.

former student of Clark's, "Some question has been raised in various quarters about the import and influence of Dr. Clark's teaching. Inasmuch as you
majored in philosophy, you should be in a position to make a fair and frank
evaluation from your point of view." Edman also wrote to John E. Woods,
another recent graduate and then student at Princeton. Although Woods
had disagreed with Clark's theological positions on a variety of grounds, he
responded to Edman with a positive appraisal of Clark's teaching methods
and noted that Clark was a "scholar and gentleman" in their theological
discussions. Woods praised Edman for "getting to the bottom of the whole
affair and learning the truth" prior to making a decision one way or the
other. Woods concluded, however, by noting, "I should personally consider
it an irreparable loss to the college if Dr. Clark were permitted to leave the
Wheaton faculty."[59]

Thiessen, however, would not back down. On June 24, 1942, he again
wrote to the board of trustees asking for Clark's resignation. This time, he
provided six specific reasons why Clark should be removed. According to
Thiessen, Clark taught the following five things: 1. God causes everything,
including evil, 2. the doctrine of double predestination, 3. the doctrine of
limited atonement, 4. God's emotions are anthropomorphic, and 5. the
figurative interpretation of Joshua's long day. Thiessen's sixth reason (not
enumerated as were the first five) for requesting Clark's resignation was the
concern that Clark's teaching tended toward absolute determinism.[60]

In response to Thiessen's claims, President Edman and a special committee of the board of trustees held a meeting on June 30, 1942. Dr. Clark was
invited to attend. The special committee consisted of thoroughgoing fundamentalists, who generally echoed the theological positions of the college.
Board members included the "Archbishop of Fundamentalism" Dr. Harry
A. Ironside (1876–1951), a popularizer of dispensationalism and pastor of
Chicago's Moody Memorial Church; David Otis Fuller (1903–1988), pastor
of the well-known Wealthy Street Baptist Church in Grand Rapids, Michigan, and an early proponent of the exclusive use of the King James Version
of the Bible; Herman A. Fischer Jr. (1882–1974), a grandson of the former
college president Jonathan Blanchard; Dr. William McCarrell (1886–1979),
pastor of Cicero Bible Church and founder of the Independent Fundamentalist Churches of America; and Mr. Robert E. Nicholas (1882–1977), a
wealthy local businessman and major donor to the college. According to
a report from the committee, they "conferred with Clark at length about
the questions that had arisen and particularly as to his personal beliefs in

59. John E. Woods to Dr. Edman, 23 June 1942, Wheaton Archives.
60. Henry Thiessen to the Board of Trustees, 24 June 1942, Wheaton Archives.

theological areas." Although admitting that Clark's beliefs for the most part did not differ from their own, the special committee concluded that "he holds certain views, originating with John Calvin, or imitators of Calvin, which go beyond what we could endorse." Ultimately, some of the committee felt that "part of the error arises from an effort to expand, by human reason and deduction, the doctrine of the person of God beyond what is definitely taught in Scripture." Apparently not wanting to get into a debate, the committee further concluded that "to attempt to directly refute such error, similarly might be to presume by human wisdom to develop doctrines about God going beyond which He has seen fit to reveal to us."[61]

Although Clark held to the fundamentalists' core beliefs, he was not a fundamentalist of the same stripe as those on the special committee of the board of trustees. In fact, Clark despised the anti-intellectualism associated with the fundamentalist movement. His commitment to the *Westminster Confession of Faith* led him to value teaching the "whole counsel of God," not just a limited set of fundamental doctrines.[62] Clark would later critique fundamentalists in general, saying, "In the twentieth century the fundamentalists, in varying degrees, advocate a faith without reason. Although they stress Bible study more than the pietists and the anarchical prophets did, they frequently inveigh against philosophy and 'mere' human reason. Even in doctrine they do not ordinarily go beyond half a dozen fundamental beliefs. Anything further is dry-as-dust theology."[63]

On August 21, 1942, Clark clarified his views in a letter to President Edman. Clark stated that he had repeatedly and explicitly informed the board that it was his belief that although God is the cause of all things, God is not the author of evil, nor is he guilty or responsible for sin. This, he argued, is because, unlike in the case of man, there is no power over God to which He can be held accountable. God, Clark believed, is not the author of sin, because nothing God does is sinful. Clark sought support for his position in the *Westminster Confession of Faith*, which states that "God from all

61. The Special Committee to the Board of Trustees of Wheaton College, August 1942, Wheaton Archives. Also: Five particular beliefs attributed to Clark which the Committee took issue with are listed in the same letter as (1) God decrees one man to be a murderer, or adulterer, or idiot; (2) God decrees some to heaven and some to hell; (3) God is emotionless, unmoved; (4) God's love is a manifestation of His will only, not of his affections (if any); (5) God never loved the non-elect.

62. Westminster Assembly, Westminster Confession of Faith (1646), Chapter I, Part VI: "The whole counsel of God concerning all things necessary for his own glory, man's salvation, faith and life, is either expressly set down in Scripture, or by good and necessary consequence may be deduced from Scripture: unto which nothing at any time is to be added, whether by new revelations of the Spirit, or traditions of men."

63. Clark, *Religion, Reason, and Revelation*, 71.

eternity, did, by the most wise and holy counsel of His own will, freely, and unchangeably ordain whatsoever comes to pass; yet so, as thereby neither is God the author of sin . . . " (WCF, Chapter III, Part I). Regarding the charge that God lacks emotions, Clark equated emotions with the passions denied of God in the *Westminster Confession*, which declares that "God is without body, parts or passions" (WCF, Chapter II, Part I).

RESIGNATION

On September 1, 1942, Edman and the special committee of the board of trustees sent three suggestions to the entire board regarding how Gordon Clark should teach:

1. *That to the largest extent possible he confine his teaching to the stated subjects, without advocating any theological beliefs which are controversial among orthodox Christians;*

2. *That if asked his personal opinion as to the group of doctrines in question, he be frank, but state the belief rather than expound his reasons,—being equally frank in admitting his susceptibility to error and that his views, in this respect, have not been those of most Christian leaders;*

3. *That he add that he by no means endorses deductions from such doctrines which have been made on such questions as personal responsibility for sin, the duty of missionary effort and evangelization, and the duty of seeking the guidance of the Spirit as to problems of both conduct and doctrine.*

The suggestions were a call for Clark to avoid his distinctive teachings. When he would not comply, the board of trustees voted unanimously on December 22, 1942, to end his tenure after the 1942–1943 school year. Clark learned about the vote when President Edman brought him in for a personal conference. Edman explained the situation to a stunned Clark, to whom he then offered an opportunity to resign.[64]

At this point Clark had not been officially removed, but he was effectively prohibited from teaching his own views. The action of denying Clark's tenure was made official in February 1943 but was not set to take effect until the end of the 1942–1943 school year, allowing him to finish his courses for the semester.

---

64. VRE to Herman August Fischer (Chairman of the Board of Trustees), 11 January 1943, Wheaton Archives.

Clark had previously sought the advice of his lawyer and high school friend, John Harper[65], asking whether he should resign or file a lawsuit against the college for breach of contract. Harper informed him that he likely did not have a winnable case since "employment is at will and may be terminated by either party at any time and without notice." In other words, if the board decided not to renew a professor's contract, a professor had no recourse. Harper recommended that Clark back away peacefully, start looking for another position, and do nothing that might harm his reputation or chances somewhere else.[66] Following this advice, on February 15, 1943, Clark sent his letter of resignation to President Edman and the board of trustees of the college. Shortly thereafter, the board accepted Clark's resignation.

On March 25, 1943, *The Presbyterian Guardian*, the semi-monthly publication commonly associated with the Orthodox Presbyterian Church, published Clark's letter of resignation. In it, Clark enumerated five points on the grounds of religious and moral conviction for his resignation. These reasons can best be summed up in his final point: "To comply with these conditions would be to repudiate my vows of ordination to the eldership." Clark's adherence as a ruling elder in the church to his denomination's confessional standards—the *Westminster Confession* and Catechisms—was thus shown to be stronger than his commitment to Wheaton College.[67]

A firestorm of letters of disapproval inundated President Edman's mailbox. Supporters of Clark who wrote to Edman included Floyd Hamilton, A. C. Gordon, LeRoy B. Oliver, Willard Wellman, Everett Hawkes, Robert H. Graham, and Elwin M. Sire. In addition to these letters of protest, Dr. Albert S. O'Brien, a chemistry professor at Wheaton, who had been involved in Clark's Creed Club, felt the college was putting a restraint on the liberty of teaching[68] and resigned in protest. O'Brien specified his reason in *The Presbyterian Guardian*: "After very serious consideration I have decided to resign my position at Wheaton. The religious and academic issues involved in Dr. Clark's removal from the faculty are the reason for my taking this action."[69]

65. "John Harper was one of my High School chums in 1916. We went to the U. of P. together."—GHC to Greg Reynolds, 31 March 1984. Letter provided by Greg Reynolds.

66. GHC and John Harper, series of letters exchanged between 1 May 1942 and 10 September 1942, PCA Archives, 309/36.

67. Birch, "Dr. Clark Resigns From Wheaton College Faculty," 86.

68. VRE to Delbert P. Jorgensen, 17 December 1943, Wheaton Archives.

69. Birch, "Another Wheaton Teacher Resigns Over Clark Issue," 160. Note also: "As I understand it, Dr. O'Brien has a Plymouth Brethren background. On returning to

The fallout continued when *The Presbyterian Guardian* printed an article titled "Wheaton College Today." Its author, Edwin H. Rian, criticized Wheaton for its inconsistency in once accepting Clark's views when hiring him and later dismissing him for holding the very same positions. Rian argued, furthermore, that Wheaton "set itself against practically every Reformed and Presbyterian church body in the world" by its actions opposing Clark's Calvinism.[70] Clark's supporters did not go away quietly, and the college's reputation in the Reformed world suffered. When a student at Wheaton informed Clark that he had found mailed OPC tracts in the trash, Clark notified Floyd Hamilton (1890–1969), a missionary who had sent the tracts on behalf of the OPC's Christian Education Committee. Hamilton sent a letter to the postal inspector.[71] President Edman then received an inquiry and visit from the postal inspector from Chicago.[72] Edman assured the inspector that the tracts were not thrown out intentionally and thus insufficient evidence was found to further the complaint.[73]

Throughout the debacle, Edman found himself in a difficult position. The complaints against Clark had not originated from him, yet he had had to make some difficult decisions about Clark's future at the college. Edman wrote, "The whole matter has been a great grief to me. I have sought to save Dr. Clark for Wheaton and for the great influence he can be for evangelical Christianity throughout the world."[74] Edman had been sympathetic to Clark's plight. To evidence this, it should be noted that Clark wrote to a friend that at an administration meeting "Thiessen tried to make another speech against me, but Edman just shut him up."[75]

After the school year was over, Clark stayed in the Wheaton area and became the Orthodox Presbyterian Church's student advisor for the 1943–1944 school year for "continuing the witness of historic Presbyterianism on the campus." In this role, he invited students to his home for Bible studies

---

Wheaton to teach, he began to attend Dr. Clark's Sunday school class; he also attended the Creed Club, an organization of students to study Calvinism."—V. Raymond Edman to Allan MacRae, 29 May 1943, PCA Archives.

70. Rian, "Wheaton College Today," 115.

71. Floyd E. Hamilton to Postal Inspector, Chicago Illinois, 25 June 1943, Wheaton College Archives and Special Collections.

72. GHC to Richard Willer Gray, 14 July 1943, PCA Archives, 309/35.

73. Floyd E. Hamilton to VRE, 18 August 1943, Wheaton College Archives and Special Collections.

74. VRE to A. C. Gordon, 12 August 1942, Wheaton College Archives and Special Collections.

75. GHC to Robert Strong, 1 July 1942, PCA Archives, 309/56.

and classes.[76] Clark's resignation from Wheaton was a low point in his life. Nevertheless, he remained optimistic and continued to pursue the call to preach the gospel, writing in his notes on this occasion, "II Timothy 4:2 Preach [the] gospel in season and out of season. This may be out of season but I shall continue to preach [under the] auspices of the Home Missions Committee of OPC."[77]

The events at Wheaton taught Clark that his Calvinist views would not be accepted at the ostensibly interdenominational Christian institution. It appears, in this case at least, that the trustees of Wheaton were more concerned with appealing to their supporters than in defining or defending true theological beliefs. It seemed obvious that Clark was more likely to be welcomed at an institution committed to the *Westminster Confession of Faith*.

---

76. Birch, "With the Standing Committees," 283.
77. Clark, teaching notes on *Westminster Confession of Faith*.

Chapter 5

The Origins of Presuppositionalism

"Instead of beginning with facts and later discovering God, unless a thinker begins with God, he can never end with God, or get the facts either."[1]
—GORDON H. CLARK

DURING THE EARLY YEARS of Gordon Clark's career, first at the University of Pennsylvania and then at Wheaton College, he began to formulate his own distinctive Christian philosophy. Clark's philosophy, which came to be called "presuppositionalism,"[2] can be seen primarily as the synthesis of two factors: (1) the rejection of empiricism and (2) the acceptance of worldview thinking. Understanding the need for a comprehensive worldview in which to orient his philosophy, and rejecting the philosophy of empiricism, Clark adopted a strictly Calvinistic approach, arguing that knowledge is entirely dependent on God's revelation in the Scriptures.

1. Clark, *Christian Philosophy of Education,* 38.

2. Other terms for Clark's philosophy include *dogmatism* (a term Clark himself used), *scripturalism* (a term coined by John Robbins), and more recently, *classical presuppositionalism* (a term coined by Dr. E. Calvin Beisner to differentiate Clark's views from Van Tillian presuppositionalism).

REJECTION OF EMPIRICISM AND THE CLASSICAL
ARGUMENTS FOR THE EXISTENCE OF GOD

Clark inherited from his reading of the ancient Greek philosophers a thorough opposition to empiricism, the philosophy that knowledge is primarily or exclusively derived from the senses. Many of the ancient Greek philosophers argued against empiricism. The Skeptics (fourth to second century BC) fully denied the existence of empirical knowledge. The ancient Sophists not only doubted empirical knowledge, but also challenged philosophers' claims of attaining knowledge in general, since in their view, generations of philosophers had failed to produce satisfactory answers to even the most simple questions. Clark took seriously the arguments of these philosophical schools and so found little to be admired among contemporary philosophical systems, which also largely rely on empirical or sensory knowledge. To Clark, it was as though modern thinkers were unaware of the problems with empiricism voiced by the ancient Greeks.

Clark was particularly concerned with the tendency of Christians to rely on empirical arguments instead of on revelation as the sole source of truth. Even many of the popular arguments for the existence of God employed by Christians, he noted, were based on empirical claims. Thomas Aquinas (1225–1274), for example, spoke of five ways we can know the existence of God, including the empirically-based teleological (or design) argument. During Clark's study of philosophy, he came to learn of and accept the refutations of these supposed proofs.

Though Clark ultimately was opposed to all non-Christian philosophies, he focused his critique against empiricism. Arguments against empiricism constitute a significant portion of his works. The reason for his emphasis is clear: various forms of empiricism, all of which Clark considered demonstrably false, dominated the philosophical landscape during his day (and continue to do so today). He knew that the ancient Sophist and Skeptic arguments against empiricism had not been refuted, but simply ignored.

Providing a definition of empiricism, Clark wrote: "Empiricism, strictly speaking, is the theory of epistemology that bases all knowledge on experience or sensation alone."[3] According to the theory of empiricism, (1) the mind is blank at birth and (2) sensations are basic. A person then is supposed to (3) infer perceptions from sensations. These perceptions are then stored in the mind as (4) memory images from which are abstracted (5) ideas or concepts. Clark critiqued the theory of empiricism at every one of these stages.

3. Clark, "Empiricism."

Regarding the first stage of empiricism, Clark argued that a mind that is blank would have no capacity to process sensations. A blank mind, in fact, is no mind at all. With such a blank mind, the process of empiricism cannot even begin. And, from a biblical perspective, Clark argued that *a priori* or innate knowledge (denied in empiricism) is necessary to explain how Adam understood the words God spoke to him shortly after he was created—an understanding impossible under the philosophy of empiricism, which requires a significant amount of time for man to learn concepts and build a language.[4]

On the second stage of empiricism he held that the senses are not trustworthy. The senses often deceive, and only a single deception of the senses is sufficient to justify doubt in them. Clark said, "If a witness in a criminal case is shown to have perjured himself, how much credence do you give to the other statements he made? If your eyes deceive you once, you can't believe any of it."[5]

Arguing against the possibility of the third stage of empiricism—that of inferring perceptions from sensations—Clark held that it is impossible to distinguish a valid perception from an invalid perception. He wrote:

> At any one time a person has impressions of red, smooth, sweet, and dozens of others. To perceive a thing, these "sensations" must be combined. Note that no one even *sees* a dog or a tree. A dog is not just black; he is also soft, fuzzy, and perhaps has an odor; combine them, and only then has he the perception of his pet. Yet there is nothing in the single qualities that forces him to select these particular ones and discard the dozens of others he has at the same time. Why does he not select the fuzzy, the sound of B flat, and the taste of Bacardi rum, all of which he senses at the same moment, and combine *them* into the perceived object?[6]

Clark critiqued this same step in the process in arguing that empiricism cannot determine individuals. He wrote:

> This massive mountain (Mt. Blanca) stands at the southern end of the Sangre de Cristo range. Is it then really a thing, an individual, a primary reality? If the entire range is the primary reality, then Mt. Blanca is not a real thing. What is worse, if we go still further, the Sangre de Cristo range may not be a thing,

4. Clark, opening remarks in "A debate between Gordon H. Clark and David Hoover on epistemology."

5. Clark, "What is Apologetics?" minute 36.

6. Clark, *Language and Theology*, 134.

but only a part of the entire Rocky Mountain chain, perhaps including the Andes as well. Which then is the individual: rock, mountain, or range? The question is embarrassing for the identification of individuals cannot be made on the empirical basis Aristotle adopts.[7]

Regarding the fourth stage, Clark argued that not everyone has memory images. Without these images, there is a major gap in the empirical path to knowledge. He wrote, "The theory of imagination, by which the sensations are supposed to be preserved and later raised to concepts, collapses on the fact that some people do not have images. Many people lack olfactory or tactual imagery; some also lack visual imagery as well. Empiricism then would have to say that these people can know nothing. But some of them are accomplished scholars."[8] In another place Clark wrote, "There are some people, and I know one fairly well, who have no images at all."[9] The person to whom Clark referred here is almost certainly himself, as he was known to claim a lack of memory images.

Against the fifth stage of empiricism Clark argued that empiricism cannot produce any universal ideas or propositions. He argued that the method employed by empiricists to generate universal propositions (such as "All emus are flightless") is to make generalizations based on a limited number of individual sensory experiences. Clark wrote, " . . . Empiricism can neither produce nor justify any universal proposition. The explanation is obvious: Experience is never universal."[10] And further, "Without universals, such as courage, liliaceae, and even red, the contents of the mind, if there be a mind at all, do not merit the name of knowledge. Without subjects and predicates there is no truth, and every predicate is a universal."[11]

In addition to these problems along empiricism's path from sensations to ideas, Clark held that there are other general issues besetting empiricism. Among these issues is the fact that empiricism cannot establish the law of contradiction, the most basic element of logical thinking. Clark wrote, "The validity of syllogistic reasoning can never be based on experience,"[12] and "Empiricism therefore is conclusively shown to be skeptical because the law

---

7. Clark, *Introduction to Christian Philosophy*, 31.

8. Clark, "The Cosmological Argument."

9. Clark, "How Does Man Know God?"

10. Clark, *Lord God of Truth*, 35.

11. Clark, *Modern Philosophy*, 62.

12. Clark, *Christian View of Men and Things*, 308.

of contradiction cannot be abstracted or obtained from temporally conditioned particulars."[13]

Furthermore, Clark argued that no normative conclusions can be deduced from descriptive premises, and thus empiricism provides no ethics. Clark held that empiricism fails to support any ethical position because it fails to surmount the Is-Ought Problem. This is the problem that an "ought" cannot be determined from an "is." In other words, from descriptive premises one cannot form normative conclusions. From what is observed in the world, one cannot conclude how we ought to act or think. Not only does empiricism fail to support any ethical theory, but it also similarly fails to produce any theory of aesthetics, any theory of what is good or what is beautiful. These limitations make empiricism inferior to those philosophies that can produce theories of ethics and aesthetics. Clark held that the Is-Ought Problem is surmounted in biblical ethics. He wrote, "Independent of descriptive empiricism, theistic ethics begins with normative propositions and escapes the fallacy of introducing terms into its conclusions that were not present in the premises."[14]

Finally, Clark maintained that empiricism is self-refuting. He said the claim that "knowledge comes only from sensory experience" cannot itself come from sensory experience, and thus on its own merits, empiricism should be rejected.

Empiricism is not only limited to secular philosophers but is also often taken up by Christians. Clark, however, believed empiricism to be incompatible with the Bible. He wrote, "The Scriptures do not discuss empiricism as such, but the doctrine of the image of God in man, the law written on the hearts of the Gentiles, and the transmission of original sin all indicate an innate, non-empirical inheritance, which precludes this philosophy."[15] Additionally, he wrote:

> But surely the most conclusive argument from Genesis centers in the word "image." If Adam was the image of God he could not have a blank mind for the simple reason that God's mind is not a blank. The account in Genesis so clearly refutes empiricism that nothing further is logically needed. But the Bible provides additional details. What is implied in Genesis is expanded in Ephesians 4:24 and Colossians 3:10. These two passages, in

13. Ibid.
14. Clark, "The Achilles Heel of Humanism," 5–6, 19.
15. Clark, "Empiricism."

explaining regeneration as a sort of new creation, teach that man was originally created in knowledge and in righteousness.[16]

Many Christians have relied on empiricism as the basis for most of the classical arguments for the existence of God. However, the failure of empiricism to produce knowledge likewise means that it can produce no knowledge about God. In addition to rejecting empiricism, Clark also rejected the classical arguments for the existence of God. He wrote:

> David Hume, who also based all knowledge on sensory experience, showed why all such "cosmological" arguments are invalid. Aside from other difficulties which Kant explained more clearly, an argument from the world, as an effect, to God, as its cause, is invalid for at least two reasons. First, there is no sensory experience that the world is an effect. Second, our experience is always finite, and a finite object cannot be shown to require an infinite cause. David Hume, to be sure, was an enemy of Christianity, but if he has disabused our minds of fallacious arguments, he has done us a service.[17]

In rejecting empiricism and taking the position that senses are untrustworthy, Clark was at odds with the school of Common Sense philosophy adhered to by many of his Presbyterian forefathers and his actual father, David Clark. David's position was far opposite of Gordon's. The elder Clark wrote:

> We know there is an external world by sight and touch. Men may quibble over the mediacy or immediacy of our sense perceptions; but that they give us knowledge of an external world no sane man can deny. If any man denies the trustworthiness of our senses, he may leap over that precipice if he pleases, the common sense of the world will not follow him. Sense perception may not give us universal knowledge, nor is it absolutely perfect, as no human thing is, but that it gives us knowledge, and such knowledge as we act on and live by, is or ought to be beyond dispute.[18]

And further, in an unpublished paper, David Clark wrote,

> The old Scottish Philosophy, toward which I confess some bias, sought to base itself on observation and induction. A true

16. Clark, "A debate between Gordon H. Clark and David Hoover on epistemology," minute 14–15.

17. Clark, "Apologetics."

18. Clark, David S. "The Reality of Me."

method must hold firmly to facts. Facts must precede theory. Empirical knowledge is necessary to a true science, and a true science is necessary to a true philosophy. We get our knowledge of the external world through our senses. If we do not accept the testimony of our sense, we will never know much about the external world.[19]

Clark's rejection of empiricism was also later a concern of his friend and fellow Presbyterian theologian, Robert Reymond (1932—2013), who wrote, "At this time, I for one am not convinced that he [Clark] is in accord with Scripture when he denies to the senses a role in knowledge acquisition and would hope that he would take the Greek skeptics less seriously and the implications in many of the 'subsidiary axioms' of Scripture more seriously than he does."[20]

But Clark later retorted:

He [Robert Reymond] thinks that I take the Greek skeptics too seriously. Of course it is not the Greek skeptics alone that I take seriously. There are also Montaigne, Descartes, Bayle, Hume, and the contemporary experiments in psychology. It would be my desire that Dr. Reymond, with his considerable ability, might take all skepticism more seriously. Responsibility to the task of apologetics demands it. Unfortunately several conservative apologetes, with whose theological views I'm in substantial agreement, seem to me to have evaded this basic problem.[21]

Neither the generation of Presbyterians which preceded Clark (like his own father) nor many of the Christian thinkers following Clark (even those like Reymond who were influenced by him) were able to reject empiricism. The full rejection of empiricism among Christians has remained unique to Clark and a few of his close-following disciples.

WORLDVIEW THINKING, A LEGACY OF JAMES ORR AND ABRAHAM KUYPER

Clark's philosophy was influenced not only by his rejection of empiricism, but also by his acceptance of "worldview thinking." A generation before Clark, two Christian thinkers, James Orr and Abraham Kuyper, laid the foundations for presuppositionalism by arguing for the necessity of understanding

19. Clark, David S. "The Intellectual Defense of Christianity."
20. Reymond, *Justification of Knowledge*, 114.
21. Clark, "Is Christianity a Religion? Part 2."

Christianity as a unified whole opposed to and separate from other worldly systems of thought. Though this antithesis between Christianity and the world had been noted by apologetes from the earliest days of the Christian church, it was Orr and Kuyper in the late nineteenth century who became more self-consciously aware of the necessity of this emphasis.

James Orr (1844–1913)

James Orr, professor of apologetics and systematic theology at the United Free Church College in Edinburgh and a contributor to *The Fundamentals*, was the first prominent forerunner of presuppositionalists. In the "Andrew Elliot Lectures in 1891," published as *The Christian View of God and the World*, Orr introduced the term *Weltanschauung* to the English-speaking world. The term had previously been employed by various German philosophers and intellectuals. Orr translated it as "view of the world." Perhaps more commonly today it is translated as "worldview." Regardless of the translation, Orr defined the term as "the widest view which the mind can take of things in the effort to grasp them together as a whole from the standpoint of some particular philosophy or theology."[22]

Rather than defending Christianity piece by piece, Orr argued that Christianity must be defended and considered in its entirety or as a system.[23] As a system, therefore, the Christian worldview should not incorporate elements from other philosophies. In fact, Orr wrote, "Between such a [modern] view of the world and Christianity, it is perfectly correct to say that there can be no kindredship."[24] For Orr, there was a radical difference between the Christian worldview and the various secular worldviews. The Christian worldview, he wrote, "stands in marked contrast with theories wrought from a purely philosophical or scientific standpoint."[25]

Realizing the distinctiveness of Christianity, Orr argued that the idea of proving the existence of God through the traditional methods was misguided. He wrote, "Proof in Theism certainly does not consist in deducing God's existence as a lower from a higher; but rather in showing that God's

---

22. Orr, *Christian View of God and the World*, 3.

23. Clark made a similar point when he wrote, "A general does not abandon half his positions to an invader. [It is] easier to defend all. [The] Bible teaches a system."—Clark, "Miracles and History."

24. Orr, *Christian View of God and the World*, 9.

25. Ibid., 4.

existence is itself the last postulate of reason—the ultimate basis on which all other knowledge, all other belief rests."[26]

Robert Knudsen has referred to Orr's kind of thinking as "transcendental"—the type of thinking that asks "What lies at the very foundation of the possibility of our experience?" Knudsen notes that as far as he is aware, Orr was the first in the English-speaking world to employ this transcendental method.[27] According to Orr's biographer, Glen Scorgie, "Ultimately, for Orr, it was the coherency of the Christian worldview, its harmony with reason and moral experience, that made it worthwhile."[28] Orr wrote, "There is a definite Christian view of things, which has character, coherence, and unity of its own . . . the Christian view of things forms a logical whole which cannot be infringed on."[29]

Clark took from Orr all three of these elements: a rejection of the proofs for God's existence, the necessity of an internally consistent worldview, and the ultimate distinctiveness of the Christian worldview. Orr's influence on Clark has been noted by David Naugle who, in *Worldview: The History of a Concept,* noted the similarity in title (and therefore suggestion of theological continuity) of Clark's *A Christian View of Men and Things* with Orr's *The Christian View of God and The World.*[30] Clark himself, in the opening page of chapter one of his *A Christian View of Men and Things,* references Orr's book of similar title.[31]

Though the influence of Orr on Clark is evident in these three elements, his influence must be considered limited in other ways. Orr was not a biblical inerrantist and was even a theistic evolutionist, positions very much at odds with Clark's theology.[32] Despite substantial differences in their theologies, however, it seems very likely that Clark gained insights into his presuppositional approach from reading James Orr.

Abraham Kuyper (1837–1920)

The theme of worldview, promulgated by Orr, was further popularized by the Dutch theologian-statesman Abraham Kuyper. This is evident in Kuyper's L. P. Stone Lectures, later published in *Lectures on Calvinism,*

26. Ibid., 94.
27. Knudsen, "Apologetics and History," 122.
28. Scorgie, *A Call for Continuity,* 49.
29. Orr, *Christian View of God and the World,* 16.
30. Naugle, *Worldview,* 14.
31. Clark, *Christian View of Men and Things,* 13.
32. Scorgie, *A Call for Continuity,* 98.

which he gave at Princeton Seminary during a visit to America in 1898. The first of his lectures, titled "Calvinism as a Life-System," spoke of two "life systems" (modernism and Christianity) wrestling with one another in mortal combat.[33] Kuyper cites Orr's *The Christian View of God and the World* for use of the "view of the world" while ultimately preferring "life system" as a translation of *Weltanschauung*.[34]

Kuyper was more specific than Orr in referring to his worldview as not only Christian but also Calvinist. Kuyper's lectures present Calvinism as the "only decisive, lawful, and consistent defence for Protestant nations against encroaching, and overwhelming Modernism."[35]

Clark found that Kuyper, like Orr, discounted the "evidences" for the existence of God. Referencing Kuyper's *Encyclopedia of Sacred Theology* (1898), Clark wrote, "Kuyper says, 'Every effort to prove the existence of God by so-called evidences must fail and has failed.' I happen to agree with Kuyper on this point."[36] Thus a line of anti-evidentialism can be traced from Orr to Kuyper to Clark, in fact growing stronger with each successive iteration until Clark rejected entirely the empirical philosophy undergirding evidentialism.

PRESUPPOSITIONALISM

Throughout the history of the Christian church, apologists, or defenders of the faith, were largely of two varieties: classical and evidentialist. The apologists of the classical variety, such as Thomas Aquinas (1225–1274) and Bishop Joseph Butler (1692–1752), argued that the nature of the world reveals that God must exist; nature, as evidence of God, thus opens a way for the convert to believe in the Christian faith. Evidential apologists, on the other hand, focused on the historical nature of the events in the Bible, particularly the death and resurrection of Christ, and on modern day miracles as evidence of the truth of Christianity.

Clark believed that the classical and evidentialist approaches were based on false, non-Christian philosophies. These approaches mostly assumed the validity of sense perception and the epistemology of empiricism, both of which Clark denied. Unsatisfied with empirical arguments for God's existence, Clark sought another foundation. He believed that one must reject non-Christian presuppositions in favor of a Christian one: the truth

33. Kuyper, *Calvinism*, 3–4.
34. Ibid., 3.
35. Ibid., 5.
36. Eggenberger, "Clark objects to review," 36–37.

of the Bible. In other words, in place of empiricism he relied on biblical revelation.[37]

More specific than Orr's "Christianity" or Kuyper's "Calvinism," Clark's philosophy and corresponding worldview were grounded in the interpretation of the Bible found in the *Westminster Confession of Faith*. Just as the *Westminster Confession* stated that "the whole counsel of God concerning all things necessary for His own glory, man's salvation, faith and life, is either expressly set down in Scripture, or by good and necessary consequence may be deduced from Scripture,"[38] Clark came to believe that all knowledge possible to man is limited to the propositions of the Bible and that which can be logically deduced from the Bible.

The Protestant church as a whole had long held to a similar view known as *Sola Scriptura*—the idea that the Bible alone is the supreme authority in matters of doctrine and practice, and provides all knowledge necessary for salvation. Clark extended this principle, however, by arguing that all available knowledge in general, not just the knowledge necessary for salvation, is to be found in the Scriptures.

Rather than setting out to prove God's existence, as Aquinas had, Clark began with the Bible and its explanation of God. He came to believe that only by starting with Scripture—the knowledge revealed by the all-knowing God—can we firmly attest to knowledge. He read verses such as Proverbs 1:7 ("The fear of the Lord is the beginning of knowledge") and 2 Timothy 3:16 ("All scripture is given by inspiration of God, and is profitable for doctrine, for reproof, for correction, for instruction in righteousness") as confirmation of this epistemological argument.

The term "presuppositionalism" itself was not coined until 1948. It first appeared in a book review in *The Bible Today* by J. Oliver Buswell, who wrote that the philosophy of presuppositionalism is "advocated in our day by a significant group of earnest Bible-believing scholars" and included among the group Clark's former student Edward Carnell, whose book the article was reviewing. Buswell credited Faith Seminary professor Dr. Allan MacRae with coining the term. Buswell also pointed out that Carnell strongly approved of Clark's views, and cited Carnell's use of Clark's *A Christian Philosophy of Education* to that effect.[39]

---

37. The Is-Ought Problem of philosophy is that no normative (or "ought") conclusion can be deduced from purely descriptive (or "is") premises. From an empirical philosophy, no norms are possible.

38. WCF, Chapter I, Part VI.

39. Buswell, "The Arguments from Nature to God." See Also: Buswell, "The Fountainhead of Presuppositionalism."

Clark used the term "presuppositionalism" only sparingly in his own writings.[40] For many, however, the term quickly became synonymous with the views of Cornelius Van Til (1895–1987) whose own philosophy gained prominence through his books and teaching at Westminster Theological Seminary. At first, though, Van Til's views were seen to be something other than presuppositionalism. In fact, Francis Schaeffer wrote a reply to a book review of Buswell's in which Schaeffer argued that the differences between traditional apologetics and presuppositionalism could be resolved by Van Til's apologetic.[41] Implied in such an argument is that Van Til's apologetic was not the presuppositionalism of Carnell (or Clark). Yet in the continued dialogue on the topic published in *The Bible Today*, Buswell referred to Van Til's views as presuppositionalism,[42] and Van Til responded in two pieces titled (perhaps by the paper's editor, Buswell) as "Presuppositionalism" and "Presuppositionalism Concluded."[43] Van Til's student John Frame has argued that "presuppositionalism" used in the sense of rejecting the use of evidence is not an adequate description of Van Til's position.[44] We can conclude that although "presuppositionalism" has been used to describe the apologetical views of a number of Christians, it historically and logically aligns best with anti-evidential views like Gordon Clark's.

THE DEVELOPMENT OF CLARK'S PHILOSOPHY

It is difficult to determine exactly when Clark came to the presuppositionalist viewpoint. His earliest extant Christian writings are sermons he gave at his father's church in the early 1920s. His earliest Christian publications, beginning in 1929, included articles in *The Evangelical Student*, the magazine of the League of Evangelical Students.[45] On a more scholarly level,

40. Perhaps one of the earliest examples is when he said, "There is a third view of truth that attempts to escape these difficulties. It might be called apriorism, presuppositionalism, or intellectualism."—Clark, "The Nature of Truth."

41. Schaeffer, "A Review of a Review"

42. Buswell, "The Fountainhead of Presuppositionalism."

43. Van Til, "Presuppositionalism." See also: Van Til, "Presuppositionalism Concluded."

44. Frame, *Apologetics to the Glory of God*, 13.

45. Gordon H. Clark, "Christian and Pagan Ethics," *The Evangelical Student: The Magazine of the League of Evangelical Students* 4, no. 1 (1929): 29–32.; ——"By Way of Welcome: An Address Before the Sixth Annual Conference of the League of Evangelical Students," *The Evangelical Student: The Magazine of the League of Evangelical Students* 5, no. 3 (1931): 33.; ——"Ethics and Theology," *The Evangelical Student: The Magazine of the League of Evangelical Students* 6, no. 2 (1932): 29–33.; ——"Leadership," *The Evangelical Student: The Magazine of the League of Evangelical Students* 6, no. 2 (1932): 6.

three articles of Clark's were published in London's *Evangelical Quarterly* starting in 1932.[46] Also of interest in gauging Clark's early thoughts are the transcripts from a radio program on which he was a guest six times between 1935 and 1938.[47]

Even though Clark's views were not yet fully developed in his early writings, there are signs of emerging presuppositionalism. For example, in Clark's 1933 article "Ethics and Theology," he wrote, "We must argue, not from our moral standards to the truth of the Bible, but from the truth of the Bible to the morality it upholds."[48]

The necessity of worldview thinking in Clark's writings first clearly shows itself in the transcript of a radio address Clark gave in 1935. Clark said,

> The Bible contains something more important than historical facts. The mere fact that Jesus Christ died, for example . . . all by itself, is of very little importance. Christianity in its earliest years would never have received a favorable hearing, if the apostles told the Gentile world merely that a man was crucified in Jerusalem. Many men had been crucified; what makes Christ's death so important above all the others is the reason, the explanation which the Bible gives of the historical fact. Christ died, is the fact; for our sins, is the explanation.[49]

This demonstrates Clark's belief that historical facts must be interpreted in light of the philosophy one already holds. In other words, he believed theory must precede facts, and facts may only be understood through theory.

The influence Kuyper and Orr had on Clark is evidenced both in the books Clark read and in the ones he wrote. In his personal book collection are Orr's *The Christian View of God and the World* and *God's Image in Man*, both of which Clark received in October of 1939 (according to notes

46. Gordon H. Clark, "Determinism and Resposibility," *The Evangelical Quarterly* 4, no. 1 (1932): 13–23.;—"Kant and Old Testament Ethics," *The Evangelical Quarterly* 7, no. 3 (1935): 232–240.;—"Miracles, History, and Natural Law," *The Evangelical Quarterly* 12, no. 1 (1940): 23–40.

47. Gordon H. Clark, "Is Faith in the Bible Reasonable" (20 March 1935), "To Be a Sinner, How Bad Must one Be?" (11 September 1935), "Christianity and Education" (18 December 1935), "The Philosophy of Miracles" (12 March 1936), "The Resurrection" (16 April 1936), and "Attitude Before God" (21 August 1938), transcripts of addresses given on *The Midweek Forum Hour* with host Erling C. Olsen, radio station WMCA New York, PCA Archives, 309/92.

48. Clark, "Ethics and Theology." 33.

49. Clark, "To Be A Sinner How Bad Must One Be?"

Clark made on the inside covers). Likewise, Kuyper's *Lectures on Calvinism* exists in Clark's personal collection, with an inscription showing that Clark acquired it in September of the same year, 1939. This does not rule out the possibility or likelihood that Clark had read all or parts of these works previously, probably from his father's library. Later, in his own *A Christian Philosophy of Education*, Clark explicitly credits Orr: "Fifty years ago James Orr in his *The Christian View of God and the World*, devoted one chapter to *The Christian View and Its Alternatives*. In that chapter he traces the non-Christian philosophical development of the nineteenth century. So convincingly did he show that the only choice is between pessimism and Christ that it is a matter of regret not to be able to reprint the entire chapter here."[50]

Although at Wheaton College in the late 1930s and early 1940s Clark was teaching presuppositionalism (and for some classes using Van Til's syllabi—i.e. his unpublished seminary books)[51], it was not until 1946 that Clark first published his own philosophical views in their essential maturity.[52] Clark's article "Criticisms of Christianity Answered" from that year clearly shows a worldview approach.[53] But it was in his *A Christian Philosophy of Education*, also published in 1946, that Clark laid out his views more fully. In fact, the first chapter was titled "The Need of a World-View."

In *A Christian Philosophy of Education*, Clark argued that particular facts about the world neither prove nor disprove Christianity and that one

50. Clark, *Christian Philosophy of Education*, 143.

51. Extant syllabi of Van Til in Dr. Clark's collection of books include *Christian Apologetics* with a note reading "Feb, 1939. Gift of Bob Rudolph," and *Junior Systematics* with a note reading "Gift of Van Til" and a date of April 1940.

52. In a letter speaking of Clark's *A Christian Philosophy of Education*, a former student wrote, "In checking over some of my notes from 7 years ago, I see some of the same patterns and some of the same illustrations that you had included in this dissertation."—Jo. A. Lininger to GHC, 21 January 1948.

53. "This psychological argument against Scriptural religion is nothing other than an attempt to browbeat Christian people. We who learned of Christ at our mother's knee are supposed to admit the fact and be ashamed of it. There is a very pertinent reply to this type of psychological argument. It should be noted that those who attack Christianity were also conditioned in their childhood. They were conditioned against God and His Word. In their homes there was no family worship. More often than not they read the Sunday paper instead of going to church. God and the Bible were ignored, if not explicitly attacked; and the whole course of their parents' conduct taught them that religion is useless and somewhat foolish. Now grown to maturity these people complain that orthodox Christians have been conditioned in childhood, and they browbeat us and deceive themselves in forgetting that they too have been equally conditioned, though in an opposite direction. Let us no longer accept such sophistry as a refutation of our beliefs or as an explanation of them."—Clark, "Criticisms of Christianity Answered," 184.

needs a worldview through which to digest these facts. For example, he wrote, "The resurrection, viewed purely as an isolated historical event, does not prove that Christ died for our sin, not only because Lazarus also rose from the dead, but also because sin is a notion which requires a particular view about God and the universe, and on such questions archaeology and history are incompetent."[54] Rather than build up a theory based on the supposed facts of the world as was traditionally done, Clark argued that theory must precede fact.[55] He wrote, "The alleged events [of history], instead of constituting Christian theism, stand themselves in need of philosophic interpretation."[56]

In the same book, Clark argued against the traditional arguments for the existence of God. He wrote, "Traditionally, three types of argument have been used to prove validly the existence of God; if any one of them should prove validly the existence of the God of the Holy Scriptures, the battle would be over and archaeology would be merely the subsequent operation of mopping up. But is any one of these three arguments valid?"[57]

In addition to the common presuppositionalist rejection of the classical arguments for the existence of God, Clark advanced the idea that all systems of thought have unproven and unprovable starting points, called axioms. He wrote, "It should be equally evident that if theism does not admit of strict proof, the same is not less true of the anti-theistic systems of pragmatism, pantheism, and materialism. In this respect therefore, theism is under no greater disadvantage than is any other system."[58] Clark argued that these axioms or "basic world-views" . . . "are never demonstrated; they are chosen."[59] This, Clark believed, was not a phenomenon unique to Christianity, but rather extended to all systems of thought. He argued, "So it is with every world-view; the first principle cannot be proved—precisely because it is first."[60]

The next step of Clark's methodology was to argue that the axiom one chooses must be judged on its own principles; it must not be

---

54. Clark, *Christian Philosophy of Education*, 35.

55. "When unbelievers object to Christianity on the basis that it views the world on the basis of undemonstrated hypotheses, the reply should plainly be made that everyone more or less consciously bases his conclusions on undemonstrated assumptions. There are no facts, no meaningful facts, apart from presuppositions."—Clark, "Concerning System and Demonstration."

56. Clark, *Christian Philosophy of Education*, 37.

57. Ibid., 38.

58. Ibid., 41.

59. Ibid., 41.

60. Ibid., 41.

self-contradictory. He wrote, "Now if such be the case, the thoughtful person is forced to make a voluntary choice. He may choose theism, or he may choose pantheism, or he may prefer to reject these various possibilities and choose skepticism. At any rate he must make a choice."[61] Clark continued:

> Still it remains true that no demonstration of God is possible; our belief is a voluntary choice; but if one must choose without a strict proof, none the less it is possible to have sane reasons of some sort to justify the choice. Ultimately these reasons reduce to the principle of consistency. A postulate must be chosen such that it makes possible a harmony or a system in all our thoughts, words, and actions.[62]

Clark's presuppositionalism reached nearly its final form with the publication of his *A Christian View of Men and Things* in 1952. Although he would further his thoughts in his Wheaton Lectures in 1965 (published in the Festschrift *The Philosophy of Gordon H. Clark*), one of Clark's students, Mary Crumpacker (1914–2007), argued that these lectures were a clarification of his previous positions, not a change in direction.[63]

PRESUPPOSITIONALISM, CLARK, AND VAN TIL

Is it possible that Cornelius Van Til influenced Clark into worldview thinking? In a letter from Clark to Van Til in 1937, Clark wrote that he was considerably interested in Van Til's system of apologetics.[64] This was over a year and a half before Clark purchased copies of both Orr's *The Christian View of Men and the World* and Kuyper's lectures on Calvinism. It is possible that Clark read Orr and Kuyper to gain understanding of where Van Til was coming from.

Though "presuppositionalism" was first used to refer to the thinking of Edward Carnell, who largely subscribed to Clark's philosophy, the term came to be most commonly associated with the philosophy of Cornelius Van Til. In fact, because of this strong association of "presuppositionalism" with Van Til's philosophy, Gordon Clark at times referred to his own philosophy as "dogmatism," at least in part to distinguish it from Van Til's.

To the degree that Van Til's philosophy can rightly be called "presuppositional," he preceded Clark in writing from that perspective by about

61. Ibid., 41.
62. Ibid., 48–49.
63. Crumpacker, "Clark's Axiom, Something New?"
64. GHC to CVT, 28 August 1937, WTS Archives.

seven years, which, coincidentally, was also the age difference between the elder Van Til and the younger Clark. According to Scott Oliphint, "Van Til was arguing presuppositionally even as far back as his doctoral dissertation in 1928."[65] David Wells affirmed a date of just one year later in *Reformed Theology in America* when he wrote, "It was not, however, until [Van Til] joined the faculty of the newly founded Westminster Theological Seminary in September of 1929 as Professor of Apologetics that he began to work out his new approach." Additionally, J. Oliver Buswell confirmed a knowledge of Van Til's presuppositional approach in the early 1930s.[66]

Van Til, like Clark, was significantly influenced by Abraham Kuyper. In fact, showing his gratitude to Kuyper, Van Til wrote in 1937, "We should surely be thankful to almighty God for the influence Kuyper has had on America."[67] Yet unlike Clark, Van Til did not fully reject empirical philosophy; nor did he reject its arguments for the existence of God. Rather, according to John Frame (b. 1939), Van Til "insisted that they [the arguments for the existence of God] be formulated in a distinctly Christian way, rejecting any 'proof' based on a non-Christian epistemology."[68]

As Van Til and Clark would later become adversaries in a church struggle over Clark's ordination, these two thinkers are frequently compared. The question arises as to who is more appropriately labeled the founder of presuppositionalism. Yet this question of bragging rights for being first is irrelevant since both Kuyper and Orr preceded Clark and Van Til into the field. Though Van Til preceded Clark, his influence on Clark's philosophy was fairly limited. By the time Clark started corresponding with Van Til and using his syllabi for classes at Wheaton in the late 1930s, Clark had already established his rejection of empiricism. It is probably best to conclude that Clark and Van Til essentially came to their views around the same time period and mostly independent of each other.

65. Oliphint, *Cornelius Van Til and the Reformation of Christian Apologetics*, 30.

66. "The presuppositionalism which denies common ground of knowledge between Christian and non-Christian, has challenged my special attention since the early 1930s, since a year or two after the founding of Westminster Theological Seminary and my first acquaintance with Professor Cornelius Van Til."—Buswell, "The Fountainhead of Presuppositionalism A Book Review."

67. Van Til, "Reflections on Dr. A. Kuyper, Sr."

68. Frame, "The Problem of Theological Paradox," 301n.

Chapter 6

Origins of the Ordination Controversy

"As you know I was active during the early thirties in arousing USA congregations to the seriousness of the apostasy in that church. I had a hand in the Reformation Fellowship, and its successor, the (poorly named) Presbyterian Constitutional Covenant Union. Not only did I speak in Penna., but I traveled as far as N.D. in this effort. Then in 1936 I had the honor of giving the nomination speech for Dr. Machen. For the next seven or eight years I taught in Wheaton, where I recommended, with some success, that ministerial students attend Westminster, rather than Dallas or elsewhere. This led to my forced resignation. Because of my continuing interest in this work, I decided to apply for ordination. To my utter astonishment, instead of being welcomed, I met hostility. It was I, who with two others, had brought charges of heresy against the Auburn Affirmationists, when the Westminster faculty excused themselves. My reaction was not so much anger as utter stupefaction and confusion."[1]

—GORDON H. CLARK TO GEORGE MARSDEN

1. GHC to George Marsden, 1 September 1980, provided by John Muether. Used with permission of George Marsden.

ON THE JOB SEARCH

IN THE AFTERMATH OF the trying events which culminated in his resignation from Wheaton College, Gordon Clark looked into a number of
career opportunities back in his home city of Philadelphia. Although he
had job prospects at Valparaiso University in Indiana and Gordon College in Massachusetts, among other places, his best chances for employment were in Philadelphia where he had lived for many years and had a
number of personal contacts.[2] Not only was Philadelphia the location
of Westminster Theological Seminary (WTS) which trained ministers for
the Orthodox Presbyterian Church (OPC) of which Clark was a member,
but the city was also the site of a planned Reformed Christian university
where Clark was a strong candidate to be hired, should it materialize.
Clark considered each of these schools as desirable places for his employment, but first turned to the Reformed Episcopal Seminary (RES)
in West Philadelphia where he had previously lectured part-time in the
early 1930s while concurrently serving as an instructor at the University
of Pennsylvania. During his job search Clark wrote to his good friend
and RES professor Robert Knight Rudolph, saying, "I consider a place in
your seminary as the most satisfactory solution to the situation."[3]

Clark's involvement in the Church also presented pastoral ministry as
a career option. While troubles were besetting him at Wheaton, he thought
God might be leading him down the path to ordination.[4] The two denominations he considered were the Orthodox Presbyterian Church and the Reformed Episcopal Church (REC). Without much deliberation, however, he
chose to stay with the OPC rather than apply to the REC. Clark's admiration
for J. Gresham Machen, the late founder of the church, greatly influenced
this decision. Clark imagined that if he were ordained in any other church
then members of the OPC might view his choice as an abandonment of the
fledgling denomination and of Machen's vision of a renewed, conservative
Presbyterian church.[5]

---

2. Edwin Rian to GHC, 27 January 1943, PCA Archives, 309/48.; GHC to Robert
Strong, 9 May 1942, PCA Archives, 309/46.; See also: "I have been preparing twenty-
seven inquiries to as many colleges (including Yale, no less) but the preceding dozen
or fifteen have not produced much."—GHC to Edwin Rian, 1 September 1942, PCA
Archives, 309/48.

3. GHC to Robert Rudolph, 1 July 1942, PCA Archives.

4. Strong, "The Gordon Clark Case."

5. "Going into your church [the Reformed Episcopal Church] might look like
leaving some of my friends while they are being attacked and leaving a work I had
begun."—GHC to Robert Rudolph, 1 July 1942, PCA Archives.

Foreseeing his fate at Wheaton College, Clark had started the process of working towards ordination almost a year prior to his resignation. On May 9, 1942, he sent a letter of application to the OPC's Presbytery of Philadelphia requesting that they ordain him to the gospel ministry.[6] Although he knew seeking ordination after the age of forty was unusual, he had good reason to seek it nonetheless. First, he had been preaching for many years as a ruling elder without having been ordained as a teaching elder. In fact, his earliest extant sermon dates from 1922 when he preached at his father's church at just twenty years of age.[7] Even while a professor at Wheaton College, he preached on occasion at a local church, the United Gospel Tabernacle, and following his resignation, remained in Illinois to be the Orthodox Presbyterian Church's representative on campus. Further good reason to seek ordination was the likelihood that he would be more warmly welcomed as a pastor in a Presbyterian church than as a professor at the colleges he had worked for (Penn and Wheaton) where his strong Calvinist convictions had made him an outsider.

Clark knew his request for ordination would raise issues about his education, since he had never attended a theological seminary, the usual path for ministers in training. He wrote about this concern to OPC ministers Clifford Smith, Robert Strong, and Burton Goddard: "About a year ago, I wrote confidentially and tentatively to [Paul] Woolley [an elder in the OPC and faculty member of WTS] about the wisdom of seeking ordination from Phila. Presbytery. The drawback of course is that I lack certain parts of seminary work; the matter would therefore have to be taken to the General Assembly. I dislike the publicity of this course, and if denied would dislike it still more."[8] This letter would prove to be prescient, as a course of events quite along the lines Clark feared would soon take place. But in regard to the expected support from Paul Woolley, Clark would be sorely disappointed.

PRESBYTERY MEETINGS

Clark's letter of application for ordination in the OPC was read at the meeting of the Presbytery of Philadelphia on March 15, 1943, less than a month after he resigned from Wheaton College.[9] He had applied for ordination

6. GHC to The Presbytery of Philadelphia of the OPC, 9 May 1942, PCA Archives.

7. Clark, "Always, Everywhere."

8. GHC to Clifford Smith, Robert Strong, and Burton Goddard, 1 May 1942, PCA Archives.

9. The Presbytery of Philadelphia, meeting minutes (Philadelphia: Mediator Orthodox Presbyterian Church, 15 March 1943).

ten months previously, but while he was still employed at Wheaton the urgency for ordination was not high, and so he did not put pressure on the presbytery's relatively slow timetable. But once he had resigned and was on the job market, the ordination process was jump-started. The OPC formally reviewed his application on May 18, 1943, when the Philadelphia Presbytery's Committee on Candidates and Credentials conducted an examination. Following the committee's examination they advised that Clark defer his request for licensure until they could consult with him further. At this point Clark was granted the floor and he asked that the presbytery adopt the recommendation of the committee. A motion to that end was made and subsequently adopted.[10]

Clark's resignation from Wheaton College brought considerable visibility to his theological views. Consequently, some ministers in the OPC were concerned about the possibility of inviting controversy into their own denomination. At Wheaton College, Clark's adherence to strict Calvinist views in his dedication to the *Westminster Confession of Faith* (WCF) generated conflict with the administration. But within the OPC, which required subscription to the system of doctrine in the WCF as the ordination vow, Clark had reason to expect that his views would be more warmly welcomed.

The presbytery's delay in granting Clark's request for liencsure was an inconvenience, of course, but it did not appear to Clark to be an impassable barrier to his goal of ordination. Rev. Richard Willer Gray, an OPC minister, believed Clark's ordination process would soon move forward. In a letter to Clark of July 9, 1943, Gray wrote, "I regret the stupid action taken by the Philadelphia Presbytery on your request for licenture [sic] and ordination. I trust that the situation might be ironed out satisfactorily."[11] Whatever the presbytery's decision, Clark was determined to preach the gospel. To Rev. Gray he replied, "The committee also judged that I did not have a call to the ministry. Whether they were within their rights in making such a judgment remains to be seen. But I will not discuss the matter, except to say that I have in my own way been preaching the gospel for the past six years at least, and it is that that has got me in trouble. And I shall continue to preach the gospel in the way I can do it best whatever the committee, Presbytery, or General Assembly does or does not do. I feel I could accomplish more if I were ordained."[12]

10. The Presbytery of Philadelphia, meeting minutes (Philadelphia: Mediator Orthodox Presbyterian Church, 18 March 1943).

11. Rev. Richard Willer Gray to GHC, 9 July 1943, PCA Archives, 309/35.

12. GHC to Rev. Richard Willer Gray, 14 July 1943, PCA Archives, 309/35.

Almost seven months passed between Clark's first examination and the time his name again appeared in the presbytery minutes. At the Presbytery of Philadelphia on January 17, 1944, it was moved and carried for "the Committee on Candidates and Credentials to seek a personal conference with Dr. Gordon H. Clark, in the matter of his application for ordination, prior to the March meeting of presbytery." A possible early sign of the trouble to come occurred when Rev. E. J. Young, Professor of Old Testament at Westminster Theological Seminary, had his dissent from the action recorded.[13]

At the "March meeting," on March 20, 1944, the Committee on Candidates reported that Clark had been examined for the purpose of considering his "experimental knowledge of religion, and the motives which influence him to the sacred office." They also reported that Clark had passed examinations in Greek, English Bible, and church history, and that he had requested a waiver of the requirements of two years of study in a theological seminary and of knowledge of Hebrew.[14] The Presbytery minutes note that Clark's examinations raised "certain questions in particular to his doctrine of miracles, and of God." They noted also that in Clark's upcoming theological examination he should be examined "with particular care on these points." With a motion passed, Clark was enrolled as a candidate for gospel ministry. He was then examined in theology. A motion was then made to "refer the licensure of Dr. Clark to the General Assembly for advice." A substitute motion was made that Clark's examination in theology be sustained. The substitute motion carried and so a vote was taken. The vote returned fifteen to thirteen in Clark's favor, but this ratio was short of the three-fourths majority necessary to waive the requirements (of seminary education and knowledge of Hebrew) at the presbytery level.[15] Though not shown in the records, the original motion to "refer the licensure of Dr. Clark to the Gen-

13. The Presbytery of Philadelphia, meeting minutes (Chestnut Hill, PA: Westminster Theological Seminary, 17 January 1944). Note: Although E. J. Young later signed *The Complaint*, the Presbytery minutes do not indicate whether his concern was about Dr. Clark's ordination or about the procedure of the motion itself.

14. The requirements for licensing and ordination in the OPC, which include two years of study in a theological seminary, are found in *THE STANDARDS of Government Discipline and Worship of The Orthodox Presbyterian Church*, 18–29.

15. The Presbytery of Philadelphia, meeting minutes (Philadelphia: New Covenant Church, 20 March 1944).; and The Eleventh General Assembly of the OPC, meeting minutes (Philadelphia: Chestnut Hill, 16 May 1944), 8. Note: Voting to sustain were Allen, Dyrness, Galbraith, Marsden, Marston, Price, Rian, Strong, Elliott, Hamilton, Smyth, Aument, Johnson, McClay, and Tichenor. Voting to not sustain: Andrews, Bradford, Clelland, Kuiper, Stonehouse, Sloat, Van Til, Woolley, Young, Oliver, Betzold, Welmers, and Thompson.

eral Assembly for advice," which soon occurred, must have been the resulting action. Both E. J. Young and Robert Strong were granted the privilege of
the floor to make statements relative to the case of Dr. Clark, but neither of
their statements were recorded.

An additional "adjourned" meeting of the presbytery was conducted
just ten days later on March 30, 1944. At this meeting a motion was passed
deeming satisfactory Clark's examination in English Bible, church history,
and Greek.

Clark received his chance to be reviewed for a waiver on the requirement for seminary education and knowledge of Hebrew at the Eleventh
General Assembly of the OPC, conducted from May 16 to 19, 1944. At
this assembly a motion was made that "in view of Dr. Clark's academic
record, remarkable gifts and personal piety, all of which demonstrate his
exceptional qualifications for the ministry, the General Assembly advised
the Presbytery of Philadelphia to waive the requirement in Hebrew and two
years of formal theological study."[16] The motion was approved and a vote
of forty-five to thirteen confirmed Clark's appeal.[17] On the final day of the
General Assembly, however, resistance to Clark's ordination arose in a written protest formally submitted by three elders.[18] It argued that the waiver
was made without discussion of the evidence concerning Clark's theological
examination.[19]

THE PROGRAM FOR ACTION AND CLARK'S
ORDINATION

Clark's request for ordination brought up greater issues regarding the structure and organization of the OPC and contributed to the creation of factions in the church even before the general assembly met to vote on his
appeal. Just days prior to the OPC's Eleventh General Assembly, a group of
four ministers (Edwin Rian, Richard Willer Gray, Robert Strong, and Clifford Smith)[20] had met to form a party of resistance to oppose what they

16. The Eleventh General Assembly of the OPC, meeting minutes (Philadelphia:
Chestnut Hill, 16 May 1944), 17.

17. Ibid., 18.

18. The three elders were Ned Stonehouse, Murray Forst Thompson, and William
Young.

19. Ibid., 65.

20. Though not all of the four ministers are explicitly mentioned in the records, by
comparing a number of sources their identities are surmisable. A key to determining
the identities of the ministers not explicitly named in the records was the following
statement: "Two of these ministers were from the Presbytery of Philadelphia, two from

perceived as the WTS faculty's centralization of control of the church. On May 11, 1944, these four ministers sent a "Program for Action" to a select group in the church asking for support on a number of objectives—four general and four specific. The general objectives of this program, briefly, were 1) to emphasize the church's ideals of combating modernism and promoting evangelism and to oppose anyone working against these ideals, 2) to cooperate with other conservative Christian groups, 3) to "keep alive" scriptural principles regarding the expedient use of Christian liberty, and 4) to recognize the primacy of the Church above all parachurch agencies and organizations. To meet these ends, four specific objectives were formulated (and likely set in desired chronological order). These objectives were 1) the ordination of Dr. Gordon H. Clark, 2) affiliation with the American Council of Christian Churches, 3) an official effort on the deliverance against the liquor traffic, and 4) to gain Church supervision over Westminster Seminary and *The Presbyterian Guardian*.[21]

Though Clark's ordination was a specific objective of the Program for Action, Clark himself was not involved in writing the document. In fact, one OPC minister later opined, "He [Clark] may all unjustly be associated with ideas in which he had no part."[22] Even though Clark was not involved in the document's formation, he substantially agreed with its objectives.

In the time between Clark's first meeting with the Presbytery and going to the general assembly for approval of the waiver regarding seminary credentials and knowledge of Hebrew, there was plenty of time for ministers in the church to consider the impact of Clark's addition to their ranks. The ministers leading the Program for Action saw Clark's ordination as their opportunity to change the direction of the denomination. Although the waiver of Clark's seminary attendance was approved, dissension showed itself with the official complaint at the end of the same general assembly. By the time the Presbytery of Philadelphia met again to consider Clark's ordination on July 7, 1944, much already had been said on the topic, both publicly and privately.

Clark, although hopeful of ordination, still kept other options open. In fact, the presbytery meeting to consider his ordination was a special session scheduled to coincide with his visit to Philadelphia on other business. Most likely Clark was visiting the Reformed Episcopal Seminary to discuss

---

the Presbytery of New Jersey as it was then constituted."—Heerema, "Whither the Orthodox Presbyterian Church."

21. Edwin Rian, Richard Willer Gray, Robert Strong, and Clifford Smith, "A Program for Action in the Orthodox Presbyterian Church," (May 1944), Ned Stonehouse's collection of papers about the "Clark Case," WTS Archives.

22. Heerema, "Whither the Orthodox Presbyterian Church."

a teaching position.[23] The special session was the best-attended session in the history of the Philadelphia Presbytery. This reflects the fact that Clark was a popular, as well as polarizing, figure. At the meeting, Ned Stonehouse, Professor of New Testament at Westminster Theological Seminary, led the standard questioning regarding the *Westminster Confession of Faith*, and the elders present conducted more specific questioning on Clark's views. In the end, a vote of thirty-four to ten approved Clark's theological examination. A similar vote of thirty-two to ten approved waiving the requirement for two years of attendance at a theological seminary, confirming the exemption the general assembly had granted. The final hurdle was for Clark to take an examination to prove his knowledge of the Hebrew language. Although he had studied Hebrew in college and prepared prior to the examination, he was not particularly able in the language (having greater proficiency in Greek, French, and German). He asked the presbytery if he might read the first chapter of the book of Genesis in Hebrew to prove his capability in the language. His reading satisfied the presbytery by a vote of thirty to ten. Having passed all examinations, he was then licensed to preach.[24]

The following month, more than two years after Clark had first applied for ordination, the process was finally complete. On August 9, 1944, he was ordained as a teaching elder in the Orthodox Presbyterian Church by the Philadelphia Presbytery into the Calvary Orthodox Presbyterian church in Willow Grove, Pennsylvania—a congregation where Robert Strong was pastor and where Cornelius Van Til attended.[25] Carrying on the tradition of his father and his paternal grandfather, Clark had become an ordained minister.[26]

THE COMPLAINT

It seemed from the outside that Clark might be able to settle into a calm career as a minister of a small church or a professor at a seminary, but inside the OPC, dissension had been brewing for some time. This dissension came

23. Tichenor, "The Answer."

24. Strong, "The Gordon Clark Case." See also: The Twelfth General Assembly of the OPC, meeting minutes (Philadelphia: Chestnut Hill, 17 May 1945), 6.; See also: The Presbytery of Philadelphia, special meeting minutes (Philadelphia: Mediator Orthodox Presbyterian Church, 7 July 1944).

25. The Presbytery of Philadelphia, special meeting minutes (Willow Grove, PA: Calvary Church, 9 August 1944).

26. In that he is the visible leader of a congregation, the teaching elder is equivalent to pastor in other denominations.

to a head as twelve elders lodged a complaint against Clark's ordination.[27] The complaint was read at a meeting in the Presbytery of Philadelphia on November 20, 1944, three months after his ordination.[28] The complainants were not just any elders, but included five of the faculty of Westminster Theological Seminary: R. B. Kuiper, Ned Stonehouse, Paul Woolley, Edward J. Young, and Cornelius Van Til. *The Complaint,* as the document was called in short, argued firstly that Clark's ordination was approved at an illegal Presbytery meeting, necessitating its nullification.[29] But of greater substance, the authors of *The Complaint* took issue with four of Clark's theological positions. *The Complaint* gave rise to a series of events which were given the name "The Clark Case" in the denomination's unofficial journal, *The Presbyterian Guardian.* More commonly though, the struggle came to be known as the "Clark-Van Til Controversy," after the two primary theological antagonists. In the words of OPC historians D. G. Hart and John Muether, it was "the greatest theological debate that has ever occurred in the denomination's history."[30] This, however, is a bit of a misnomer; although the theological issues became topics of great discussion among members of the church, no formal debate was ever actually held.

Clark must have been somewhat surprised that some of the faculty members of Westminster Theological Seminary would find cause to complain about his ordination. He had been the commencement speaker at Westminster in 1941 and had for years been successful in encouraging graduating Wheaton College students to attend seminary there. In fact, at the time of the complaint, WTS had a considerable number of former Clark students enrolled. A Wheaton College alumni magazine from 1944 lists thirteen Wheaton graduates then enrolled at WTS, approximately one quarter of the seminary's student body.[31] In addition, at least five other Wheaton alumni had recently graduated from Westminster[32], many of

27. The twelve elders were John Wister Betzold, Eugene Bradford, R. B. Kuiper, Leroy B. Oliver, N. B. Stonehouse, Murray Forst Thompson, William E. Welmers, Paul Woolley, Cornelius Van Til, Edward J. Young, David Freeman, and Arthur W. Kuschke, Jr.

28. The Presbytery of Philadelphia, meeting minutes (Wilmington, DE: Eastlake Church, 20 November 1944).

29. Betzold, "The Complaint."

30. Hart and Muether, *Fighting the Good Fight,* 106.

31. "The following Wheaton College alumni are at present enrolled in Westminster Seminary: Alton Bean '43, Herbert Bird '44, Ralph Clough '42, Warren Davis '44, Robert Hamilton '43, Everett Hawkes '43, Paul Jewett '41, Roy Lambert '43, John MacDonald '43, Charles Mason '43, Elwin Sire '43, Charles Svendsen '43, and James Tompkins '42."—"Further Study: Westminster," 6.

32. Edward Carnell, Edwards Elliott, Francis Mahaffy, Delbert Schowalter, George Vanderpoel

them from the freshman class of 1939. In fact, six of the seven members of that class had also participated in Clark's Creed Club at Wheaton College.[33] Even if the faculty at Westminster had never read a word Clark had written in formal publication, they would have learned much of his philosophy second-hand from Clark's former students.

Also of surprise to Clark was that Paul Woolley had signed *The Complaint*. Clark had written to Woolley when he applied for ordination, "In view of our friendship for the past ten years, and to conclude a matter that has been revolving in my mind for a little while, would you be so kind as to join with Bob Strong in presenting the enclosed paper to the Philadelphia Presbytery?"[34] Clark trusted Woolley with giving his application for ordination to the Presbytery and believed at that time that Woolley would support him.

Clark even had reason to think Cornelius Van Til might support his ordination. While dealing with the difficulties at Wheaton, Clark received a letter from OPC minister Robert Strong which showed how Van Til appreciated Clark's influence on students' decision to attend Westminster. Strong wrote:

> Let me report some of the things that were said last night about developments at Wheaton. Van Til was especially outspoken in his regret at the course of events. He paid the highest tribute to your work out there, pointing out that the Wheaton group at Westminster is at the seminary because of your influence and that, whereas he used to have to spend a large part of his time in the first year in rooting out Arminian notions from Wheaton-trained minds, now, thanks to you, the Wheaton men come Calvinists already.[35]

In the same letter, Strong thought Clark's ordination would be a sure bet, saying:

> Now about your ordination. I think we could put that through all right. Your prestige in our group is very high. All recognize that you have selflessly served the cause. If it is your judgment

---

33. Davis, "John Frame's Pastoral Method," 696.

34. GHC to Paul Woolley, 9 May 1942, PCA Archives, 309/62. Note: Clark's friendship with Woolley can be attributed, at least in part, to their shared connection in the Penn chapter of the League of Evangelical Students where Woolley was Secretary and Clark was the chapter advisor. In fact, Clark wrote to Ned Stonehouse as far back as 1929 expressing favor of Woolley: "Now if you can only get Woolley to lead the League again."—GHC to Ned Stonehouse, 8 August 1929, WTS Archives.

35. Robert Strong to GHC, 6 May 1942, PCA Archives, 309/56.

that you are now ready for the step of ordination there will be mighty few who won't be ready to go along wholeheartedly. I cannot think that anyone will impugn your motives. Instead of that the men will rally around a man who has stood to his guns in a hard place of battle. That's my judgment."[36]

So why the sudden change? Why the complaint? It seemed Clark had support of the church. He certainly had Strong's support. Paul Woolley had been a friend, and even Cornelius Van Til had expressed appreciation of Clark's influence on incoming WTS students. There were, as will be seen, multiple factors which gave rise to the composition of *The Complaint*.

CAUSES OF THE COMPLAINT

The Complaint, an attempt to block Clark's ordination in the OPC, was lodged both in opposition to Clark's theological views and in reaction to the Program for Action. The Program for Action sought to have Clark ordained, but it also encouraged the OPC to cooperate with other churches via an affiliation with the American Council of Christian Churches, to produce an official statement affirming the benefit of alcohol abstinence, and to establish church control over Westminster Theological Seminary and *The Presbyterian Guardian*. The WTS-led faction opposed each of these policies and the occasion of Clark's ordination was their first opportunity to thwart its objectives. Rather than waiting for motions on these political topics to arise at the general assembly, they decided to make their stand on Clark's ordination. The theological issues addressed, however, were so complex that many of the OPC pastors, not to mention lay people, struggled to follow the arguments.

It is apparent that the causes of *The Complaint* against Clark, however, were not solely the philosophical and theological doctrines it addressed but also the ecclesiastical and political positions that Clark's ordination supported. A number of issues were included in *The Complaint,* building a coalition for its support. Each of the charges in *The Complaint* regarded theological issues Van Til had with Clark, which they had previously discussed in letters and in person. The issues were not isolated doctrinal points but a series of related doctrines over which the theological systems of Van Til and Clark conflicted. The fourth issue, however—on the Free Offer of the Gospel—was not solely an issue raised by Van Til. It had strong support also from Ned Stonehouse and R. B. Kuiper, both of whom, like Van Til,

36. Ibid.

had come from the Christian Reformed Church where the doctrine was a hot-button issue. The intended results of the complaint, to declare Clark's ordination invalid and solidify control of the denomination and seminary, may have been enough to secure the support of any of the rest who signed the complaint, like Paul Woolley, who seems to have been concerned more about the political issues in the church than with Clark's theology.

That the complainants were not concerned merely with Clark's theology, but with the political situation in the church, is also shown in the fact that they questioned the procedure of Clark's ordination in the presbytery. If the authors of *The Complaint* were opposed only to Clark's theological positions, in order to be consistent, they would have had to oppose other ordinations as well. Pointing this out, OPC missionary Henry W. Coray wrote to Van Til, "It has been suggested that a graduate named [Francis] Mahaffy, who accepts Dr. Clark's apologetic, I understand, passed thru Presbytery without any objections on the part of those who blocked Clark. This would seem to be an inconsistency, if the case against Clark was on apologetic grounds."[37]

Clark was not the only figure in the OPC who had views at variance with the WTS faculty. There was a large diversity of views across the ministers of the young denomination, but these views were tolerated as long as they were kept sufficiently private.[38] Clark's views, however, were visible to all, due to his publicized resignation from Wheaton. A letter written just a few months after Clark's ordination reported how the Westminster faculty viewed Clark as a liability:

> Dr. N. B. Stonehouse came to Dr. Edman . . . to say in substance, "You folks at Wheaton had a Clark problem; now we at Westminster have that problem. The difficulties have arisen quite largely out of the move to have Dr. Clark ordained in the Orthodox Presbyterian Church. We at Westminster have very high regard for Dr. Clark as a person and as a scholar, but we believe that his view of the Gospel is out of focus. We believe in the presentation of the Gospel and in evangelism. We understand that Dr. Clark's concept of the Gospel message is purely an intellectual one, with emphasis on preaching and acceptance

37. Henry W. Coray to CVT, 15 April 1944, WTS Archives.

38. For example, Rev. Edward Kellogg wrote to Van Til, "Is it not possible that you are taking some of Clark's statements which, for the sake of argument, let us say are wrong. And you are trying to drive those statements to their logical conclusions and by so doing you are attributing to Clark positions he does not hold? There are doubtless many errors in my views and if one should take the implications of them or drive them to their logical conclusion I would appear to be a very terrible heretic."—Rev. Edward L. Kellogg to CVT, 29 April 1944, WTS Archives.

of substitutionary atonement. Because the faculty members at Westminster have felt constrained to take a stand against his position, which they believe to be an extreme form, or even a distortion, of Calvinism, the faculty is receiving criticism from Dr. Clark's friends much as Wheaton did a year or two ago."

The letter concludes, "This material was given wholly spontaneously on Dr. Stonehouse's part, in a very friendly and cordial spirit."[39]

The Program for Action—specifically the desire of its authors to cooperate with other conservative Christian groups like the ACCC—contributed to Paul Woolley joining the complaint against Clark. Woolley had written an article for *The Presbyterian Guardian* titled "Discontent!" just weeks after Clark had been ordained. In it he identified two types of discontent in the church; he called one *malignant* and the other *healthy*. Woolley cited discontent over lack of numerical growth of the church a malignant type, but concern for "lack of enthusiasm over the Reformed Faith" as healthy discontent. He argued that the two goals were incompatible and that the denomination must therefore choose one of them. He wrote, "The question is really a very simple one. Does the Orthodox Presbyterian Church want to have a growing revival of the preaching, teaching, and application of the Biblical and Reformed Faith in these United States in the year 1944? Or does the Orthodox Presbyterian Church want to have many members and much money and read about itself often in the newspapers? It can have either one, but it cannot have both."[40]

Cause of the Controversy #1: Van Til's concerns about Clark's philosophy

Though there were ecclesiastical and political causes of the controversy, the central cause was that Cornelius Van Til had serious misgivings about the philosophy and theology of Gordon Clark. The earliest recorded reference to theological issues between Clark and Van Til is in a comment of Rev. Richard Willer Gray in the *Calvin Forum*. Referring back to the time of Clark's nomination of Machen as moderator of the general assembly in 1936, Gray wrote, "At that time his [Clark's] differences with Dr. Cornelius Van Til were well known, as those who were students at Westminster Seminary at that time can testify."[41]

39. Letter dated 10 November 1944, Wheaton Archives. Neither an author nor a recipient is listed.

40. Woolley, "Discontent!" 213–14.

41. Gray, "The O.P.C. and the University Project," 99.

The primary theological concern Van Til had with Clark regarded a doctrine called "The Creator-creature distinction." Van Til's understanding of this doctrine was at the core of his thinking. In his 1939 syllabus, *Christian Apologetics*, he stressed the Creator-creature distinction, saying that man, as a created entity, is different from God and "can never outgrow his creaturehood."[42] Van Til believed the Creator-creature distinction necessitated a qualitative difference between man's knowledge and God's knowledge. Van Til viewed Clark as opposing such a qualitative difference. Van Til thus regarded Clark's view as an insufficient account of the qualitative difference between God and Man, which he believed led to a denial of the fundamental distinction between Creator and creature.[43] Van Til wrote in a letter to a minister in the OPC, "Clark has for a number of years maintained openly and vigorously a position which would do away with the Creator-creature relation."[44]

The reason Van Til took this position may have come from his interpretation of the implications of the doctrine of divine simplicity. Van Til may have concluded based on this doctrine that since God and His attributes are identical, if a man were to have any of God's knowledge he would therefore also have God, or be God—an impossibility.[45]

Van Til believed that this theological difference between himself and Clark was sufficient reason to warrant *The Complaint*. The political issues in the church may have been more important to other signers of *The Complaint*, but for Van Til the primary issues were theological. He wrote to OPC minister Ed Kellogg before *The Complaint* to indicate the main points of difficulty with what he understood to be Clark's position. In the letter Van Til concluded, "Let me say again how much I dislike having to oppose Clark. I am simply conscience-bound before God to do so."[46] And later he wrote, "Clark's position therefore involves the rejection of the Reformed concept of God's revelation to man and a reduction of it to Greek specifications. I

42. Van Til, *Christian Apologetics*, 8.

43. "I pointed out to him [Clark] then that for a creature to seek to know God comprehensively was to seek to wipe out the Creator-creature distinction. When he fell back on the distinction between God's being and His knowledge saying that it would be sin for men to aim for identity with God's being but no sin for man to seek for omniscience in knowledge I indicated that such a distinction would cut a rift in the very nature of God. But to no avail."—CVT to Charles Stanton, 27 December 1945, WTS Archives.

44. CVT to "Cal" (Rev. Calvin Knox Cummings), 2 July 1944, WTS archives.

45. That Van Til held to the doctrine of divine simplicity is shown in one of his letters to Clark: "God's consciousness and His being are coextensive; His being and His attributes are one."—CVT to GHC, 5 December 1938, PCA Archives, 309/58.

46. CVT to Ed Kellogg, 16 April 1944, WTS Archives.

shall oppose it with every ounce of strength God may be pleased to give me."[47] Van Til also defended himself against suggestions that his motivations, and those of all the signers alike, were personal rather than theological. He wrote, "In the first place I may say that I did not and as far as I know my colleagues on the faculty did not entertain any personal feelings against Dr. Clark. On the contrary we have always had the highest respect for him and his work. He has no doubt been instrumental in bringing several men to the Seminary. If we had been willing to follow policy we would have kept silence."[48]

Van Til is to be credited with attempting to resolve the issues in person prior to the filing of *The Complaint*. In a letter of April 16, 1944 (five months before the complaint was written), Van Til mentions a "recent conversation" he had with Clark about the primacy of the intellect and other topics which were later included in *The Complaint*.[49] Referring apparently to this same meeting, Van Til wrote in a letter of July 2, 1944,

> Just before presbytery meeting of last spring Clark and I spent about two hours together at my house. I tried as several times before to show him that his article on the primacy of the intellect failed to make the distinction between the creator and creature fundamental. He dismissed the whole matter. At presbytery I discussed his three articles, the one mentioned, the one on the question of predestination and the one on miracles, showing how in each case they would involve the rejection of the doctrines of the historic Christian faith. Clark dismissed the whole thing with a wave of the hand.[50]

As these specific theological issues Van Til brought up will be addressed more thoroughly in the following chapter, we shall move on to other causes of the controversy.

47. CVT to Charles Stanton, 27 December 1945, WTS Archives.

48. Ibid.

49. CVT to Edward L. Kellogg, 16 April 1944, WTS Archives.

50. CVT to "Cal" (Rev. Calvin Knox Cummings), 2 July 1944, WTS Archives. This same meeting is referred to in another of Van Til's letters, in which he wrote, "I have personally tried as best I knew how to deal in as friendly and kind a way as I knew how in the whole matter. This is no claim to perfection but before God I dare say that I have tried to do what I could at every stage of discussion to make Dr. Clark feel that it was purely a matter of principle. So on the occasion of his visit to the city for the presbytery examination I asked him to come to our house in advance for lunch so that we might talk things over."—CVT to Charles Stanton, 27 December 1945, WTS Archives.

Cause of the Controversy #2:
Whether to include other fundamentalists

The second of the four major causes of the Clark-Van Til controversy was related to the OPC's stance toward fundamentalist churches. The OPC's membership growth had stagnated and an expected exodus of conservatives out of the PCUSA never materialized. Despite the stagnation, Clark continued to hope for growth in the OPC through the addition of fundamentalist members and congregations transferring from other denominations. In 1942 he wrote, "I have maintained a hope that the OPC could lead a considerable section of the fundamentalists."[51] And in an article titled "An Appeal to Fundamentalists," he encouraged like-minded Christians to come out of their faltering denominations and join the OPC. He was clear, however, to invite unity with fundamentalists only on the basis of following the doctrines of the original Reformers, namely the whole Reformed faith, not simply the basic tenets of fundamentalism which Clark likened to a house with a foundation but no roof. Clark's vision was that the OPC would lead the fundamentalists under the banner of the teachings of the *Westminster Confession of Faith* in their entirety. Thus, whereas Paul Woolley, in his article "Discontent!," stated his belief that the goals of church growth and commitment to Reformed principles were mutually exclusive, Clark held that the two goals were compatible.[52]

The WTS faction disagreed with Clark and his supporters over the inclusivity of membership in the church. If church membership grew to include fundamentalists—who did not share the WTS faction's particular views—the WTS faction would lose its majority control in the denomination. As Woolley's article showed, the WTS faction preferred their perception of Reformed purity over numerical growth in the church.

Edwin Rian, chairman of the board of trustees at WTS, did not support the majority WTS faction's position. He had pushed for and got a "Committee of Nine" three years earlier at the Eighth General Assembly in 1941 for the stated purpose to "study the relationship between the Orthodox Presbyterian Church to society in general, and to other ecclesiastical bodies in particular" and to suggest "ways and means whereby the message and methods of our church may be better implemented to meet the needs of this generation."[53] Elected to the committee were six elders, including Rian

51. GHC to Robert Strong, 9 May 1942, PCA Archives, 309/56.

52. Clark, "An Appeal to Fundamentalists," 66–67.

53. The Eighth General Assembly of the Orthodox Presbyterian Church, meeting minutes (Philadelphia: Chestnut Hill, 3 June 1941), 24.

and Clark, who favored the committee's purpose, and three elders, including Van Til and Kuiper, who believed the committee's goals compromised the Reformed identify of the OPC.[54] The next year, at the Ninth General Assembly in 1942, the Committee of Nine gave a report of its findings and recommended that the general assembly elect another committee of five to study the matter of cooperation with evangelical churches.[55] But a minority report presented by Van Til and Murray Forst Thompson concluded against such an additional committee. The minority report stated, "We believe that the committee, however laudable the purposes underlying its formation and actions, represents a most unfortunate concentration of power and will tend to disrupt and to impede the work of our church."[56] In critique of the minority report's appraisal, Clark wrote to Edwin Rian, "Since it was not an administrative committee, and could merely report to the assembly, the charges made against it were preposterous."[57]

The Committee of Nine was ultimately disbanded, striking a blow to Clark's hopes for OPC cooperation with evangelicals. He wrote, "The discontinuance of the Committee of Nine is quite a disappointment."[58] He also wrote of his frustration regarding the committee saying, "This past year I was on a Com. of Nine, and the two above [Van Til and Thompson] were merely obstructionists. MFT [Murray Forst Thompson] objected to everything proposed; I hardly believe there was a single matter of which he approved; and Van Til objected to nearly everything."[59]

Cause of the Controversy #3:
Clark's resolution for alcohol abstinence

Another cause of the controversy was Clark's position on how the church should address alcohol use and abuse. The OPC in general, and WTS in particular, had long had an image problem with regard to alcohol. By today's standards their level of alcohol acceptance would hardly be questioned, but in the first half of the twentieth century—not far removed from the era of

---

54. The six elders in favor of the goals of the committee were Edwin Rian, Gordon Clark, Robert Strong, Clifford Smith, Burton Goddard, and C. A. Freytag. Those opposed were Cornelius Van Til, R. B. Kuiper, and Murray Forst Thompson.

55. The Ninth General Assembly of the Orthodox Presbyterian Church, meeting minutes (Rochester, NY: 2–5 June 1942), 28.

56. Ibid., 31.

57. GHC to Edwin Rian, 27 June 1942, PCA Archives, 309/48.

58. Ibid.

59. GHC to Robert Rudolph, 1 July 1942, PCA Archives.

alcohol prohibition—a church which did not outrightly condemn alcohol was likely to be held in suspicion. Rumors had long plagued the OPC that the family of its late founder J. Gresham Machen had made their fortune in the manufacture of alcohol.[60] These rumors are addressed in Machen's biography, written by WTS professor Ned Stonehouse:

> Such is the mischief caused by slanderous and malicious re-ports, and the perversity of men to believe the evil rather than the good, that throughout the rest of Machen's life, and indeed for many years afterwards, credence has been widely given outright falsehoods concerning his attitude toward intoxicating beverages. They sometimes took the form that he was a "wet" and even a drunkard. Most frequently it was stated that the Machen money was made in the brewery business and that he continued to depend on that source for his income. Such reports were in circulation in the far west in 1934, for example, and were being spread by one of the leading clergymen of the denomina-tion [PCUSA] as a basic reason why Machen had to be opposed. Graduates of Westminster have frequently encountered such charges, and the present writer has been told by a number of persons, that regardless of what he might say to the contrary, there was absolute proof of their veracity. . . . Such charges were completely without foundation in fact. It is true that Machen did not consider the 18th Amendment as wise, but this was basically due to his political philosophy with its antipathy to centralized government. . . . His family background was hardly prohibition-ist, though the godly and exemplary character of the lives of his parents is beyond cavil. Nor was Machen committed himself to total abstinence as a principle. . . . Unfortunately commitment to the Biblical principle of temperance, or moderation, as dis-tinguished from total abstinence, is identified by some persons as license, and no allowance is made for the possibility that the defender of Christian Liberty may consistently refrain from the exercise of that liberty. . . . As for the charges concerning the source of Machen's income, it can confidently be asserted that they were pure inventions.[61]

After Machen's death, the denomination's public image with regard to alcohol worsened. At the Third General Assembly in 1937 the moderator disposed of a motion to "refrain, as a matter of expediency, from indulging

---

60. White, *Van Til, Defender of the Faith*, 55.

61. Stonehouse, *J. Gresham Machen, A Biographical Memoir*, 391.

in the use of intoxicating beverages" without a vote.[62] A protest was filed later in the same general assembly over the fact that the resolution was disposed. But it was to no avail. In response to this and other issues, a group of ministers left the denomination immediately after the general assembly and formed the Bible Presbyterian Church. The Bible Presbyterians took a strong stance against alcohol and earned a reputation as a dry church. By comparison to the BPC, the OPC earned the undesirable reputation as a "wet" church.[63]

The church's image as "wet" was partially but unfairly based on the rumors surrounding Machen's family and comparison to the dry BPC. But at Westminster Theological Seminary the liberty to use alcohol was seen by some as license. The situation was so dire that, prior to the split in the denomination, J. Oliver Buswell submitted to Machen an extensive critique of Westminster Seminary highlighting the issue of alcohol abstinence (or the lack thereof).[64]

Clark saw the acceptance of alcohol at Westminster Theological Seminary as a further detriment to the image of the church. With such a stain on the church's image, the reality of Clark's hope that the OPC could lead the fundamentalists, most of whom were teetotalers, waned. He believed the fundamentalists would not join the OPC without the church adopting an official policy on abstinence from alcohol.[65] Therefore, Clark desired to commend, but not absolutely require, abstinence from alcoholic beverages to improve the image of the church and remove a stumbling block to the fundamentalists looking to the OPC for leadership. Clark wrote of the issue:

> In the present circumstances our Church faces a deplorable situation. Because the General Assembly of 1937 did not make a complete pronouncement on the liquor question the church has been called a wet church. Because of rumors of drinking by persons connected with Westminster (popularly identified with the Church [OPC]), students have chosen to go to other seminaries. Insofar as these rumors are true, the individuals concerned are responsible for placing a stumbling block in the path of prospective students. The attitude of the faculty and students of Westminster, on this and similar matters, is widely and plausibly interpreted as smugness and stubbornness. Well-authenticated cases can be produced of students making

62. The Third General Assembly of the Orthodox Presbyterian Church, meeting minutes (Philadelphia: OPC, 1 June 1937), 8.

63. Stonehouse, *J. Gresham Machen, A Biographical Memoir*, 504.

64. Ibid.

65. Clark, "An Appeal to Fundamentalists," 66–67.

themselves un-reasonably objectionable and bringing reproach upon the Church. The matter of drinking alcoholic beverages seems to be the center or at least a prominent part of this attitude. The faculty of the seminary has been requested privately to remedy the situation but the reply was completely unsatisfactory. Unless something unforeseen should happen, the only Presbyterian procedure remaining is to bring the matter before the Assembly."[66]

Bringing the issue before the Assembly was exactly what Clark desired to do when he wrote a proposal for a denominational resolution on abstinence.[67]

The WTS faculty who had signed *The Complaint* held to a position of Christian liberty in the matter of alcohol use. Professor John Murray, for example, explained the seminary's position well in an article for the *Westminster Theological Journal*. He wrote, "The progress of knowledge, of faith, of edification, and of fellowship within the body of Christ is not to be secured by legislation that prohibits the strong from the exercise of their God-given privileges and liberties, whether this legislation be civil or ecclesiastical."[68] On the particular matter at hand Murray commented in a letter to Ned Stonehouse, "Dr. Clark's minority report which will no doubt be presented to the general assembly in the form of a resolution gives me grave concern."[69] These professors who supported Christian liberty in writing were also known to indulge themselves. A number of them were known to smoke pipes, a common practice of those who were of Dutch heritage, and Murray, of Scottish heritage, smoked cigars and occasionally drank single malt whisky.[70] To the WTS faculty, and many in the OPC, the issue of alcohol abstinence had already been dealt with at the Third General Assembly of the OPC in 1937, which, by not voting on the issue, essentially affirmed their position on Christian liberty. Thus Clark's resolution for abstinence would not find any support among the professors.

Clark saw the level of alcohol acceptance at WTS as a real problem. He wrote to Rev. Strong:

66. Clark, "Resolution on Total Abstinence."

67. GHC to the ministers and ruling elders of the Orthodox Presbyterian Church, n.d., PCA Archives.

68. Murray, "The Weak and the Strong."

69. John Murray to Ned Stonehouse, 7 May 1942, WTS Archives.

70. MacLeod, *W. Stanford Reid*, 57–58. See also: William Edgar, *Schaeffer on the Christian Life*, 44.

And I must confess that, rightly or wrongly, I think the seminary men are woefully blind to the situation. Kuiper speaks of having a course introduced to take care of the matter. In my judgment no course on ethics is needed for this matter. Unless the professors change their attitude, a course will be no good. And if they change their attitude, a course would not be necessary. But what hope is there of the professors changing their attitude? For this reason I want to push the resolution. . . . I have maintained a hope that the OPC could lead a considerable section of the fundamentalists. They need leadership, and it ought to fall to us. But to lead them, we must have their confidence. . . . Well, you can continue the line of thought for yourself.[71]

It is important to note that Clark's position on abstinence shifted over time or at least became more nuanced. In 1936 he had written to Buswell, "I have always supported the prohibition movement."[72] And again to Buswell in 1938, "I want you also to know that in 1934 or '35, I wanted to raise the liquor question in the Independent Board, because I knew that at least one member of the board was drinking. Griffiths persuaded me not to because it would result in such an explosion that the whole case would be injured."[73] But by 1942 Clark, it seems, had changed his position when he wrote to three OPC ministers saying, "I affirm my belief in the doctrine of Christian liberty. Spurgeon smoked, Luther drank beer (the stinking stuff), and with the statement prepared by the committee of nine on the matter I am in complete agreement."[74]

By the time of his proposal in 1942, Clark sought to correct the alcohol image of the OPC without forming laws opposed to it. His resolution was not to create a law regarding abstinence in the church, but simply to commend abstinence as beneficial. Continuing the same letter to the three OPC ministers, he wrote,

I sympathize, more than the seminary men image [*imagine*] I judge, with their unwillingness to make even an apparent concession to the Wheaton group, the perfectionists, the victorious life group, and that type of people. I know very well that my resolution would not change their attitude one bit toward us. The people whom the resolution is aimed at are good, humble Christians here and there who have been deeply grieved at our

71. GHC to Robert Strong, 9 May 1942, PCA Archives, 309/56.

72. GHC to JOB, 3 March 1936, Wheaton Archives.

73. GHC to JOB, 22 February 1938, Wheaton Archives.

74. GHC to Clifford Smith, Robert Strong, and Burt Goddard, 1 May 1942, PCA Archives.

mess. It is a fact that the students at Westminster, and perhaps the younger ministers, have said and done unjustifiable things. People still no doubt always call us (as Burt [Goddard] so cautiously expressed it to me) 'unbending.' And our men must be ready to take it on the chin. Guts are required. But I do believe that some of our number have voted unwisely even taking into consideration either their youth, their more prominent position, or any and all considerations.[75]

Clark wrote a motion regarding abstinence from alcohol and brought it up at a meeting of the Committee of Nine, the committee on which WTS professors Cornelius Van Til and R. B. Kuiper were also members.[76] The motion read:

> WHEREAS false statements and malicious rumors have been published by irresponsible persons and have been spread, to the detriment of the Orthodox Presbyterian Church, by some who may be well intentioned but ill informed;
> AND WHEREAS the ninth commandment forbids all prejudicing of the truth, including our good name;
> AND WHEREAS the apostle Paul, though not obliged by the law of God, voluntarily made a vow in order to silence slander; and the late and beloved J. Gresham Machen followed this procedure in abstaining from alcoholic beverages;
> AND WHEREAS the Scriptures give authority to the Church to make pronouncement on matters expedient;
> THEREFORE BE IT RESOLVED that this General Assembly do hereby denounce the efforts to besmirch the good name of the Church, and commend total abstinence as expedient conduct in the propagation of the reformed faith."[77]

The faculty at WTS, however, were unmoved by Clark's appeals. Paul Woolley wrote to fellow professor Ned Stonehouse:

> You will be interested in knowing that Gordon Clark wrote a very cordial and friendly reply to my letter on behalf of the faculty, but indicated that the only real solution of the difficulty regarding alcoholic beverages, in his opinion, would be a letter from me stating that the members of the faculty do not use such beverages. I read his letter to the faculty, and while it was appreciated, there seemed to be no need for any further official reply

75. Ibid.
76. Paul Woolley to Ned Stonehouse, 12 January 1942, WTS Archives.
77. Clark, "Resolution on Total Abstinence."

and we, therefore, agreed that I would write him a short, personal, informal note. I did this, indicating that the chances of his receiving any such statement from me were exceedingly remote, since I, myself, would consider such a statement as calculated to damage the maintenance of the principle for which we have so long fought, and stating that I considered that principle a very important one to emphasize in these days.[78]

Stonehouse agreed, later writing to Woolley, "I am pretty much upset by Gordon Clark's resolution, and even more so by the 'argument.'"[79]

Despite opposition from the WTS professors, Clark continued moving forward with his proposal. Woolley wrote to Stonehouse about a Committee of Nine meeting, "By a vote of five to two I think, Van Til and Thompson being the minority, it was decided to adopt in principle a resolution setting forth the general scriptural teaching on expediency and Christian liberty, the exact text to be worked over further. I believe John Murray has been revising Cliff Smith's original proposal. I understand that if any resolution at all is to be passed this has some hope of being all right. Gordon Clark indicated that it would not, however, prevent his introducing his minority report."[80] Woolley again wrote to Stonehouse, "I understand that Gordon Clark predicts that his resolution will pass the General Assembly by a two-thirds majority."[81] And Stonehouse replied, "I trust no one takes Clark's predictions seriously."[82]

A number of OPC ministers recommended to Clark that he not present his resolution. Robert Strong wrote to him, "Now about your resolution. I still feel that it would be better not to present it. . . . Might not a big row on the abstin. question do harm at this point?"[83] Clark responded to Strong, "Clifford [Smith] wrote me an almost overpowering letter to get me to withdraw it, and maybe I shall have to, but it will be a bitter disappointment."[84] And finally, Ned Stonehouse wrote to Clark objecting to the resolution and its argument.[85]

Stonehouse was strongly opposed to Clark's resolution. He wrote to Rev. Strong, "My conviction is that it would be nothing short of tragic if

78. Paul Woolley to Ned Stonehouse, 30 January 1942, WTS Archives.
79. Ned Stonehouse to Paul Woolley, 7 April 1942, WTS Archives.
80. Paul Woolley to Ned Stonehouse, 13 April 1942, WTS Archives.
81. Paul Woolley to Ned Stonehouse, 27 April 1942, WTS Archives.
82. Ned Stonehouse to Paul Woolley, 29 April 1942, WTS Archives.
83. Robert Strong to GHC, 6 May 1942, PCA Archives, 309/56.
84. GHC to Robert Strong, 9 May 1942, PCA Archives, 309/56.
85. Ned Stonehouse to GHC, 3 June 1942, WTS Archives.

this resolution, or a similar one, was passed, or even if it received any ap-
preciable amount of support." His reasoning was that Clark's resolution and
argument made a "fatal concession" to the modernist view that attacked the
protestant view that the "church is so bound to the Scriptures that it may not
make pronouncements not derived from them." Rather, Stonehouse argued
that "the contents of [Clark's] resolution are not derived from the Word of
God, but he insists nevertheless that the church has the right to make such
a pronouncement on the basis of its judgment as to its expediency."[86] In
Stonehouse's view, Clark was making the same type of mistake the PCUSA
had made many times in its actions during the Fundamentalist-Modernist
Controversy. In Stonehouse's letter to Clark he wrote, "I am in fundamental
disagreement with your approach to this problem. Although I deeply appreciate your high motive, it is my judgement that your approach is fundamentally unsound. The main thrust of my statement is to point out that, in my
judgement, the appeal to Acts 15 is not pertinent. I am concerned as you, I
believe, to counteract malicious rumors, but I am persuaded that nothing of
real worth can come out of the method that your resolution advocates."[87]

E. J. Young also was opposed to Clark's motion. He wrote to Stonehouse, "No doubt you have heard fairly detailed reports of the General Assembly. Best of all, to my mind, is the fact that the Committee of Nine is
now out of existence. This major victory, so it seems to me was the great
achievement of this Assembly. Also, I am inclined to think that no 'total
abstinence' overture would ever be able to poll more than a few votes. Possibly I am somewhat too optimistic in that."[88]

Ultimately Clark heeded the warnings and chose not to present his
proposal at the general assembly.[89] According to a letter Strong wrote to
Stonehouse, Strong had seen a copy of a letter Clark had written to Paul
Woolley which read, "Owing to the fear, expressed by several of the pastors,
that an acrimonious opposition to the resolution I proposed as a minority
report of the Committee of Nine would produce more dissension in local

86. Ned Stonehouse to Robert Strong, 26 May 1942, WTS Archives.

87. Ned Stonehouse to GHC, 3 June 1942, WTS Archives. Cornelius Van Til
also opposed Clark's argument related to Acts 15: "There is one point we ought to be
prepared to meet. That is the point with respect to the council of Jerusalem spoken of
in Acts 15. It is to that chapter that Gordon Clark appeals in his overture. He claims
that church assemblies have the right to make pronouncements on things indifferent
inasmuch as the council at Jerusalem did so. I feel I can meet his argument, but if you
have any suggestions as to good literature on the subject I should be glad to know about
it."—CVT to Ned Stonehouse, 31 March 1942, WTS Archives.

88. E. J. Young to Ned Stonehouse, 23 June 1942, WTS Archives.

89. "Gordon Clark withdrew his minority report entirely, before the assembly . . . "
—Paul Woolley to Ned Stonehouse, 8 June 1942, WTS Archives.

congregations than the resolution would produce good, I hereby regretfully withdraw it."[90] Even though Clark did not present his motion, his view on abstinence became known to the faculty of WTS. Seeing that Clark was essentially calling out the leadership of WTS with his view and could potentially bring it back up at a later general assembly, the WTS faculty were alarmed.

Without the resolution, Clark had to rely on the Committee of Nine to develop positive relationships with other church bodies. Clark wrote to Edwin Rian, "On withdrawing my resolution I wrote to all who had written to me urging them to support the [Committee of] Nine."[91] But the Committee of Nine was disbanded, leaving Clark and those supporting his policies with less say, and directly causing the Program for Action to be written.

Cause of the Controversy #4:
Seminary control and the denomination's theology

The last of the four causes of the controversy addressed in this chapter is that of control over the Westminster Theological Seminary. At the time of the controversy the professors at WTS (whether siding with Clark or against) held complete control of the affairs of the school. They had neither a denomination overseeing them, nor a president to direct them. Since its founding in 1929, WTS had remained an independent institution and the professors had full say in handling its affairs.

The status quo of professorial leadership at the seminary was threatened by two issues directly related to Clark's ordination. First, Clark's motion to commend abstinence of alcohol, although never presented, was particularly aimed at the seminary and the drinking issues there. Second, the Program for Action called for denominational oversight of the seminary.

The WTS professors had good reason to be concerned about church control over the seminary. Nearly all of them had previously taught at Princeton Theological Seminary, where church control had led to the modernists' control of the Board of Trustees and the conservative professors' departure to form Westminster. Thus the faculty at Westminster desired to choose for themselves who would be on the board. They chose mostly recent graduates of Westminster who supported the faculty's positions. As a result of the experience at Princeton, WTS had been administered by consensus at faculty meetings since its founding.[92] History taught them that the seminaries are

90. Robert Strong to Ned Stonehouse, 29 May 1942, WTS Archives.

91. GHC to Edwin Rian, 27 June 1942, PCA Archives, 309/48.

92. MacLeod, *W. Stanford Reid*, 176. Also note: "You see, the reason Machen didn't

the heart of the denomination. A popular phrase in Christianity, "As the seminary goes, so goes the church," is quite fitting to this situation. This was the case in the PCUSA where the seminaries were all liberal by the 1930s, long before the majority of the church members themselves followed suit. Westminster Theological Seminary, by remaining independent, sought to avoid any shift to modernism or to other views divergent from the professors' own.

Clark expressed what he believed to be dangers of independency in years prior regarding missionary societies in the church. To fellow members of an OPC committee, Clark wrote, "An independent society is responsible to no one but itself and involves all the dangers of un-Presbyterian independency."[93] There can be little doubt that Clark extended this same concern to an independent seminary.[94]

While Clark's alcohol abstinence motion and the Program for Action threatened the seminary's status quo from the outside, Clark's theology threatened it from the inside. WTS had struggled through the years to enroll enough students to remain financially sound. In its early years, the seminary often survived only because J. Gresham Machen was personally wealthy and could himself make up for budgetary shortfalls.[95] So when, with Clark's direction, students from Wheaton College started attending the seminary, it was of great financial help to the institution. But the students who came from Wheaton also came versed in Clark's thought. The WTS faculty had to do battle for the theological mind of the students, but many who had studied under Clark remained committed to his teachings. A prime example of this was Edward Carnell who came to Westminster having been taught by Clark at Wheaton and, despite having professed that he had learned more from Van Til and the impressive faculty of the seminary than he had at Wheaton, nevertheless remained committed to the "consistency criterion" of Clark's apologetic method.[96] This concerned Van Til, as shown in a letter a few years later in which a disappointed Van Til wrote of Carnell's prize-winning

want a president was because of J. Ross Stevenson."—Van Til, "transcript of interview by Jim Payton, Jack Sawyer, and Peter Lillback," 4.

93. GHC to members of the Committee on Home Missions and Church Extensions of the Presbyterian Church of America, 24 March 1937, Wheaton Archives.

94. That it was Clark's opinion that a seminary should be under the authority of a church, not an independent institution, is confirmed by a recollection of Genevieve Long, widow of Clark's friend Howard Long.—Email to the author from Ellen Schulze, daughter of Genevieve Long, 11 November 2015.

95. Stonehouse, J. Gresham Machen, A Biographical Memoir, 393.

96. Nelson, The Making and Unmaking of an Evangelical Mind, 45, 64.

book *An Introduction to Christian Apologetics*, saying, "Have you seen the book by Carnell? It is Clark through and through."[97]

Clark's ordination brought with it the possibility that he could teach at the seminary or at the newly planned Reformed university and even further impact the future ministers of the denomination. Robert Rudolph wrote, "Dr. Van Til said that Clark was probably the most effective teacher he knew and that therefore he was afraid of the great influence he would have on students and that Clark's effectiveness would do much harm—more so than most other men."[98] A letter from one OPC pastor to another raised the concern saying, "Cross currents of emotional pressure are present in the presbytery, currents originating from men who would seek to use Clark as a spearhead about the seminary."[99]

It was clear to Ned Stonehouse that the force of those aligning against the seminary caused *The Complaint* to be written in reaction. He wrote, "The issue, to state it again, is whether we are in our approaches to be distinctly Presbyterian. The Clark case is only one aspect of that; indeed it would not have arisen, in my judgment, unless there had been the anti-seminary left-wing group." However, because the seminary power struggle was intertwined with the Clark case, Stonehouse had to point out that there was a case against Clark on its own merits and that false accusations had flown in the direction of the professors. He wrote, "Unless we had felt that there was something wrong in Dr. Clark's outlook, we would never have taken the step of challenging his qualifications. But what happened. Immediately people's minds were poisoned with charges that we had personal animosity towards Dr. Clark, that we were afraid of him, and all sorts of false and unChristian statements of that kind."[100]

THE MEANING OF THE COMPLAINT

Rev. Ed Kellogg warned Van Til of the repercussions of lodging the complaint. He wrote to Van Til, "I also feel that if Clark does hold errors of sufficient magnitude to make him unfit for the ministry that the Commissioners to the Assembly will expect you as a teacher and apologete to present the error in a very clear and understandable manner. If you are not able to make the error very apparent and show from Scripture the seriousness of it I'm

97. CVT to "Ted," 30 April 1948, WTS Archives.

98. Rudolph, "A Truly Great and Brilliant Friend," 104.

99. Edwards E. Elliott to "Prosper" (Edmund Prosper Clowney), 13 January 1945, WTS Archives.

100. Ned Stonehouse to Rev. Robert H. Graham, 30 April 1946, WTS Archives.

afraid your opposition may arouse a certain distrust. I do not want you to conclude from this last statement that I distrust you for I certainly do not but I do feel that perhaps at this point you have made a mistake."[101]

Although many of the differences between the WTS faction and Clark were of political and ecclesiastical nature, with *The Complaint*, the WTS faction chose to make their stand on theological and philosophical grounds. Clark, an Old School Presbyterian, was a strict subscriptionist to the Westminster Standards, but *The Complaint* asked him to subscribe to Van Til's particular views. Not only did this go beyond the requirements for ordination, but Clark believed that Van Til's views were novel and in error. Because of this, Clark concluded, "The Complaint would have denied ordination to both [respected former Princeton professors] Hodge and Green, and even Machen."[102]

PRESUPPOSITIONALISM AND THE ABANDONMENT OF OLD PRINCETON

A disagreement in apologetics between B. B. Warfield and Abraham Kuyper a generation prior sheds light on the origins of the Clark-Van Til controversy.

Warfield followed a long line of Princeton professors in his apologetic approach. In fact, the Princeton approach itself was a continuation of Scottish Common Sense Realism philosophy, traceable to the eighteenth century. Warfield, like his precursors, held an evidentialist view of apologetics that appealed to general revelation to provide one with knowledge of God's existence prior to building a case for accepting the validity of the Bible. He believed the existence of God was knowable through the evidence of general revelation—through what was seen in the world—and by this, man was made inexcusable before God. Warfield also believed that by logic—the rules of logical inference—the consistency of the believer and the inconsistency of the unbeliever could be shown.

Where Warfield had an evidentialist approach to apologetics, Kuyper had a presuppositional (or proto-presuppositional) one. Rather than starting with general revelation, Kuyper began with special revelation, the Scriptures. He believed reason should not judge revelation. Kuyper saw the believer's and unbeliever's worldviews as completely separate, with no point of common ground. For Kuyper, all beliefs were relative to one's worldview; there was no neutral item on which the worldviews could agree.

---

101. Rev. Edward Kellogg to CVT, 28 April 1944, WTS Archives.

102. GHC to Michael A. Hakkenberg, 11 July 1980, provided by John Muether.

The disagreement between Warfield and Kuyper comes into view in the introduction to Francis Beattie's *Apologetics,* where Warfield called Kuyper "a striking instance" of those mystics who have the tendency to "deprecate Apologetics because they feel no need of 'reasons' to ground a faith which they are sure they have received immediately from God." Warfield then argued that in the face of rationalist attacks against Christianity, believers need better arguments for faith, rather than a retreat in the form of saying faith is an "immediate creation of the Holy Spirit in a man's heart." Clarifying his own position, Warfield wrote, "It is just as essential that grounds of faith should be present to the mind as that the Giver of faith should act creatively upon the heart" and "that faith is, in all its exercises alike, a form of conviction, and is necessarily grounded on evidence."[103] In short, Warfield saw Kuyper's approach, lacking arguments for faith, as purely fideistic.

Cornelius Van Til, according Owen Anderson in *B. B. Warfield and Right Reason,* "attempted to formulate a third position that takes the best of both of these [Warfield and Kuyper] and yet avoids what he saw as weaknesses in each." Some, however, like R. C. Sproul, accuse Van Til of being fully a Kuyperian (see Sproul's *Classical Apologetics*). Other students of Van Til, such as Greg Bahnsen, denied this and pointed to explicit statements by Van Til to the contrary (see Bahnsen's *Van Til's Apologetics: Reading and Analysis*).[104] W. Robert Godfrey, another student of Van Til, however, lends credence to Sproul's view that Van Til was far closer to Kuyper than to Warfield. Godfrey wrote, "Van Til maintained the strong anti-modernism and unmodified Calvinism of Old Princeton. But he did decisively change the apologetic direction of the seminary. He built not on the evidentialism of Warfield, but on the work of Abraham Kuyper."[105] In fact, this has become the common view. Evidencing this, Greenville Presbyterian Theological Seminary Professor Morton H. Smith has written, "The apologetics of Dr. Van Til has come to be known as presuppositional apologetics, as opposed to the traditional evidential apologetics of Old Princeton."[106]

Van Til's acceptance of Kuyper's apologetic over Warfield's effectively ended the continuance of the tradition passed down through the Princeton theologians from Charles Hodge to A. A. Hodge to B. B. Warfield to J. Gresham Machen. Even Van Til's strongly supportive biographer, William White, admitted to the significance of the change from Old Princeton to Van Tillian apologetics. He wrote, "Throughout the last hectic months at Princeton and

---

103. Warfield, "Introduction to Beattie's Apologetics."

104. Anderson, *Benjamin B. Warfield and Right Reason,* 46.

105. Godfrey, "The Westminster School," 96.

106. Smith, "The Southern Tradition," 204.

the early segment of seminary life in Philadelphia, it is not clear how many of the Westminster men were aware of the basic and far-reaching revolution going on in the orbit of apologetics. Did Machen understand how far from the Old Princeton apologetic the new Westminster apologetic really was? Did Machen realize that Van Til, R. B. Kuiper, and Ned Stonehouse had brought to Philadelphia the best of Amsterdam?"[107] In Van Til's own work, *The Defense of the Faith* he confirmed "what has been advocated in this syllabus has in large measure been prepared under the influence of Kuyper" and argued that "it is only in Apologetics Warfield wanted to operate in neutral territory with the unbeliever. He thought this was the only way to show the unbeliever that theism and Christianity are objectively true." But on one point—the usefulness of reasoning with unbelievers—Van Til sided with Warfield. He wrote, "I am unable to follow [Kuyper] on the uselessness of reasoning with the natural man," and "Warfield was quite right in maintaining that Christianity is objectively defensible. And the natural man has the ability to understand intellectually, though not spiritually, the challenge presented to him. And no challenge is presented to him unless it is shown him that on his principle he would destroy all truth and meaning."[108]

Clark believed that Van Til's (and Kuyper's) apologetics went too far in rejecting logic as a common ground between the believer and unbeliever.[109] Despite Van Til's desire to avoid the use of logic to determine his worldview, he still had to employ logic. Clark, realizing the impossibility and hypocrisy of such a position, retained logic in his apologetics while Van Til denied common ground of any sort, including logic. Clark argued that all men, believer and unbeliever alike, shared the same logical mental structure because this structure was part of the image of God in which all men were created.[110] In this respect, Clark continued part of the tradition of Warfield

107. White, *Van Til, Defender of the Faith*, 99.

108. Van Til, *The Defense of the Faith*, 361–364.

109. "Dr. Cornelius Van Til of Westminster Seminary has annoyed the empirical apologetes by insisting that there is no common ground shared by believers and unbelievers—that is if both are consistent with their principles. The empirical aim is to discover some point of agreement which they can use in convincing any man of the truth of Christianity. Dr. Van Til denies that there is such an agreement."—Clark, *Lord God of Truth*, 37.

110. Clark wrote to J. Oliver Buswell (a follower of the Warfield / Old Princeton approach), "It amuses me somewhat to compare what you say of my thought with what Dr. Van Til says. You complain that I do not allow for a 'common ground' while Dr. Van Til condemns me because I do. Probably I suffer from inability to express myself clearly. . . . I hold that Christ is the light and logos that lighteth every man that cometh into the world. I hold that every man is made in the image of God, and that every man has what may be conveniently be called an innate idea of God. All this is common ground between the Christian and the unbeliever. But there is no common ground between

and Old Princeton, even if he rejected other aspects such as the thesis that general revelation necessarily preceded special revelation of the Bible.

Explaining Clark's view, Dr. Gary Crampton wrote in *The Scripturalism of Gordon H. Clark*:

> After demonstrating the internal incoherence of the non-Christian views, the biblical apologete will argue for truth and the logical consistency of the Scriptures and the Christian worldview revealed therein. He will show how Christianity is self-consistent, how it gives us a coherent understanding of the world. It answers questions and solves problems that other worldviews cannot. This method is not to be considered as a proof for the existence of God or the truth of Scripture, but as proof that the non-Christian view is false. It shows that intelligibility can only be maintained by viewing all things as dependent on the God of Scripture, who is truth itself. This is the proper "presuppositional" approach to apologetics.[111]

Clark believed that because of the shared logical nature of all men, Christians can legitimately argue with unbelievers on two grounds; firstly, the Christian can argue that the unbeliever's worldview is inconsistent, and secondly, the Christian can argue that Christianity is consistent.

Van Til diverged from the Old Princeton tradition further than Clark by largely accepting Kuyper's formulations.[112] Clark later pointed out the fact that Van Til was outside of the Old Princeton tradition. He wrote, "Machen was more opposed to the Van Til apologetics than I am. Machen accepted Hodge."[113]

Clark, however, did not continue in the Old Princeton tradition either and admitted such. He wrote, "I never followed the Old Princeton apologetic. I certainly never had any sympathy with the Common Sense school."[114] In another place Clark criticized Scottish Common Sense Philosophy as "one of the most incompetent types of philosophy in the history of the subject."[115] With neither party legitimately able to claim that they followed

---

Christianity and a non-Christian system."—GHC to JOB, 10 November 1947, SDCS Library, 1/52.

111. Crampton, *The Scripturalism of Gordon H. Clark*, 44.

112. See: Anderson, "Chapter 4: Benjamin B. Warfield and Cornelius Van Til . . . " in *Benjamin B. Warfield and Right Reason*.

113. GHC to Michael A. Hakkenberg, 11 July 1980, provided by John Muether.

114. Ibid.

115. Clark, *The Incarnation*, 41.

the Old Princeton apologetics, the Clark-Van Til controversy functioned to determine the new orthodoxy in the church's apologetics.

Westminster Theological Seminary might have been friendly to Clark's ideas in an earlier age—Princeton graduates from past generations would have appreciated his rigorous method, his uncompromising stance, his intellectualism, and his commitment to logical argumentation—but by 1944, the year of *The Complaint*, much of this had changed. WTS had lost many of its ties to Old Princeton. When Machen formed WTS in 1929, a number of professors left Princeton to join the new seminary. But by the time of *The Complaint*, all of the WTS professors who had significant experience at Princeton were gone. Robert Dick Wilson, an expert scholar of biblical languages, had died in 1930; the independently wealthy Oswald T. Allis resigned in 1935 to focus on his writing; and Machen had died in 1937. These three had been long-time Princeton professors, steeped in "Princeton Theology." With the departure of these professors, WTS was no longer Old Princeton. It was a new seminary, with new professors, mostly young and with lesser ties to Princeton. The younger professors at WTS (Cornelius Van Til, Ned Stonehouse, R. B. Kuiper, and Paul Woolley) had all been students at Princeton, but only Van Til had taught there, and even then, only briefly. John Murray also had taught at Princeton, but for only one year. The influence from Old Princeton remained, but it was mixed with and muted by other theologies, particularly those of the Christian Reformed Church in which Van Til, Kuiper, and Stonehouse had been raised. Influenced by the Dutch Reformed traditions, the WTS faculty had difficulty recognizing the fidelity to the Presbyterian tradition in Clark's theology.

Chapter 7

The Arguments of the Ordination Controversy

WITH THE COMPLAINT FILED against the Presbytery of Philadelphia alleging faults in the ordination of Gordon Clark, issues in the Orthodox Presbyterian Church that had been brewing behind the scenes came to the forefront. The church leaders who had founded the OPC were united in their opposition to modernism, but on a number of other doctrines there remained diverse views.

Gordon Clark and Cornelius Van Til were among those who had coexisted in the young church despite the theological diversity. Their coexistence can be attributed at least partially to the fact that, since the beginning of the OPC, Clark had been at Wheaton College, distant from the center of the church structure in the Philadelphia area. Clark's application for ordination, his departure from Wheaton, and his subsequent return to Philadelphia brought the two thinkers into close proximity and brought their disagreements to a head. Van Til and eleven others had filed their complaint against Clark in the presbytery and the presbytery prepared to respond.

THE ANSWER

At the meeting of the Philadelphia Presbytery on November 20, 1944, following the reading of *The Complaint*, Clark took the floor and made a personal protest against its contents. Following his protest, the presbytery elected a committee to prepare an answer to the complaint.[1] The commit-

1. Philadelphia Presbytery, meeting minutes (Wilmington, DE: Eastlake Church, 20 November 1944), courtesy of Rev. Thomas A. Foh, stated clerk of the Presbytery of

tee, by rules of the church, could not have as members any of those who signed the complaint and therefore was composed entirely of the remaining members of the presbytery who all were Clark supporters. Included on the committee were ministers Alan Tichenor (an assistant professor at WTS and former Clark student), Robert Strong (pastor of Calvary Church—one of the largest congregations in the denomination), Floyd Hamilton (a missionary to Korea), and Edwin Rian (the President of the Board of Trustees at WTS). Clark himself was also on committee as he was the one most capable of responding to the philosophical arguments.

The committee presented *The Answer* to the Presbytery of Philadelphia at their stated meeting of March 19, 1945.[2] Not surprisingly, considering the members elected to write it, *The Answer* defended the decision to ordain Clark and supported his theological positions.[3] At this same meeting it was moved that the complaint be dismissed. The vote of the presbytery came back a tie—twenty in favor and twenty against—and the motion was declared to be lost. Ten days later, on March 29, after providing time for all to more thoroughly review *The Answer*, the presbytery reconvened and an additional series of votes was held. The first vote sided 23 to 14 in Clark's favor, denying that the special meeting of the presbytery was illegal. A second vote of 20 to 16 in Clark's favor denied the theological components of the complaint.[4] These votes effectively ended the complaint at the presbytery. The complaint, however, would later re-emerge at the general assembly.

In the time between his ordination and *The Complaint*, Clark and his family had relocated from Wheaton, Illinois, to Philadelphia. They briefly stayed at the house of fellow church member Floyd Graf in the summer of 1944, and then purchased a house of their own in Jenkintown, a suburb of Philadelphia. Clark accepted a visiting lecturer position at the Reformed Episcopal Seminary for the fall semester of the 1944–1945 school year and taught courses in ethics and philosophy.[5] His daughter, Lois, was enrolled in the Willow Grove Christian School, then just in its second year of existence. Although she was only eight years of age, she was placed in 5th grade, skipping two grades because of her advanced reading level. Among Lois's

---

Philadelphia.

2. Philadelphia Presbytery, meeting minutes (Philadelphia, PA: Mediator Church, 19 March 1945), courtesy of Rev. Thomas A. Foh, stated clerk of the Presbytery of Philadelphia.

3. Tichenor, "The Answer," 6.

4. Philadelphia Presbytery, meeting minutes (Philadelphia, PA: Mediator Church, 29 March 1945), courtesy of Rev. Thomas A. Foh, stated clerk of the Presbytery of Philadelphia.

5. Acker, *History of the Reformed Episcopal Seminary*, 45.

friends in her class was Jean Young, the daughter of WTS professor E. J. Young. Other students at the school included Chip Stonehouse (the son of Ned Stonehouse) and Patty Strong (the daughter of Robert Strong).[6]

The move back to Philadelphia was short-lived as Clark accepted an associate professor position at Butler University in Indianapolis and started there at the beginning of the winter semester of 1945. While Clark moved to Indianapolis, his wife and their two daughters, Lois and Betsy, stayed in Philadelphia to finish out the school year and to sell their house. Following his move to Indiana, Clark sought a transfer of his ministerial credentials from the OPC's Philadelphia Presbytery to the OPC's Presbytery of Ohio (which also had jurisdiction over Indiana). On October 9, 1945, he was examined in theology at his new home in Indianapolis and, after passing the exam, was accepted into the Presbytery of Ohio as a teaching elder.[7]

Before *The Answer* was presented to the Philadelphia Presbytery, Clark addressed the situation in the church in an article in *The Presbyterian Guardian*. The article, titled "Blest River of Salvation," was published in the first issue for the new year of 1945. In it Clark recalled the founding days of the church and the founders' united opposition to modernism, but lamented the changing emphases of the church. He critiqued the present situation in the OPC, writing, "Instead of leading the Christian forces of our country, we have assumed the position of an isolationist porcupine." He wished for a "return to the ideals and emphasis that characterized our church when it was formed in 1936."[8] In the same issue, Thomas Birch, the editor of the paper, wrote a three-page editorial critiquing (and preceding) Clark's shorter two-page article. *The Presbyterian Guardian* had been under suspicion of being biased towards the WTS faction of the church. That they published Clark's article would seem to indicate their neutrality if it were not for the fact that Birch's editorial apologized ahead of time for publishing Clark's article at all. The editorial warned, "Dr. Clark's article was submitted to it through a third party who vigorously champions the position Dr. Clark outlines and who indicated to the editorial council that, unless the article were published with reasonable promptness, he would consider that he and those who agree with him were being 'given the brush-off.'"[9]

The argument that *The Presbyterian Guardian* was biased was not unfounded. Even before the controversy erupted, six ministers sent a letter to

6. Lois (née Clark) Zeller, interview by Douglas Douma, Sangre de Cristo Seminary, 2014.

7. Strong, "Presbytery of Ohio," 332.

8. Clark, "Blest River of Salvation," 10, 16.

9. Clelland, "Have We Changed?" 7–9.

The Presbyterian Guardian urging them, for the benefit of the denomination, to withhold publication of the minority's complaint, or at least wait until the majority's answer could be included alongside.[10] From the perspective of many of Clark's supporters, publishing *The Complaint* alone or even at all risked harming the OPC's reputation. *The Presbyterian Guardian* acknowledged both this letter and a vote by the Philadelphia Presbytery advising them not to publish the complaint. Technically speaking, the magazine did not print it. Instead, the editorial staff sent the text of *The Complaint* to a private printer and then offered it as supplemental material included as part of a regular issue on December 10, 1944.[11] This allowed *The Presbyterian Guardian* to claim to have heeded the plea of Clark's supporters while still pursuing their own agenda. Regardless of who printed it, the damage was done.

THE THEOLOGICAL ISSUES

There were four theological topics addressed in *The Complaint* and *The Answer*, summarized by the following titles: 1) The incomprehensibility of God, 2) The relationship of the faculty of knowledge to other faculties of the soul, 3) The relationship between divine sovereignty and human responsibility, and 4) the Free Offer of the Gospel. A fifth topic, however, related to each of the others, was Clark's alleged rationalism.

Issue 1: The incomprehensibility of God

The theological portion of the complaint centered on the first of the four issues, the incomprehensibility of God. More time and discussions were spent on this point during the controversy than perhaps on all of the other points combined. Both parties agreed that God is incomprehensible—that man can never fully and exhaustively know God. The issue between the two parties, rather, was over how man's knowledge relates to God's knowledge.

10. Robert Strong et. al. to the editors of *The Presbyterian Guardian*, 18 September 1944, Reformed Theological Seminary Archives. See also: Philadelphia Presbytery, meeting minutes (Wilmington, DE: Eastlake Church, 20 November 1944), courtesy of Rev. Thomas A. Foh, stated clerk of the Presbytery of Philadelphia.

11. Birch, "The Text of the Complaint," 349. See also: Birch, "Phila. Presbytery Hears Complaint in Clark Case," 355.; Note also that Ned Stonehouse wanted to see *The Complaint* published. He wrote, "You will recall that I held that it was proper and wise to publish the Complaint as soon as it became available. Some of the brethren including a few members of the faculty, however, were inclined to think that we would be on stronger ground if we waited until it was actually read in the Presbytery."—Ned Stonehouse to G. A. Andreas, 25 September 1944, WTS Archives.

Clark believed that for man to know any truth at all, there must be a common point of contact between man's knowledge and God's knowledge. This point of contact was, for Clark, the proposition known.[12] He believed that the propositions which man knows must be identical to the propositions which God knows in order for man to know anything at all.

Clark also held to a number of distinctions between man's knowledge and God's knowledge. First, because man will never know everything, whereas God has always known everything, Clark believed it is necessary to acknowledge a quantitative distinction between man's knowledge as limited and God's knowledge as not limited by anything outside of himself. Likewise, Clark held to a quantitative distinction regarding the implications of propositions—that for any given proposition, God knows all of its implications, whereas man knows only some of its implications at best. In addition to these two quantitative distinctions, Clark held to a qualitative distinction in the mode or manner of knowing. He believed God's knowledge is intuitive (that is, God knows all truth immediately and essentially), whereas man's knowledge is discursive (that is, man knows truth in part, via revelation and deduction).

The Complaint, however, argued that Clark's distinctions were insufficient and that a further qualitative distinction is also needed. *The Complaint's* argument was worded: "Because God is God, the creator, and man is man, the creature, the difference between the divine knowledge and the knowledge possible to man may never be conceived of merely in quantitative terms, as a difference in degree rather than a difference in kind."[13] *The Complaint* held that Clark's distinction in "mode" was insufficient to account for this qualitative distinction. *The Complaint* read, "We gladly concede this point [Clark's distinction in mode] . . . However, this admission does not affect the whole point at issue here since the doctrine of the mode of the divine knowledge is not a part of the doctrine of the incomprehensibility of his knowledge. The latter is concerned only with the contents of the divine knowledge. Dr. Clark distinguishes between the knowledge of God and of man so far as mode of knowledge is concerned, but it is a tragic fact that his dialectic has led him to obliterate the qualitative distinction between the contents of the divine mind and the knowledge which is possible to the creature."[14] Thus it was argued that in addition to Clark's qualitative distinction in mode there must be a

12. A proposition is defined as the meaning of a declarative sentence. See: Clark, *Logic*, 28.

13. Kuiper, *The Complaint*, 3.

14. Ibid, 6.

qualitative distinction in "content." The use and meaning of the term *content* would become a central element of the controversy.

Van Til and the complainants believed that Clark's claim—that there must be an identical point of knowledge between God and man—ignored the fundamental distinction between Creator and creature. Van Til was concerned to uphold a specific formulation of the "Creator-creature distinction." He wrote in his 1940 syllabus, *Junior Systematics*, "Christians believe in two levels of existence, the level of God's existence as self-contained and the level of man's existence as derived from the level of God's existence. For this reason, Christians must also believe in two levels of knowledge: the level of God's knowledge, which is absolutely comprehensive, and the level of man's knowledge, which is derivative and reinterpretive." Echoing Van Til, *The Complaint* declared, "Because of his very nature as infinite and absolute the knowledge which God possesses of himself and of all things must remain a mystery which the finite mind of man cannot penetrate."[15] And in the strongest form possible, the phrase for which *The Complaint* became most well known, "We dare not maintain that [God's] knowledge and our knowledge coincide at any single point."[16]

Clark, however, did not deny a Creator-creature distinction; he merely denied Van Til's formulation of the doctrine. For Clark, God (the Creator) *is* ontologically[17] distinct from man (the creature) in that God is eternal, omnipotent, and omniscient while man is created, temporal, and limited in both power and knowledge. Yet Van Til wanted more from the Creator-creature distinction. He believed that not only are man and God distinct in these aspects of their beings, but they must also be distinct in all items of knowledge. Thus Van Til's Creator-creature distinction was both ontological (with respect to being) and epistemological (with respect to knowledge).

Van Til used the term "analogy" to describe the relationship between God's knowledge and man's knowledge. In a 1937 letter from Van Til to Clark, he referred to "analogical reasoning" as "keeping in mind the

15. Kuiper, *The Complaint*, 3.

16. Kuiper, *The Complaint*, 5.

17. Since ontology is the branch of metaphysics that deals with the nature of being, an ontological distinction is one of being.

distinction between the pagan system which starts with man's autonomy and the Christian system which starts with God's autonomy."[18] [19]

As argued by Gilbert Weaver in his master's thesis "The Concept of Truth in the Apologetic Systems of Gordon Haddon Clark and Cornelius Van Til", the term "analogy" as Van Til used it should not be confused with Thomas Aquinas's use of the term.[20] Whereas Aquinas contended that man could know God via analogy—a middle path between univocism and equivocation—Van Til used "analogy" to mean that man's knowledge itself is an analogy of God's knowledge. Van Til emphasized that man's knowledge is derivative of God's knowledge.

Despite the validity of Weaver's point, Clark perceived that when Van Til spoke of "two levels" of knowledge without a single "point of contact," Van Til still relied on Aquinas's rejection of any and all univocal predication of God. Thus Clark critiqued Van Til as holding to Aquinas's position.[21]

---

18. "When the 'pagan' concludes that the 'supreme principle' 'is deprived of volition' [it] is due to the fact that in his starting point he *assumes* 'the continuity of the universe' both metaphysically and epistemologically. He assumes that the only 'god' he will allow for is one who is not more ultimate than himself. He cannot allow for a sovereign God. His God, granted his starting point can only be a correlative to man. Now by analogical reasoning I mean nothing else but constantly knowing this distinction between paganism and Christianity in the mind at all times."—CVT to GHC, 24 September 1937, WTS Archives.

19. Another definition of Van Til's "analogous reasoning" has been given by John Frame as "reasoning which presupposes as its ultimate basis the reality of the biblical God and the authority of His revelation."—Frame, "The Problem of Theological Paradox," 311.

20. "Van Til's use of the term is to be distinguished from certain other uses of 'analogy,' both common and literary and philosophical uses and a special theological use by St. Thomas Aquinas."—Weaver, "The Concept of Truth," 6, 15, 25.; See also: "For Aquinas analogy purports to be a middle way between univocal and equivocal predication of names or words to subjects. This is not the case for Van Til. For him analogy applies not to terms, but to the overall process of human thought."—Weaver, "Man: Analogue of God," 327.; Paul Moser, however, in agreement with Robert Reymond has noted: "Weaver has overlooked some of the pertinent literature. Van Til's analogy does concern words and predication. . . . Admittedly, Van Til's theory of analogy is not identical with that of Thomas; but the distinction between the two is not one that commends Van Til's theory; for his view, if held consistently, implies pure equivocism."—Moser, *Reformed Apologetics and First Principles*, 111.; See also: Reymond, *Justification of Knowledge*, 104.

21. It is not clear whether Clark ever allowed for Van Til's definition of analogy to distance itself from Aquinas. Much later, connecting the two, Clark said, "Unless the analogy is based on a literal and univocal similarity, there could be no analogy at all. And I use this argument to pay my respects to Thomas Aquinas and Cornelius Van Til."—Clark, "Language, Truth, and Revelation, Part 1," minute 27.

In critiquing Van Til's theory of analogy, Clark argued that if God's knowledge has no point in common with ours, then we know nothing that is true, for God knows all truths. Therefore, Clark believed, Van Til's theory of analogy resulted in skepticism. In *The Answer*, his argument for this conclusion is presented: "The Presbytery wishes to suggest that if man does not know at least one truth that God knows, if man's knowledge and God's knowledge do not coincide in at least one detail, then man knows nothing at all. God knows all truth, and if man's mind cannot grasp one truth, then man's mind grasps no truth. Far from being a test of orthodoxy, this test imposed by *The Complaint* is nothing else than skepticism and irrationalism."[22]

A further area of disagreement between Clark and Van Til regarded the nature of truth. Clark believed that truth is a property of propositions alone. At Clark's theological examination before presbytery, he was asked: "Is all truth in the mind of God capable of being addressed [sic, expressed] in propositions intelligent to the mind of man?" Clark answered, "I would not know what the word 'truth' meant unless as a quality of proposition. I cannot conceive of anything that is of truth that is not a proposition."[23] *The Complaint* therefore argued that "the fundamental assumption made by Dr. Clark is that truth, whether in the divine mind or in the human mind, is always propositional. . . . It will be observed that Dr. Clark does not claim to derive this judgment from Scripture; it is rather regarded as an axiom of reason."[24] But *The Answer* responded, "The presbytery replies to this assertion by pointing out that there is nothing in the transcript to justify it. . . . Dr. Clark has said that all truth can be expressed in propositions, but this does not mean that God thinks in propositions."[25] Clark, however, later did affirm his belief that God's knowledge is exclusively propositional, drawing a conceptual distinction between propositional objective knowledge and the subjective manner of how one thinks (e.g. intuitively or discursively).[26] More details on this topic will be covered in the following chapter.

Although the overwhelming percentage of time and effort spent in the ordination controversy surrounded this first issue, the other issues each brought up a significant discussion, with OPC members supporting Clark or Van Til, respectively, along party lines in each case.

22. Tichenor, *The Answer*, 21.

23. The Philadelphia Presbytery, examination in theology of Gordon H. Clark (Philadelphia, PA: Mediator Orthodox Presbyterian Church, 7 July 1944), 2, PCA Archives, 309/100.

24. Kuiper, *The Complaint*, 5.

25. Tichenor, *The Answer*, 14–15.

26. Clark, *God's Hammer*, 35.

Issue 2: The relationship of the faculties of the soul

The authors of *The Complaint* came to know of Clark's view on the topic of the relationship of the faculties of the soul through his then recently published article "On the Primacy of the Intellect" in the May 1943 issue of the *Westminster Theological Journal*. While specifying that a person is a unity, not a compound of his mental functions or conscious states, the goal of Clark's article was to answer the question with which faculties of the soul (given as intellect, will, and emotion) does "a man best respond, most fully grasp God, most perfectly worship, and most closely commune with Him."[27] Critiquing emotion and will, Clark argued for the primacy of intellect, saying, "Now if in Christianity the end of all human endeavor is to see or contemplate God, evidently the desire for God or the love of God is subordinate, since one can love God without seeing him, or at least without seeing him with that clarity which characterizes the final object of desire. In other words, desire and love, because they are means to the end, cannot be the end itself."[28] Clark furthermore argued,

> Certainly it is clear that historic Christianity with its acceptance of a written revelation is more in accord with intellectualism than with either of the rival theories. Now the creed is the most accurate expression possible of so much truth as has been discovered in the Scriptures. It is therefore the object of explicit faith. God himself is revealed in the words of Scripture; their truth is his truth; in understanding them we understand him, and in contemning truth we contemn God.[29]

On this issue *The Complaint* brought up discussion on two related points. First, as did Clark's article, it discussed the relationship of the faculties of the soul in man. Secondly, it discussed the faculties, not of man, but of God. Arguing that the discussion of one point necessitated a discussion of the other, *The Complaint* said, "Any statement on the relation between the intellect and other spiritual faculties must needs be concerned with God as well as with man."[30]

The Complaint took issue with Clark's denial of emotions in God. Clark used the term "emotions" synonymously with the term "passions," and the complainants did concede that with that definition, to attribute such to God would be opposed to the Confession.

27. Clark, "The Primacy of the Intellect," 183.
28. Ibid., 192.
29. Ibid., 195.
30. Kuiper, *The Complaint*, 7.

After describing Clark's views, *The Complaint* stated, "Dr. Clark deserves the highest commendation for his faithful opposition to any form of humanistic emotionalism in theology . . . However . . . it unfortunately begins to appear that he is in grave danger of falling into the equally serious error of humanistic intellectualism."[31] In a later place the document is even more forthright: "Dr. Clark's view of the primacy of the intellect is at serious variance with Scripture. . . . This variance is of no minor matter; it is the product of a rationalistic dialectic."[32]

Responding to *The Complaint*'s accusation that Clark had a "forthright denial of anything that might be called 'emotion' in God," *The Answer* responded that such attributes as love and wrath God does certainly have, but that they are better called "volitions," or acts of will, rather than emotions.[33]

This second issue of the controversy was the least discussed, being mostly overshadowed by the other three issues.

Issue 3: Divine sovereignty and human responsibility

The third charge in *The Complaint* stemmed from Clark's views as presented in his 1932 article "Determinism and Responsibility." In this article, Clark aimed "to show that determinism is consistent with responsibility, indeed responsibility requires determinism."[34] To put it another way, Clark believed there was no contradiction or even apparent contradiction between the doctrine that God is the fully sovereign cause of all things and the doctrine that man is responsible for his own sins. Clark was not alone in holding to this view. But unlike other theologians who held these views, Clark set out to prove that the doctrines were without contradiction. He wrote, "[My own] denomination [at that time the PCUSA] has stated that the reconciliation of man's free agency and God's sovereignty is an inscrutable mystery. Rather, the mystery is—recognising that God is the ultimate cause of the man's nature—how the Calvinistic solution could have been so long overlooked."[35] Here, as was his common practice, Clark first defined his terms. Regarding "responsibility" he wrote, "By calling a man responsible we mean he may be justly punished by God. For this definitional truth is the key to the explanation of why a man is responsible for the act God

31. Kuiper, *The Complaint*, 7.

32. Kuiper, *The Complaint*, 10.

33. Tichenor, *The Answer*, 27.

34. Clark, "Determinism and Responsibility," 14.

35. Ibid., 16.

determined him to do."[36] Taking the key to his solution from John Calvin, Clark wrote, "God is Sovereign; whatever He does is just, for this very reason, because He does it. If He punishes a man, the man is punished justly and hence the man is responsible."[37]

According to *The Complaint*, "Dr. Clark asserts that the relationship of divine sovereignty and human responsibility to each other presents no difficulty for his thinking and that the two are easily reconcilable before the bar of human reason."[38] *The Complaint* listed theologians who had wrestled with these doctrines and then argued that "there is a problem that has baffled the greatest theologians of history. Not even Holy Scripture offers a solution. But Dr. Clark asserts unblushingly that for his thinking the problem has ceased being a problem. Here is something phenomenal. What accounts for it? The most charitable, and no doubt the correct, explanation is that Dr. Clark has come under the spell of rationalism."[39]

The issue of divine sovereignty and human responsibility brought up a more general disagreement between the two factions: the nature of Scripture. *The Complaint* argued that reconciling these two doctrines is impossible for man; it is an unsolved and unsolvable paradox. In *The Answer*, however, Clark responded, "The Scriptures nowhere prohibit us from attempting to solve revealed paradoxes."[40] Clark then turned the tables, arguing that "anyone who argues that a given revealed paradox cannot be solved is virtually claiming omniscience. He who says a given paradox cannot be solved, logically implies that he has examined every verse in Scripture, that he has exhausted every implication of every verse, and that there is in all this no hint of a solution. Such a person must have a tremendous knowledge of the Bible. And this is exactly what the complainants claim."[41] In fact, Clark lampooned the complainants' principle, describing it as the view that "a man, to be subject to God's Word, must fail to understand it."[42]

---

36. Ibid., 20.

37. Ibid., 21.

38. Kuiper, *The Complaint*, 10.

39. Kuiper, *The Complaint*, 12.

40. Tichenor, *The Answer*, 35.

41. Tichenor, *The Answer*, 36.

42. GHC to Presbytery of Philadelphia, 20 November 1944, Gordon H. Clark Papers, A.E. 0.4, 1/96.

Issue 4: The Free Offer of the Gospel

On a fourth issue, *The Complaint* charged:

> In the course of Dr. Clark's examination by presbytery it became abundantly clear that his rationalism keeps him from doing justice to the precious teaching of Scripture that in the Gospel God sincerely offers salvation in Christ to all who hear, reprobate as well as elect, and that he has no pleasure in any one's rejecting this offer but, contrariwise, would have all who hear accept it and be saved.[43]

Clark's hesitancy in his theological examination to apply the term "sincere" to the call in the gospel concerned the complainants. The topic of debate was over what is known as the "sincere," "well-meant," or "Free Offer" of the gospel. The crux of this doctrinal question concerns not to whom the Christian should preach the gospel, but the very content or message of that preaching. Both Clark and the complainants agreed that the gospel should be preached to all people (what is often referred to as the "General Call of the Gospel"), but Clark did not agree with the complainants' supposition that God desires the salvation of all men, reprobate included (what is called the "Free Offer of the Gospel"). Rather, Clark and his supporters held that God desires the salvation of only those whom He actually saves: the elect only.[44]

Controversy over the doctrine of the Free Offer of the Gospel did not arise for the first time at the Clark controversy but had precedent in at least two previous occurrences in Protestant church history.

The first of these occurrences was the Marrow Controversy in Scotland, which began when the book *The Marrow of Modern Divinity* (originally published by Edward Fisher in 1645) was reprinted in 1718.[45] A number of the book's views, including support of the doctrine of the Free Offer of the Gospel, were quickly brought to the attention of prominent church leaders. Led by James Hadow (1667–1743), professor of divinity and principal of St. Mary's College in the University of St. Andrews, they argued, among other points, that the book's support of the Free Offer of the Gospel led to or logically necessitated universal atonement, the dreaded error of the

43. Kuiper, *The Complaint*, 13.

44. The distinction between the General Call of the Gospel and the Free Offer of the Gospel is of critical import. Often those, like Clark, who have denied the latter are wrongly accused of denying the former. Frequently, those who support the Free Offer of the Gospel fail to make the distinction between the two doctrines, conflating the Free Offer of the Gospel with the General Call of the Gospel.

45. Lachman, *The Marrow Controversy*, 201.

Arminians. The book was thus viewed as contrary to the *Westminster Confession of Faith* and condemned at the 1720 General Assembly of the Church of Scotland.[46] However, a group of twelve ministers, who later came to be called the "Marrow men," including James Hog (1658?–1734) and Thomas Boston (1676–1732), objected to the general assembly's condemnation of the book. Although the Marrow men rejected universal atonement, they held, in agreement with *The Marrow of Modern Divinity*, that the atoning work of Christ was universal in God's desire to have all men come to faith.[47] They responded to the general assembly's condemnation with a petition requesting the Act of 1720 be rescinded, and argued that the book had been misrepresented and taken out of context. Despite their arguments, the 1722 General Assembly of the Church of Scotland reaffirmed the 1720 General Assembly's act condemning *The Marrow of Modern Divinity*.[48] The vote was nearly unanimous.[49] Theological disagreements between the two groups continued, however, and some of the Marrow Men seceded from the Church of Scotland, forming the Associate Presbytery in 1733.

The second occurrence of controversy that arose over the doctrine of the Free Offer of the Gospel was in the United States in the early 1920s in the Common Grace controversy of the Christian Reformed Church (CRC). The Common Grace controversy found its logical origins in the "Janssen Affair," when, in 1922, a debate arose at Calvin College over the views of the college's Old Testament professor, Ralph Janssen, who was under suspicion of teaching higher criticism in his classes. Herman Hoeksema, pastor of Eastern Avenue Christian Reformed Church in Grand Rapids, and three other ministers led the battle against Janssen. Janssen's views were ultimately condemned at the CRC's 1922 synod of Orange City, Iowa, but the end of this controversy led quickly to the beginning of another (the Common Grace controversy).[50]

Janssen, in his own defense, had appealed to what was called the doctrine of "common grace." The Dutch theologian and statesman Abraham

---

46. Ibid., 22, 276.

47. "In answer to the question what is that warrant [to believe], the Marrowmen replied that it was the Father's 'deed of gift and grant of His Son to sinners of mankind.' It was this mode of expression that laid them open to the charge of teaching the doctrine of a universal atonement, but in reality the real crucial point of the controversy was not so much the extent of the atonement as the effort on the part of the Marrowmen to solve the old problem of a universal call and a definite atonement. Never before, perhaps, in Scottish preaching was such stress laid on the free offer of the Gospel to every sinner of the human race."—Beaton, "The Marrow of Modern Divinity," 331.

48. Lachman, *The Marrow Controversy*, 372, 418.

49. Ibid., 477.

50. Hoeksema, *The Protestant Reformed Churches in America*," 20.

Kuyper had developed a doctrine of "common grace" whereby he held (based on Matthew 5:45)[51] that "God has good things happen on earth to even the reprobate." But this doctrine had developed in the CRC to mean also that even non-Christians can do civil good and that God desires the salvation of the non-elect. In defending himself and diverting the discussion, Janssen brought up the fact that Hoeksema denied this doctrine.

In an effort aimed directly at condemning Hoeksema, the 1924 Synod of Kalamazoo of the CRC approved a motion on "Three Points on Common Grace." The first of these points contained approval of the phrase "the favorable attitude of God towards humanity in general and not only towards the elect" and a confession of the "general offer of the Gospel" as evidence of a grace of God, not to the elect alone, but to all humans. The authors of "Three Points on Common Grace" argued for support of their position in the writings of Abraham Kuyper. The three points, however, went beyond Kuyper's doctrine to affirm that not only does God allow good things to happen to the reprobate, but also that God actually has a favorable attitude toward them. Kuyper, in fact, had warned at the very beginning of his three volumes on common grace that no one should mistake his doctrine of common grace for the teaching of a saving grace of God toward all. Kuyper went so far as to distinguish his cultural common grace from the universal saving grace of Arminianism by calling his common grace *gemeene gratie*, in distinction from *algemeene genade*, the saving grace of God.[52] Three ministers, Herman Hoeksema, George M. Ophoff, and Henry Danhof, openly rejected the Three Points on Common Grace. In addition, the three points, they argued, went beyond the formula of subscription that ministers were required to sign.[53] Hoeksema's refusal to accept the three points led to the local classis (or group of churches) suspending him from ministry and deposing the consistory of his church.[54] The same fate soon thereafter also befell Ophoff, Danhoff, and their respective church consistories.[55] The departing ministers then founded the Protestant Reformed Churches (PRC).[56]

51. "That ye may be the children of your Father which is in heaven: for he maketh his sun to rise on the evil and on the good, and sendeth rain on the just and on the unjust."—Matthew 5:45 (KJV).

52. Kuyper, *Common Grace: Noah–Adam*, 11, 12, 239–241. See also: Hoeksema, *The Protestant Reformed Churches in America*, 309. See also: Engelsma, *Hyper-Calvinism and the Call of the Gospel*, 164–168.

53. Hoeksema, *The Protestant Reformed Churches in America*, 155.

54. Ibid., 213. Note: The action of the classis contravened Reformed polity, which vests power to call and dismiss ministers in the consistory.

55. Ibid., 250–52.

56. Ibid., 258, 286–87.

The CRC's 1924 Synod of Kalamazoo was a prominent event in the denomination's history. Cornelius Van Til, R. B. Kuiper, and Ned Stonehouse, all members of the church, would have closely followed the events.

In 1922 Van Til was a senior at Calvin College and wrote on the Janssen affair in the student paper, saying it was an opportunity for students to profit from studying the issues rather than making rash judgments.[57] Van Til had heard Hoeksema preach at least once during his college days and, according to biographer John Muether, "had tremendous respect for Hoeksema" but "was in essential agreement with the Kalamazoo decision" though "never quite settled with its particular formulations."[58] Van Til later involved himself in the continuing debate on common grace, writing a paper on the topic in 1941 which was published as three articles in the *Westminster Theological Journal* in 1945–1946. The second of these articles included a critique of Hoeksema.[59] Later, in 1956, in response to some who questioned his commitment to the doctrines, Van Til explicitly affirmed that he agreed with the Three Points of Common Grace and gave his signing of *The Complaint* against Clark as evidence of holding to that position.[60]

Upset at the CRC synod's decision to fire Janssen, R. B. Kuiper (who was Janssen's brother-in-law) transferred for a period of time to the Reformed Church in America (RCA) before returning to the CRC and later holding the presidency of Calvin College from 1930–1933.[61] Kuiper wrote in favor of Common Grace as early as 1924 in a paper presented at the Western Conference of the RCA.[62] He continued to oppose Hoeksema and Hoeksema's doctrine of the gospel call for many years, first from the RCA, then from the CRC after his return.[63]

While Kuiper was in the RCA and Van Til was studying at Princeton (though still a CRC member) at the time of the Synod of Kalamazoo in the summer of 1924, Ned Stonehouse was a senior at Calvin College and was surely following the events unfolding in the denomination and at the

57. Van Til, "Students and Controversies," 87–91.

58. Muether, *Cornelius Van Til, Reformed Apologist and Churchman*, 42, 49.

59. Cornelius Van Til, "Common Grace," *Proceedings of the Calvinistic Philosophy Club*, ed. Edward Heerema, Autumn 1941.; ——"Common Grace Part I: The Christian Philosophy of History," *Westminster Theological Journal* 8, no. 1 (1945): 39–60.;——"Common Grace Part II: The Latest Debate about Common Grace," *Westminster Theological Journal* 8, no. 2 (1946): 166–200.; ——"Common Grace Part III," *Westminster Theological Journal* 9, no. 1 (1946): 47–84.

60. Van Til, "Letters to the Editor," 20–21.

61. Muether, *Cornelius Van Til, Reformed Apologist and Churchman*, 42, 48.

62. Van Andel, "The Importance of Common Grace," 50–51.

63. Kuiper, *As to Being Reformed*, 51, 61, 109–120.

nearby seminary. Unfortunately, no extant writings by Stonehouse on this topic from that period have been located in research for this present book. Nonetheless, as Stonehouse remained with the majority CRC, it is clear what position he held.

The CRC's teaching on the Free Offer of the Gospel came to the OPC and the Clark controversy via the former CRC ministers Van Til, Stonehouse, and Kuiper, and it was through the lens of this teaching that they viewed Clark's theology. In fact, among the theologians *The Complaint* cited against Clark was Herman Kuiper, a CRC theologian and brother of R. B. Kuiper.[64]

The doctrine of the Free Offer of the Gospel was not one that arose in the Orthodox Presbyterian Church from consulting their own Presbyterian history. Protestant Reformed Church theologian Herman Hanko has argued:

> It has been pointed out that the General Assembly of the Church of Scotland has officially condemned the idea of the free offer of the gospel, and that, therefore, all the Scottish Presbyterian Churches which trace their origin to the Church of Scotland are bound by that decision. Some, in the interests of maintaining the free offer, have denied this; but the evidence nevertheless supports this contention. That decision of 1720, reaffirmed in 1722, has never been retracted."[65]

In the Scottish Presbyterian tradition, the main church body had rejected the doctrine of the Free Offer, but in the Dutch Reformed tradition the opposite occurred; the largest of their America churches, the CRC, accepted the doctrine. The doctrine of the Free Offer of the Gospel therefore was an imposition on the (Scottish) Presbyterian tradition from the Dutch Reformed tradition or more exactly, by the CRC.[66]

The influence of the CRC on the Clark case was evident to Herman Hoeksema. Writing during the controversy, he surmised:

64. Kuiper, *The Complaint*, 14.

65. Hanko, "Chapter 6: The Marrow Controversy," footnote 46.

66. It should be noted that although the *Westminster Confession of Faith* reads "[God] freely *offered* unto sinners life and salvation by Jesus Christ" (WCF, VII, III), the term "offer" was used at that time to mean "bringing to someone" or "presenting something or someone to somebody." Thus Christ is presented (offered) to all who hear the preaching. God is not feebly hoping that men will accept his "offer" of Christ as a sacrifice, but powerfully presenting Christ as savior. See: Engelsma, *Hyper-Calvinism and the Call of the Gospel*, 48.

The Complaint leaves the impression that it was chiefly written by Christian Reformed men that are trying to defend the Christian Reformed tradition in the Orthodox Presbyterian Church and to introduce into the latter the errors of 1924. In fact, this impression is so strong that I make bold to conjecture that *The Complaint* was written by more than one author, and that I could point out the writer of the last part merely on the basis of internal evidence.[67]

Based on the historical evidence, it is probable that Hoeksema is referring to R. B. Kuiper.

Van Til was also motivated to promote the CRC's views. This is evidenced in a letter from 1943 in which Van Til considered a job offer at the CRC's Calvin Seminary. He wrote, "If I do not accept, it will be because I still feel that I ought to spread the beliefs of the Christian Reformed Church outside of that Church."[68] In another letter a few weeks later, Van Til explained his reasons for ultimately declining the job offer: "My declination is decidedly not due to any indifference toward the Christian Reformed Church. It is in fact the reverse of it. I simply feel conscience bound at present to continue to teach what the Christian Reformed Church teaches, where I am."[69]

Even *The Complaint* explicitly ties in events in the CRC from two decades prior. It reads, "Incidentally, it may be remarked here that when, in 1924, one of the very few churches in this country which takes the Reformed faith seriously deposed certain ministers of the gospel, one ground, among others, for this action was the denial by these ministers of the sincerity of the divine offer of salvation to all men."[70]

Historically, those who have agreed with the Free Offer of the Gospel contend that God has both a perfect will and a permissive will. On the former (perfect will), God has certain desires for what should occur in the world, but on the latter (permissive will), he allows other events to come to fruition—events he does not desire in his perfect will.

In a letter to J. Oliver Buswell, Clark argued against this twofold distinction in the will (or wills) of God. He wrote,

> When we examine our own experience of permission we see that always it implies an independent power in another person.

67. Hoeksema, *The Clark-Van Til Controversy*, 11. Originally published in articles in *The Standard Bearer* from 1944–1946. Note: It seems likely that Hoeksema is referring to R. B. Kuiper as the writer of the fourth point of the complaint.

68. CVT to H. J. Kuiper, 23 June 1943, WTS Archives.

69. CVT to Rev. John De Haan, Jr., 8 July 1943, WTS Archives.

70. Kuiper, *The Complaint*, 14.

We permit a man to do something; that is, we do not hinder him from doing it; but his is the power and frequently enough we could not have forced him to do it if he had not wanted to. But there is no power independent of God; in the case of omnipotence the distinction between permission and something else vanishes, and I want to stick by the proposition of the catechism: God has foreordained whatsoever comes to pass. Further, the introduction of permission, which was intended to relieve God of responsibility for sin, does not accomplish its end. The historic objection to Christianity runs: Either God could have prevented sin and did not want to, or else he wanted to and could not; therefore God is either not omnipotent or not good. I cannot see how permission enables us to escape that dilemma. If we could prevent a suicide but permit it, we seem as morally reprehensible as if we had actually goaded the person to his act. Permission, therefore, does not solve the problem for which it was invented.[71]

And in another letter to Buswell, "It seems to me impossible to produce any definition of permission, as distinct from something not permission, that would apply to an omniscient and omnipotent Being. It is one of the standing flaws of those who speak about permission that they do not say clearly what they mean. . . . Calvin I think is with me."[72] For Clark the doctrine of two wills in God added to the problem of the Free Offer of the Gospel instead of solving it.

Opponents of the CRC's position on the Free Offer of the Gospel have seen affinities between that doctrine and the doctrine of French Protestant theologian Moïse Amyraut (1596–1664), for whom the term "Amyraldism" was coined. Amyraut held that Christ died for *all* men even if some are not saved, a view also called hypothetical universalism. The supporters of the Free Offer of the Gospel denied Amyraut's universalism, instead holding that Christ died for *some* men (i.e. limited atonement); but they, like Amyraut, did contend that God *desires* the salvation of *all* men. This latter position, held by John Murray in his 1948 report in the OPC (in the wake of the Clark controversy), was viewed as contradictory by Clark and his supporters. It is possible that Clark would have looked to critiques of Amyraldism such as that of B. B. Warfield who wrote that Amyraldism is "an inconsistent form of Calvinism and therefore an unstable form of Calvinism."[73] If consistency is

---

71. GHC to JOB, 28 December 1935, Wheaton Archives.

72. GHC to JOB, 14 December 1948, PCA Archives, 309/27.

73. Warfield, *The Plan of Salvation,* 119–20.

critical, as Clark held, then Warfield's same critique would apply with equal force to supporters of the Free Offer of the Gospel.

The complainants, however, did not believe Scripture was inherently and systematically understandable to man; they denied that consistency was always to be the rule of interpretation. Rather, they held to a theory of paradox, or apparent contradiction. In other words, they held that from man's perspective, some doctrines of Scripture appear contradictory and irreconcilable, but are, nevertheless, reconcilable by God. Eugene Bradford, a supporter of the complainants, further explained the idea of paradox: "It may not appear possible to reconcile these two doctrines of Scripture, but this difficulty should not prevent our hearty acceptance of these two truths, both of which come to us as the Word of God who will not deceive us."[74] Clark's argument concerning the logical impossibility of God having two (apparently) contradictory wills was of no effect to those who held to the existence of apparent contradictions in Scripture.

A committee formed at the OPC's 1947 General Assembly presented two reports regarding the Free Offer of the Gospel at the OPC's 1948 General Assembly.[75] The minority report of William Young and Floyd Hamilton opposed the doctrine. The majority report of Arthur Kuschke Jr., John Murray, and Ned Stonehouse argued in favor of the doctrine.

After the majority report's publication the doctrine of the Free Offer of the Gospel, aided by the reputation of both Murray and Westminster Theological Seminary, rose in popularity in the Presbyterian and Reformed world. For the acceptance of the doctrine of the Free Offer of the Gospel within the Presbyterian and broader Calvinistic world the events of the Clark case should be recognized as being of pivotal importance.[76]

However, not all Presbyterian theologians familiar with the 1948 report on the Free Offer of the Gospel have approved of it. Pittsburgh Theological Seminary professor John Gerstner (1914–1996) critiqued the Murray-Stonehouse report and lamented the impact of its doctrines in the Presbyterian world:

74. Bradford, "The Controversy," 5.

75. Arthur Kuschke, John Murray, and Ned Stonehouse, "The Free Offer of the Gospel: Report to the Fifteenth General Assembly of the Orthodox Presbyterian Church," meeting minutes (13 May 1948), Appendix 51–63.

76. Morton Smith of the PCA is among those in non-OPC Presbyterian churches who accept the doctrine that God desires the salvation of each and every person. Among those Smith quotes for support of his position are John Murray and Ned Stonehouse. Smith writes, "The offer of the Gospel is to be made to all men, and it is to be understood as a sincere offer," and, "He [God] loves all men. His love is universal in this sense. . . . It is a love that is directed to all men."—Smith, *Reformed Evangelism*, 12, 18.

> One may sadly say that Westminster Theological Seminary
> stands for this misunderstanding of the Reformed doctrine
> since not only John Murray and Ned Stonehouse but also Cor-
> nelius Van Til, R. B. Kuiper, John Frame, and so far as we know,
> all of the faculty, have favored it. . . . They recognize theirs as a
> very *dangerous* position and appeal to great mystery . . . How-
> ever this is not "mystery" but bald contradiction.[77]

Gerstner later concluded, "With tears in my heart, I nevertheless confidently assert that they erred profoundly in the Free Offer of the Gospel
and died before they seem to have realized their error which . . . still does
incalculable damage to the cause of Jesus Christ and the proclamation of
His Gospel."[78]

Clark continued throughout his life to support his position in the
controversy, arguing that the theory of paradox, rather than displaying
the theologian's humility, was a theory of utmost arrogance. He reasoned
that the claim that there are apparent contradictions in Scripture which are
irresolvable is a claim that, because its holder hasn't solved the Scriptural
problem, no one else can. In an unpublished manuscript, Clark wrote at
length on this issue:

> John Murray, late of Westminster Seminary in Philadelphia, im-
> pressed many people with his devoutness. He was also an assidu-
> ous scholar. And many people considered him very modest and
> humble. Now, in his booklet, "The Free Offer of the Gospel," in
> which his colleague Ned B. Stonehouse cooperated to an unde-
> termined degree, John Murray considered the paradox between
> the Free Offer of the Gospel and the doctrines of election and
> irresistible grace. His conclusion is, "We have found that God
> himself expresses an ardent desire for the fulfillment of certain
> things which he has not decreed in his inscrutable counsel to
> come to pass. This means that there is a will to the realization of
> what he has not decretively willed, a pleasure toward that which
> he has not been pleased to decree. This is indeed mysterious . . .
> " Here I do not wish to emphasize what I believe is Murray's
> incorrect notion of what the phrase "the Free Offer of the Gos-
> pel" means. What strikes me is that their author could not see
> any logical consistency between the Free Offer and the divine
> decree. His word inscrutable seems to suggest that nobody else
> can understand it either. Such a viewpoint, however, is not one
> of humility, but of arrogance. It means that if he cannot see the

77. Gerstner, *Wrongly Dividing the Word of Truth,* 142–146.
78. Gerstner, foreword to *Hyper-Calvinism and the Call of the Gospel,* xii–xiii.

answer, the answer is just not in the Bible at all. But has he traced out all the possible implications of Scripture and shown by a complete induction that a solution is impossible? In view of the fact that Christ pointed out implications; implications no one had thought of before, and condemned his hearers for not having done so themselves, we, when our thoughts lead us to an assertion of contradictions, should be warned that our thinking has been fallacious. Then instead of appealing with pseudo-piety to inscrutable mysteries, we can review our thinking and perhaps discover our mistakes. This would be a more modest procedure.[79]

The Overriding Issue: Charges of rationalism

Alongside each of the four issues brought against Clark in *The Complaint* was the charge of rationalism. Clark was not a rationalist according to the philosophical definition of "one who bases knowledge on human reason," for he clearly bowed to Scripture as his base. Yet while arguing that only Scripture can give man knowledge, Clark believed logic played an integral part in the process. The fact that humans can reason at all, Clark believed, was because man was made in the image of God. Logic, *i.e.* rationality, he held, is the image of God that separates man from the animals. Using logic, Clark argued, man can deduce further truths from the explicit truths of Scripture—a position for which he found support in the *Westminster Confession*'s statement accepting doctrines that can be deduced from Scripture "by good and necessary consequence."[80] It was ultimately because Clark was unwilling to accept paradox—unwilling, that is, to let allegedly apparently contradictory Scripture passages remain unsystematized—that he was called a rationalist. In fact, Clark later called paradox a "charley horse between the ears" and said the fear of "being too logical" was a "fear without a corresponding danger."[81]

At the time of the controversy, Herman Hoeksema of the Protestant Reformed Church wrote on the alleged rationalism of Clark in his denomination's publication *The Standard Bearer*. He wrote, "There is here, indeed, something that is more than amazing, that is really unbelievable, that almost might be catalogued as another paradox: the phenomenon that theologians

79. Clark, "Desultory New Testament Curiosities," 22–23.
80. WCF, Chapter I, Part VI.
81. Clark, "The Wheaton Lectures," 26.

accuse a brother theologian of heresy because he tries to solve problems!"[82] Hoeksema then rhetorically asked, "Is it really rationalism to attempt to bring Scripture in harmony with itself?"[83] Hoeksema also argued that the theological issues in the Clark-Van Til controversy were of a nature that they should have been an academic debate, not a test for ordination. He wrote, "And this renders the whole dispute rather abstract—a matter, it would seem, to be discussed by a conference of theologians rather than to be used as a ground for protest against the licensure of a candidate for the ministry."[84]

Van Til argued that Clark, in not accepting paradox, employed "Greek conceptions" of revelation rather than the Christian conception of revelation. In a letter to Charles Stanton, Van Til wrote:

> The old Princeton Apologetic was defective because in maintaining that there must be identity of content at some point between the system of the believer and the system of the unbeliever it virtually held also that there must be identity of content as between the mind of man and the mind of God. The natural man will not accept a God who stands essentially above him; he will allow a sort of great scientist God who is an expert and knows a lot more about a field than man does at the present moment. But now Clark is seeking to introduce into the very heart of systematic theology what the Princeton theologians with inconsistency allowed in the field of apologetics. Clark's position therefore involved the rejection of the Reformed concept of God's revelation to man and a reduction of it to Greek specifications.[85]

In one of the articles Van Til wrote on Common Grace during the Clark controversy, he critiqued Herman Hoeksema on the same basis. Van Til wrote:

> It may perhaps be said that much of the abstract reasoning of Hoeksema comes from his failure to distinguish between Christian and non-Christian logic. We do not mean, of course, that the rules of the syllogism are different for Christians and non-Christians. Hoeksema refers to the idea of insanity, saying that sin has not made us insane. We may agree if he means merely that the unbeliever can follow the technical processes of intellectual procedure as well as, or often better than, the believer. But when

82. Hoeksema, *The Clark-Van Til Controversy*, 24.
83. Ibid.
84. Ibid., 6.
85. CVT to Charles Stanton, 27 December 1945, WTS Archives.

he says or assumes that God's revelation in Scripture may be expected to reveal nothing which will be apparently self-contradictory, we demur. He attempts to "harmonize" the revealed and the secret will of God, prayer and the counsel of God.[86]

Clark on the other hand believed revelation is inherently understandable; revelation reveals something. Clark and Hoeksema alike held that there are parts of God's will which are a secret to man, but that the Bible is what is revealed. Thus, harmonizing the texts of the Scriptures was not an attempt to find God's secret will (as that would be futile), but was rather an attempt to better understand His revealed will.

How Van Til came to believe that the Christian approach to Scripture must be welcoming of paradox might be traced to his reaction to the liberal higher critics who made the case for there being actual contradictions in the Scripture. Clark, and those like him, answered the charge of there being contradictions in Scripture with a resounding "no" and sought to demonstrate Scripture's consistency at all costs. Van Til and those like him, however, took a different approach: admitting that contradictions of a sort existed in Scripture, but arguing that these contradictions were merely apparent and ultimately reconcilable by God.

Alternatively, Van Til's acceptance of paradox might be found in the nineteenth-century irrationalistic philosophers. Clark may have had Van Til in mind when in 1956 he wrote:

> In contrast with the Greek philosophies of Plato and Aristotle, in contrast also with the earlier modern systems of Spinoza and Hegel, the late nineteenth and twentieth centuries have seen the development of avowedly irrationalistic viewpoints. Nietzsche, Dewey, Heidegger, and Sartre are examples. The themes of this contemporary irrationalism have been applied to the problem of religion and have infiltrated even moderately conservative Christian thought.[87]

While *The Complaint* and *The Answer* remained at the crux of the controversy, the effects of the disparate philosophical and ideological positions could soon be felt beyond the Clark case in the denomination at large. Denominational politics would unfold and decisions would be made that clearly reflected the underlying division between the two camps. Sadly, obstinacy on the part of many OPC ministers made compromise and understanding an impossibility.

---

86. Van Til, "Common Grace Part II," 170–171.
87. Clark, "Logic and Language," 3.

Gordon Clark as a boy.

Gordon with his dog Victor.

Gordon with his parents.

Gordon during his university years.

Gordon and Ruth

At Wheaton College.

Students gather at the Clark home.

Clark with his daughter.

A Clark painting at Sangre de Cristo Seminary.

Chapter 8

The Continued Controversy and Its Results

"That assembly [1946] upheld the ordination of Dr. Gordon H. Clark by a vote of nearly two to one. A member of Westminster Seminary faculty in an impassioned speech said that no one should think that the so-called Clark case was over, that he for one would keep fighting it until his 'dying breath.' They opposed the ordination of Mr. Tichenor. They successfully opposed the going out of Rev. Floyd E. Hamilton to teach in a seminary in Korea that had urgently requested his services. And all because these two men supported the views of Dr. Clark at certain points. The result has been that minister after minister has withdrawn from the denomination to seek a happier connection."[1]

—THE SESSION OF CALVARY CHURCH, WILLOW GROVE, ON LEAVING THE OPC

THE COMPLAINT CONTINUED

THOUGH *THE COMPLAINT* WAS defeated at the Philadelphia Presbytery on March 29, 1945, it was re-introduced at the OPC's Twelfth General Assembly in May of the same year.[2] To address *The Complaint*, a com-

1. "Calvary Church Leaving the OPC" (unpublished document, 31 December 1948), WTS Archives. Note: The WTS faculty member who made the "impassioned speech" was R. B. Kuiper.—Heerema, "The Orthodox Presbyterian Church," 26.
2. Twelfth General Assembly of the Orthodox Presbyterian Church, meeting

mittee of five was formed at the general assembly. These members, by rules of the church, were required to come from outside the Philadelphia Presbytery, the presbytery from which *The Complaint* had arisen. The five elected to the committee were Richard Willer Gray, Edmund Clowney, Lawrence Gilmore, Burton Goddard, and John Murray.[3] Dr. Murray, a professor at WTS, was sure to favor the views of the complainants. Dr. Goddard, of Gordon College, and Rev. Gray were close friends of Clark and were doubtless on his side. Thus the deciding opinions would be those of Rev. Gilmore, a minister of a church in New Jersey, and Rev. Clowney, a former Clark student at Wheaton College and recent graduate of Westminster Theological Seminary. Clowney was elected as the chair of the committee. His involvement would be crucial.

In preparing to write the report to be presented at the following year's general assembly, Clowney wrote to Clark to clarify his understanding of Clark's views. Although Clowney's original letter is not extant, Clark's response is. Clark's letter shows his disgust with the whole situation. It is worthy of quoting at length. It reads in part:

> It is always a pleasure to reply personally to a personal letter that asks for my views. The committee of which you are a member has not asked me to appear. I argued at the last Assembly that the procedure set up was in fact an administrative procedure applied to a judicial case, and that the injustice of it is no less than that heaped on Dr. Machen in his trial. I could ask for no better persons as judges, but the present committee is not judicial. So much for the record.[4]

Regarding one of the theological questions on which Clowney requested clarification, Clark's response brought out what he saw as the key fault in the view of the complainants: the introduction of the term "content" to the object-mode distinction of knowledge to which he held. Clark wrote,

> The mode of knowing, as I use the word, is simply the psychological activity of the knower. The object is what the knower knows. An answer to the question, How do you know, would state the mode of your knowing. An answer to the question, What do you know, would state the object. And so far throughout all the discussion I have failed to see any reason for introducing any

minutes (Philadelphia, PA: Chestnut Hill, 17–23 May 1945), 5–30.

3. Ibid., 53.

4. GHC to Edmund Clowney, 20 February 1946, WTS Archives.

other element; in particular the third element [content] that has been introduced is simply unintelligible to me.[5]

At the Thirteenth General Assembly of the OPC in May of 1946, the committee of five, with the exception of John Murray, brought their conclusions in Clark's favor. More precisely, they concluded that the presbytery had not erred in ordaining Clark. Edmund Clowney presented the report which concluded that Clark's view on the incomprehensibility of God did not substantially differ from the view of the complainants.[6] Their majority report read in part:

> It has been shown that the major specific charge of *The Complaint* cannot be supported from the stenographic record. Dr. Clark cannot be accused of failing to distinguish between Divine and human knowledge as to "content" when he analyzes knowledge into only two parts, mode and object. We have seen that it is possible, and even likely that Dr. Clark's distinction of the mode of knowledge includes much of what the complainants require in their distinction of content. This question must be examined somewhat more closely. To declare that the mode-content-object schematization of knowledge cannot be insisted upon is not to declare that no doctrine conveyed in such a schematization can be insisted upon. The difficulty emerges in determining just what difference the complainants are insisting upon in speaking of content, a term which they do not define.[7]

Referring to *The Complaint* as it relates to the *Westminster Confession*, the report concluded, "Our committee is of the opinion that [*The Complaint*] requires the Presbytery of Philadelphia to exact a more specialized theory of knowledge than our standards demand."[8]

Following the general assembly's report in his favor, Clark analyzed *The Complaint* and *The Answer* in a document he titled "Studies of the Doctrine of the Complaint" in the winter of 1946/1947. In this document,

5. Ibid.

6. Thirteenth General Assembly of the Presbyterian Church of America, meeting minutes (Philadelphia, PA: Chestnut Hill, 21–28 May 1945), 36–68.

7. Ibid., 49. Repeating this same point, Clark would later write, "There was a question I asked the complainants which they refused to answer. If *mode* answers *how* we know, and *object* answers *what* we know, what question is answered by the idea of content? They have (to this day, as far as I know) refused to define content so as to distinguish it from mode and object."—GHC to D. Clair Davis, 14 October 1952, provided by D. Clair Davis.

8. Thirteenth General Assembly of the Presbyterian Church of America, meeting minutes (Philadelphia, PA: Chestnut Hill, 21–28 May 1946), 49.

never published but found among Clark's papers, he aimed to show that "the source of the difficulty and the chief issue between the two parties is epistemological." He explained, "The men who wrote *The Answer* maintain the position of Warfield, Hodge, Charnock, and Calvin. That *The Complaint* does not consistently hold this position, but that it alters and vitiates the doctrine by an untenable epistemology, it is the aim of this paper to prove."[9] His full argument is too lengthy to include here, but it is worth reading and has therefore been included as an appendix to this volume.

After the "Clark Case" was officially resolved in Clark's favor, the faculty of Westminster Theological Seminary turned their attention to those who had supported Clark.[10] Clark's supporters became targets in the WTS faction's attempt to purify the church (toward their views of Reformed theology) by setting up roadblocks to their influence. Three situations where the "Clark Case" spilled over into other church-related business were (1) the attempt to found a Reformed Christian university, (2) the ordination of Alan Tichenor, and (3) the decision not to renew the professorship of the missionary Floyd Hamilton at the Korean seminary.

THE CHRISTIAN UNIVERSITY ASSOCIATION

In the early 1940s, a movement began among members of the Orthodox Presbyterian Church to found a Christian university. The denomination already had a seminary (although officially an independent one) in Westminster Theological Seminary for the theological education of their prospective pastors, but the desire arose to have also an institution for the education of students pursuing graduate degrees in other areas of study. At that time, many of the church leaders of the OPC believed that the nation's universities were antithetical to Christianity. In fact, these universities, it was argued, ultimately based their teaching on secular principles. According to one editor

---

9. Clark, "Studies of the Doctrine of The Complaint."

10. That this would occur was the concern of the OPC missionary Francis Mahaffy who wrote to the Clarks from Eritrea, Africa: "The news we have been hearing of things in the church lately has not been at all encouraging; it is evident that our Church cannot go forward as she should at home or abroad with all this quarreling and strife constantly. . . . On the whole I was very pleased with the stand the G.A. [general assembly] took but I am not so optimistic as to think that is the conclusion of the matter. I think I know some of the Seminary men well enough to realize that they will not graciously take a defeat but will become even more militant in their opposition to some of us 'left-wingers.'"—Francis Mahaffy to Ruth Clark, 25 September 1946, in the possession of the Clark family.

of *The Presbyterian Guardian,* there was not a single graduate school which based its instruction upon the Protestant Christian life and worldview.[11]

The Christian University Association was formed to bring the idea of a thoroughly Christian university to fruition. Edwin H. Rian was elected as general secretary of the committee of the Association. Led by Rian, who was the primary fundraiser, the Association called for a "great center of Christian learning" and offered the Free University in Amsterdam as an exemplar of such an institution.[12] According to the Association's adopted constitution, the new university was to be committed to Reformed doctrine but free of denominational control. Membership in the Association came from across the Reformed and Presbyterian denominations in North America. Included were members of the Orthodox Presbyterian Church, the Christian Reformed Church, the Reformed Presbyterian Church General Synod, the Presbyterian Church in the United States, the Reformed Church in America, and the Presbyterian Church in Canada.[13] The Association was truly a pan-Reformed venture, at least at its beginning.

In 1942 Gordon Clark was contemplating resignation from Wheaton College and began searching for a professor position elsewhere. At this time he received a letter from Rian about the new university project. Rian wrote to Clark:

> You will be delighted to know that four denominations . . . have appointed committees to confer about a Federation of Presbyterian and Reformed Churches. . . . If this federation becomes a reality we can establish a university association, separate from the federation but encouraged by all the groups in it. If our plans go forward as I hope we might be able to have as large a number as 300,000 who would get in back of this university. It very likely will be several years before we can start.[14]

Rian knew of Clark's impact on Wheaton students and he saw Clark as an important constituent for the new university to reach the broader evangelical world.

Clark agreed with Rian regarding the need to found a Christian university. He wrote in *The Presbyterian Guardian:*

> Practically everything that appears in print is in the broad sense humanistic. Such a situation shows clearly what is needed. A

11. Clelland, "The Christian University," 221.
12. Rian, "Needed: An American Christian University," 289–90, 299–301.
13. Birch, "Group Looks to Founding of Christian University," 318–19.
14. Edwin Rian to GHC, 26 August 1942, PCA Archives, 309/48.

center of Christian learning must be established in which investigation in all fields of study will be pursued. A Christian college
is not sufficient. Several Christian colleges exist at the present
time. Some do respectable work; some are rather incompetent.
A list of the faculty's publications is the criterion. And there is
enough room in the country for other Christian colleges, if they
are to be competent. But the greater need is the need of a university. This includes a law school . . . it must include a graduate
school for the granting of the doctorate, and it must be administered by a faculty which through research, mutual criticism, and
publication will develop the philosophy to coordinate Christian
thought and action.[15]

There can be little doubt that Clark, with his many publications and
proven dissatisfaction with the interdenominational atmosphere of Wheaton College, envisioned himself as part of this proposed faculty. Other
church leaders also saw Clark as the right hire. Robert K. Rudolph of Reformed Episcopal Seminary wrote of the board of the Christian University
Association, "We had begun to try to choose an opening faculty. Many of us
deemed Gordon Clark the right man to head the Philosophy Department."[16]

The Association took an important step toward their goal of founding the new university when, in 1944, they purchased thirty-four acres
along with Lynnewood Hall at the P. A. B. Widener Estate in Elkins Park,
Philadelphia for their campus.[17] The plan for the Christian University was
as grandiose as the 110-room neoclassical revival mansion that was Lynnewood Hall. The university was to be "second to none" and grant both
undergraduate and graduate degrees. The Association placed a four-page
article in *The Presbyterian Guardian* with pictures of the newly-purchased
campus and an advertisement seeking contributions and applications for
membership. The article also listed the trustees of the association. Among
them were John Murray and Cornelius Van Til of Westminster Theological
Seminary, as well as Edwin Rian and Robert K. Rudolph. But the list of
trustees did not include Gordon Clark.[18]

A contest in 1946 to determine the name for the university produced
as the winning entry "The Christian University of America," but this would
prove to be the last positive development for the ill-fated venture.[19] The

15. Clark, "The Next War," 71–72.

16. Rudolph, "A Truly Great and Brilliant Friend," 105.

17. P. A. B. Widener (1834–1915) was a wealthy Philadelphia businessman and a
founding organizer of U.S. Steel and the American Tobacco Company.

18. Birch, "An American Christian University," 363–65.

19. Marsden, "University Association Holds Stormy Meeting," 218–19.

formation of the university progressed far more slowly than Edwin Rian desired. Two factions arose within the Association. The majority of the Association's board of trustees was controlled by men (including a number of Westminster Theological Seminary professors—Ned Stonehouse, John Murray, R. B. Kuiper, and Cornelius Van Til) who wanted the Association's membership limited to those who shared their own view of Reformed theology; a second group, led by Rian, argued for broader appeal. These two groups broke down along the same lines as the ongoing controversy over Clark's ordination.

Dr. Rudolph, a longtime friend of Clark, charged the majority on the board with responsibility for the problems then present in the Association. He said the majority had "certain convictions concerning the nature of Calvinism, and concerning theology and apologetics which in fact commit the Association to a position that will make the founding of a University impossible,"[20] and that "in particular the Board should ease its requirements for candidates for future membership on the Board, if the work committed to the Board was to be performed."[21]

For Dr. Rudolph it was clear that the two factions arose along the same lines and for many of the same reasons that they did in the dispute regarding Gordon Clark's ordination. He believed "people were nominated for the Board who were against Dr. Clark, and apparently only such people had a chance of being nominated."[22] To evidence his point, at one of the early meetings of the Association, Clark's name was proposed as a possible board member and was immediately rejected by the majority.[23] Rian too was at odds with the board of trustees. According to Dr. Rudolph, the board accused Rian of not being Calvinistic enough, an accusation that Rudolph believed arose because Rian had supported Clark in the ordination controversy.

Lack of sufficient membership and support from other denominations affected the finances of the Association. The Christian Reformed Church concluded in its synod minutes:

> That because unfortunately there are indications of internal dissension even at this early date within the ranks of the Orthodox

20. Sloat, "University Association Meets," 315.

21. Ibid., 315.

22. Ibid., 316.

23. Ibid., 316. (However, the reason Clark was not a board member was not only due to opposition to him. Edwin Rian wrote to Clark, "I became convinced that since you would be given most serious consideration as a faculty member, it would be embarrassing for you to serve on the association."—Edwin Rian to GHC, 25 March 1943, PCA Archives, 309/48.

Presbyterian Church, whose leaders are the chief proponents of the Calvinistic University (witness the Clark case), Synod declares that we must therefore be hesitant in lending support to the establishment of a so-called Calvinistic University when the leaders of this movement are not thoroughly agreed among themselves as to what constitutes true Calvinism.[24]

Payments were due on the property, but because of the lack of support, the Association struggled to pay them.

On September 11, 1946, the Association's board terminated the services of Edwin Rian by an eighteen to five vote. The reason given by Ned Stonehouse for Rian's dismissal was that "over a period of time it became increasingly evident that Dr. Rian was out of accord with certain policies of the Board of Trustees, policies which deeply affect the character of the movement and of the University which it seeks to establish and maintain." Evidences provided for this accusation were that Rian thought the Board of Trustees was failing to carry out its responsibilities by being too selective with board membership, and that relative to the Board of Trustees, Rian had a differing conception of the Constitution of the Association believing it gave him, as president, power over the board even to remove members from it. Thus it was, as in the "Clark case," a power struggle, but this time the struggle was for control of the University Association instead of the denomination or seminary.[25]

The connection between Rian's dismissal and the complaint against Clark is evidenced by a comment from Thomas Birch, editor of the pro-WTS *Presbyterian Guardian*. For Birch and those in the WTS faction, only their own views (which in many ways originated in the traditions of the Dutch Reformed Churches in both America and the Netherlands) were acceptable in the denomination. Birch wrote, "The Christian Reformed Church has no militant left wing of the type seeking domination of the OPC. It has no Clarkian theology, no devotees of piosity [sic], no diluters or soft-pedallers of its Calvinism. I am not overly fond of the Christian Reformed Church, but I'd prefer it any day to what the OPC will be if the Clark-Strong-Rian wing ever, God forbid, gains control."[26] And in the same letter Birch wrote, "A man whose attitude is unfriendly toward Westminster Seminary is a man whose true zeal for the principles and furtherance of Calvinism I must

24. Bouma, "That University Project," 157.

25. Ned Stonehouse to members of the Christian University Association, 2 October 1946, Christian University Association Files, WTS Archives.

26. Thomas Birch to Rev. Fred Kuehner, 23 September 1946, Christian University Association Files, WTS Archives.

gravely question. That goes, whether the man's name is Eerdmans, Strong, Rian, Clark, or Plotnick."[27]

On the opposing side of the issue, the view of the "Clark-Strong-Rian" wing and the general dissatisfaction with the leadership of the Association are seen in a comment from one member of the board, John MacDonald, who wrote, "That the University project should have come to this point at all is a shame and surely cannot be pleasing to God. The reason for this condition seems to me to be an entirely unchristian attitude on the part of such members of the Board who have insisted that their brand of Calvinism is the only acceptable form for the University."[28]

Criticism of Rian's forced resignation came to Stonehouse in a letter from Rev. Robert Moody Holmes that read:

> Years ago, Dr. Rian was vitally interested in establishing a Christian University. He talked with me about it as well as others. And just when he was about to see his dream come true, after years of untiring labor to that end, you ruthlessly cut the ground from under him and destroy the work to which he had given his life. You knew from the beginning that his policy was ecumenical. On what other basis could the University serve the Reformed faith? That was its only excuse for being. Why, then, did you associate yourselves with him and the movement, if you disagreed with that principle? It looks like usurpation from one angle and sabotage from another. Are you and your colleagues bent on eliminating everyone in the Reformed family who does not fit your own peculiar personality pattern? You are destroying, whether you realize it or not, the noble and much-needed work of Westminster Seminary, the Orthodox Presbyterian Church, and the Christian University Association.[29]

In the wake of Rian's dismissal, Dr. Rudolph resigned from the board.[30] In his resignation letter, Rudolph explained his reasons for resigning:

27. Ibid.

28. John A. MacDonald to the Board of Trustees of the Christian University Association, 8 October 1946, Christian University Association Files, WTS Archives.

29. Robert Moody Holmes to Ned Stonehouse, 7 October 1946, Christian University Association Files, WTS Archives.

30. The following men also resigned from the board around the same time: Howard D. Higgins, a bishop in the Reformed Episcopal Church; Lawrence Gilmore and Richard Willer Gray, OPC pastors; John R. Richardson and R. E. Hough, PCUS pastors; and P. E. Jobson of an independent church.—Ned Stonehouse to unknown recipient, 3 November 1946, WTS Archives. See also: Gray, "The O.P.C. and the University Project," 99.

An increasing understanding that the leadership of the majority is incapable of running a University with the many minds that would have to compose its sincere and Calvinistic trustees and faculty, when that leadership has taken part in seeking to bring heresy charges against such a staunch and well-known Calvinist and believer in the Westminster Confession as Gordon H. Clark, PhD. Dr. Clark has been falsely accused of disloyalty to the Reformed faith because the leadership of the majority charged him with (their own understanding of) the implications of his theological and epistemological positions, not because of proven denials or disloyalty to any provision of the Westminster Confession. Who in Faculty or on Trustees would be safe from such persecution?[31]

The in-fighting in the OPC surrounded the question of subscription to the *Westminster Confession of Faith*. The WTS faction believed they were continuing the tradition of Old School Presbyterianism in requiring subscription to the standards. The opposition, however, equally desirous of maintaining the Confession, felt that the WTS faction was going beyond the Confession in making their particular views the standard.

One complaint to Ned Stonehouse of the actions of the board against Edwin Rian saw the action as a continuance of the Clark case and even referred to Gordon Clark as "that persecuted saint."[32] Not all spoke so favorably of Clark, however. One donor to the project wrote to Ned Stonehouse:

I've been reading the letter that was sent to me a short time ago about the discontent of several members of the University Association, living more or less in the near neighborhood of the university property except a few of them, like Dr. Gordon H. Clark and *cum suis*. I have read the missive more than once, to get a clear understanding of the matter. . . . It seems to me there is an element in the association that is not sound to the core in regard to Calvinism and now that they see that those, who are stronger Calvinists than they are, may get the upper hand in regard to the university control, they rather wreck the affair than go along with them for future support.[33]

Following Rian's departure, a conspicuous anomaly was noticed in the books of the Association. Stonehouse wrote to Rian, "In connection with the

31. Robert K. Rudolph to Ned Stonehouse, President of the Christian University Association, 19 October 1946, PCA Archives.

32. Miss Alice R. Lee to Ned Stonehouse, 8 October 1946, WTS Archives.

33. D. Vander Wagen to Ned Stonehouse, 30 September 1946, WTS Archives.

sale of the Widener Estate, it has developed that there are persons enrolled as members who were quite unaware they were members . . . In checking over the applications, it further develops that these people never personally subscribed the application for membership, but that their names were typed in by another person. . . . In view of the very clear provisions of the Constitution of the Christian University Association concerning applications for membership, I am greatly interested to learn if there is anything that you can say in extenuation of this procedure."[34] Further inquiry into Rian's mailings to members who had paid more than their required five dollar fee found that Rian was allowing each additional five dollars to be used to sign up additional members.[35] Shortly after problems in the bookkeeping were discovered, Rian announced that he was returning to the PCUSA, ten years after originally breaking away from the PCUSA to join the OPC.[36] As Rian had been the right-hand man of J. Gresham Machen, the late leader of the OPC, Rian's return to the PCUSA was an embarrassment to the OPC.

As evidenced by the failure of the Christian University Association, the unity of the OPC and of Westminster Theological Seminary had fallen apart since J. Gresham Machen's death. Machen was the linchpin in both organizations. In his day there had been a common enemy (modernism), and the many differences among the fundamentalists who formed the OPC and WTS were set aside. The new factions which developed came as a result of the leadership void produced by Machen's absence.

The Christian University Association lasted only a short time after Rian's departure. The Association defaulted on its loans for the campus property.[37] The campus was sold at a sheriff's sale to a real estate developer in 1948 who had thoughts of turning it into a country club.[38] The property finally realized its academic destiny in 1952 when Faith Theological Seminary purchased it for their new campus.[39]

In 1945, Clark had no way of knowing that the Christian University of America was a doomed endeavor, and he expected to only stay at his new post at Butler University for a few years until the Christian University could be established. With connections on the board and the desire to find a teaching position at a Christian university, Clark was a likely candidate—despite

34. Ned Stonehouse to Edwin Rian, 14 March 1947, WTS Archives.

35. Ned Stonehouse to Edwin Rian, 9 April 1947, WTS Archives.

36. Sloat, "Withdrawal of Dr. Rian," 157.; —— ed., "Rian Returns to U.S.A. Church," 190.

37. Law Offices of Ballard, Spahr, Andrews, & Ingersoll to Ned Stonehouse, 5 January 1948 and 16 January 1948, Christian University Association Files, WTS Archives.

38. Roy, "Widener Mansion May Become Club," 5.

39. Rhoads and Anderson, *McIntire: Defender of Faith and Freedom*, 170.

some board members' poor opinion of his theology—for a position as professor of philosophy at the university, if it should develop. Interest in the proposed university among the WTS faculty, however, was never more than lukewarm, since there was insufficient donor money available for both the seminary (which itself was not on a sure financial footing) and a university.

Edwin Rian's expectations for the Christian University were wildly optimistic. His expectation of 300,000 backers for the university never materialized. The 300,000 figure seems to be just his summation of the entire membership of the denominations involved, not any study of actual interest among the members. Considering the lack of agreement even within the relatively small Orthodox Presbyterian Church, the idea that all of the Reformed Christian denominations could cooperate on a project as massive as a university seems ludicrous in hindsight.

THE TICHENOR CASE

The battle over Clark's ordination negatively impacted another ordination in the OPC—that of Charles Alan Tichenor. Tichenor was well acquainted with the issues being debated in the church. He had been one of Clark's students at Wheaton College and graduated from there in 1938.[40] He then attended WTS where he earned his Master's in Theology in 1941 and later became an assistant for the Old Testament professor E. J. Young from 1943–1945.[41] As a licentiate, Tichenor supplied the pulpit of Westminster Church in Bend, Oregon, in the summer of 1944 and the next year was stated supply at Mediator Church in Philadelphia.[42]

Tichenor supported Clark's ordination and was one of the five men in the Philadelphia Presbytery who collaborated to write *The Answer* in Clark's defense. That Tichenor supported Clark is also shown in *The Presbyterian Guardian* which recorded:

> Mr. Tichenor, speaking against the motion, said that Dr. Clark's abilities exceeded those of many Orthodox Presbyterian Church ministers, that he was not ignorant of Hebrew, that he had taught the Reformed faith at Wheaton College, and had been zealous in spreading Reformed truth in countless ways. Mr. Tichenor added that his own interest in the Orthodox Presbyterian

40. Dyrness, *Bulletin of Wheaton College* 1939–1940, 112.

41. Yeo, *Plundering the Egyptians*, 158.

42. Birch, "Orthodox Presbyterian Church News," 219.; —— "Presbytery of Philadelphia," 64.

Church would be dulled, if not killed, if Dr. Clark were lost to the movement.[43]

Tichenor sought ordination in the OPC himself in 1946 and found resistance just as Clark had. At his ordination *The Presbyterian Guardian* noted that "as he was one of five who presented to presbytery a proposed Answer to the complaint against the presbytery in connection with the licensure and ordination of Dr. G. H. Clark, he was questioned at somewhat greater length than usual," but that "the presbytery finally determined by majority vote to proceed with the ordination."[44] The extent of the resistance to Tichenor's ordination is not evident from the record, but testimony being passed around the church in 1948 and printed in *The Presbyterian Guardian* read:

> There was a long and persistent effort in the Presbytery of Philadelphia and in the General Assembly to prevent and then to bring into question the ordination of Dr. Gordon H. Clark. And during this past year there was a similar determined opposition to the ordination of Mr. C. Alan Tichenor, in spite of the fact that the previous General Assembly had upheld the Presbytery of Philadelphia in approving the theological examination of Dr. Clark who had expressed essentially the same views."[45]

Robert Strong's lecture "The Gordon H. Clark Case" corroborates this story, recording: "Alan Tichenor had been a teacher at Westminster Seminary; he was very nearly refused ordination because of supporting Clark's position."[46]

THE HAMILTON CASE

In 1947 the danger of sharing Clark's views became apparent once again when the Foreign Missions Committee of the OPC at the Fourteenth General Assembly rejected the request of Floyd Hamilton, a long-time missionary to Korea, to return to Koryu Theological Seminary in Korea where he had taught until World War II forced his retreat. They reported, "The Committee, on the basis of Mr. Hamilton's testimony before the Committee, and some recent publications of his views, was not assured of the wisdom of sending Mr. Hamilton at the present time to teach in a theological seminary

43. Birch, "The Clark Case," 172.
44. Clowney, "Tichenor to be Ordained," 281.
45. Sloat, "Testimony Being Circulated," 14.
46. Strong, "The Gordon Clark Case," 6.

in Korea."[47] Although the committee chose not to send Hamilton to teach at the seminary, they did desire for him to continue with general missionary service in Korea.[48]

Hamilton recognized that the committee's decision was directly related to his having sided with Clark in the controversy. Hamilton, upset at the actions, resigned from the committee and wrote, "The committee obviously took such action because it felt I was doctrinally unsound," referring to the fact that he had sided with Clark's positions in the controversy.[49] Later at the General Assembly, all of the members of the Foreign Missions Committee (who had chosen not to send Hamilton) were themselves re-elected. Hamilton and others viewed this as an approval by the majority of the denomination of the committee's decision not to send him.

The battle in the church continued into the next year at the Fifteenth General Assembly in 1948. Here three notable actions were taken by the supporters of Clark and Hamilton. Firstly, Martin Bohn, who was then Clark's pastor at Covenant OPC in Indianapolis, made an overture on behalf of the Presbytery of Ohio asking for the signers of the complaint against Clark to present to the next year's General Assembly a "statement acknowledging their errors of judgment and reprehensible defect of charity in circulating the aforementioned allegations."[50]

Bohn's second overture, also on behalf of the Presbytery of Ohio, addressed Hamilton's situation requesting to "terminate the services of all present members" of multiple committees including the Foreign Missions Committee responsible for the "refusal to send" Floyd Hamilton to Korea to teach at the theological seminary.[51] The moderator of the General Assembly, John Galbraith, ruled that these overtures were out of order because they "contemplated judicial action which was not the prerogative of this

47. Fourteenth General Assembly of the Orthodox Presbyterian Church, meeting minutes (Cedar Grove, WI: 22 May 1947), 17.

48. Sloat, "Hamilton to Korea Under Independent Board," 30.

49. Fourteenth General Assembly of the Orthodox Presbyterian Church, meeting minutes (Cedar Grove, WI: 22 May 1947), 17. See also: Rev. Floyd E. Hamilton, "Classification and Mutual Relation of the Mental Faculties" (unpublished paper, c. 1947), PCA Archives, 309/3.; —— "The Teaching of Scripture on The Offer of the Gospel" (unpublished paper, c. 1947), WTS Archives, Stonehouse/Box 6, 1945–1962, folder: Gordon H. Clark controversy.; and Clark, "Studies of the Doctrine of 'The Complaint.'"

50. Martin Bohn, "Paper 15: Overture to the Fifteenth General Assembly of the Orthodox Presbyterian Church," in meeting minutes (Wildwood, NJ: 13 April 1948), 13.

51. Martin Bohn, "Paper 16: Overture to the Fifteenth General Assembly of the Orthodox Presbyterian Church," in meeting minutes (Wildwood, NJ: 13 April 1948), 13.

Assembly."[52] A number of ministers, including Hamilton, requested that their negative votes be recorded.[53] Hamilton was so upset that he requested permission to be excused for the remainder of the Assembly. The third action taken by supporters of Clark was a protest lodged by twenty-one ministers and read by Rev. Richard Willer Gray to the general assembly for failing to pass an amendment that would have assured that the four doctrines of the Clark Case "not be considered as tests of theological soundness" as they were "extra-confessional."[54]

SAMUEL ALLEN'S SEVEN LETTERS

As the controversy spread to other areas of the church, the resistance movement made plans for a final stand at the general assembly. This stand was organized by the Rev. Samuel J. Allen. If Samuel Allen is remembered at all today, it is as the minister of the congregation in North Dakota which J. Gresham Machen was visiting when Machen fell ill and died on the first of January, 1937. Allen's involvement in the Clark ordination controversy had been fairly limited until he sent seven letters to ministers of the OPC (and perhaps to laypersons as well) explaining his views on the current state of the church and severely critiquing the WTS faction.

Allen's first letter, "Teach, Evangelize, Contend" (April 14, 1947), praised the OPC for being a great church but ended with a suspense-inducing question to be pondered until his next letter arrived. The question he posed was simply, "What is the primary cause of the division?"[55]

Allen's second letter, "Cause of Division" (April 21, 1947), again praised the greatness of the OPC for its emphasis on doctrine in a non-doctrinal age and for its opposition to modernism. Returning to answer the question posed in his first letter, Allen wrote:

> The chief cause of division in the O.P.C. is the opposition of many ministers and laymen to the leadership of the professors of Westminster Seminary. The professors have a very definite idea of what constitutes the Reformed faith and practice. . . .

52. Fifteenth General Assembly of the Orthodox Presbyterian Church, meeting minutes (Wildwood, NJ: 13 April 1948), 18.

53. Ibid.

54. Mr. Richard W. Gray and signatories, official protest lodged during the Fifteenth General Assembly of the Orthodox Presbyterian Church, in meeting minutes (Wildwood, NJ: 13 April 1948), 54.

55. Samuel J. Allen to ministers of the OPC, "Teach, Evangelize, Contend," 14 April 1947, PCA Archives, 309/18.

The professors have looked upon anyone who veered from their conception as not being truly Reformed. The list of those who are considered as not truly Reformed has grown throughout the years. It includes men who have given their time, energy, and lives for what they considered the Reformed Faith; . . . such men were and are barred from teaching at Westminster Seminary or being members of its Board of Trustees or having anything to say about the editorial policy of *The Presbyterian Guardian*. This list includes Carl McIntire, Allan MacRae, Charles Woodbridge, Cary N. Weisiger who left our Church and Robert Strong, Clifford Smith, Gordon Clark, Edwin Rian, Floyd Hamilton, the writer, and probably a majority of the ministers in the O.P.C.[56]

Allen's third letter, "Forthrightness" (April 28, 1947), continued:

If the issues raised are not principle but matters upon which truly Reformed people can and do differ, then the professors are not forthright but schismatic. . . . There have always been men in truly Reformed Churches who have opposed Premillennial doctrine very strongly, who have opposed what they considered a piety not taught in Scripture, who have opposed an emotional type of evangelism which they thought minimized the importance of sound doctrine, and who have opposed cooperation of any kind with other church bodies as a lowering of Reformed distinctiveness; but very few in America indeed have maintained that such men should not be in a truly Reformed Church. Even the professors have not been forthright enough to say that. . . . They are willing that such should remain in the Church and that such should have liberty within the Church and that such should support the agencies of the Church, plus institutions like Westminster Seminary and *The Presbyterian Guardian*; but they are not willing to see anyone whom they consider to be tainted with these errors to have any real influence in deciding the policy of Westminster Seminary or *The Presbyterian Guardian*. That is why they are so afraid of letting the O.P.C. have anything to say about the policy of these institutions. That is why they do not trust the O.P.C. That is why they are apparently willing to work and split the O.P.C. rather than permit it to have a say as to the education of its future ministers or a voice in the running of a magazine that is looked upon by many as an organ of the Church. THAT IS APPARENTLY THE REASON WHY THEY HAVE ALWAYS MADE THE O.P.C. FEEL THAT THEY

---

56. Samuel J. Allen to ministers of the OPC, "Cause of Division," 21 April 1947, PCA Archives, 309/18.

WOULD LEAVE ITS MEMBERSHIP IF THE ISSUES THEY
RAISE ARE NOT DECIDED FAVORABLY."[57]

Allen's fourth letter, "Consistency" (May 5, 1947), continued his critique of the Westminster faculty. He wrote that "consistency had a jewel-like
quality when the professors pointed out the errors of modern-dispensa-
tionalism and the errors and tendencies of 'fundamentalism' in general." He
continued, saying,

> But it was foolish consistency that caused them to take the
> stand that a church could not say that it was expedient to ab-
> stain from drinking of alcoholic beverages. It was and is fool-
> ish consistency to make hobgoblins out of men like McIntire,
> Strong, Smith, Clark, Hamilton, and others. It is foolish con-
> sistency which compels men to go on the defensive and spend
> their lives and energies repelling as enemies those who want
> to be friends, whose enthusiasm and talents are needed in the
> common cause. It is foolish consistency which causes the best
> minds in our Church to argue for four years without reaching a
> common understanding as to the definition of terms. It is this
> foolish consistency which makes the professors unfit to exercise
> practical and inspirational leadership.[58]

In Allen's fifth letter, "Militancy" (May 12, 1947), he continued the
critique, writing:

> The professors of Westminster Seminary in the present contro-
> versy firmly believe that they are standing where Dr. Machen
> would have them stand. I do not presume to know where Dr.
> Machen would stand in the Clark case, the Mahaffy case,[59] the
> Rian case, the Tichenor case, the Gregory case,[60] the Hamil-
> ton case (only one of these was an official case, but the others
> were relentlessly grilled to ascertain whether or not they held to

57. Samuel J. Allen to ministers of the OPC, "Forthrightness," 28 April 1947, PCA
Archives, 309/18.

58. Samuel J. Allen to ministers of the OPC, "Consistency," 5 May 1947, PCA Archives, 309/18.

59. Note: Francis E. Mahaffy was a missionary to Eritrea from 1945–1968. He
graduated from Wheaton College in 1941 and from WTS in 1944. He was ordained in
1944. That same year, he faced opposition from the Committee on Foreign Missions
regarding his being sent out to Eritrea. See: Sloat, "Testimony Being Circulated," 14.

60. Note: Thomas Gregory graduated from WTS in 1946 and was ordained in
1947. "The complainants have vigorously opposed two candidates for licensure and
ordination. One is Alan E. Tichenor . . . the other is Thomas Gregory."—Gray, "The
O.P.C. and the University Project," 99.

the alleged heresy or heresies of Dr. Clark). But I do know and unhesitatingly state that regardless of where he stood he would not have become less militant against modernism than against Bible-believing Christians, particularly those who claimed to be Reformed and have suffered for what they considered the Reformed faith.[61]

The purpose of Allen's sixth and seventh letters, sent on the same day, was to garner support for the upcoming Fourteenth General Assembly to vote against the Westminster professors. He writes on May 19, 1947:

> The most important business at that Assembly is in my opinion the election of members to the various Standing Committees of the Church. These Committees furnish leadership for the denomination in its mission and educational work. I do not think that it would serve the best interests of our Church to have these Committees dominated by the professors and those who apparently approve their policy 100%."

Allen then reiterated his reasons for opposition from his previous letters and gives Clark's case as an example of the problem with the professors:

> Take the case of Dr. Clark—In the report on the doctrine of incomprehensibility signed by Professors Stonehouse and Murray, there is an admission that the complainants erred in assuming that the teaching of Reformed theologians on the subject was uniform; there is also an admission that some of the statements of the Complainants were infelicitous and misleading. But these men hold in the same report that Dr. Clark should have seen that in its main thrust the Complaint could not possibly have meant that man cannot know God. They are demanding of Dr. Clark and the men who wrote the Answer to the Complaint a discernment and a charitable attitude which if they themselves had exercised the same attitude . . . would have spared the Church the awful experience through which it is passing. They have treated and continue to treat former friends as the basest of heretics; and despite the admissions of the above-mentioned report, they insist on making the so-called Clark case a test of orthodoxy for ministers of the O.P.C. In my opinion it would be catastrophic to continue such men in leadership."[62]

61. Samuel J. Allen to ministers of the OPC, "Militancy," 12 May 1947, PCA Archives, 309/18.

62. Samuel J. Allen to ministers of the OPC, "General Assembly," 19 May 1947, PCA Archives, 309/18.

These seven letters of Samuel Allen exemplify the lowest point of the situation in the OPC resulting from the ordination controversy and signaled the approaching dissolution of the church which began not long after, with the departure of numerous pastors and congregations.

THE UNRAVELING OF THE ORTHODOX PRESBYTERIAN CHURCH AND THE CONTINUED DEBATE

What Clark perceived as the WTS faction's obstructionist votes (on Clark's and Tichenor's ordinations, on Hamilton's teaching in Korea, and in the Christian University Association), their skeptical epistemology, and that the OPC was infighting rather than leading the nation's fundamentalists, brought Clark to conclude that he could "more effectively bring the truths of the Bible to human minds in another connection."[63] On October 14, 1948, Clark left the OPC and joined the United Presbyterian Church, the denomination in which his grandfather had ministered.[64] Clark was not the only casualty. Edwin Rian had already left the OPC and returned to the PCUSA in 1947. Alan Tichenor transferred, like Clark, to the United Presbyterian Church in 1948.[65] Robert Strong, with his large congregation (Calvary Church in Willow Grove, Pennsylvania), left the OPC in 1949 for the Presbyterian Church, U.S. (PCUS).[66] Floyd Hamilton joined the PCUS in 1955. Clark supporters Franklin Dyrness and Richard Willer Gray also left the denomination. All told, approximately 15 percent of congregations, ministers, and members left the OPC over matters related to the Clark case and the Hamilton issue.[67]

Clark's reasons for leaving come to light in a letter he wrote on March 1, 1948, six months prior to his actual departure from the OPC. In the letter, written to the directors of Covenant House (a pro-Clark group in the

63. GHC to the directors of Covenant House, 1 March 1948, PCA Archives, 309/67.

64. Stonehouse, "Dr. Clark Dismissed to U.P. Church," 260.

65. Stonehouse, "Philadelphia Presbytery," 242.

66. Sloat, "Orthodox Presbyterian Church News: The Church in 1949," 16.

67. Ministers whose departures from the OPC were related to the Clark ordination controversy include the following: Samuel J. Allen (PCUS, 1948), Martin J. Bohn (UPCNA, 1949), Gordon H. Clark (UPCNA, 1948), Franklin Dyrness (unaffiliated Presbyterian, 1949), Thomas Gregory (UPCNA, 1949), Floyd Hamilton (PCUS, 1955), Richard Willer Gray (independent Presbyterian, 1949), Alan Tichenor (UPCNA, 1948), Edwin Rian (PCUSA, 1947), Clifford Smith (UPCNA, 1947), and Robert Strong (PCUS, 1949).

OPC first formed to publish gospel tracts[68] and who later published *The Witness*), Clark listed evidences that a "Sectarian party" had frequently attacked the American Presbyterian heritage which the OPC was to continue per its founding as the "true spiritual succession of the Presbyterian Church in the U.S.A." Among these evidences of sectarianism, Clark cited a recent article in *The Presbyterian Guardian* which referred to Arminianism and modernism as "equally dangerous." Clark, however, believed that although "Arminianism misinterprets Scripture on some important points," it still accepts the Bible, and that "sincere Arminians are predestinated, all persevere in grace, and are perfectly sanctified in heaven." Modernism, on the other hand, Clark wrote, is dangerous because "it denies the infallibility of the Bible," it "denies the vicarious atonement of Christ," and ultimately "leads to hell." In the sectarian parties' grouping of these two errors, it grouped Christians and non-Christians, condemning them both. The sectarian party admitted that there were mistakes in *The Complaint* but still had it published without correcting them. They also, according to Clark, attacked the character of Floyd Hamilton, which he found outrageous considering Hamilton's twenty years of service as a foreign missionary. Yet more than anything else, the sectarian party outraged Clark most severely in implying that "the human mind can never know any truth whatsoever" and thus ultimately leading Clark to conclude that they were skeptics. Clark wrote:

> Of course the General Assembly has the legal right to choose who shall administer the affairs of the church. But inasmuch as the Sectarian party won such a victory—inasmuch as the General Assembly, after seeing clearly that it was faced with the definite choice between the two parties, chose the skeptics, there comes a question that we must ask and answer: Is it worthwhile to expend more energy trying to maintain the purpose for which the OPC was founded? Is there any hope in continuing with a group who prefer skepticism and slander to truth? Can we not better bring the truths of the Bible to human minds more effectively in some other connection? These are hard questions. The answers may be harder. But answers must be given shortly. Some of our friends have already decided.[69]

The departure of so many ministers and congregations from the already small OPC, and along with them much of the evangelistic zeal, essentially ended any likelihood of the denomination becoming a noticeable

---

68. E. J. Young to GHC, 6 May 1942, SDCS, 1/81.

69. GHC to the directors of the Covenant House, 1 March 1948, PCA Archives, 309/67.

THE CONTINUED CONTROVERSY AND ITS RESULTS   155

numerical presence in the American Christian landscape. This fracturing of the church left the OPC weak. During the twentieth century, the OPC would have only slow growth, never having more than thirty thousand members[70] while the liberal PCUSA continued as the most prominent national Presbyterian church.

MISUNDERSTANDINGS AND CONFUSION

There has been significant misunderstanding regarding the ordination controversy. For example, in William White's biography of Van Til he writes, "The ultimate outcome of the controversy was that, for better or worse, the complaint carried."[71] But the complaint did not carry. Either this confusion stems from the fact that Clark left the church, making it appear as if the complaint carried, or from wishful thinking on White's behalf. In another case, a factual error was made by D. G. Hart and John Muether who wrote, "[Clark] was licensed to preach and ordained at the same meeting" indicating that his ordination process was rushed.[72] But, in truth, there was a month between Clark's licensing (July 7, 1944) and ordination (Aug 9, 1944). Furthermore, Clark's application for ordination (May 9, 1942) was more than two years prior to these events. His ordination was anything but rushed.

The participants in the Clark case themselves were often confused. The documents presented at OPC general assemblies were not actually solely authored by Clark and Van Til, respectively, but by representatives of their viewpoints. This can be likened to a proxy war. According to Robert Strong,

> One of the difficulties of this subject is that the opponents of Clark on the floor of the presbytery and in the drawing up of *The Complaint* did not include Cornelius Van Til. It was Van Til for whom they were speaking; it was his thought they were trying to express. It was essentially opposition between these two thinkers, Gordon H. Clark and Cornelius Van Til, which was coming to expression in the controversy. But not once did Van Til take the floor of the presbytery to speak, to explain, or to protest; and nothing came from his hand either about this issue.[73]

---

70. Orthodox Presbyterian Church, membership data 1937–2009, The Association of Religion Data Archives, http://www.thearda.com/Denoms/D_1307.asp.

71. White, *Van Til, Defender of the Faith*, 128.

72. Hart and Muether, "The OPC and the New Evangelicalism," 107.

73. Strong, "The Gordon Clark Case," 9.

According to the OPC General Assembly minutes, Van Til did not contribute to any of the study committees on the controversial doctrines. Rather, it was John Murray who championed the WTS faculty's position. In fact, because of this, Van Til's biographer, John Muether, has called the ordeal the "Clark-Murray debate."[74]

Still, it was clear to Clark that Van Til was the impetus behind *The Complaint*. Clark wrote, "Dr. Van Til's views are obviously the philosophic background of the Complaint."[75] And again he wrote, "It must be clear to anyone who has studied that document that its ideas and accusations are largely based on Dr. Van Til's views."[76] Van Til later affirmed his involvement himself, writing, "There was no one in the General Assembly . . . who did not know that I had signed *The Text of a Complaint* against Clark."[77] Even if Van Til didn't contribute to the study committees, he published three articles on Common Grace in the *Westminster Theological Journal* during the controversy.[78]

Some members of presbytery went along with *The Complaint* solely based on the reputation of those who made it, without understanding the doctrines involved. Referring to this fact, Clark wrote, "The necessity of examining the philosophic background of the Complaint is seen in the fact that certain members of the Assembly openly admitted that they did not understand the issues and accordingly based their votes on their confidence in the ability and scholarship of the complainants."[79] Rev. Gray wrote similarly to Ned Stonehouse, "As you and others virtually have put it, the theological reputation of the Complainants has been at stake in this controversy. Men have admittedly stood with them because of that reputation."[80] Mentioning one of these men specifically, another elder involved commented, "At this point I feel something like Bradford as he sat next to me at the July presbytery meeting, twitching nervously, 'I don't know how to vote'—so

---

74. Muether, *Cornelius Van Til, Reformed Apologist and Churchman*, 105.

75. Clark, "Studies of the Doctrine of The Complaint," 4.; John Robbins would later write, "Cornelius Van Til . . . furnished the basic content of A Complaint."—Robbins, introduction to *Clark Speaks from the Grave*, 8.

76. Clark, "Studies of the Doctrine of The Complaint," 4.

77. Van Til, "Letter to The Editor," 20.

78. Cornelius Van Til, "Common Grace Part I: The Christian Philosophy of History," *Westminster Theological Journal* 8, no. 1 (1945): 39–60.;—"Common Grace Part II: The Latest Debate about Common Grace," *Westminster Theological Journal* 8, no. 2 (1946): 166–200.;—"Common Grace Part III," *Westminster Theological Journal* 9, no. 1 (1946): 47–84.

79. Clark, "Studies of the Doctrine of The Complaint," 4.

80. Richard Willer Gray to Ned Stonehouse, 7 January 1946, WTS Archives.

he voted for Clark, and when he felt uncomfortable there, he changed and signed the complaint."[81] Lest one think it was only in the direction of the complainants that reputation was a factor, it should be noted that Clark's reputation gained him backing as well. Ned Stonehouse pointed this out to another minister, "One minister . . . told me that the entire matter might be looked at in an entirely different light if only the status of Dr. Clark were not bound up with it."[82]

Not only were the participants in the controversy confused, but according to John Frame, Clark and Van Til made mistakes as well. Frame wrote, "Neither man was at his best in this discussion; each seriously misunderstood the other."[83] Taking the opposite of Frame's view that "neither man was at his best," John Muether argues that "Van Til's role in the controversy, far from being an embarrassment, should be interpreted as one of his finest moments."[84] Muether praises Van Til's role, though he also acknowledges that it was rather minimal, noting that "most analyses tend to overstate [Van Til's] involvement in the debate"[85] and that "Not once did [Van Til] take the floor of the presbytery to speak, nor did he write anything during the controversy. Nor did he serve on the General Assembly study committees."[86]

Sadly, it seems few ministers in the OPC approached the controversy in a balanced manner. From the outset nearly every minister had chosen a camp—Clark or the WTS faculty—and never relented from their positions. The only known exception to this was the Rev. Edward F. Hills who wrote letters to both Clark and the WTS faculty calling attention to "the underlying doctrinal unity which still exists in our Church" and suggesting potential philosophical ways around the impasse.[87] But Rev. Hills's suggestions, whether plausible or not, went unheeded.

CHANGES IN THE POSITION OF THE COMPLAINANTS

The final salvo in the Clark case in the OPC was made at the Fifteenth General Assembly in 1948 when reports from study committees were included

81. Edwards Elliott to Bob Marsden, 13 January 1946, WTS Archives.

82. Ned Stonehouse to Robert K. Churchill, 25 July 1946, WTS Archives.

83. Frame, *The Doctrine of the Knowledge of God*, 21.

84. Muether, *Cornelius Van Til: Reformed Apologist and Churchman*, 108.

85. Ibid., 98.

86. Ibid., 98.

87. Edward F. Hills to GHC, 29 April 1947 and 8 May 1947, PCA Archives, 309/39.; Edward F. Hills to Paul Woolley, 29 April 1947, WTS Archives.; See also: Edward F. Hills to Ned Stonehouse, 29 April 1947, WTS Archives.

in the minutes. A majority report, written by Murray, Stonehouse, and Kuschke, especially clarified *The Complaint*, arguing that the complaint never intended to be skeptical or divide into two the content of the knowledge of man and God. The majority report conceded Clark's major argument that not allowing for a connection between God's knowledge and man's knowledge would result in skepticism. The report read: "The second statement [in the original complaint] is also misleading, particularly because of the words, 'single point.' The whole clause, taken by itself, is liable to create the impression that our knowledge does not come into contact with the objects of the divine knowledge at any point. This would, of course, be incorrect and would also be skeptical in character."[88] Yet despite admitting to *The Complaint's* misleading character, the report concluded:

> Careful examination should have shown that the Complaint was not contending for any qualitative distinction between the "objects" of knowledge known to God and man nor that a true proposition in its "narrowest and minimal significance, is qualitatively different for God" (*Answer*, p. 21), nor that a true proposition has one import or signification for God and another for man, nor that man can have no cognitive contact with the objects of divine knowledge, but rather was contending for a qualitative distinction in some other respect, namely, what *The Complaint* denotes as "content," distinguished from "mode," on the one hand, and from the 'truth known' on the other. Hence we conclude that, though *The Complaint* failed in the matter of clear definition and lucidity, it is not defensible to charge it with error in the direction of skepticism.[89]

It seems the complainants felt the weight of Clark's criticism that their position results in skepticism, and in the wake of this critique modified their position. This modification was made in two ways: (1) a changed definition of "content" and (2) an acceptance of a "point of contact" which at the start of the controversy had been categorically denied.

In order to maintain that their position in fact did not entail skepticism, it is evident that the complainants changed their definition of "content" in the time between *The Complaint* (1944) and the majority report in 1948. The majority report explained "content" as distinct from "object." The majority report read, "It is not with the objects of knowledge the Complaint is concerned but with the difference between the character of

88. Fifteenth General Assembly of the Orthodox Presbyterian Church, meeting minutes (Wildwood, NJ: 13 May 1948), Appendix 21.

89. Ibid., Appendix 25.

God's understanding and man's understanding even when the same object is contemplated."[90] Thus in the majority report that thing beyond "object" with which they were concerned (i.e. "content") was taken to mean "the character of understanding." But in *The Complaint*, "content" had meant the very item of knowledge itself in the mind.

In a minority report, Floyd Hamilton raised a red flag that this change of definition had occurred. First Hamilton pointed out that "the crucial definitional question is that of content, which the Complainants insist is qualitatively different for man and for God."[91] Next he argued that *The Complaint* had used "content" to mean the items of knowledge in the mind. He wrote:

> In the Complaint itself, the meaning of the term is . . . the things which the knowledge of God contains, i.e., the truths in His mind. . . . Having stated, as the proposition to be proved, that Dr. Clark denies a qualitative difference between the contents of the knowledge of God and the contents of the knowledge possible to man, the Complaint proceeds to adduce evidence by asserting first that Dr. Clark assumes that truth, whether in the divine mind or in the human mind, is always propositional. . . . The trouble is, the argument asserts, that on this assumption "there is no single item of knowledge in God's mind which may not be shared by the human mind."[92]

Clark understood *The Complaint's* meaning of "content" just as Hamilton did. He wrote, "The important question arises, what are the *contents* of one's knowledge? Obviously the *contents* of one's knowledge are the *truths* one knows. . . . The contents of God's knowledge are the truth he knows, and the contents of a man's knowledge are the truth the man knows. The Complaint maintains that these two sets of truths are qualitatively different."[93]

Given the original definition of "content" as "items of knowledge" or "the truths one knows," Clark's critique of the position of *The Complaint* was devastating. To avoid this result, "content" was changed to mean "character of understanding" in the 1948 majority report. But what character is this meant to refer to? One character of knowledge is its truth value; that is, whether it is true or false. In this respect, if the character of man's knowledge is different from God's knowledge, and God's knowledge is true, then man's knowledge can only be false. Alternatively, "character of understanding"

90. Ibid., Appendix 22.
91. Ibid., Appendix 88.
92. Ibid., Appendix 88.
93. Clark, "Studies of the Doctrine of The Complaint."

perhaps is meant to be the way one knows. But the "way" of knowing must, it seems, be the same as "mode." And Clark's distinction of mode was deemed insufficient in the complaint. Based on the complainants' new definition of "content," the original complaint no longer made sense.

Though the report changed the definition of "content," Van Til later refused to define it at all. In response to *The Answer*'s request that the complainants "state clearly what the qualitative difference is" (i.e. what is meant by "content"), Van Til wrote:

> Suppose now that the complainants should try to "state clearly" in Dr. Clark's sense the qualitative difference between the divine and the human knowledge of the proposition that two times two are [sic] four. They would have to first deny their basic contention with respect to the Christian concept of revelation . . . It is precisely because they are concerned to defend the Christian doctrine of revelation as basic to all intelligible human predication that they refuse to make any attempt at "stating clearly" any Christian doctrine . . . [94]

The second change in position occurred in 1948, when a letter of retraction signed by all the original signers of *The Complaint* was sent out to the church. In a key paragraph it read:

> Since certain expressions used in the Complaint have been understood as skeptical in character and since the Complaint cannot disavow all responsibility for producing such misunderstandings of its intent, we gladly affirm that, when the objects of knowledge are contemplated, human knowledge does have contact with the objects of divine knowledge within the compass of the divine revelation, and that within that sphere of revelation the objects of knowledge as such are the same for God and man.[95]

This admission was a far cry from *The Complaint*'s original statement that "We dare not maintain that [God's] knowledge and our knowledge coincide at any single point."[96] In fact, the admission that "the objects of knowledge as such are the same for God and man" is nothing other than a complete reversal of the original position.

---

94. Van Til, *An Introduction to Systematic Theology*, 171–72.

95. The eleven elders of *The Complaint* to the ministers and sessions of the Orthodox Presbyterian Church, 26 April 1948, WTS Archives.

96. Kuiper, *The Complaint*.

In 1949, just a year after the Clark case, Van Til made his first and only official foray into the controversy writing about the issues in his syllabus, *An Introduction to Systematic Theology*.[97] In the syllabus he affirmed that his views agreed with *The Complaint*.[98] But he took the retraction from the 1948 letter a step further. He elaborated:

> In the first place, it is possible in this way to see that the knowledge of God and the knowledge of man coincide at *every* point in the sense that always and everywhere man confronts that which is already fully known or interpreted by God. *The point of reference cannot but be the same for man as for God.* There is no fact that man meets in any of his investigation where the face of God does not confront him. On the other hand in this way it is possible to see that the knowledge of God and the knowledge of man coincide at no point in the sense that in his awareness of meaning of anything, in his mental grasp or understanding of anything, man is at each point dependent upon a prior act of unchanging understanding and revelation on the part of God."[99]

Van Til thus clarified in which sense he believed there is a point of contact and in which sense he believed there is not. But because *The Complaint* was clear and adamant on affirming that there was no point of contact in any sense, the conclusion must be that Van Til's view changed, or that *The Complaint*, written by others, yet signed by Van Til, never adequately reflected his view in the first place.[100]

Van Til's 1949 syllabus argued that the qualitative distinction between man's knowledge and God's knowledge is that the former is dependent and the latter independent. It seems unlikely that Clark would have found much difficulty in agreeing with this formulation. In fact, the dependency or dependent nature of man's knowledge on God's knowledge was precisely Clark's position from the beginning. It seems by 1949 Van Til had almost fully come around to Clark's position.[101]

97. Van Til, *An Introduction to Systematic Theology*.

98. "The Complaint set forth is essentially the same view as this chapter."—Van Til, *An Introduction to Systematic Theology*, 163.

99. Van Til, *An Introduction to Systematic Theology*, 159–160.

100. Yet in 1948, Van Til used language similar to that of *The Complaint* when he wrote, "Being based upon God's revelation, [Scripture] is on the one hand, fully true, and on the other hand, at no point identical with the content of God's mind."—Van Til, "Introduction" In *The Inspiration and Authority of the Bible*, 33.

101. Greg Bahnsen wrote that Clark and Clark's supporters misunderstood Van Til's "analogy." Bahnsen explained what he believed to be an important distinction between

Having admitted to Clark's view but needing something against Clark to justify the complaint, Van Til took Clark's univocism (by which Clark meant a point of contact) to mean that Clark thought of man as autonomous, capable of knowledge apart from God. Van Til wrote that Clark "overlooks" that it is "little possible to reach the transcendent God of Christianity" by means of Aristotelian logic.[102] Clark's presuppositionalism, however, never held that such logic-based proof of God was possible. In fact it was a key tenet of Clark's views that God's existence cannot be determined by so-called proofs made by man, but rather that knowledge of God is innate in man's mind and that His existence is assumed, rather than proven, in the Bible. Van Til continued, saying that "Dr. Clark understood the incomprehensibility of God in a way which would be in accord with the Romanist or Arminian view of it, and out of accord with the Reformed view of it," and that Clark "seems to hold that man may obtain a certain amount of information about God apart from revelation. Presumably this knowledge is to be obtained by 'reason' operating independently of revelation."[103]

Van Til so obviously misunderstood Clark on these points that John Frame wrote, "I must say that I find this criticism of Clark quite preposterous," and "Again, I am rather shocked at Van Til's distortion of Clark's position." Frame concludes, "It would have been more helpful if Van Til, like the Report, had straightforwardly conceded Clark's point that there is such common meaning."[104]

PROPOSITIONAL TRUTH

The reports presented in 1948 at the OPC's Fifteenth General Assembly did not end the debate. In addition to Van Til's syllabus in 1949, there was an article by Clark in 1957 titled "The Bible as Truth." In this article Clark

---

analogy and "analogously." He wrote, "Van Til did not teach that what we know is only an analogy of God (or truth about Him), much less that univocal predication regarding God must be rejected, but rather that we know God (as well as His creation) *analogously* to His knowing Himself (and His Creation)."—Bahnsen, *Van Til's Apologetic,* 228–229. Whether Bahnsen's adverb *"analogously"* modifies the verb "know" or "knowing," it must in either case refer to the action of knowing, i.e. the mode, rather than the object of knowledge. Thus Bahnsen must be considered mistaken, at least insofar as his view applies to the early views of Van Til, as the *The Complaint* clearly and repeatedly emphasized that Clark's distinction of mode was insufficient.

102. Van Til, *An Introduction to Systematic Theology,* 156.

103. Ibid., 163.

104. Frame, *Cornelius Van Til: An Analysis of His Thought,* 108–113.

clarified that his position is that all truth is propositional.[105] Because of the lack of clarity in the transcript of Clark's original examination, Edmund Clowney and the committee to review Clark's theology in the general assembly seem to have prematurely dismissed the charge made against Clark on this issue. *The Complaint* made the accusation that "the fundamental assumption made by Dr. Clark is that truth, whether in the divine mind or in the human mind, is always propositional." But the report of Clowney and the committee denied this accusation saying:

> The Committee feels that, in all justice, this allegation cannot be regarded as a completely accurate representation of Dr. Clark's views as they are expressed in the Transcript. . . . It is evident from the record that Dr. Clark ascribes a propositional character to truth in the human mind. He declares, "I would not know what the word 'truth' meant unless as a quality of a proposition. I cannot conceive of anything that is a truth that is not a proposition." But it is by no means evident from the record that Dr. Clark ascribes a propositional character to God's knowledge.[106]

Yet it seems from his original examination answer that Clark did believe God's knowledge to be propositional. But apparently this was not inferred by Clowney and the committee and so they denied the accusation of *The Complaint* on this point. Alternatively, perhaps Clowney was speaking to the manner of God's knowledge, not its object. The position of Clark in "The Bible as Truth" was essentially the same as in his theological examination—he believed all truth, whether known by God or man, to be propositional. Had Clowney and the committee found that Clark's position was that God's knowledge, as well as man's, was propositional, one wonders what they might have concluded. However, even if Clowney would have agreed with the complaint's accusation, it is hard to see what repercussions this would have had either in the report or in theology itself. Does thinking of God's knowledge as propositional unjustly reduce God to human dimensions? Does such thinking fall prey to arguments, made famous by Ludwig Feuerbach, that man has created God in man's image? Ultimately Clark felt that the burden of proof was on the Westminster professors to give evidence for the existence of "nonpropositional truth" and suggested that it may be "a phrase without meaning."[107]

105. Clark, *God's Hammer*, 25, 34–35.

106. Thirteenth General Assembly of the Orthodox Presbyterian Church, meeting minutes (Philadelphia, PA: Chestnut Hill, 21 May 1946), 40.

107. Clark, *God's Hammer*, 25, 34–35.

CONCLUSION

Perhaps the best summary of the whole controversy, commenting on its almost complete futility, was made by Rev. Strong, who wrote, "This controversy was very unfortunate. It wasted a great many men's time . . . But perhaps value does attach to the exploration of the subject of incomprehensibility. One hopes that some benefits have accrued."[108] Despite the controversy and all of the personal pain which must have resulted, Clark was able to joke about the situation, writing to J. Oliver Buswell, "Is it not amusing that you and Van Til and I think severally that the other two are hopelessly confused?"[109]

108. Strong, "The Gordon Clark Case," 6.
109. GHC to JOB, 14 December 1948, PCA Archives, 309/27.

Chapter 9

The Butler University Years (1945–1973)

"To those of my generation—college undergraduates, 1955–1959—Dr. Clark was the philosopher-hero of the post-fundamentalism Evangelical Renaissance."[1]

—DAVID CLYDE JONES

A FRESH START AT A SECULAR UNIVERSITY

THE CONTROVERSY OVER GORDON Clark's ordination in the Orthodox Presbyterian Church was still ongoing when he began teaching at Indiana's Butler University in the winter semester of the 1944–1945 academic year. The professorship position had opened up due to the retirement of Elijah Jordan (1875–1953) who taught philosophy at Butler from 1913 to 1944.[2] Originally intending to stay at Butler for only a short period, Clark remained there twenty-eight years, from 1945 to 1973, during which time he wrote prolifically, detailing his own Christian philosophy and criticizing both secular and religious philosophical rivals.[3]

---

1. E-mail to the author from Dr. David Clyde Jones, Professor Emeritus of Systematic Theology and Ethics, Covenant College, 11 August 2015.

2. Butler President M. O. Ross to VRE, 23 October 1944, Wheaton Archives. Note: Elijah Jordan was an American philosopher who specialized in social and legal thought.

3. "As for the College [Butler] itself, it is just another secular institution. I aim to do an honest professional job, make as good a reputation as possible, and leave when more congenial associations are available."—GHC to JOB, 30 January 1945, PCA Archives,

Butler was founded by the Disciples of Christ, a Christian denomination, but the university had long since ceased to have any religious affiliation. It was, for all practical purposes, a standard secular American university. Butler had prestige as a private university with scholarship of its own, but it certainly did not have the reputation of Clark's alma mater, the University of Pennsylvania, nor did it produce the Christian scholars of the "Fundamentalist Harvard" (Wheaton College) where Clark had last held a regular professorship. Though Butler University was non-religious, there was a small, independently-run Butler School of Religion on the same campus. The Butler School of Religion, however, had no impact on Clark nor did he have any involvement or interest in it. In fact, disparaging the neighboring school in a letter to Carl F. H. Henry, the editor of *Christianity Today*, Clark described it as "about the most radical place imaginable" and noted "it seems most improbable that anyone faintly evangelical could be appointed to any position there."[4]

As Butler was a secular institution, Clark did not have any theological battles to fight as was the case at Wheaton College. There were no separatists making waves like Wheaton's President Buswell or complaints from zealous Bible teachers like Wheaton's Professor Theissen. Although Butler was peaceful in these regards, and consequently provided Clark with a beneficial atmosphere in which to continue his writing, it came at a price for him as there were few Christian students for him to mold into scholarly defenders of the faith as he had done at Wheaton College.

Without many Christian students interested in his teachings it seemed he would perhaps live out his backup plan of being a Plotinian scholar. Clark had written a few years previously about this plan while considering leaving Wheaton, "Of course I could write articles on Plotinus and show his effect on Augustinianism. I am already making my small way in the American Philosophical Assn. with Plotinus. I could achieve the distinction of being a mediocre Plotinian. It would be a relatively easy, comfortable, and enjoyable life; provided I could get a job."[5] Rather than focusing on Plotinus, however, Clark set out on an ambitious path writing on a variety of Christian topics.

Spurred on by the events leading up to his resignation at Wheaton College and the controversy surrounding his ordination in the OPC, the beginning of Clark's time at Butler was the turning point in his scholarship. It was at this point that he began to put into writing his own Christian philosophy,

4. GHC to CFHH, 12 February 1958, BGC Archives.

5. GHC to Robert Strong, 9 May 1942, PCA Archives, 309/56.

rarely again writing on ancient Greek philosophy, with the exception of *Thales to Dewey*, a popular textbook on the history of philosophy, published in 1957. There is no better example of Clark's Christian philosophy than his seminal work and magnum opus, *A Christian View of Men and Things*, published in 1952, which broadly addresses his views on a number of topics.

In his books, Clark's constructions of a Christian view often consisted of just a brief few pages following chapters of refuting other philosophies. He was at his best when critiquing non-Christian philosophies, having a thorough understanding of them from his years studying secular thinkers at the University of Pennsylvania. His refutations of secular (and also often religious) thought were presented first in his works with the intent of clearing the room for a presentation of the Christian alternative. He dealt with the primary philosophical alternatives prominent in his day in books on *Dewey* (1960), *Karl Barth's Theological Method* (1963), *William James* (1963), and *The Philosophy of Science and Belief in God* (1964). Clark's own Christian philosophy was given a fuller exhibition in *A Christian Philosophy of Education* (1946), *A Christian View of Men and Things* (1952), *What Presbyterians Believe* (1956), *Religion, Reason, and Revelation* (1961), and *Three Types of Religious Philosophy* (1973).

TEACHING AT BUTLER

Part of what must have enticed Clark to accept the position at Butler University was the fact that, in addition to his job as professor, he would have autonomy in directing the philosophy major as chairman of the department. However, the department's faculty at the relatively small university never grew beyond just Clark and at most two assistant professors. The professors who taught in the department during Clark's tenure included William Young (1918–2015), Thomas M. Gregory (1920–1993), Robert Crafton Gilpin (1920–1983), and Bernard Baumrin (b. circa 1935). Both Young and Gregory were contacts Clark had from his time in the Orthodox Presbyterian Church. Young, who taught at Butler from 1948 to 1955[6], had been involved in Clark's ordination controversy in the OPC. He had not signed the original complaint, but his name appears on a later complaint which argued that the previous General Assembly (1945) ought to have declared that the Presbytery of Philadelphia had erred in failing to find ground for the original complaint against Clark's ordination.[7] Despite opposition to

6. Butler University, "Annual Catalogue."

7. The Thirteenth General Assembly of the Orthodox Presbyterian Church, meeting minutes (Philadelphia, PA: Chestnut Hill, 21–28 May 1946), 89.

Clark on some issues in the ordination controversy, Young's name was included on minority reports in support of Clark's positions at the Fourteenth General Assembly of the OPC in 1947.[8] Gregory, who taught at Butler from 1948 to 1952, had been ordained in the OPC in 1947 despite some apparent resistance to his ordination, possibly related to his views on the Clark case. He, like Clark, left the OPC in the wake of the controversy, transferring to the UPCNA. Gregory later attended Clark's alma mater, the University of Pennsylvania, earning a PhD in philosophy in 1958.

As chair of the department, Clark was in charge of designing the curriculum. During his tenure at Butler, he added new courses to the philosophy department, increasing the department's offerings from eight courses in 1945 to seventeen by the time of his retirement in 1973.[9] Yet throughout his years at Butler, the core curriculum remained relatively unchanged. In addition to core courses on the history of medieval philosophy and on ancient philosophy, there were two courses on logic and later a course on the theory of knowledge, each specialties of his. All of the courses remained 400 level or below as there was no graduate program in philosophy.

Most of Clark's classes remained small. One former student commented that with Clark's general lack of emotion, "a chill pervaded the classroom."[10] Despite this "chill," some students were genuinely affected by Clark's faith. Former student Chris Williams recalled, "The approach that GC took to the believability of the Bible had an almost instantaneous effect on me. His clarity and rigor of thought (as well as his boldness) was completely disarming and I found myself accepting the truth of the scriptures without much resistance."[11]

Other characteristics of Clark as a professor can be seen in the recollections of former Butler student Ed Harris, who recalled, "Whenever we had exams, he would leave the room to go play chess with the religion professor [Dr. Andry]," and "I remember very well the last final exam I took from him. The blue book exams were three hours long and he only asked one question with three words: 'summarize the course.'"[12]

---

8. The Fifteenth General Assembly of the Orthodox Presbyterian Church, meeting minutes (Wildwood, NJ: 13–18 May 1948), Appendix 65, 70.

9. Butler University, "Annual Catalogue."

10. Craig Pinkus (former Clark student at Butler from 1961–1965), interview by Douglas Douma, phone, 30 October 2014.

11. E-mail to the author from Chris Williams (former Clark student at Butler from 1962–1965), 17 November 2014.

12. Ed Harris (former Clark student at Butler in 1962), interview by Douglas Douma, phone, 4 June 2014.

Another Butler student and star halfback on the university's football team, John Floyd Brown, enrolled in Clark's philosophy courses, not because of any desire for religious indoctrination, but because they were challenging. Brown recalled thinking at the time, "I can play football. That's easy. But Aristotle is interesting." According to Brown, Clark would sit back while he (Brown) and another student debated philosophy vigorously. Brown recalled, "In class Clark would let a student go on a tangent and then when they were really proud of themselves, he would get a twinkle in his eyes just knowing what was coming next, and then he'd hit them with a one-liner which showed they didn't know what they were talking about."

An anomaly in Clark's philosophy courses as an African-American, John Floyd Brown also recalled that for Clark "color had nothing to do with intellectual progress; but how you thought [did]." If Clark had any prejudice at all it was against athletes, something Clark himself certainly was not. Brown took five courses from Clark over the years he studied at Butler and visited Clark's house a number of times, but had never mentioned to Clark that he played on the football team. Brown recalled, "Every book where [Clark] had to make a bad point, he'd use an athlete. I didn't say anything for years. In my Senior year, at my last game, the paper had a picture of me. Dr. Clark saw the paper. He looked at the paper and then looked at me and asked, 'Is that you?' And it was. We had quite a laugh because all this time he talked about athletes as dumb dodos."[13] [14]

It is not difficult to see that Clark had a profound influence on many of his students. Even after his resignation from Wheaton College in 1943, his influence continued to be perpetuated there through the beliefs and behaviors of his former students. For example, a 1950 visit by Clark's former student Carl F. H. Henry to the Wheaton campus and Henry's description of his own time as a student of Clark aroused the interest of D. Clair Davis, a freshman philosophy major. After reading Clark's *A Christian Philosophy*

13. Dr. John Floyd Brown (former football player and Clark student at Butler, 1954–1956 and 1960–1962, serving in the Air Force during the intervening years), interview by Douglas Douma, phone, 21 October 2014. Note: John Brown is the brother of Timothy Brown, a National Football League halfback who played for the Philadelphia Eagles in the 1960s.

14. One such example of Clark lambasting athletes is found in a recorded lecture in which he said, "If a college student in a Logic class complains about the age-old and worn out syllogism, namely 'All men are mortal; Socrates is a man; therefore, Socrates is mortal,' and remarks,—the football player in the back row whose weight is twice his IQ—if he [that football player] remarks, 'I agree that all men are mortal and that Socrates is a man, but you can't force on me the idea that by mere human logic that Socrates is mortal;' If that is his objection, the professor must reply, 'If you do not grasp implication, you cannot understand anything, for nothing else is clearer.'"—Clark, "Predestination in the Old Testament," minute 28.

of Education, which he found fascinating and crystal clear, Davis transferred to Butler in 1951 to study under Clark for two semesters. Of this time Davis recalled,

> My experience at Butler was simply invaluable, I would humbly say evidenced by my showing later in the Graduate Record Examination in Philosophy in the 99th percentile. The best course was one on epistemology using Brand Blanshard's *Nature of Thought.* Blanshard was worthy of Clark's mind and the interaction between the two in class was just amazing. But in general the caliber of student in his classes was not very high, and since GHC was a master of the Socratic method by drawing out students with probing questions, and since most students there didn't have that much that could be drawn out, he was seldom able to display his Socratic skill.[15]

After taking nearly all of Dr. Clark's courses at Butler, Davis returned to Wheaton. When Davis sought ordination in the Orthodox Presbyterian Church, his history as a student of Dr. Clark prompted his presbytery to thoroughly question him on the topic of the incomprehensibility of God. Davis recalled that the majority of the questioning was on this one doctrine.[16] By taking a moderate position on the incomprehensibility of God he passed the interview.[17] Davis later became a professor at Westminster Theological Seminary, teaching Church History there from 1966–2003.

During Clark's tenure at Butler he received a number of accolades. He was promoted to full professor in 1949 and won the Holcomb Award from the university for his teaching in 1951. He helped found the Evangelical Theological Society in 1949, was a member of its first executive committee, and helped draw up the society's belief statement: "The Bible alone, and the Bible in its entirety, is the word of God written and is therefore inerrant in its autographs."[18] He was elected vice president of the Evangelical Theologi-

---

15. Dr. D. Clair Davis, e-mail to the author, 31 March 2014.

16. Dr. D. Clair Davis, e-mail to the author, 10 December 2013.

17. Dr. D. Clair Davis explained, "I was ordained by the OPC Presbytery of Wisconsin in 1963. My exam was led by Bob Churchill, and 2 hr of the 2.5 exam was on incomprehensibility. I didn't say CVT was wrong, but said that God had revealed the truth to us, though we didn't and never would understand all implications. I suppose I was 'moderate' but I think by avoiding CVT's analogy theory I was closer to GHC."—Dr. D. Clair Davis, e-mail to the author, 29 March 2015.

18. Evangelical Theological Society, founding meeting documents (Cincinnati, OH: 27–28 December 1949), BGC Archives, records of the Evangelical Theological Society, coll. 243, founding meeting and constitution by-laws folders 1–1, 1–2. See also: Wiseman, "The Evangelical Theological Society, Yesterday and Today," 5.

cal Society for 1964 and then president for 1965.[19] He was chosen to be the moderator of the 138th General Assembly of the Reformed Presbyterian Church, General Synod in 1961.[20] Finally, as the commencement speaker in 1966 at the Reformed Episcopal Seminary, he was awarded an honorary doctorate of divinity degree.[21]

Although he found himself fitting in more comfortably at Butler than he did at Wheaton, Clark was nevertheless still regarded highly by many at Wheaton. On the invitation of Wheaton College's professor Arthur Holmes, Clark returned to Wheaton to give three lectures in November of 1965.[22] The lectures consisted of a critique of secular philosophy and a construction of his Christian worldview from the axiom of revelation. These lectures were later published in 1968 in Clark's Festschrift, *The Philosophy of Gordon H. Clark.*

CHURCH AND DENOMINATIONAL INVOLVEMENT IN INDIANAPOLIS

Clark's activities and responsibilities were not limited to his work as a professor at the university. He also was actively preaching and teaching in the church as well as contributing to a variety of national periodicals and newspapers.

When the Clark family (Gordon, his wife Ruth, and their two daughters, Lois and Betsy) moved to Indianapolis in 1945, they first joined Covenant Orthodox Presbyterian Church. The pastor of Covenant, Martin "Marty" Bohn, was in sympathy with Clark's position in the ordination controversy. When Clark left the OPC three years later, he and his family joined the United Presbyterian Church of North America (UPCNA) and, on October 14, 1948, his ministerial credentials were transferred to their Presbytery of Indiana.[23] Many of the other pastors who left the OPC in the 1940s joined the Presbyterian Church United States (PCUS), but this

19. The Evangelical Theological Society, meeting minutes (1964–1965), Records of the Evangelical Theological Society, BGC Archives, Wheaton College.

20. Taylor, "Clark Elected by RPC," 4.

21. Henry, "A Wide and Deep Swath," 49–50. See Also: Invitation to the 79th Commencement of the Theological Seminary of the Reformed Episcopal Church, 19 May 1966 at Christ Memorial Church, Philadelphia, PA, Sangre de Cristo Seminary, Clark Library, 1/91.

22. Arthur F. Holmes (1924–2011) taught philosophy at Wheaton College from 1951–1994. During the eight years between Clark's departure and Holmes's arrival, Wheaton went without a philosophy professor.

23. Dennison, *Ministerial Register*, 17.

denomination was primarily located in the southern states and so was not an option for Clark at that time. In 1949, the year after Clark switched denominations, Marty Bohn also left the OPC for the UPCNA.[24] Covenant OPC Indianapolis soon after became one of the casualties of the ordination controversy, officially closing on October 20, 1952.[25] According to Clark's daughter Betsy, "My dad never complained about the OP church. I grew up with a very high estimation of that church. He never expressed," and here she laughed, "any *emotion* about it." Also, according to Betsy, her father never spoke about the OPC ordination problem in their daily lives, although her mother had been furious regarding the situation.[26]

Clark and his family joined First United Presbyterian Church in Indianapolis, a member church of UPCNA pastored by Rev. Clarence Paul Blekking. Clark led Bible studies at the church, preached as a substitute pastor, and preached at various other UPCNA churches within the presbytery in central Indiana when called upon.[27]

The UPCNA had originated almost a century earlier when immigrants from Scottish Seceder and Covenanter denominations came to America in sufficient numbers to warrant the formation of their own churches. The majority of the Seceder and Covenanter churches united as a single denomination in 1858, forming the UPCNA. The denomination originally had conservative convictions, including the exclusive use of Psalms in singing during the worship service, but over time the UPCNA deviated from its roots and began to accept more and more liberal theology. In the 1950s, when the transition of the denomination to liberalism was sufficiently thorough, the UPCNA sought a merger with the liberal PCUSA, to Clark's dismay.

Rev. Blekking at the First United Presbyterian Church did not put up resistance to the denomination's decision to merge with the PCUSA. Clark, who often preached in Blekking's absence, and who had a better understanding of what was at stake, was decidedly opposed to the merger. It was the PCUSA from which Clark had left at the formation of the OPC in 1936. He certainly did not want to be brought back into that denomination through a merger.[28] Clark wrote to Carl F. H. Henry with hope that there might be

24. Ibid., 9.

25. The Nineteenth General Assembly of the Orthodox Presbyterian Church, meeting minutes (Denver, CO: 10–15 July 1952), 64.

26. Betsy Clark George, interview by Douglas Douma, at her home in Murphysboro, IL, December 2013.

27. George, "Life with Father," 21.

28. Hutchinson, *History Behind the Reformed Presbyterian Church, Evangelical Synod*, 356.

sufficient resistance within the UPCNA to prevent the merger: "This week I received some good news about the UP church. The men opposing union are slowly beginning to move, and we have made one important convert, the editor of the denominational paper. If we can pick up 200 votes out of a total of 1300, we shall safely have won. But it is the hardest thing in the world to get the UP ministers to do anything except pure routine."[29] Ultimately the effort was to no avail, and the UPCNA voted in favor of merging with the PCUSA. On May 28, 1958, the two denominations officially became one.[30] Looking back later that year, Clark wrote to *Christianity Today* calling the merger "another defeat for the Christian faith."[31]

Clark's local church, however, managed to avoid the merger. In a sudden turn of events, Rev. Blekking died of a heart attack on Easter Sunday morning, April 21, 1957. This happened just as the congregation was preparing to vote on whether to stay with the UPCNA, which was joining the PCUSA, or switch to another denomination. With Rev. Blekking's death, Clark was appointed Stated Supply for the congregation.[32] Under Clark's leadership the church left the UPCNA and joined the Reformed Presbyterian Church, General Synod (RPCGS), a small conservative Presbyterian denomination. The congregation stated its reasons as follows for rejecting the merger: "The Presbyterian Church in the U.S.A. ordains men who do not believe in the inerrancy of Scripture, the virgin birth, the substitutionary atonement, and the resurrection of Christ, and considers them ministers worthy of all confidence and fellowship."[33] These reasons clearly harkened back to the "Five Fundamentals" of the Fundamentalist-Modernist controversy which caused Clark to leave the PCUSA for the OPC in the 1930s.

Clark was unanimously received into the ministry of the Western Presbytery of the RPCGS. The local congregation itself was renamed the First Reformed Presbyterian Church. Soon following Clark into the RPCGS were two former OPC pastors and close associates of his, Franklin Dyrness

29. GHC to CFHH, 28 April 1956, BGC Archives, Wheaton College.

30. Smylie, *Brief History of the Presbyterians*, 124.

31. Gordon H. Clark, letter to the editor, *Christianity Today*, December 1957, BGC Archives.

32. "An Historical Sketch of Grace PCA and The Presbyterian Church in America" (unpublished document, c. 2000), from the "archives" of Grace Presbyterian Church, Indianapolis, courtesy of church member Craig Lukowiak.

33. First United Presbyterian Church of Indianapolis, special session meeting minutes (Indianapolis: 14 March 1958), Sangre de Cristo Seminary, Clark Library.

and Richard Willer Gray.[34] Within a year the small denomination nearly doubled in size.[35]

When the Clark family became members of the denomination with the name "Reformed" in its title for the first time, Clark's younger daughter Betsy, then fifteen years of age, was unfamiliar with the use of the word as it applied to a church. She recalls saying, "Daddy, you don't want to go to a reformed church. That sounds like a prison! [Troubled] kids go to reformed school!"[36] Fortunately for Betsy, her father was a master of explaining confusing concepts. Unfortunately, however, the little church had far bigger problems in its future than confusion over name changes.

Switching from one denomination to another brought difficult circumstances to the small church. On June 28, 1960, the Indianapolis Presbytery of the United Presbyterian Church (formerly of the UPCNA) filed suit against the congregation to recover the property.[37] The local presbytery of UPCNA had given the congregation a quitclaim deed a few years before the merger. This deed gave the property on Park Avenue in Indianapolis to the congregation. However, when the congregation broke away from the denomination, the newly-formed Presbytery of Indianapolis of the UPUSA initiated legal action to recover the deed. Initially the congregation prevailed in the case. Then an appeal was filed by the UPUSA. Although the congregation eventually lost the case, they had already relocated from Park Avenue to a new facility on Allisonville Road in the north part of the city.[38] The church property dispute was finally decided in favor of the UPUSA at the Court of Appeals of Indiana in the court case *The Presbytery of Indpls. etc., v. First United Presbyterian Church (of Indpls.).*[39] The loss of the property was a financial burden to the congregation, but with the support of some large donations, including one from the Clark family, the congregation remained solvent.[40]

34. Hutchinson, *History Behind the Reformed Presbyterian Church, Evangelical Synod*, 357.

35. Membership grew from 1121 to 2020 members. See: Clark, Nancy Elizabeth. "A History of the Reformed Presbyterian Church," 85–86.

36. Betsy Clark George, interview by Douglas Douma, at her home in Murphysboro, IL, December 2013.

37. "An Historical Sketch of Grace PCA and The Presbyterian Church in America" (unpublished document, c. 2000), from the "archives" of Grace Presbyterian Church, Indianapolis, courtesy of church member Craig Lukowiak.

38. "An Old Church Begins a New Era" (flyer, c. late 1960s), from the files of First Reformed Presbyterian Church of Indianapolis, now Grace PCA Indianapolis.

39. *Presbytery of Indpls. etc., v. First United Presbyterian Church (of Indpls.),* 238 N.E.2d 479, 667A14 (Ind. Ct. App. 1968).

40. Clark briefly recounts this history in one of his recorded lectures: "My own

The congregation made do without winning back the old property. Clark preached every Sunday for over eight years until the church grew in membership sufficiently to afford a full-time pastor. One of the members of the church and a student in Dr. Clark's Sunday school classes recalled:

> As much as Ruth Clark was vivacious and outgoing, her husband was pensive and reserved. Although his preaching was not of the fire and brimstone style and some might describe it a bit dry, he did however choose his words very carefully and did not go too deep theologically where it was difficult for new Christians to follow nor would I say he was feeding the listener pablum.[41]

Clark enjoyed the preaching, but the administrative duties of the church wore on him. He was a busy man in these years. Not only was he simultaneously teaching full-time at Butler and leading the church, but he was also busy writing books and making regular contributions to a number of Christian periodicals. His former student Carl F. H. Henry was the editor for many years at *Christianity Today* and frequently sent requests to Clark to write articles on a variety of topics. During this time Clark also wrote a number of articles for *The Southern Presbyterian Journal*, including a series of articles explaining the doctrines of the *Westminster Confession of Faith*.

Yet Clark still made time to minister to his flock. His patience was displayed to one church member who recalled that Clark once sat down to lunch with him and answered his questions on the doctrine of predestination for three and a half hours. Members of the church also recalled Ruth's dedication to the church community. Among her efforts, Ruth helped take care of an elderly couple, even going to their house and washing their feet.[42] Although Gordon and Ruth Clark were dedicated servants of this church, they welcomed the change when, in July of 1965, the Rev. James Ransom accepted a call to the church and relieved Clark of his preaching and administrative duties.[43]

---

congregation voted unanimously not to merge with an apostate organization. Moreover, our congregation had a quitclaim deed to its property. Yet those who gave us the quitclaim deed changed their minds after the merger, invalidated the deed in court, and took the property."—Clark, "The Decline of Theology in America," minute 11.

41. Craig Lukowiak, e-mail to the author, 1 April 2014.

42. Grace PCA members who have attended the church since Dr. Clark's time there (Craig and Arlene Lukowiak, Bob and Pat Cloud, and Greg and Marcia Bogan), interview by Douglas Douma, Indianapolis, 24 May 2015.

43. "Waiting to Relocate," 6.

In the same year, 1965, Clark was involved in arranging a merger between the RPCGS and the Evangelical Presbyterian Church (EPC).[44] The EPC was the larger branch of the 1956 division of the Bible Presbyterian Church, itself having originated in 1937 from a division in the Orthodox Presbyterian Church. In 1961, this branch of the BPC, called the Columbus Synod, renamed itself the Evangelical Presbyterian Church, holding this name from 1961 until the 1965 union with the RPCGS. The new merged denomination took the name Reformed Presbyterian Church, Evangelical Synod (RPCES). The merger with the EPC brought to the newly combined denomination J. Oliver Buswell, Clark's longtime friend who had originally hired him at Wheaton College almost thirty years prior. Also from the EPC came Francis Schaeffer, a Christian apologist and founder of L'Abri, a Christian ministry in Switzerland. Furthermore, the EPC brought into the merger Covenant College and Covenant Seminary. The merger would prove to be beneficial as the new denomination grew in the subsequent years.

LIFE OUTSIDE OF WORK

As Clark became increasingly comfortable in his position at Butler University, he was able to settle into a routine in both his professional life and in his personal life. In the Clark household there was almost constant quiet. If Gordon was not studying, he was playing chess or napping. He studied diligently and deliberately, planning out his studies far in advance. In addition to teaching full-time and writing books and articles, he maintained continual correspondence, often on difficult theological matters. Besides regular business letters exchanged with Carl F. H. Henry, Clark's correspondence was the most frequent with J. Oliver Buswell. Extant correspondence between Clark and Buswell consists of 149 letters written between 1933 and 1962.

Though he was not afraid to speak his mind or convey his thoughts regularly through letters and publications, Clark was nevertheless reserved. His wife Ruth, on the other hand, was hospitable and outgoing. She managed the household's activities and frequently entertained guests, many of whom were students of Clark. She was known to be an exceedingly kind woman.

44. "Dr. Gordon H. Clark, Professor of Philosophy at Butler University in Indianapolis and chairman of the joint fraternal relations committee which has discussed details of the union since 1958, presided at the joint sessions of the two denominations while mutual problems were discussed. Both churches have laid plans to meet April 2–8, 1965, at the new Lookout Mountain campus of Covenant College near Chattanooga, Tennessee."—Nicholas, "EP-RP Churches Vote to Unite in 1965," 61–62.

The Clarks all had sharp minds. Former Wheaton student, Genevieve Long, related memories of Ruth speaking French, standing on the sidewalk at Wheaton and talking to a girl from a diplomat's family. Additionally, Long recalled her sister once having said, "Mrs. Clark is smart enough to be President of the USA."[45] During the Butler years, Ruth taught as a substitute teacher at a number of high schools in Indianapolis including a full semester at Shortridge High School.[46] Dr. Clark regularly played chess, even achieving some notoriety. In 1966 he received a plaque for being champion of a local Indianapolis chess club, the King's Men Chess Club. Among those with whom he frequently played chess (sometimes in person and sometimes via mail) were Dr. E. Robert Andry (a religion professor at Butler), Robert Strong (a Presbyterian minister), John Harper (an attorney friend from Clark's youth in Philadelphia), C. W. Efroymson (an Economics professor at Butler), and later J. C. Keister (a professor of physics at Covenant College).

Clark often used chess as a means of fellowship with other students and professors, even if the matches were generally one-sided. One account of Clark's chess prowess, given by family friend Tom Jones, is worth quoting at length:

> I bumped into Dr. Clark back in the late sixties when he was visiting his daughter Betsy on Lookout Mountain, Tennessee, where Betsy taught at Covenant College. I knew he was a chess champion and suggested that it would be fun to play with him sometime. He was eager to do so, and later that week he dropped by our home for an evening of chess. My wife had gone shopping and left me at home with our two small children.
>
> We played two games. In the first game I thought I did reasonably well for about a half an hour but then, rather abruptly, the entire left side of my board seemed to collapse and Dr. Clark swept me away. So, we played a second game in which he defeated me unceremoniously in about ten minutes.
>
> Feeling properly humiliated I asked a question, "Dr. Clark, I want to learn from you. So, tell me if you will, in that first game I thought I did fairly well for a while but then you just clobbered me at the end. Can you remember anything about where I made my mistakes?"
>
> With that Dr. Clark proceeded to set up that first game and replay the entire thing. He reached a point where he said, "Now,

---

45. Genevieve Long via her daughter, Ellen Schulze, e-mail to the author, 9 August 2014.

46. Lois Zeller interview by Douglas Douma, Sangre de Cristo Seminary, 13 June 2015.

at this point, I expected that you would move your queen thus so, at which point I was prepared to counter with my knight, like so, and then . . . " (with this he made about six hypothetical moves which he had anticipated), "but you didn't do that" (he said as he put all the pieces back in place). "Instead, you moved your rook over here" (and with that he finished the game, explaining each move in the swift demise of my game).

It was by now at least forty-five minutes after the first game had been played and he had remembered every single move in that game! I was amazed and thoroughly in submission to the master by now.

But the thing that humiliated me the most was that the entire time that we had been playing he was holding my four-year-old son, Bradley, on his lap and was reading a story book to him. He would glance up after my moves, take a brief look at the board, make his move nonchalantly, and go back to reading the story. HE HAD NOT EVEN BEEN PAYING ATTENTION! Or so it seemed. What a mind![47]

As a college professor, Clark often had the summers free from his regular work. He always kept busy, but he and his family still made time for vacations. Starting in May of 1954 the Clark family went on a four-month vacation to Europe. They stayed a month in Paris and a month in London (August).[48] In between there were visits to Lausanne, Lucerne, Heidelberg (July)[49] where Clark had studied in 1927, Amsterdam, and Edinburgh (July).[50] On the trip they visited L'Institut Biblique in Paris run by M. Jules-Marcel Nicole (the brother of Roger Nicole of Gordon Divinity School) and the Emmaus Bible Institute in Switzerland where they met with Swiss theologian Dr. René Pache.[51]

The family also regularly vacationed in Arizona, New Mexico, and western Texas, where Clark spent much of his time painting landscapes of the surroundings. He fulfilled numerous speaking engagements during these trips.

47. E-mail to the author from Tom Jones, Clark family friend, 8 August 2015.

48. "London Aug. 1954," an inscription in Clark's handwriting on the inside cover of Jean Wahl's *Pluralist Philosophies of England and America*, Sangre de Cristo's Clark Library.

49. "Heidelberg July 6 1954," an inscription in Clark's handwriting on the inside cover of Karl Lowith's *Von Hegel Zu Nietsche*, Sangre de Cristo's Clark Library.

50. "Edinburgh July 1954," an inscription in Clark's handwriting on the inside cover of *Blackwood's Philosophical Classics: Hegel*, Sangre de Cristo's Clark Library.

51. Clark, "Religious Travelogue," 19–20.

In the summers starting in 1958 and continuing most years until 1969, Clark taught two-week-long seminars at the Winona Lake School of Theology in Indiana at the invitation of their president, John A. Huffman.[52] One of Clark's students there was Erwin Lutzer, today the senior pastor of the historic Moody Church in Chicago. Lutzer recalled taking a couple of classes at Winona Lake School of Theology under Dr. Clark, including one in which he turned out to be the only student in the course. For this course, Lutzer worked one-on-one with Clark to review the latter's yet-to-be-published manuscript of *Historiography: Secular and Religious*. Lutzer credits Clark as a significant influence on him.[53] He wrote, "[Clark's] emphasis on logic aroused my philosophic mind to think through certain issues from a rational standpoint." And "He also increased my understanding of Calvinism and solidified many doctrines that I had already come to accept."[54]

Yet Lutzer found Clark's philosophy ultimately difficult to reconcile with the world in which we live. According to Lutzer,

> Because of his disdain for empirical evidence, I felt his epistemology ultimately was lacking. I studied with him during the summer of 1969 when Teddy Kennedy's car ran off a bridge and Mary Jo Kopechne drowned. Dr. Clark was grousing about the Kennedy family and this incident. I said to him, "How do you know that this incident happened since it is based on empirical observation?" He answered, "I'm willing to go on insufficient evidence." It was difficult for me to live with such a rational approach to all knowledge.[55]

Although Gordon Clark's public image and reputation revolved around his academic and philosophical accomplishments and battles, he was still just a man. He valued and loved his friends and family, and in some ways was like many other men of his generation. He owned a home, had a wife and children, and pursued hobbies. He had his own peculiarities. For example, he compartmentalized his food, eating one entrée or side fully before moving to the next. He loved chocolate ice cream, devoured scrapple (a pork, cornmeal, and spice dish popular in Pennsylvania), and, for health

52. John A. Huffman, President of Winona Lake School of Theology, to GHC, 10 September 1958, Sangre de Cristo Seminary, Clark Library, 1/63.

53. Erwin Lutzer, interview by Douglas Douma, phone, August 2014. Note: Clark wrote a foreword to Lutzer's *The Morality Gap, An Evangelical Response to Situation Ethic* (Chicago: Moody Press, 1972).

54. E-mail to the author from Dr. Erwin W. Lutzer, Senior Pastor of The Moody Church in Chicago, 8 July 2015.

55. Ibid.

reasons, drank postum (a powdered roasted-grain beverage) as a coffee substitute.

Clark even owned a dog for a time. The dog, Zephi (short for Zephaniah), was a gift from his daughter Lois and her husband Dwight, a chaplain in the U.S. Navy who, together with Lois, had been sent to Guam on a two-year assignment. In 1962, the small-standard dachshund was put on a train in Albuquerque and picked up by Clark in Indianapolis. Zephi remained a beloved member of the family for more than a decade.

KARL BARTH AND THE VOLKER FUND

In 1959 Clark received a visit from a representative of the Volker Fund who invited him to submit an application for a grant.[56] The Volker Fund had been established in 1932 by William Volker (1859–1947), a wealthy businessman, to underwrite a number of charitable causes in the Kansas City, Missouri, area.[57] Following Volker's death, his nephew Harold Lunhow (1895–1978) expanded the fund's mission to include support of free-market economic theory and contributed money to conservative and libertarian authors. Clark was awarded a Volker Fund grant which funded a sabbatical during the 1961–1962 school year for him to write a book on the theologian Karl Barth. This book was to be a refutation of Barth's theology. Sensing the importance of this topic and the efforts Clark put into his writing, Carl F. H. Henry wrote to Clark with great expectation, "I trust 1962 proves to be your best year yet."[58]

Clark's study and writing on Barth was just in time for what turned out to be Barth's first and only visit to America, in 1962. Barth gave speeches on his theology that year at both Princeton Theological Seminary and Chicago University. Clark attended the Chicago event.

Cornelius Van Til was also a theological opponent of Karl Barth, and like Clark, Van Til was working on a book against Barth's theology. In a letter to Carl F. H. Henry, Clark expressed joy when he found out from Henry that publication of his own book on Barth would precede Van Til's. Clark wrote, "P.S. So, I'll beat Van Til in the race to publish? Good."[59] Clark's book *The*

---

56. GHC to CFHH, 18 November 1959, BGC Archives, Wheaton College. (The representative was Kenneth S. Templeton)

57. William Volker (1859–1947) made his fortune in the picture frame and window shade businesses.

58. CFHH to GHC, 28 December 1961, BGC Archives, Wheaton College, CN8, 15–13.

59. GHC to CFHH, 1961, BGC Archives, Wheaton College, CN8, 15–13.

Theological Method of Karl Barth made it to the printers in 1963, and Van Til's *Christianity and Barthianism* came out the following year. Although Clark and Van Til were not on the most cordial terms, Clark sought to avoid any new conflict. When Henry asked him to review Van Til's book for *Christianity Today*, Clark responded with his own idea, one likely to exhaust the energies of two other Christian thinkers and give himself a good laugh. He wrote, "I, too, have Van Til's book on Barth. So far I have read only thirty pages. Why don't you get Buswell to review it, and get Van Til to review Buswell's Theology. That would be a malicious combination, would it not?"[60]

CLARK'S COMEDY

Although caricatured as a strict, logical professor, Clark was also known for his comedic wit, often to the surprise of those who would expect the professor of logic to not have a funny bone in his body. Sometimes he even used comedy in explaining the principles of logic. In one recorded lecture, Clark said, "The law of contradiction requires that a word have a definite meaning. Now if a word has all possible meanings, it means nothing. Suppose there was a word in the dictionary and you look it up in the dictionary and the meanings were all other words in the dictionary. Suppose the word were automobile. The word automobile means cat, it means tree, it means the square root of minus one and so on and so on. In order to write a book all you'd have to say is, 'Auto auto auto auto auto auto auto,' and that means 'The New York Yankees are going to win the pennant and the World Series next October.'"[61]

Emotion (which Clark was often accused of lacking) was a topic that sometimes led to comedic situations. Former Covenant Seminary president and WTS professor William Barker recalled, "That leads me to a story that I have only second-hand, but reported to me by a reliable source, namely my brother Nick. Nick, a professor of English [at Covenant College] and something of a poet, made a presentation to a faculty forum meeting, at which he argued for a proper use of emotion in Christian art by referring to George Frederick Handel's manuscript of the libretto for *The Messiah* as having tear stains on it. Dr. Clark, congratulating Nick after the discussion, said that the stains were not from tears, but from sweat!"[62]

---

60. GHC to CFHH, 29 October 1962, BGC Archives, Wheaton College, CN8, 15–13.

61. Clark, "Is Christianity a Religion? Part 2," minute 41.

62. William S. Barker, e-mail to the author, 21 March 2014.

Some of Clark's comedy was not intentional but was the product of his philosophical views. For example, in 1958 Carl F. H. Henry sent a letter to Clark saying, "Our news editor tells me that he recently asked [you] for fifty words of commentary on the projected U.S. shot to the moon. Your own comment was a bit facetious, indicating that you could find no significance in the event."[63] On other occasions Clark would refer back to philosophical examples in his comedy. In a lecture where he had explained the paradox of Zeno which intends to show that motion is impossible, Clark joked about his publisher's slowness, saying, "Well, I guess we need a definition of faith or something. How do you distinguish between saving faith and temporary faith? If you will wait a year, as I have already done, my treatise on faith and saving faith will be printed. But, oh boy, Craig [Publisher Charles H. Craig (1912–1983) of Presbyterian and Reformed Publishing] is the slowest person on earth. He would have pleased Zeno the Eleatic with his exhibition of no motion."[64] Finally, as seen in a chapter on eschatology in his unpublished systematic theology, Clark used humor to take jabs at his theological opposition. Critiquing dispensationalism, he wrote, "Another indefensible aberration of the dispensationalists is their insertion, between Rev. 3:22 and Rev. 4:1, of a rapture so secret that there is no reference to it in the whole Bible."[65] Clark's wit was in many ways typical of an intellectual: somewhat biting, often sarcastic, and always sharp. For those who would claim Clark was somber and stern, there is plenty of evidence that Clark could crack wise with the best of his peers.

CLARK'S DAUGHTERS

Despite all of the work at the university, writing books, and pastoring churches, Clark still regularly made time for his family. His wife and daughters were especially dear to him. Both of his children married ministers. Clark's elder daughter, Lois, married Dwight Zeller, who was then a chaplain in the U.S. Navy. His younger daughter, Betsy, married Wyatt George, who pastored PCA churches in Illinois for many years.

Lois married a few months after graduating from Butler in 1956 with a bachelor's degree in French and German. Her father had hoped she would go to France to study, but the marriage temporarily put an end to her academic work. As a chaplain's wife she was able to use her musical gifts serving

63. CFHH to GHC, 12 September 1958, BGC Archives, Wheaton College, CN8, 15–12.
64. Clark, "Is Christianity a Religion? Part 3," minute 37.
65. Clark, "First Lessons in Theology," chapter 9, 85.

as an organist in many military chapels during her husband's career. She also taught piano lessons to children of servicemembers and to others in years afterwards. Her academic background prepared her for positions teaching French and English for two years in New York and subbing in schools in Pennsylvania and Colorado after leaving military life.

Lois and Dwight are the parents of six sons and two daughters. When Dwight founded Sangre de Cristo Seminary, Lois taught the Church Music course (every third year for thirty years), and completed a Masters of Divinity degree in 1985, a few months after her father's death. In fact, she recalled studying Hebrew for class at her father's bedside in his final days. In addition to the music jobs, she served as the librarian for the seminary. Lois married young and admits that it was her father's wish for her to not do so; he would have preferred she continue her studies. Clark's hopes for a scholar-daughter then shifted to his younger daughter Betsy.

Betsy followed a more ambitious academic career. While her father was still teaching at Butler, Betsy earned there a bachelor's degree in French and German in 1962 and a master's degree in history in 1966. Her master's thesis was titled *A History of the Reformed Presbyterian Church.*[66] Then, blazing the trail that Lois declined to pursue, Betsy went to France to study at L'Institut Biblique de Nogent, which made her father very happy.

Along with her husband Wyatt, who served three pastorates in the PCA, Betsy raised four sons. Later in life, after teaching at multiple institutions—Tudor Hall in Indianapolis, and Covenant College, where she met her husband—Betsy earned a PhD in History at Southern Illinois University in 1996. She taught French, Latin, and Church History at Trinity Christian School in Carbondale, Illinois, and served as school principal until her retirement in 2015.

BUTLER YEARS: CONCLUSION

Clark ultimately spent the bulk of his career at Butler University. Being isolated there as a Christian thinker, there was no chance of him falling into groupthink on theological matters as can be the case when working in a denominational seminary. His own collegiate training, already unusual for a theologian (having studied philosophy at a secular university rather than theology at a seminary), and this isolation at Butler both contributed to many unique theological conclusions. Some of these conclusions are detailed in the following chapter.

66. Clark, Nancy Elizabeth. "A History of the Reformed Presbyterian Church."

Chapter 10

Four Theological Contributions of Gordon H. Clark

"The construction I am aiming at is the deduction of the Westminster Confession from Scripture, and this I take it is a step toward axiomatization, or systemization."[1]

—GORDON H. CLARK

THE GOAL OF THIS chapter is to explain four of Gordon Clark's significant doctrinal contributions. Namely, these are (1) an axiomatized epistemological system, (2) teleological supralapsarianism, (3) a solution to the problem of evil, and (4) arguments for a return to traditional logic.

CONTRIBUTION #1:
AN AXIOMATIZED EPISTEMOLOGICAL SYSTEM

The first of these four doctrinal contributions, and the one on which the whole of Clark's thought rests, is his view of knowledge as a system of thought based on the axiom of Scripture. Clark saw epistemology, the study of knowledge, as the foremost branch of philosophy. His own epistemology consisted of two primary elements: a starting point and a method by which to acquire knowledge.

---

1. GHC to George Mavrodes, 2 May 1968, PCA Arhives, 309/44.

Clark's epistemological starting point was the truth of the Bible. In arguing for the necessity of a starting point, Clark held to foundational-ism, the theory that knowledge must rest upon some secure foundation for certainty. By assuming a foundation, Clark argued, the problem of infinite regress (that the necessity of providing justification for every proposition requires also that such a justification requires its own justification and this logic goes on ad infinitum) is circumvented. To start a philosophy, he argued, one must begin somewhere. Each and every philosophy has a starting point. The truth of the Bible is a starting point that should be considered along with other starting points, such as assuming the validity of one's own senses.

Regarding the method of gaining knowledge, Clark rejected the popular inductive method of science and argued that deduction was the Christian method, for the simple reason that induction always commits a logical fallacy. Clark wrote of his epistemology, "My position has been that the axiomatization of theology is at least an ideal toward which we should press, even if we cannot attain it. . . . The construction I am aiming at is the deduction of the *Westminster Confession* from Scripture, and this I take it is a step toward axiomatization, or systemization."[2] In *Karl Barth's Theological Method*, Clark explained axiomatization as "simply the perfecting and exhibiting of the logical consistency of a system of thought."[3]

Clark likened his axiomatized system to Euclidean geometry which has given postulates and derived theorems. Christianity, by analogy, Clark claimed, has the postulate of "the Bible is truth" and as the theorems, the doctrines derived from the Bible's contents.

According to Clark, to determine the best starting point there is a two-fold test: the starting point must possess greater explanatory power, and it must pass the test of internal coherence or consistency.[4] He wrote, "It has been argued that Christianity is self-consistent, that it gives meaning to life and morality, and that it supports the existence of truth and the possibility of knowledge,"[5]and, "A choice must be made between skeptical futility and a word from God."[6]

2. Ibid.

3. Clark, *Karl Barth's Theological Method*, 95.

4. "We can judge the acceptability of an axiom only by its success in producing a system . . . And by the systems they produce, axioms must be judged."—Clark, *An Introduction to Christian Philosophy*, 60.

5. Clark, *Christian View of Men and Things*, 324.

6. Clark, *Thales to Dewey*, 534.

The units, or bits, of Clark's axiomatized system were propositions—the propositions of Scripture. He wrote, "Propositions, not concepts, are the objects of knowledge because only propositions can be true."[7]

Scripturalism, as Clark's philosophy later came to be called, aimed at answering philosophical questions in a consistent, systematic fashion, starting with the Christian Bible and its unique and central role in revealing truth from God to man. All truth available to man, Clark argued, comes either directly from the Bible or indirectly from it, via deductions from doctrines contained therein. The basis of scripturalism is the idea that no knowledge can be had by man apart from God's revelation. Clark argued that the truth of the Bible is systematic—each doctrine relates to all the others. The philosophy of scripturalism is related to the Reformation principle of *Sola Scriptura*. Where *Sola Scriptura* affirmed that the Bible is the sole source of all Christian doctrine, Clark went further and claimed that the Bible is the sole source of all human knowledge.

Perhaps the most common critique leveled at Clark's philosophy of scripturalism was in asking him the question, "Don't you have to read the Bible?" For if, as Clark contended, all knowledge comes from the Scriptures, does not one have to use the senses (particularly sight) to acquire that knowledge? If the knowledge does not come through the senses, how is it to be understood? Clark argued that those who raised this question had presupposed the philosophy of empiricism. As Clark had so thoroughly critiqued empiricism, there was not much left of the philosophy for anyone who would actually consider his arguments. Those who ask, "Don't you have to read your Bible?" are, according to Clark, not only ignoring the problems Clark raised with empiricism, but were also skipping over the necessity of explaining the mechanics of empiricism: how sensations produce perceptions and then memory images on the way to becoming knowledge. Clark held that the assumption of empiricism committed the fallacy of *petitio principii*, an appeal to the principle without proof of it.[8]

The question for Clark was not whether sensations provide knowledge, but rather, "what is the role of the senses in knowledge acquisition?"[9] Cer-

7. Clark, "A Christian Construction, Part 1."

8. "Don't you have to *read* the Bible? Well do I know the objections that this immediately raises. Evidentialist apologists and secular philosophies alike exclaim, 'But that assumes the point at issue; you are begging the question; you are arguing in a circle.' The reply to this objection should be obvious. The opponents, both secular and religious, assume the authority of experience, the inerrancy of experience, the validity of induction. But this assumes the point at issue, this begs the question, and the one is as circular as the other."—Clark, "Empiricism," minute 35.

9. Clark, *Lord God of Truth*, 23.

tainly, the senses were involved in some way when reading, but not in the way empiricism would have them. To answer the question, Clark looked to the theory of divine illumination developed by Augustine in his *De Magistro* and other works. According to the theory of divine illumination, God gives knowledge directly to man's mind through the divine light of His Logos. According to this theory, the purpose of sensation is in preserving the body from danger,[10] and the role given to the senses in knowledge acquisition is one of "a stimulus to intellectual intuition." Sensation occurs at the same instant as knowledge is given to man, but it is not sensation itself that gives knowledge.[11] This theory goes hand-in-hand with the theory of occasional-ism held by Nicolas Malebranche (1638–1715), a French theologian whom Clark admired. According to the theory of occasionalism, God is the sole and indefeasibly effective cause of everything throughout the universe. God speaks and it is done. God produces mental events and physical events si-multaneously.[12] Created things are at best "occasions" for divine activity.[13]

On November 4 and 5 of 1965, Gordon Clark gave three lectures at Wheaton College on the axiom of revelation. These lectures later were print-ed as part of his Festschrift, *The Philosophy of Gordon H. Clark*, and printed in a stand-alone volume as *An Introduction to Christian Philosophy*. There was immediate resistance to his lectures by those in attendance. George I. Mavrodes of the University of Michigan held that Clark's axiom was too limiting in allowing knowledge only from Scripture. Wheaton's philosophy professor Arthur F. Holmes, despite referring to Clark as "the foremost evangelical philosopher," also questioned Clark's choice of axiom.[14]

10. "Malebranche, following Augustine, defines the purpose of sensation to be that of preserving the body from danger."—Clark, *Lord God of Truth*, 18.

11. "St. Augustine, though he altered his view as he grew older, gave a different role to sensation; without too much distortion one might call it a stimulus to intellectual intuition."—Clark, *Language and Theology*, 114.

12. Clark, *The Biblical Doctrine of Man*, 91.

13. "While Hume denied all miracles, there was a medieval Moslem who antici-pated Hume's arguments against causality and concluded that every event is a miracle. Since no sensation can be the cause of another sensation, every event is immediately caused by God . . . We now concur with the Islamic anti-aristotelian Al Gazali: God and God alone is the cause, for only God can guarantee the occurrence of Y, and indeed of X as well. Even the Westminster Divines timidly agree, for after asserting that God foreordains whatsoever comes to pass, and that 'no purpose of yours can be withheld from you' (Job 42:2), they add, 'Although . . . all things come to pass immutably and infallibly, yet by the same providence he ordereth them to fall out according to the nature of second causes . . . ' What they called second causes, Malebranche had called occasions. But an occasion is neither a fiat lux nor a differential equation."—Clark, *Lord God of Truth*, 24–25, 27.

14. Newsome, "Clark Probes Resultants of Secular Philosophy." See also:

In the decades since Clark's lectures on axioms, his views failed to gain widespread popularity. To some, his views perhaps seem quite unusual or too dogmatically biblical. People are not quick to discount their own sensory perception and ideas, tossing them all aside for reliance on the Bible. Yet this is Clark's approach: the Bible has a monopoly on the truth. There are no competitors. We, as Christians, cannot serve two masters—the teachings of the Bible and the supposed truths gained from experience.

CONTRIBUTION #2: TELEOLOGICAL SUPRALAPSARIANISM

The study of the logical order of God's decrees in salvation is known as lapsarianism from the Latin *lapsus*, meaning "to fall." The majority view on this topic, in both Calvinist and non-Calvinist circles, is (and historically has been) infralapsarianism, the doctrine that God's decree of election and reprobation logically *follow* His decree of the fall. Less commonly held, supralapsarianism is the doctrine that God's decrees of election and reprobation logically *precede* His decree of the fall. Gordon Clark held to the latter view, but with modifications, as will be explained.

Clark's view was described as "teleological supralapsarianism" by Samuel Storms in *Chosen for Life, The Case for Divine Election*.[15] That this view is called "teleological" comes from the idea that all God's decrees are ultimately arranged to accomplish his ends or results (from the Greek *teleos*). Clark first explained his argument for this view in a letter to J. Oliver Buswell, President of Wheaton College, in 1935:

> This leads to the question of infra—versus supra—lapsarianism. On this question I hold that logical order is *the exact reverse* [emphasis added] of temporal order. For example, 1. I must buy a Christmas present, 2. at Wanamaker's, 3. which means I must take the trolley, 4. therefore I must walk to the corner. Such is the plan in its logical order; its execution is the exact reverse. The execution of the decrees is as follows: creation, fall, work of redemption, consummation including the reprobation of some and the glorification of others. The logical order is the exact reverse. Unless the two orders stand in this reverse relationship I do not know of any principle by which any answer to the question can be given.[16]

Abrahamson, "Visiting Philosophers React Against Clark's Epistemology."

15. Storms, *Chosen for Life*, 215–16.

16. GHC to JOB, 28 December 1935, Wheaton Archives.

To make the analogy from Clark's Christmas present example to the order of God's decrees in salvation, the following correlations must be considered:

A1. Clark's goal is to buy a Christmas present.

B1. God's goal is his own glory, including the glorification of some and the damnation of others.

A2. Clark goes to the store.

B2. God decrees salvation for some and destruction for others.

A3. Clark takes the trolley.

B3. God decrees the fall.

A4. Clark walks to the corner.

B4. God decrees creation.

The temporal order for buying the Christmas present is A4 → A3 → A2 → A1 (i.e. Clark walks to the corner, takes the trolley, goes to the store, and buys a Christmas present). And the temporal order of God's plan of salvation is B4 → B3 → B2 → B1 (i.e. God creates the world, causes the fall, provides salvation for some and condemns others, for his glory).[17]

The temporal order is agreed upon by both infralapsarians and supra-lapsarians. It is the logical order which is debated. Emphasizing this point, in typical Clarkian confidence, Clark explained to one of his students:

> You ask, Does God condemn man before he decrees the fall? The word *before* here causes trouble, for it introduces an element of time in a non-temporal situation. Several theologians it is true insist that the problem is *logical* and not temporal; but then they either follow a temporal order, or as often fail to say what they

---

17. It is not clear whether Clark was the originator of this teleological version of supralapsarianism. For one, supralapsarian proponent Herman Hoeksema used the teleological principle to order God's decrees in his *Reformed Dogmatics*. He wrote, "What is first in decree is last in the execution of it."—Hoeksema, *Reformed Dogmatics*, 232. Although this book was first published posthumously in 1966, Hoeksema's former student David Engelsma relays that *Reformed Dogmatics* is "basically [Hoeksema's] teaching in the PR Seminary from 1924 onwards."—Email to the author from David Engelsma, 24 October 2015. If what Engelsma says is so, this would mean Hoeksema held to teleological supralapsarianism prior to the earliest evidence of Clark holding to the view (a letter of Clark's from 1935). Also note that Robert Reymond also lists "(possibly)" Jerome Zanchius (1516–1590) and Johannes Piscator (1546–1625) as holding to this doctrine. (See Reymond, *A New Systematic Theology of the Christian Faith,* 489)

mean by logical order. Once a person grasps the *order*, i.e. what the word *order* means, the problem is easily solved.[18]

Clark critiqued those who held to the infralapsarian position by saying that they confused the logical order with the temporal order.[19] The "easy solution," according to Clark, is rather to consider the logical order as the reverse of the temporal order.

Clark's view can be considered a form of supralapsarianism in that the decree to save some and condemn others *precedes* the decree of the fall. Yet in reversing the entire temporal order, Clark's formula differs from the traditional supralapsarian position in a number of ways. A helpful way to understand the differences in the three positions is to consult the table below.

	Infralapsarianism	Supralapsarianisn	Teleological Supralapsarianism (Clark)
1	Decree of creation	Decree to save some and condemn others	Decree to save some and condemn others
2	Decree of the fall	Decree of creation	Decree to provide salvation only for the elect
3	Decree to save some and condemn others	Decree of the fall	Decree of the fall
4	Decree to provide salvation only for the elect	Decree to provide salvation only for the elect	Decree of creation

Having explained his view, Clark remarked to Buswell that he did "not know of any other principle by which any other answer to the question can be given." But should Christians not be primarily concerned with the relevant biblical passages rather than any logical principle? Fortunately, in *What do Presbyterians Believe?*, Clark addressed such a relevant biblical passage:

> Many, in a sense most, passages in the Bible explain the steps in God's plan. . . . But while hints and implications are abundant, there are few passages that explicitly and in so many words

18. GHC to Tim Deal, 28 October 1982, provided by Dennis Bills.

19. "If you wish to check various theologians you can look up Henry Bradford Smith, Louis Berkhof, my father, and oh well maybe Charles Hodge and I think you will find in all of them that they put the decree of election after the decree of the fall. My criticism of this is that they confuse logical sequence with temporal sequence. And my contention is that the logical sequence is precisely the reverse of the temporal sequence. A person chooses an end and then works back from the end to where he is now on something that he can do."—Clark, "Predestination in the Old Testament," minute 136.

connect the act of creation with God's final and comprehensive purpose. Some people say there is only one such passage. We shall therefore examine with all the greater care that one passage. It is found in Ephesians 3:9–10 . . . The main exegetical problem of Ephesians 3:9–10 is the identification of the antecedence of the purpose clause: "in order that the manifold wisdom of God might now be known, by means of the Church, to the principalities and powers in heavenly places, according to the eternal purpose which he purposed in Christ Jesus our Lord." Something happened in the preceding verses for the purpose of revealing God's wisdom. What was it that had this purpose . . . There are three and apparently only three possible antecedents: (1) Paul was called to preach in order that, (2) the mystery was hid in order that, and (3) God created the world in order that."

After disposing of (1) and (2), Clark concluded: "When we say that God created the world for the purpose of displaying his manifold wisdom, we connect the purpose clause with the nearest antecedent." Harkening back to his earlier letter to Buswell, Clark wrote:

> The connection between supralapsarianism and the fact that God always acts purposefully depends on the observation that the logical order of any plan is the exact reverse of its temporal execution. The first step in any planning is the end to be achieved; then the means are decided upon, until last of all the first thing to be done is discovered. The execution in time reverses the order of planning. Thus creation, since it is first in history, must be logically last in the divine decrees. Every biblical passage therefore that refers to God's wisdom also supports Ephesians 3:10.[20]

In his commentary on Ephesians, Clark, addressing the same verses (Ephesians 3:9–10), wrote, "Every mention of an eternal all-embracing plan contributes to a teleological and therefore supralsapsarian view of God's control of history."[21]

Clark's teleological reversal provides not only a solution to the question of lapsarianism, but also aligns with his view of history as an outworking of God's plan. For example, in *A Christian View of Men and Things*, Clark wrote, "God has not only controlled history so far, but he will bring it to its end and culmination."[22] Clark further discussed his view of supralapsarian-

20. Clark, *What Do Presbyterians Believe?* 49–54.
21. Clark, *Ephesians*, 112.
22. Clark, *Christian View of Men and Things*, 89.

ism and its relation to history in his unpublished systematic theology, where he wrote:

> Supralapsarianism, for all its insistence on a certain logical or-
> der among the divine decrees, is essentially, so it seems to us, the
> unobjectionable view that God controls the universe purpose-
> fully. God acts with a purpose. He has an end in view and sees
> the end from the beginning. Every verse in Scripture that in one
> way or another refers to God's manifold wisdom, every state-
> ment indicating that a prior event is for the purpose of causing
> a subsequent event, every mention of an eternal, all-embracing
> plan contributes to a teleological and therefore supralapsarian
> view of God's control of history. In this light, Ephesians 3:10
> clearly does not stand alone.[23]

CONTRIBUTION #3:
A SOLUTION TO THE PROBLEM OF EVIL

A frequent argument posed against orthodox Christianity is the so-called "problem of evil" (POE). The argument asserts that the Christian worldview is not logically valid, as it cannot consistently and simultaneously believe the following three doctrines: (1) God is loving, (2) God is omnipotent (all-powerful), and (3) there is evil in the world. It is argued that acceptance of any two of these doctrines requires a denial of the third. Yet Christians hold to all three simultaneously. Hence, a problem. Are Christians being illogical? Are their doctrines inconsistent?

Naturally, Gordon Clark, in his desire for a systematic (and non-paradoxical) Christianity, addressed this supposed problem. In his chapter "God and Evil" in *Religion, Reason, and Revelation* (1961), he presented an answer to the POE consistent with Reformed theology and the *Westminster Confession of Faith*.

A common Christian answer is to assume God gave man free will which man then exercised for evil (preceded by Satan's similar choice). This answer is intended to protect God from charges of creating evil by putting the responsibility on man and angels. However, according to Clark, it only moves the issue one step further. It begs the question: why does God allow there to be evil? Permission, Clark argued, only makes sense where there is a force independent of the actor. The idea of permission is inconsistent with

---

23. Clark, "First Lessons in Theology," chapter 4. Note: This exact quote is reproduced in Clark, *Ephesians*, 112.

a sovereign, omnipotent God who has no force independent of him. Clark pointed to John Calvin as supporting the same position.[24]

Closely related to the idea of permission is the idea that man has "free will"—the ability to choose between two incompatible actions, or said another way, that the will is ultimately free from any outside factor or influence. Clark rejected the idea of free will but accepted "free agency"—that man's will is free from outside forces in the world, but not free from God. Thus man makes choices as he is a free agent, but these choices are only made within God's will or plan. Clark took a compatibilistic view between the free agent's ability to choose and the deterministic necessity of that choice occurring as God has willed it. He wrote, "A choice is still a deliberate volition even if it could not have been different."[25]

Clark's view was that God is the cause of all things; therefore, God is the cause of evil. Clark pulled no punches, saying, "Let it be unequivocally said that this view certainly makes God the cause of sin. *God is the sole ultimate cause of everything* [emphasis added]. There is absolutely nothing independent of him. He alone is the eternal being. He alone is omnipotent. He alone is sovereign."[26] Clark found support for this doctrine in the *Westminster Confession of Faith* which states that God ordains whatsoever comes to pass and foreordained even the means by which everything is accomplished.[27] Yet while God is the ultimate *cause* of sin, He is not the *author* of sin. The author is the immediate cause, whereas God is only the ultimate cause of sin.

Man's responsibility, Clark argued, does not derive from free will but from God's sanction. Man is responsible for his actions, not because he has the ability to choose otherwise (he does not), but because God set punishments for those actions.

---

24. "Here they have recourse to the distinction between will and permission. By this they would maintain that the wicked perish because God permits it, not because he so wills. But why shall we say 'permission' unless it is because God so wills? Still, it is not in itself likely that man brought destruction upon himself through himself, by God's mere permission and without any ordaining. As if God did not establish the condition in which he wills the chief of his creatures to be! I shall not hesitate, then, simply to confess with Augustine that 'the will of God is the necessity of things,' and that what he has willed will of necessity come to pass."—Calvin's Institutes (III, xxiii, 8 & II, iv., 3).

25. Clark, *Religion, Reason, and Revelation*, 229.

26. Ibid., 238.

27. WCF, Chapter III, Part I, "God from all eternity did, by the most wise and holy counsel of his own will, freely and unchangeably ordain whatsoever comes to pass," and Part VI, "As God has appointed the elect unto glory, so has he, by the eternal and most free purpose of his will, foreordained all the means thereunto."

God, on the other hand, cannot sin. Whatever God decrees is right simply because he decrees it. Whatever God does is just. What he commands men to do or not to do is similarly just or not just. Clark wrote, "God is neither responsible nor sinful, even though he is the only ultimate cause of everything. He is not sinful because in the first place whatever God does is just and right. It is just and right simply in virtue of the fact that he does it. *Justice or Righteousness is not a standard external to God* to which God is obligated to submit. Righteousness is what God does."[28]

So why is there evil in a world created and sustained by a loving, omnipotent God? Almost hidden in Clark's writing on God and evil is his answer. In his refutation of a non-Christian professor and speaking of that professor's view Clark wrote, "To suppose that God created the good and the evil for his own glory, to bestow his love on the good and his wrath on the evil is [in the view of the non-Christian] to lower God to the level of the most degenerate human tyrant." This is Clark's answer, and it is a biblical one. God created the good and the evil for his own glory, to bestow love on the good and wrath on the evil. This doctrine likely came from Paul's letter to the Romans where Paul wrote, "What if God, desiring to show his wrath and to make known his power, has endured with much patience vessels of wrath prepared for destruction, in order to make known the riches of his glory for vessels of mercy, which he has prepared beforehand for glory?" (Romans 9:22–23).

CONTRIBUTION #4:
ARGUMENTS FOR A RETURN TO TRADITIONAL LOGIC

In *History of Western Philosophy and Theology*, John Frame, speaking of Clark's views on logic, wrote,

> He believed that God's mind included, not merely logic in general or the law of noncontradiction, but a specific system of logic. But who was right? Aristotle or [Bertrand] Russell? Or is there a third alternative? In a post-lecture discussion, Clark did not hesitate to answer the question: Aristotle was right and Russell was wrong. But how can we be sure of that? Clark said he had written a paper that established Aristotle's position. But how can we be sure that Clark's paper is correct? Clark said, in effect, well, if my paper is not correct, then there is no possibility of coherent thought or intelligible discourse.[29]

28. Clark, *Religion, Reason, and Revelation*, 240.
29. Frame, *History of Western Philosophy and Theology*, 529.

Although the paper of Clark's which Frame referenced does not seem to be extant, Clark addressed the same topics in a chapter on Bertrand Russell in his book *Language and Theology*, published in 1980, and again more thoroughly in the book *Logic*, published in 1985. To understand Clark's position, one must first understand some of the history of logic and in particular the terms *subalternation* and *existential import*.

Traditional logic, as exemplified by Aristotle, holds that there are twenty-four valid syllogisms, or forms of logical argumentation.[30] The theory can be diagrammed well with the square of opposition.

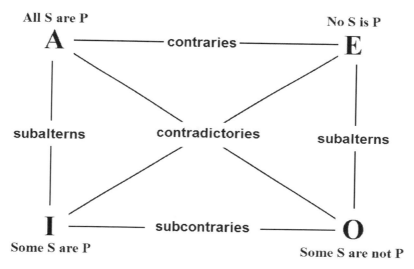

Square of Opposition

To understand the terms of the square of opposition, a table is helpful:

Letter Designation	Description	Subject/Predicate Relationship
A	Universal Affirmative	All S are P
I	Particular Affirmative	Some S are P
E	Universal Negative	No S is P
O	Particular Negative	Some S are not P

30. The twenty-four valid syllogisms are labeled as: AAA-1, EAE-1, AII-1, EIO-1, EAE-2, EIO-2, AEE-2, AOO-2, IAI-3, AII-3, OAO-3, EIO-3, AEE-4, IAI-4, EIO-4, AAI-1, EAO-1, AEO-2, EAO-2, AAI-3, EAO-3, AEO-4, EAO-4, and AAI-4.

In the square of opposition, there are two relations which are called subalterns. The first subaltern is the immediate inference between A and I, a syllogism of the type:

"All S are P, therefore Some S is P."

The second subaltern is the immediate inference between O and E, a syllogism of the type:

"No S is P, therefore Some S are not P."

Employing either of these syllogisms is called subalternation.

Working toward Clark's solution requires an understanding of subalternation and another aspect of traditional logic called existential import. Existential import is the concept that a universal proposition implies the existence of that proposition's subject. Given existential import, subalternation is valid. For example, under existential import, the proposition "All parakeets are blue" implies the existence of parakeets, and thus affirms the validity of the subaltern, "Some parakeets are blue."

However, starting in the late nineteenth century with the philosopher Franz Brentano, a new theory arose which denied the validity of existential import.[31] According to this new theory, called "modern logic," universal propositions have no existential import—that is, they do not imply the existence of the subject, and therefore they do not imply the subalternate particular propositions. The form of argument of modern logic is, for example, that "All lions in the room next door have sharp teeth" does not mean that "some lions in the room next door have sharp teeth" because there might be no lions at all.

Bertrand Russell is the most well-known proponent of modern logic.[32] As such, modern logic has become synonymous with his name. Like all proponents of modern logic, Russell denied existential import, and therefore denied the validity of subalternation. This left Russell with fifteen valid syllogisms instead of the twenty-four of Aristotle.[33] Clark explained Russell's involvement in the development of modern logic:

> In order to avoid all the ambiguities of ordinary English, and in order to solve some logical puzzles which he did not think otherwise soluble, Bertrand Russell proposed a completely symbolic, artificial language. While his ideal proposal was rejected even by his immediate disciple, Ludwig Wittgenstein,

31. Brentano, *Psychology from an Empirical Standpoint,* ii, ch. 7.

32. Russell and MacColl, "The Existential Import of Propositions," 398–402.

33. Removing the nine "conditionally valid" syllogisms from traditional logic, modern logic holds to the validity of fifteen syllogisms labeled as: AAA-1, EAE-1, AII-1, EIO-1, EAE-2, EIO-2, AEE-2, AOO-2, IAI-3, AII-3, OAO-3, EIO-3, AEE-4, IAI-4, and EIO-4.

his symbolism for logic has become standard. He reduced the sentence "All Athenians are Greek," not merely to A(ab), but further to (a<b); that is to say, class *a* is included in class *b*. If this definition is accepted, modern symbolic logic follows without a hitch. Its conclusions follow necessarily.[34]

Nearly all logicians have come to accept Russell's view. Clark, however, argued in favor of Aristotle's traditional logic, believing modern logic to be in error. How then do we decide between the two theories of logic? Back to Frame's question: Who was right? Aristotle or Russell? Or is there a third alternative?

In arguing for his choice of the axiom of revelation over and above other philosophical axioms, Clark held that the only way to evaluate axioms is to examine the implications which respectively follow from each of them.[35] Similarly, in the field of logic also, Clark held that the explanatory ability of each coherent system is the basis on which they can be compared, and the greater chosen. He wrote, "Since definitions are not deductions, they can only be judged by their consequences; and the consequences of modern symbolic logic are a restricted sub-system of logic. Aristotelian logic has the nineteen syllogisms that modern logic has, but it also has five more. Surely, if at all possible, it is better to have a less restricted system than merely a sub-set."[36] And again, "Modern logic has failed to put Aristotelian logic into symbolic form. Its language cannot say as much as ordinary language can."[37]

According to Clark, not only is modern logic inferior to traditional logic, but it also fails to accurately represent actual language. Clark wrote,

> I now assert that Russell made a great blunder, not in his deductions, but in his definition of the term *All*. Remember, he explained *All a is b as a is included in b*. However obvious Russell's definition seems, and it seems so to the immense majority of logicians, it is not a correct analysis of the English word *All*."[38]

34. Clark, *Logic*, 81.

35. "Axioms, whatever they may be and in whatever subject they are used, are never deduced from more original principles. They are always tested in another way. . . . We can judge the acceptability of an axiom only by its success in producing a system. . . . By the systems they produce, axioms must be judged."—Clark, *Introduction to Christian Philosophy*, 60.

36. Clark, *Logic*, 82.

37. Clark, *Language and Theology*, 23.

38. Clark, *In Defense of Theology*, 51.

For those who want to explore it further, Clark's argument in longer form is as follows:

> One is the class that contains all classes. Zero is the class that contains nothing. Now, since zero is a class, a class used extensively in modern logic, and since one is the class that contains all classes, it follows that (o<i), that is, zero is contained in one. Now try to follow carefully. Since on Russell's view (a<b) defines "All *a* is *b*," then on Russell's view (o<i) means "All zero is one." But it cannot mean this. When we say, in English, that "All dogs are animals," we mean that every dog is an animal. Hence, if we say with Russell that All zero is one, we would mean that every zero, every class that contains nothing, is a one, a class that contains all classes. Or to make it still clearer, since zero not only means an empty or null class, but also a false proposition, (o<i) would mean, All false statements are true. Let it be true that zero is included in one: Since zero is a class, and since one is the class that contains all classes, (o<i) must be true. But it is not the definition of *All*. Zero is included in one, but it is false to say, "All zero is one." Hence Russell's definition of *All* is faulty, and his completely valid deductions from his faulty definition have nothing to do with *All*, *Some*, or subalternation.[39]

Note especially the conclusion Clark reaches regarding Russell's view: it would mean all false statements are true. This is the answer to Frame. It shows why Russell's view presents "no possibility of coherent thought or intelligible discourse."[40] Thus, Russell's view cannot compete with traditional logic. There is only one valid logic known, and that is Aristotle's traditional logic.

---

39. Ibid., 82–83.

40. Clark brings forth essentially the same arguments in *Language and Theology*. He wrote, "The source of the flaw is the initial definition. If (all a is b) means (a is included in b), subordination cannot be defended. But should not this result have prompted the logician to find a formula for all that would have expressed the English meaning? After all, (a<b) is an arbitrary choice. . . . When Aristotle said all the a's are b's he meant that every a is a b. But when Russell asserts, as the definition of all, that (o<i), he cannot say that every zero is a one. This means that Russell's definition of all does not reproduce the English meaning of all."—Clark, *Language and Theology*, 24.

Chapter 11

"Clark's Boys"

"Dr. Clark was heartbroken that his 'boys' were turning in the wrong direction."
—A FRIEND[1]

IN A BIOGRAPHY OF Clark's Wheaton College student Edward Carnell, *The Making and Unmaking of an Evangelical Mind* by Rudolph Nelson, there is a telling recollection from a classmate of a scene from their college days:

> I recall on one occasion, following a particularly lively session with Clark, that we trooped out together across the campus. Clark (who, I suppose, was about five feet seven inches in height) was in the lead. Ed, who may have been five-ten or eleven, fell in behind Clark, walking in his footsteps with Paul Jewett next in step, etc. The order may not have been just so, but at least there were four or five of us imitating Clark's gait and manner like goslings following their mother goose.[2]

True to form, like nature's goslings, many of Clark's students followed theologically in the ways of their teacher. But others, in time, came to reject Clark's teaching, specifically on the doctrine of biblical inerrancy, even wandering astray on paths which led away from historic Christianity.

---

1. A letter to the author from a close contact of Paul Jewett who prefers anonymity, 10 February 2014.
2. Nelson, *The Making and Unmaking of an Evangelical Mind*, 37.

From among Clark's students at Wheaton College came a number of prominent leaders in American Christianity including Harold Lindsell (class of 1938), Carl F. H. Henry (class of 1938 and M.A. 1941), Edmund Clowney (class of 1939), Edward J. Carnell (class of 1941), and Paul King Jewett (class of 1941). Though Clark had no biological sons, these Wheaton students were "Clark's boys." This chapter tells the story of how their individual relationships with Clark influenced them during their college days and on into the inerrancy controversy that embroiled American evangelicals in the middle of the twentieth century.

Through his boys, Clark's sphere of influence was extended beyond his own classroom and books. Ronald Nash wrote, "It is important to remember that much of Clark's important work occurred during the deep theological valley that marked the lowest point in the fortunes of American fundamentalism. It is also important to note that evangelicalism was led out of that pit largely through the efforts of Clark and two of his philosophy students at Wheaton College, Carl Henry and E. J. Carnell."[3] The importance of these two students is also noted by Gary Dorrien in *The Remaking of Evangelical Theology*: "The Modern origins of a post-conservative evangelicalism can be traced to a cluster of thinkers who began the process of rethinking evangelicalism a half century ago. In the mid-1940s Carl F. H. Henry and Edward J. Carnell committed themselves to the task of reforming American Fundamentalism."[4]

CLARK'S BOYS AT WESTMINSTER AND HARVARD

Edward Carnell (1919–1967), Edmund Clowney (1917–2005), and Paul King Jewett (1920–1991) were among the many students Clark influenced to attend Westminster Theological Seminary following their respective graduations from Wheaton. While at Wheaton each was greatly influenced by Clark's teaching. Carnell, who had been a mediocre student in high school, came to Wheaton as a freshman in 1937, the same year Gordon Clark began teaching there, and with the single exception of his performance in Clark's philosophy courses, in which he received high marks, his academic performance at Wheaton remained unremarkable. According to Carnell's biographer, "The evidence from his Wheaton transcript clearly indicates it was philosophy that captured his mind." Because of this newfound interest, nurtured by Clark, Carnell chose philosophy as his major.[5]

3. Nash, "Clark and Contemporary Thought," 87.
4. Dorrien, *The Remaking of Evangelical Theology*, 6–7.
5. Nelson, *The Making and Unmaking of an Evangelical Mind*, 36.

Jewett was also impressed by Clark. During Clark's struggles with the administration of the college in 1942, Jewett wrote a letter to the board of trustees in support of Clark. Although Jewett's letter is not extant, a response from a member of the board of trustees, Dr. David Otis Fuller, shows that Jewett had "gathered together some eight or ten testimonies in favor of Dr. Clark and sent them to me trying to prejudice me instead of leaving it to the Lord."[6] Jewett had taken to Clark's view of predestination so enthusiastically that he was warned twice on the topic by Dr. Fuller: "Don't ride hobbies."[7]

Clowney was likewise influenced significantly by Clark's philosophy courses. According to Clowney's son David, "To the best of my recollection, he [Edmund] attended a Presbyterian church with my grandparents. The church, I think, was more generally evangelical and dispensationalist than anything else, though my grandfather was a Calvinist. Dad, if I remember what he told me, felt comfortable with what he was getting from that church until he studied with Clark."[8]

In studying first at Wheaton and then at Westminster, these students were of a small but fortunate group to have had the privilege to study under both Gordon Clark and Cornelius Van Til, two of the most prominent Reformed Christian philosophers of the era.

Following their studies at Westminster, Carnell and Jewett enrolled at Harvard. Carnell was a rising star of the evangelical world. In fact, he enrolled at both Harvard University and Boston College and earned doctoral degrees from both schools, a Th.D. from Harvard and a PhD from Boston College. His education, however, was not handed to him on a silver platter. Without financial backing from his parents (his father was a minister and not a wealthy man) he needed to work his way through college to pay for it. At Wheaton he worked nearly full-time in the cafeteria. As he progressed to higher educational degrees he studied more hours and put himself under extreme pressure to succeed. These efforts paid off academically but were a detriment to his health. During his doctoral studies, Carnell's aggressive nature drove him to write *An Introduction to Christian Apologetics* for which he won a $5,000 book prize from Eerdmans Publishing. But while at Harvard he began to feel that, despite his years with Clark and Van Til, he still had no answers to some of the major objections against Christianity.

Carnell's classmate Paul Jewett wrote a critical PhD dissertation at Harvard on the neo-orthodox theologian Emil Brunner. According to D.

6. David Otis Fuller to Paul Jewett, 24 July 1942, Wheaton Archives.
7. Ibid.
8. David Clowney, e-mail to the author, 8 April 2014.

Clair Davis, a student of Clark's at Butler University in 1951–1952, Clark appreciated the comprehensiveness and fairness of Jewett's treatment and subsequently decided to use Jewett's dissertation on Brunner for his philosophy of religion course.[9] The dissertation was published by the pro-inerrancy Evangelical Theological Society in 1954 as *Emil Brunner's Concept of Revelation* and was dedicated to "Gordon H. Clark, Teacher and Friend."[10]

CLARK'S BOYS REUNITED AS FACULTY AT FULLER SEMINARY

Though graduated from college, many of Clark's boys would not remain geographically separate for long as they reunited as faculty at Fuller Seminary in the 1950s. In 1947 the wealthy radio evangelist Charles Fuller founded Fuller Seminary with funds raised from his *Old Fashioned Revival Hour*, a nationally syndicated radio program. Clark's former Wheaton student Carl F. H. Henry (1913–2003) was one of the first members recruited to the faculty of the new seminary. After graduating from Wheaton, Henry had completed a doctorate at Northern Baptist Theological Seminary near Chicago and was on his way to completing a PhD at Boston University. After accepting the job at Fuller Seminary, Henry recommended to Charles Fuller that his former Wheaton colleague and fellow Clark student Harold Lindsell (1913–1998) be included on the new staff. Following graduation from Wheaton College, Lindsell had earned degrees from both UC Berkeley and NYU. At Fuller, Lindsell was chosen to be the registrar and acting professor of missions while Henry became the acting dean. Edward Carnell arrived at Fuller a year later to teach apologetics and systematics, bringing the number of former Clark students teaching at Fuller to three.[11]

The impact of Clark on Henry is shown in Bob E. Patterson's biography on Carl Henry titled *Makers of the Modern Mind*. Patterson wrote, "Henry's guiding instrument for separating truth from error is the law of noncontradiction. He freely admits that he was drawn to this position by Gordon Clark, an evangelical philosopher under whom he studied at Wheaton."[12]

The hiring of these highly educated young scholars to Fuller Seminary was an attempt to bring greater intellectual reputability to the seminary and to mimic, in some respects, Princeton Seminary as it was prior to its collapse into modernism. For support of this contention, one need only look

9. Dr. D. Clair Davis, e-mail to the author, 11 August 2014.

10. Jewett, *Emil Brunner's Concept of Revelation*.

11. Marsden, *Reforming Fundamentalism* 26–27, 54, 59, 97.

12. Patterson, *Carl F. H. Henry: Makers of the Modern Theological Mind*, 62–63.

to Gary Dorrien's *The Remaking of Evangelical Theology* where he writes, "To Ockenga and most of the faculty he hired, including Henry and Carnell, the ideal of a reformed fundamentalism was Old Princeton."[13] Part of this Princeton tradition was the acceptance of the doctrine of biblical inerrancy. The story of Fuller Seminary, including the accounts of Clark's boys who taught there, is a story of a battle over this doctrine. But while Fuller Seminary did attempt to mimic Princeton, it also sought to avoid duplicating the strong reformed distinctiveness of Princeton's conservative heir, Westminster Seminary.

Carnell hoped that Clark would also come to teach at Fuller Seminary. He wrote to Clark for that purpose saying, "I am still deeply anxious to see you with us here, and I trust that during this time of interim between now and the Payton Lectures you will feel the call more and more strongly to be with us."[14] Although Clark never accepted a position at Fuller, he visited in 1951 to give the Payton Lectures, named after the parents-in-law of the seminary president. These lectures were published the following year as *A Christian View of Men and Things.*[15]

CLARK'S BOYS AND THE BEGINNINGS OF NEO-EVANGELICALISM

Around the same time as the founding of Fuller Seminary, a new movement emerged called neo-evangelicalism of which a number Clark's students were seen as the leaders of. The term itself was coined in 1947 by Harold Ockenga (1905–1985), the pastor of Park Street Church in Boston and the first president of Fuller Seminary.[16] Along with Ockenga, former Clark student's Carl Henry and Edward Carnell have been included among the ranks of neo-evangelicals. The neo-evangelicals sought to rid themselves of the embarrassing fundamentalist label and its perceived anti-intellectualism and separatism. Carnell, for one, had been raised by a fundamentalist pastor, but

13. Dorrien, *The Remaking of Evangelical Theology*, 47.

14. EJC to GHC, 4 May 1950, Fuller Seminary Archives, 4/27.

15. Although Clark never taught at Fuller Seminary, during the 1960s he taught at the Winona Lake School of Theology, where President John Huffman was in discussions with Fuller to merge institutes. At one point Winona Lake was slated to be a summer school location for Fuller students. Credits completed at Winona Lake would be transferrable to Fuller. However, due to the inerrancy controversy, in which Winona Lake remained conservative, Huffman terminated the merger. See: Marsden, *Reforming Fundamentalism*, 226, 227.

16. Lightner, *Neo-Evangelicalism*, 5.

came to reject that faith as legalistic and anti-intellectual, and embraced the neo-evangelical movement.[17]

Neo-evangelicalism can be seen as a mixture of American fundamentalism and Reformed orthodoxy. Henry, Carnell, and Jewett had brought their fundamentalist convictions to Wheaton where they encountered Clark's Reformed theology and intellectualism. Seeking to escape the stigma of fundamentalist anti-intellectualism and gain legitimacy, the neo-evangelicals adopted certain elements of Reformed thought, including a greater acceptance of millennial differences and some aspects of Clark's presuppositionalism. They sought to move past the fundamentalist-modernist divide and provide positive formulations of Christianity rather than focus on critiques of either the fundamentalists or the modernists.

Not all of the founders of the neo-evangelical movement, however, were students of Clark. Bernard Ramm and Harold Ockenga were prominent neo-evangelicals who never studied under Clark. Yet like Carnell, Lindsell, and Henry, they all had fundamentalist (and Baptist) backgrounds, not discovering Reformed theology until their college days. The leader of the movement, Billy Graham, although he was one of Clark's former students at Wheaton, never embraced Clark's distinctive theological views.

Clark himself was never a neo-evangelical, and the neo-evangelicals never fully embraced the Reformed orthodoxy he held. Yet Clark was a substantial force behind the emergence of the movement. Ronald Nash wrote, "This writer has noticed that lately Clark's name has been left out in discussions of neo-evangelicalism. Nevertheless, he was one of its 'founding fathers' and still represents its basic position."[18] In that Clark represented the basic position is only true to the extent that the neo-evangelicals embraced Reformed theology. Despite being associated with neo-evangelicalism by some, Clark opposed much of its theology. He believed neo-evangelicals were inconsistent in that they did not accept the *system* of faith of the *Westminster Confession of Faith*. And Clark saw little value in disjointed doctrines.

Clark influenced the neo-evangelicals towards the Reformed faith in doctrines such as predestination and biblical inerrancy, but he had less success in converting them into baby-baptizing Presbyterians supportive of elder-led church governance. According to Christian historian George Marsden (b. 1939), "Clark's Wheaton protégés who later went to Fuller proved to be more moderate ecclesiastically than their Orthodox Presbyterian mentor,

17. Nelson, *The Making and Unmaking of an Evangelical Mind*, 1988.
18. Nash, *The New Evangelicalism*, 17.

though they shared most of his concerns."[19] They added Clark's intellectual approach to their Christianity but remained fundamentalist Baptists rather than embracing the entire Reformed heritage Clark so admired. Henry and Carnell never departed from the Baptist convictions they carried into college, and Lindsell, in fact, left the Presbyterian church and was ordained a Baptist minister in 1944.

The most noticeable divergence, however, began as some neo-evangelicals drifted away from their commitment to the doctrine of biblical inerrancy. In place of biblical inerrancy, some of them shifted towards the position that the Bible was true in matters of faith and practice, but was not necessarily true in matters of science and history. Among those who would accept this position were Jewett and Bernard Ramm. Henry and Lindsell, on the other hand, held to inerrancy. Carnell seemed to attempt to straddle the fence, as will be seen later in this chapter. Clark, a scriptural inerrantist, felt alienated by the efforts of those who wanted to limit scriptural authority to matters of faith. This sense of alienation was the primary cause of rifts between Clark and his former students, Jewett and Carnell.

CLARK'S BOYS: REJECTING INERRANCY

From the early days of Fuller Seminary, Harold Ockenga, while actively ministering at Boston's well-known Park Street Church, had served as the president *in absentia*. He had initially planned on relocating to the seminary full-time but was ultimately unwilling to leave his pastorate. Finally, in 1954, after having waited seven years, Fuller Seminary decided to move on without Ockenga and, after an aggressive search, chose Edward Carnell as president. Carnell wrote to his old mentor Clark explaining his reasoning for accepting the job. "To see this school fall into the hands of those who would let it develop into a mediocre, fundamentalist institution, would be more than I could stand."[20] Carl Henry was disappointed by the choice, thinking that as he was older and generally a better leader, that he would have been chosen before Carnell.[21] Henry, a few years later, while working for *Christianity Today*, may still have been upset at the choice of Carnell as president. Henry wrote to Clark:

> Up to three weeks ago I was fully persuaded that I ought to return to Fuller this fall. Not even the happy result of the survey

19. Marsden, *Reforming Fundamentalism*, 46.
20. EJC to GHC, 25 October 1954, PCA Archives, 309/30.
21. Dorrien, *The Remaking of Evangelical Theology*, 76.

of readers, mentioned in a recent note, outweighed that inclination. In the meantime Carnell offered me a third year of leave, and I have somewhat the feeling that he would be more happy if I were to stay here than to return there. I do not think I have ever had a letter from an administrator like the last one I had from him, throbbing with somewhat of a messiah-complex.[22]

As president, Carnell hired Paul Jewett in 1955 to fill Carnell's former position as a professor of systematic theology. Jewett not only joined Fuller, but he also joined the neo-evangelical camp and rejected biblical inerrancy. Lindsell, who remained a stalwart for inerrancy his entire life, later wrote of him, "More recently Paul King Jewett . . . has taken the next step away from a trustworthy Scripture. The seminary statement of faith proclaims a belief in an infallible Bible in matters having to do with faith and practice. But Dr. Jewett now says that it is defective in at least one area having to do with faith and practice."[23] In *Man as Male and Female*, Jewett wrote that the apostle Paul's patriarchal view of women in the church is in error.[24] As Jewett held that at least one biblical doctrine was wrong, he therefore held that the Bible was not inerrant.

Whereas Clark was solidifying his already stalwart opinion of the Bible's inerrancy and helping found the Evangelical Theological Society for just that purpose, the neo-evangelicals including Carnell and Jewett were drifting slowly away from a commitment to the doctrine. Clark suspected Carnell's drift as early as 1953 when he wrote to Carnell saying, "You say you have not scuttled the Reformation view of Inspiration. Then how is it that you assert that the Psalmist told a lie in his teaching. Where in the Reformation view do you get the distinction between doctrinal and non-doctrinal passages. Paul says all scripture is profitable . . . for doctrine."[25]

Although Clark was certainly upset with Carnell for his weak stance on inerrancy, Clark was livid when Carnell critiqued Clark's hero, J. Gresham Machen. In *The Case for Orthodox Theology*, Carnell wrote, "While Machen was a foe of the fundamentalist movement, he was a friend of the fundamentalist mentality, for he took an absolute stand on a relative issue, and the

22. CFHH to GHC, Feb 1958, BGC Archives, Wheaton College, CN8, 15–12.

23. Lindsell, *The Battle for the Bible*, 117.

24. "Paul [the apostle] is not only basing his argument exclusively on the second creation narrative, but is assuming the traditional rabbinic understanding of that narrative whereby the order of their creation is made to yield the primacy of the man over the woman. Is this rabbinic understanding of Genesis 2:18f. correct? We do not think that it is."—Jewett, *MAN as Male and Female*, 119.

25. GHC to EJC, 31 March 1953, PCA Archives, 309/30.

wrong issue at that."[26] Also, "Machen was so fixed on the evil of modernism that he did not see the evil of anarchy."[27] In response to these critiques of Machen, Clark wrote to Henry in 1959, "As for Carnell, someone ought to tell him off. He has now taken to distorting the facts. He rebukes Machen for having left the church. When Carnell was a student, he knew quite well that Machen was tried in ecclesiastical court, denied the elementary justice of presenting his defense, and excommunicated. Machen tried to stay in the church; the church put him out. Now Carnell distorts the facts, and apparently sympathizes with the injustice."[28] Clark continued to suspect Carnell's theology. He wrote again to Henry in 1960, "By this time I find it hard to classify Carnell as an evangelical. Is he not pretty totally neo-orthodox?"[29]

Jewett came out against biblical inerrancy as well. He wrote, "Our all important Protestant conviction of biblical authority needs revitalizing."[30] Clark viewed the departure of Carnell and Jewett from this tenet as a sign of the downfall of their faith. Clark's concern for these men took a toll on him. A close contact of Paul Jewett interviewed for this biography summarized the ordeal well:

> After Wheaton, Paul went to Westminster Seminary and we felt that a change was taking place in his beliefs about this time. He wrote his master's thesis on paedobaptism and won a scholarship to go abroad to study under Barth and Brunner. Things were never the same after that. Dr. Clark was "heartbroken" that his "boys" were turning in the wrong direction. The inerrancy of the Scriptures was the central thing being talked about at the time and Paul's position was not our position. This was difficult for us to understand.[31]

Back at Fuller, accepting the presidency proved a mistake for Carnell. Truly, he was a scholar, not an administrator. His driven nature and desire to see the seminary go the direction he chose led him to accept the position. However, in 1959, after only four and a half years as president, with his health in decline and with the seminary struggling financially under his

---

26. Carnell, *The Case for Orthodox Theology*, 115. See also: Nelson, *The Making and Unmaking of an Evangelical Mind*, 112.

27. Carnell, *The Case for Orthodox Theology*, 115.

28. GHC to CFHH, 5 October 1959, records of *Christianity Today*, BGC Archives, Wheaton College, CN8, 15–12.

29. GHC to CFHH, 30 January 1960, records of *Christianity Today*, BGC Archives, Wheaton College, CN8, 15–12.

30. Jewett, "Biblical authority a crucial issue in Protestantism," 9.

31. Letter to the author from a close contact of Paul Jewett who prefers anonymity, 10 February 2014.

leadership, Carnell stepped down. After a sabbatical he returned to Fuller as a professor of ethics.

The friction between Clark and Carnell came to a head in 1962 when Karl Barth, the famous Swiss theologian, came to speak in America for the first and only time. Chicago was one of the two locations at which Barth spoke, and Clark and Carnell were sure to be there. Carnell was one of six panel members chosen to pose questions to Barth. Henry, who had been the editor of *Christianity Today* since leaving Fuller Seminary in 1956, was unable to attend the speech due to previously scheduled business in Canada.[32] In his place, Henry hired Clark to be the field correspondent for the magazine.[33] Clark had taken the preceding year as a sabbatical from Butler University to write a book titled *Karl Barth's Theological Method*. Thus Clark knew Barth's theology as well as anyone. Clark saw the inevitable direction Barth's theology would go—the rejection of the central tenet of biblical inerrancy. It was Clark's goal to warn others, through his book, of what he saw as Barth's pernicious teachings.

What happened at the Barth event to affect Clark and Carnell's relationship can perhaps be best shown in Clark's report for *Christianity Today*. Clark felt that Carnell should have pressed the issue with Barth regarding the standard by which the Bible should be judged. Although Carnell would later claim to hold to inerrancy, Clark was extremely upset with Carnell due to the latter's failure to press Barth with more difficult questions. Carnell's position created a permanent rift between Clark and Carnell.[34] Recalling Carnell's questioning of Barth, Clark wrote:

> "How does Dr. Barth," asks Carnell, "harmonize his appeal to Scripture as an objective Word of God with his admission that Scripture is sullied by errors, theological as well as historical or factual?" Carnell confessed parenthetically that, "this is a problem for me, too." . . . Barth's answer does not seem to meet the question. He asserted that the Bible is a fitting instrument to point men to God, who alone is infallible. The Bible is a human document and not sinless as Christ was. Then a large part of the overflow audience—possibly 500 were standing in the aisles or sitting on the stone floor—applauded Barth's assertion that there are "contradictions and errors" in the Bible. After and possibly because of this expression of hostility, Carnell professed to be

---

32. CFHH to GHC, 11 December 1961, records of *Christianity Today*, BCG Archives, Wheaton College, CN8, 15–13.

33. CFHH to GHC, 15 January 1962, records of *Christianity Today*, BGC Archives, Wheaton College, CN8, 15–13.

34. Rudolph, "A Truly Great and Brilliant Friend," 103.

satisfied and did not press the matter of a non-biblical criterion by which to judge what is a theological error in the Bible.[35] [36]

According to theologian Richard Mouw (b. 1940), who was sitting next to Clark in the audience, upon Carnell's admission "This is a problem for me too," Clark "muttered something like 'betrayal!'"[37]

Carnell wrote an article for *The Christian Century* discussing his thoughts on the Barth event. In the article, Carnell made a number of criticisms of Barth, but, more importantly to the point of Carnell's relationship with Clark, he distanced himself from the critiques of Barth that the fundamentalists had made. Carnell wrote, "I suffered some disappointments in my encounter with Barth. But if extreme fundamentalists think I am going to join their 'holy war' against Barth, they are sadly mistaken. I am convinced that Barth is an inconsistent evangelical rather than an inconsistent liberal." Carnell's criticism was, in fact, directed not so much toward Gordon Clark as it was toward Cornelius Van Til, who had often critiqued Barth in print. Carnell wrote, "I am utterly ashamed of the manner in which extreme fundamentalists in America continue to attack Barth. I felt actual physical pain when I read in *Time* magazine that Cornelius Van Til, one of my former professors, had said Barthianism is more hostile to the Reformers than is Roman Catholicism."[38]

Following the Barth event, Clark wrote to Henry, "I had breakfast with Carnell twice. Pleasant. His wife is lovely. But I took Carnell aside to tell him face to face that I was greatly disappointed in him, particularly about his distortion of Machen's case. I also noted in my report to you that Carnell had said he shares the problem of harmonizing the authority of Scripture with the errors in it. To me it is obvious that this problem can be shared

35. Clark, "Special Report: Encountering Barth in Chicago," 35–36. See also: Nelson, *The Making and Unmaking of an Evangelical Mind*, 188.

36. After hearing an audio recording of the Barth event, Nelson contested Clark's recollection that the audience's response was applause. Nelson rather called the response "a slight murmur." Clark described his memories of the event and the poor acoustics: "Barth never came to this country until 1962 when he spoke in the Rockefeller Chapel at the University of Chicago, and his lectures were awfully dull. I listened to them, I read some of them. And besides, the Rockefeller Chapel is a horrible place for anybody to speak in. The acoustics are impossible, and Barth has a strong German accent, and he gargled all the way down the nave, and it resounded from all sides. Of course, I was with the press, and I sat on the second row. I could hear him. I could even understand some of his words. But it's a terrible place to speak in. He lectured in English. I think I could have better understood it if he had lectured in German."—Clark, "Irrationalism," minute 32.

37. Dr. Richard Mouw, e-mail to the author, 29 November 2014.

38. Carnell, "Barth as Inconsistent Evangelical," 713–714.

only by one who has decided that there are errors in Scripture. I did not however, stress this inference in the news article. But Pelican [theologian Jaroslav Pelikan] publicly said to Carnell, upon this problem, 'Welcome to the club.'"[39]

Carnell had modified Clark's apologetic by adding an empirical justification to Clark's consistency approach, but it was the two men's disagreement on the question of biblical inerrancy that caused the rift. Rudolph Nelson writes in his biography of Carnell that Clark was mistaken about Carnell's approval of Barth, citing a professor at Fuller who argued that Carnell did, in fact, support inerrancy.[40] But regardless of whether or not Carnell was weak on Barth or not, he had been flirting with rejection of the doctrine of inerrancy for some time. For fundamentalists like Clark, this was about the worst possible theological crime a Christian could commit.

Lindsell defended Carnell against Clark's report in an editorial two issues later in *Christianity Today*. To correct that "Dr. Clark apparently was left with the impression that Dr. Carnell does not himself believe in an inerrant Scripture," he quoted a statement Carnell had made in the Fuller Seminary Chapel that "I [Carnell] want to make it as clear as the English language can put it, that I now believe and always have believed plenary inspiration of Scripture and the inerrancy of Scripture."[41]

Clark disputed Lindsell in a letter he wrote to Henry, "I was scrupulously accurate in my news report of Carnell at the Barth lectures. Lindsell has no leg to stand on, if he questions the truth of any of my sentences. In fact I leaned over backwards to be fair to Carnell."[42] In fact, Clark wrote a reply to Lindsell for Henry to use if necessary for *Christianity Today* saying,

> The precise point of my news report on the Barth lectures to which Dr. Lindsell objects is hard to ascertain. If he intends to imply that the report is inaccurate, I can only reassert that I believe every sentence of it is true. Yes, I made one guess. When Barth refused to answer Dr. Carnell's question, and when the audience expressed its hostility to biblical infallibility, I guessed that many a man might have concluded that it was useless to press such a question under those circumstances. That this was a guess, and was not an attribution of motives to Dr. Carnell was made clear by the word *perhaps*. If, as Dr. Lindsell now asserts, this was not the motivation, and Dr. Carnell did not continue

39. GHC to CFHH, 7 May 1962, BGC Archives, Wheaton College, CN8, 15–13.
40. Nelson, *The Making and Unmaking of an Evangelical Mind*, 11.
41. Lindsell, "Carnell on Scripture," 19–20.
42. GHC to CFHH, 18 May 1962, BGC Archives, Wheaton College, CN8, 15–13.

through lack of time, still every statement of my report in this connection remains true.[43]

L. Nelson Bell, Henry's boss, chose not to run Clark's letter, but commented, "For years I have feared that Carnell's pride in intellect had blunted his testimony at the place most needed. Should he leave Fuller watch out where he lands! Let us hope this episode will have shocked him into a clearer affirmation of his faith in liberal circles."[44]

By the time of the Barth event, Carnell was (according to Nelson) "a seriously disabled man."[45] In fact, Henry notified Clark of Carnell's condition prior to the event saying, "My last word, through Paul Jewett, is that he [Carnell] is confined and that only his wife has access to him, but perhaps he has taken a turn for the better."[46]

Clark continued to critique Carnell in letters he wrote to Henry. He wrote:

> Perhaps you surmize [sic] my own opinions of Carnell. I resent his misrepresentation of Machen; I resent his choosing Machen to criticize without a word of criticism of Machen's opposition; and I doubt that when Carnell resigned from ETS [The Evangelical Theological Society] and gave as a reason that he could not 'afford' to belong, the trouble was a matter of five dollars a year.[47]

Also, "My conclusion is that Carnell does not believe the infallibility of the Bible and that his principles allow anyone to reject anything."[48]

Carnell's relentless work habits had turned him into an insomniac, and in combating the disorder he became addicted to sleeping pills. In 1967 Carnell was scheduled to speak at a Roman Catholic conference. When he did not show up for his speech, a search found him dead in his hotel room from a (probably accidental) sleeping pill overdose. He was just forty-seven years of age.[49]

---

43. GHC to CFHH with enclosed reply to Dr. Lindsell, 18 May 1962, BGC Archives, Wheaton College.

44. L. Nelson Bell to CFHH, referred to in CFHH to GHC, 22 May 1962, BGC Archives, Wheaton College.

45. Nelson, *The Making and Unmaking of an Evangelical Mind*, 11.

46. CFHH to GHC, 19 March 1962, BGC Archives, Wheaton College, CN8, 15–13.

47. GHC to CFHH, 18 May 1962, BGC Archives, Wheaton College, CN8, 15–13.

48. GHC to CFHH, 16 September 1965, BGC Archives, Wheaton College, CN8, 15–13.

49. Nelson, *The Making and Unmaking of an Evangelical Mind*, 120.

CLARK'S BOYS: KEEPING INERRANCY

Whereas Carnell and Jewett each departed from Clark's view of biblical inerrancy, the three other students of Clark's from Wheaton—Carl Henry, Harold Lindsell, and Edmund Clowney—continued to believe in the inspiration
of Scripture and supported much of Clark's teaching. Lindsell, a stalwart
supporter of biblical inerrancy, was best known for his 1976 book *The Battle
for the Bible* in which he argued for the Bible's inerrancy and chronicled
the demise of the doctrine at Fuller Theological Seminary. Lindsell resigned
from Fuller Seminary in 1964 over his growing divergence from the seminary's increasingly liberal position on inerrancy. He then took a position
at *Christianity Today*, again following Carl F. H. Henry as he had done in
coming to Fuller. A letter from L. Nelson Bell of *Christianity Today* does
a fair job of summarizing Lindsell's history at Fuller: "He taught at Fuller,
then was Dean of Students, then Dean of the Faculty and Vice-President. As
a matter of fact he ran Fuller for nine years but left when things changed and
he could not control the situation. He stands unswervingly on the *complete*
inspiration of and authority of the Bible. He came to us as Associate Editor.
He and Carl were close personal friends."[50]

Clark also continued to have a positive relationship with Carl F. H.
Henry and wrote the introduction to Henry's *Remaking the Modern Mind*,
the same book Henry dedicated to Clark. Later, Henry penned the introduction to *The Philosophy of Gordon H. Clark: A Festschrift*. Henry notes Clark
in the preface of *God, Revelation, and Authority*, his six-volume magnum
opus completed in 1983. In it Henry acknowledged, "To no contemporary
do I owe a profounder debt, however, than to Gordon Clark, as numerous
index references will attest. Since the thirties when he taught me medieval
and modern philosophy at Wheaton, I have considered him the peer of
evangelical philosophers in identifying the logical inconsistencies that beset
non-evangelical alternatives and in exhibiting the intellectual superiority of
Christian theism."[51] Henry concluded the work by stating, "If we humans
say anything authentic about God, we can do so only on the basis of divine
self-revelation; all other God-talk is conjectural."

Clark's relationship with Henry is revealed in their correspondence
while Henry was editor of *Christianity Today*, as he frequently called upon
Clark to contribute articles. In fact, there are more extant letters between
Clark and Henry than between Clark and any other individual.[52] (This is

50. L. Nelson Bell, Executive Editor, to J. Howard Pew, 2 February 1968, files of
Christianity Today, BGC Archives, Wheaton College.

51. Henry, *God, Revelation, and Authority*, 10.

52. There are 240 extant letters with Henry. A total of 888 Clark letters were

largely because these items and records of *Christianity Today* have been preserved at the Billy Graham Center Archives at Wheaton College.)

Another former Clark student who maintained his belief in the inerrancy of Scripture was Edmund Clowney. Within the Orthodox Presbyterian Church, Clowney was known to support Clark during Clark's ordination controversy. Clowney had even included his name on a protest in support of Floyd Hamilton[53] and on a minority report supporting Clark at the 1948 General Assembly.[54] OPC historian Charles Dennison, himself opposed to Clark's apologetics, wrote that Edmund Clowney was a man whose "stand was disappointing to many in the Van Til/Clark debate."[55] Clowney continued his support for Clark at Westminster Theological Seminary, where he became upset whenever someone called Clark a rationalist.[56]

Clowney graduated from Westminster Theological Seminary and was hired there in 1952 as professor of Practical Theology. He later became the first president of Westminster Theological Seminary (1966–1984). For the first 37 years of the seminary's existence it operated without a president; the faculty themselves were responsible for the administrative work and took turns filling a rotation-style leadership role. But in 1966, in something of a surprise considering the pro-Van Til and therefore often anti-Clark perspective of the seminary, Clowney became the first official president of the school.

Clowney brought significant change to the seminary. His views were closer to Clark's than to many of the then-retiring professors who had complained about Clark's ordination two decades earlier. But instead of focusing on battling liberalism, Clowney implemented a more positive agenda, emphasizing what the school stood for, rather than what it stood against. Clowney brought in many students from non-OPC and non-Reformed backgrounds to learn at the seminary, effectively ending the OPC hegemony at the "independent" seminary. His vision for the school was much more inclusive.[57]

Clowney's inclusive vision was in line with Clark's vision during his own OPC days, but Clark's views at WTS were still overshadowed by Van Til and his legacy. At Fuller, the acceptance of Clark's views may have been

identified in research for this biography.

53. The Fifteenth General Assembly of the Orthodox Presbyterian Church, meeting minutes (Philadelphia: OPC, 13 May 1948), 54.

54. Ibid., Appendix 70.

55. Dennison, et. al. *History for a Pilgrim People*, 137.

56. Dr. D. Clair Davis, e-mail to the author, 10 December 2013.

57. Dennison, et. al. *History for a Pilgrim People*, 138.

more noticeable, but the school's rejection of inerrancy ultimately dissolved any link between Fuller Seminary and Gordon Clark.[58] Thus even though Clark's presence was felt strongly at both Fuller and Westminster, neither seminary should be considered the model of what he would have desired.

58. Critiquing Fuller Seminary's lack of commitment to inerrancy as it was essential to the historical use of the term *evangelical*, Clark said, "I've been carrying on a controversy with Fuller seminary for some years, challenging them to define the word evangelical. I can't get them to do it. They like to use the word, you know. But they carefully refrain from telling you what they mean by it. And they certainly don't mean what the word has meant in the history from the time of Luther to the early part of this century."—Clark, "Language, Truth, and Revelation, Part 3." minute 36.

Chapter 12

Persons, the Trinity, and the Incarnation

"A man is what he thinks."[1]

—GORDON H. CLARK

IN GORDON CLARK'S LATER years, he wrote *The Trinity* and *The Incarnation*, two books in which he sought to improve the philosophical formulations on two historically difficult questions of Christian doctrine: (1) how God is both one and three, and (2) how Christ is both man and God. A lifetime of philosophical study and learning went into these books, but the formulations that Clark presented (particularly the latter, on Christ) were not warmly embraced by many theologians. Even some who would agree with him on most other issues rejected his formulations on these two doctrines.

The Trinity had originally been a chapter in Clark's systematic theology, an unpublished work titled *Introduction to Theology*.[2] A section of *The*

---

1. Clark, *The Trinity*, 106.

2. Clark had started writing *Introduction to Theology* (also known by its earlier working title, *First Lessons in Theology*) by 1974 (as evidenced by an undated letter he sent to Howard Long, circa August of 1974) and finished in 1977. See GHC to John Robbins, 25 August 1977, letter courtesy of The Trinity Foundation. Clark submitted the manuscript in 1978 to Presbyterian and Reformed Publishing (GHC to Mr. Craig, 17 August 1978, letter courtesy of The Trinity Foundation.) and in 1980 to Baker Book House for publication. Both publishers turned down the 938-page manuscript, with Baker claiming it was too large to be profitable. Individual chapters of the book were later printed separately by the Trinity Foundation as *The Biblical Doctrine of Man* (1984), *The Trinity* (1985), *The Atonement* (1987), and *Sanctification* (1993). Additional

Trinity (with some modifications) was published as an article also titled "The Trinity" in 1979. The book itself was published as a stand-alone volume out of the systematic theology in 1985. The second book, *The Incarnation*, was unfinished when Clark died. It was published posthumously in 1988, after Clark's disciple, John Robbins, completed it.[3]

For Clark, one crucial element involved in formulating possible solutions to both doctrines was the necessity of a clear definition of the term *person*. The "define or discard" method was a hallmark of Clark's approach to solving theological puzzles. In both books, Clark argued that theologians, especially on these two doctrines, had failed to define their terms adequately, and without clear and consistent definitions, their formulations suffered from ambiguity. In order to make sense of the trinitarian idea that God is one essence and three persons, and of the orthodox Christian idea that Jesus is both man and God, Clark believed clear definitions of terms were of utmost importance.

THE TRINITY

To understand the task Clark set out to achieve in *The Trinity*, a brief historical overview is necessary. The doctrine of the Trinity has historically differentiated orthodox Christianity from various heretical sects. Alternative views on the nature of God have included unitarianism (that God is but one person), modalism (that the Father, Son, and Holy Spirit are not three distinct persons, but rather three modes of God's existence according to their respective functions), and tritheism (that there are three gods). Opposed to these views, the orthodox Christian doctrine of the Trinity asserts that there are three persons in one God. But what does "person" mean and how are three of them, whatever they are, united in, or united as, one God? These are the questions with which Clark grappled.

---

chapters on the Scriptures, God, creation, salvation, and eschatology remain unpublished as of this biography. The provenance of the manuscript is as follows: two copies (one complete and one nearly so) were in Clark's possession at the time of his death at Sangre de Cristo Seminary. These were stored in the basement of the house in which he died. In March of 2014, while searching for other extant documents of Dr. Clark's for use in research for this biography, Sangre de Cristo Seminary's president, Andrew Zeller, discovered the systematic theology manuscripts.

3. Based on Clark's letters with John Robbins and this author's interviews with Tom Juodaitis of The Trinity Foundation during the writing of this biography, it became clear and is important to note that "The Incarnation" was almost entirely complete at the time of Clark's death. Robbins's work to complete the book was minimal.

With a view toward clarifying the orthodox expression of the Trinity, Clark sought a definition of *person*. He found it in the Bible itself, in Proverbs 23:7—"As he thinketh in his heart, so is he." From this verse Clark asked rhetorically, "Cannot we infer that a man is what he thinks?"[4] Elaborating upon this and forming a definition, Clark wrote, "Accordingly the proposal is that a man [person] is a congeries, a system, sometimes an agglomeration of miscellany, but at any rate a collection of thoughts. A man is what he thinks: and no two men are precisely the same combination."[5] Regarding God's threeness, Clark then employed his definition of *person* to conclude, "Since also the three Persons do not have precisely the same set of thoughts, they are not one Person, but three."[6] It was, according to Clark, the uniqueness of the respective sets of thoughts which made each of the persons of the Trinity distinct.

The doctrine of the Trinity, however, also requires an explanation of the "oneness" of God. How are the three persons one God? Taking his cue from the philosophical notion of idealism, which affirms the reality of individuals and of the ideal Form, Clark wrote:

> Now, when we face the subject of the Trinity—the common unity in the three Persons—may we not say that the three Persons share or communicate the common characteristics of omnipotence, omniscience, and so forth, and so constitute one essence? The Platonic point of view makes this essence a reality, as truly as Man and Beauty are real. Were the essence not a reality, and the Persons therefore the only realities, we should have tritheism instead of monotheism.[7]

In an article entitled "The Intellectual Triunity of God," Joel Parkinson explains Clark's view as providing a distinction between subjective knowledge and objective knowledge, with the former applying to the persons and the latter applying to the omniscience of divinity. By asserting that there are differing subjective thoughts for each person of the Trinity, Clark's view, Parkinson argues, sufficiently provides distinctions among the persons to preclude the heresy of modalism. Parkinson also argues that Clark's view negates the three separable gods of tritheism by maintaining an (inseparable) unity among the persons in their shared and identical objective knowledge.[8]

4. Clark, *The Trinity*, 105.
5. Ibid., 106.
6. Ibid., 106.
7. Clark, "The Trinity."
8. Parkinson, "The Intellectual Triunity of God."

Parkinson's explanation is contrary to the view of Roman Catholic theologian John O'Donnell, who, in *The Mystery of the Triune God*, argued that such views of "persons" amount to tritheism. O'Donnell wrote, "For if we say that God is one being in three persons, and if we understand by person centre of consciousness and freedom, then God becomes three centres of consciousness and there are three '*I think*'s in God. But such an understanding is obviously the same as tritheism."[9] But, with Parkinson's explanation of Clark's view, three personal minds or consciousnesses is not tritheism; it is tri-personalism. It would be tritheism if indeed, as O'Donnell states, these persons have "freedom." But in Clark's view the persons of the Trinity are not free from each other; rather, they are united in one essence and one single interpenetrating will.[10]

THE INCARNATION

In addition to working to better understand the doctrine of the Trinity, Clark set his sights on explaining the incarnation of Christ. Debates about the nature of Jesus Christ consumed the Christian church through much of the first seven centuries following Christ's death. Was Christ God? Was he man? Was he both? Various attempts to solve this question were rejected as heresies in the early Christian church. These heresies included docetism (that Christ's human form was merely an illusion), Arianism (that Christ was only a man and not God), Apollinarianism (that Christ had a human body but only a divine, not human, mind), Nestorianism (that Christ was two distinct *hypostases* or persons: the Logos and Jesus of Nazareth), Eutychianism (that the human and divine natures of Christ were mixed into a single new nature), and Monothelitism (that Christ had both the nature of God and man, but only one will). The condemnation of these various teachings as heretical was made official through a number of church councils. The First Council of Nicea (AD 325) produced the Nicene Creed, which stated that Jesus Christ is of one and the same substance as God the Father,

9. O'Donnell, *The Mystery of the Triune God*, 103.

10. Robert Reymond defends Clark's view against tri-theism, saying, "Every form of real tritheism requires three separable and distinguishable gods, that is to say, one could be eliminated without impinging on the 'godness' of the others in any way. But if any one of the three 'centers of self-consciousness' within the Trinity were to be eliminated from the Godhead, that elimination would immediately and directly necessitate eliminating data from the knowledge of the other two, which in turn would impinge upon their omniscience, which is immutable. Simply the immutable, shared omniscience possessed by the three Persons of the Godhead means that all tritheistic separability is out of the question."—Reymond, *A New Systematic Theology*, 323–24.

rejecting both docetism and Arianism. The First Council of Constantinople (AD 381) rejected Apollinarianism, the Council of Ephesus (AD 431) rejected Nestorianism, the Council of Chalcedon (AD 451) rejected Eutychianism, and the Third Council of Constantinople (AD 681) denounced Monothelitism as heretical.

Despite the credal statements produced at the ecumenical councils of the church, Clark saw that ambiguity remained regarding certain aspects of the doctrine of the incarnation. Perhaps the best explanation of the doctrine of Christ was that of the "hypostatic union" formulated at the Council of Chalcedon. This doctrine stated that Christ is one person of two natures, one human and one divine, with the natures neither confused nor divided.[11] Clark did not disagree with this formula so much as he simply criticized it for using vague language.[12] For Clark, there were two major issues that needed clarification. The first problem, Clark believed, was that the council never clearly defined *person*. Secondly, he believed Christ's human-ness was always presented in the Bible as total. In other words, Christ does not only have the nature of a man; he *is* a man.

To address the first problem, i.e. the vagueness of Chalcedon on the meaning of *person*, Clark again utilized his definition of *person* as "a composite of truths," saying, "A man is what he thinks."[13] To address the second problem, that Christ must be present as an actual man, he argued that in order to be "fully human" as Chalcedon stated, a human must also have a mind, for without a mind a man would not be fully human. Having a mind, Jesus was therefore a human *person*. Thus Clark employed his definition of *person* to arrive at the conclusion that Christ was two persons, one fully human, and one fully divine.

Clark specifically critiqued the position that Christ was a divine person only, and not a human person. Clark wrote,

---

11. The Creed of Chalcedon reads in part: "Following, then, the holy Fathers, we all unanimously teach that our Lord Jesus Christ is to us One and the same Son, the Self-same Perfect in Godhead, the Self-same Perfect in Manhood; truly God and truly Man; the Self-same of a rational soul and body; co-essential with the Father according to the Godhead, the Self-same co-essential with us according to the Manhood; acknowledged in Two Natures unconfusedly, unchangeably, indivisibly, inseparably; the difference of the Natures being in no way removed because of the Union, but rather the properties of each Nature being preserved, and (both) concurring into One Person and One Hypostasis."

12. "The great defect in the Creed is the absence of definitions."—Clark, *The Incarnation*, 15.

13. "Since God is Truth, we shall define *person* . . . as a composite of truths. A bit more exactly . . . the definition must be a composite of propositions. As a man thinketh in his (figurative) heart, so is he. A man *is* what he *thinks*."—Clark, *The Incarnation*, 54.

> If Jesus was not a human person, who or what suffered on the cross? The Second Person [of the Trinity] could not have suffered, for Deity is impassible. One of the heresies of the early ages . . . was Patripassianism. Substituting a modal trinity for the three distinct Persons, the theory requires the Father to have been crucified. But to require The Second Person, as such, to suffer is equally impossible. The Westminster Confession describes him as "a most pure spirit, invisible, without body, parts, or passions" (II, 1). If then the Second Person could not suffer, could a "nature" suffer?[14]

Clark's theory of Christology, using the term "person" to describe both Christ as man and Christ as God, opened him up to criticism, with some alleging that he held to the heresy of Nestorianism. This charge he anticipated in his writings. Clark wrote, "Some unfriendly critics will instantly brand the following defense of Christ's humanity as the heresy of Nestorianism."[15] Yet he dismissed the critique as unable to "be sustained either logically or historically."[16]

David Engelsma, however, of the Protestant Reformed Churches, who was "friendly" to Clark's views on many other topics, still saw Clark's view as Nestorian. In a review of Clark's book on the incarnation, Engelsma wrote, "Clark's doctrine is the boldest, most advanced Nestorianism, suffering, fatally, from the weaknesses because of which the church rejected Nestorianism—its failure to unite the two natures of the Savior and its inability to unify the work of redemption."[17] Engelsma answered Clark's question

---

14. Clark, *The Incarnation*, 67.

15. Ibid., 75.

16. It should be noted that Nestorius himself very well might not have held to the doctrine which now bears his name. Clark wrote, "Nestorius . . . taught, or was supposed to have taught, that the Incarnation of the Logos results in two persons. This view of Nestorius, with its accompanying condemnation, cannot be sustained either logically or historically."—Gordon H. Clark, *The Incarnation* (Jefferson, MD: Trinity Foundation, 1988), 75. Also: "Nestorius himself indignantly repudiated this account [that the God-man was split into two distinct persons], and in recent times the whole question what in fact it amounted to has been opened afresh. The discovery early this century of the Book of Heracleides—a prolix apologia which he wrote some twenty years after the main controversy and in which he avowed himself satisfied with the Christology of Leo canonized at Chalcedon—has seemed to make a reassessment necessary. Modern students are sharply divided, some regarding him as essentially orthodox but the victim of ecclesiastical politics, others concurring in differing degrees in the traditional verdict."—Kelly, *Early Christian Doctrines*, 312.

17. Engelsma, "Review of 'The Incarnation.'"

about who died on the cross, saying, "The answer is, The person of the eternal Son of God suffered and died in the human nature."[18]

Clark, in fact, was opposed to Nestorianism. He had just written a few years prior to *The Incarnation* in his commentary on *Philippians* (written circa 1982) a statement sounding much more like the traditional Chalcedonian view: "We must insist that Christ was not a human person somehow associated with a divine person. . . . we must avoid Nestorianism."[19] And he noted that "Nestorianism faces worse difficulties" than the orthodox doctrine.[20] Yet in the same book, Clark noted that the Westminster Larger Catechism explained that Christ took "to himself a true body and reasonable soul." On this basis, that Christ took both a body and a soul, Clark asked, "Does not this make him a human person?"[21] This may indicate the early development of views Clark later articulated in *The Incarnation*.

As Clark was writing the book, he was acutely aware of the dangers of Nestorianism and was engrossed in solving the problem of the doctrine of the incarnation. He wrote to John Robbins, "[An] extremely difficult problem is the doctrine of the Incarnation. I have been working on it constantly since moving here [to Sangre de Cristo Seminary], and have some 150 handwritten pages. I can alleviate or eliminate several impossibilities in the doctrine as usually stated; but it is hard to avoid Nestorianism. I write and sleep, and sleep and write, and sometimes eat."[22] Later that month Clark wrote again, "My MS [manuscript] on the Incarnation may have 230 handwritten pages. It needs perhaps 25 more as a good conclusion. But there are so many complications in the subject, that putting them all together in a conclusion is really a very difficult problem."[23]

How then was Clark's later view not Nestorianism, if he came to hold that there are two persons in Christ? In addition to the fact that he explicitly denied the charges of Nestorianism, Clark held that the ancient theologians, Nestorius included, never defined *person*, and therefore did not have a clear, unified idea of what the term meant. Since Clark had defined *person* in a unique way, the claim that Clark held the same view as Nestorius (or his followers) cannot be sustained. Secondly, rebutting the charges of Nestorianism in Clark's doctrine, Gary Crampton and Kenneth Talbot have written,

18. Ibid.

19. Clark, *Philippians*, 63.

20. Ibid., 65.

21. Ibid., 64.

22. GHC to John Robbins, 3 January 1985, letter courtesy of The Trinity Foundation.

23. GHC to John Robbins, 25 January 1985, letter courtesy of The Trinity Foundation.

"It should be noted that Gordon Clark does not separate the two persons of Christ, as Nestorians do; rather, he 'distinguishes' between them. It is important to understand the difference between 'separation' and 'distinction.'"[24] This idea of "distinct but not separate" applies in that Clark held there are two persons, but these persons are united in one Christ.

So Clark's view was not Nestorianism, but was it correct? Or perhaps the question is better phrased: Is Clark's formulation an improvement upon Chalcedon? Returning to Engelsma's objection, is Clark's view unable to "unify the work of redemption" in his "failure to unite the two natures?" In previous works Clark wrote: "[The] Chalcedonian doctrine is necessary to support the function of Christ's mediatorial office,"[25] and also, " . . . the incarnate Jesus has two wills, one divine, and one human; and yet even with a human will, and a 'reasonable soul,' he is not a human person. Nestorianism, with its assertion that Christ was two persons, though plausible on the ground of this psychology, is nonetheless on the ground of the mediatorial atonement, a heresy."[26] Can Clark be said to have changed his views on this subject, or merely his terminology? Crampton and Talbot, holding Clark's positions, respond, "God is impassible and cannot suffer. Orthodox Christianity maintains that Christ suffered on the cross as touching His humanity, not His divinity."[27]

Because *The Incarnation* was published posthumously, Clark was not around to see his readers' reactions to the book, nor to continue to discuss the theology or defend his position. For many, Clark's defense of two persons in Christ, even if not intentionally Nestorian, sounded Nestorian. This somewhat soured his reputation. Coupled with the various other controversies Clark was involved in, this has made him appear to be a controversial figure, even one whose writings some choose to avoid.

There was an inevitable tension between Clark's desire to have a standard (the Westminster Standards along with the early church creeds) and his desire to see improved formulations of certain doctrines, such as the doctrine of the incarnation. Improving the formulation and understanding of doctrine is critical to the "always reforming" (*semper reformanda*) directive of the Reformed faith, but avoiding philosophical speculation is equally crucial. Readers of Clark's work should consider for themselves whether Clark toed the line or fell into speculation over the doctrine of the incarnation.

24. Crampton and Talbot, "Was Gordon Clark a Nestorian?"
25. Clark, *What do Presbyterians Believe?* 95.
26. Clark, *The Trinity*, 59.
27. Crampton and Talbot, "Was Gordon Clark a Nestorian?"

The very last extant letter written by Clark suggests that he felt a fair amount of frustration at not being able to fully resolve the difficulties the doctrine of the incarnation presented. At the same time it also leaves room to conclude that, had someone been able to show him a position better than his own, he would have gladly entertained their arguments. In this letter, of February 1985, he wrote to John Robbins, "Maybe I am all wrong, but I won't admit it until my critics define substance, being, subsistence, essence, etc., as well as person and nature."[28] As evidenced by similar positions expressed in the final published manuscript of *The Incarnation*, Clark continued to grapple with these questions right up until his death, just two months after the February letter.

28. GHC to John Robbins, 3 February 1985, letter courtesy of The Trinity Foundation.

Chapter 13

Gordon Clark's Later Years

Got a problem? Just ask Dr. Clark,
Who finds thinking simply a lark
But of your logic be certain,
Or you could be hurtin',
And you'll wind up even more in the dark.

—A STUDENT'S POEM, 1979[1]

A BRIEF RETIREMENT

THERE WERE A NUMBER of signs that suggested Gordon Clark would retire from teaching at the customary age of sixty-five if not earlier. During
the 1961–1962 school year, when Clark was on sabbatical from Butler
University, writing a book on Karl Barth with a grant from the Volker
Fund, he wrote to Carl Henry that he wished he could have a grant indefi-
nitely, be done with teaching, and focus instead on his writings.[2] He also
wrote to Henry, who was working long hours as editor of *Christianity
Today*, "My whole inclination is to buy a hogan on the Arizona desert and
hole up for the rest of my life. Maybe you enjoy your merry-go-round;
it seems more like the whip to me and it jerks my neck."[3] Another sign
pointing to his imminent retirement occurred in 1968, when a Festschrift

1. *Tartan 1979 Yearbook,* 162.
2. GHC to CFHH, 8 April 1961, BGC Archives, Wheaton College, CN8, 15–13.
3. GHC to CFHH, 17 May 1962, BGC Archives, Wheaton College, CN8, 15–13.

in Clark's honor was made with contributions from a number of fellow philosophers and edited by his colleague, philosophy professor Ronald H. Nash.[4] It had been a long career of work for Clark. He had taught college courses since 1924. He had preached many sermons and written many books, and the years of controversy in the church were enough to wear down any man.

But as the years rolled along and Clark reached and then passed his 65th birthday, he found it difficult to leave his professor position and the college atmosphere he had so long been surrounded by. There were a number of reasons why he stayed at Butler. In addition to continuing to receive a good salary, Clark was head of the department and therefore had the luxury of setting his own schedule. He also had a number of good friends at Butler. And he probably realized that there was scarcely a hogan in the world large enough to house his ever-growing book collection. Thus, retirement held little allure.

As Clark continued at Butler University, however, he knew that his tenure would be limited by the college's policy requiring retirement by age 70. He expected to retire at the end of the 1971–1972 school year, as he would turn 70 the following summer. The dean, however, mistakenly thought Clark was one year younger than he actually was, and, still in the process of searching for a replacement to head the philosophy department, asked Clark to stay one more year. In December of 1972 Clark wrote to his longtime pen-pal in Germany, Frau Schulze, "This is my last year in the university. I'll be 71 years old in August, and that is a year over the ordinary retirement age. I should have had to retire last August. I have no specific plans, except that I'm going to write."[5] Finally, at the end of the 1972–1973 year, his retirement commenced. Clark's regular chess-playing associate and the head of the religion department at Butler, Dr. E. Robert Andry, who had started at Butler in 1944 one year prior to Clark, retired alongside him that same year.[6]

4. Nash was a long-time philosophy professor at Western Kentucky University who found much to agree with in Clark's philosophy. The Festschrift is titled *The Philosophy of Gordon H. Clark* and was published in 1968 by the Presbyterian and Reformed Publishing Co.

5. "Diese Jahr ist mein letztes in der Universität. Ich werde 71 Jahre alt in August sein, und das ist ein Jahr uber das gewöhnliche Pensionsalter. Ich sollte mich letzten August zurückziehen gehabt. Ich habe keine bestimmte Plane, ausser dass ich zu schreiben zartsetzen werden."—GHC to Frau Schulze, December 1972, translated by Douglas Douma, PCA Archives.

6. "Butler Reports" (news bulletin, PR office of Butler University, Indianapolis, IN, April 1973), from Gordon H. Clark's personnel file at Butler University.

Despite retirement, Clark was not willing to end his teaching career so unceremoniously. Some may have expected that he would retire from teaching and spend his time on other passions: writing, chess, and landscape drawing. Even so, for a man dedicated to loving God with his whole mind, and for whom teaching philosophy was a passion, Clark's official retirement from Butler did not keep him out of the classroom for long. In fact, as he neared retirement at Butler, there were multiple schools knocking on his door, hoping to lure the eminent philosopher to their rosters. In his final year teaching at Butler, Clark received a letter from William Barker, the dean of faculty at Covenant Theological Seminary, who was hopeful that Clark's upcoming retirement from Butler may allow him to teach a course or speak at Covenant the following year.[7] Clark received an offer to teach at Reformed Episcopal Seminary as well.[8] He turned down the offers from both seminaries but later accepted a position at Covenant College. Before relocating to this new teaching post, Clark took a full year off.

GORDON CLARK AGAINST THE TORONTO SCHOOL

Clark's full-time position at Covenant College started in the fall of 1974, though he had a prior commitment to fulfill before he could focus entirely on Covenant. To that end, Clark went to Geneva College in Beaver Falls, Pennsylvania, for part of the fall semester of 1974.[9] His former Wheaton student Howard Long helped arrange the Geneva job connection.[10]

At this time a growing influence at Geneva College was emerging from a school of thought known as the Toronto School, which followed the teachings of the Dutch philosopher Herman Dooyeweerd. Although Dooyeweerdians built institutions with the names "Association for the Advancement of Christian Scholarship" and "Institute for Christian Studies," the Toronto School's main focus was not teaching accepted Christian doctrine, but advancing Dooyeweerd's particular philosophy. Part and parcel of this philosophy was the belief in various forms of the Word of

---

7. William S. Barker, dean of faculty at Covenant College, to GHC, 12 February 1973, Sangre de Cristo Seminary's Clark Library, 1/47.

8. Dr. Milton C. Fisher, secretary to the faculty, to GHC, 7 May 1974, PCA Archives, 309/32.

9. GHC to Richard Chewning, 14 November 1974, PCA Archives. See also: GHC to John H. White, 26 July 1974, Sangre de Cristo Seminary, Clark Library.; and John H. White, former professor and president of Geneva College, e-mail to the author, 3 October 2014.

10. GHC to Howard Long, 1974, from the personal files of Howard and Genevieve Long.

God, including what Dooyeweerd called the "Creation Word" rivalling the Bible itself as an epistemological basis.[11] Johannes Vos, the longtime professor of philosophy at Geneva, had retired in the previous year (1973) but remained concerned about the presence of Dooyeweerdian thought on campus. One proponent of the Toronto School had then recently been hired on at Geneva only to be let go for his views a short while later. It seems that Clark was hired to fill some open lecture times while Geneva was searching for a long-term philosophy professor who was not associated with the Toronto School. In February 1973, during his last year as chairman of the Bible and Philosophy Department, Vos wrote a letter to the administration of Geneva College warning them of the teachings of the Toronto School with its "marks of a sub-Christian cult" and hoping "that there will be the most thorough and careful consideration before another advocate of the Amsterdam [Dooyeweerdian] school is appointed to the Geneva faculty."[12] Vos also wrote a letter to the members of the student senate of Geneva College expressing and explaining reasons for his opposition to the formation of a Dooyeweerdian club on campus.[13] According to a note on this same letter, Vos's advice was heeded, and the proposal to have a Dooyeweerdian club on campus was defeated at the student senate by a vote of 11 to 0. Vos wrote of his opposition to the Toronto School, "I am 71 years old and cannot expect to live in this world many more years. But as God gives me strength I intend to oppose the Toronto movement until I die."[14]

To combat the Toronto School, Vos asked Howard Long to write a review of *The Challenge of Our Age* by Hendrick Hart, a Dooyewerdian. Long in turn deferred to Clark to write the review, writing to Clark, "My review would be just a pop-gun and yours would be big caliber."[15] Long also wrote, "At this time we [The Reformed Presbyterian Church] need a scholarly demolition of the Toronto philosophy because there will be a report on it at our next Synod."[16] Referring to the review, Vos acknowledged to Clark, "I am very glad you are willing to undertake this."[17] Clark took up the task and

11. Vos, "The Cultic Character of the Toronto Movement."

12. Johannes G. Vos to the administration of Geneva College, 5 February 1974, PCA Archives, 309/60.

13. Johannes G. Vos, Professor Emeritus, to the members of the student senate of Geneva College, 8 February 1974, PCA Archives.

14. Johannes G. Vos to ministers of Midwest Presbytery, 3 April 1974, PCA Archives, 309/60.

15. Howard Long to GHC, 31 July 1974, from the personal files of Howard and Genevieve Long.

16. Ibid.

17. Johannes G. Vos to GHC, 6 August 1974, PCA Archives, 309/60.

the review came out later that year in the Reformed Presbyterian Church's journal, *Blue Banner Faith and Life*. Clark continued to work against the Toronto School as a member of a group called the Study Committee on Amsterdam Philosophy for the RPCES which reported to the 153rd General Assembly in 1975.[18]

MAJOR CHANGES FOR DR. CLARK

Following Clark's brief time at Geneva College, he returned to a permanent position at Covenant College. The college, in Lookout Mountain, Georgia, was then the denominational college of the Reformed Presbyterian Church, Evangelical Synod (RPCES), of which Clark was a member. He had an established friendship there with, among others, John W. Sanderson Jr., who had previously taught philosophy at the college and was vice president at the time of Clark's hire. Sanderson pleaded with Clark to come and add a strong dose of rigor to the Covenant curriculum.[19] Clark accepted, and beginning in 1974, taught philosophy courses at Covenant College for ten years.[20]

Unlike secular Butler University where few Presbyterians attended, Covenant provided Clark the pleasure of teaching Christian students from his own denomination. Covenant also provided a Christian environment in which he was able to impact students not only philosophically, but in their Christian lives and ministries as well. Noted students of Clark's from Covenant College include Paul Moser, a philosophy professor currently at Loyola University in Chicago; Dr. Kenneth Talbot, the founder and president of Whitefield Theological Seminary; Clark's grandson Dr. Andrew Zeller, the president of Sangre de Cristo Seminary; and Dr. Frank Walker, the president of City Seminary Sacramento.

Teaching past his eightieth birthday at Covenant College, Clark had a wealth of historical as well as philosophical information to impart to his students. He had lived through and had been intimately involved in many important events in twentieth-century American Presbyterian church history. Many students at Covenant enrolled in philosophy courses solely because Clark was teaching them.

18. GHC to Richard Chewning, 14 November 1974, PCA Archives, 309/31. See also: Richard Chewning to GHC, 21 November 1974, PCA Archives, 309/31.; and Richard Chewning to GHC, 21 April 1975, PCA Archives, 309/31.

19. J. C. Keister, e-mail to the author, 5 May 2015.

20. The courses Clark regularly taught at Covenant College included Philosophy of Religion, History of Modern Philosophy, Philosophy of Language, Political Philosophy, and Philosophy of Science.—Covenant College, undergraduate course catalogs, 1974–75 to 1983–84, https://portal.covenant.edu/archives/Academic_Catalog.

In July of 1977, after Clark's third year at Covenant College, his wife, Ruth, died of leukemia. Later that year Clark wrote to Frau Schulze, "I know quite well what it means to be sad. It is useless to soften the message: my dear wife died in July, and I am alone. Physically healthy, but alone."[21] The previous year, in order to help care for his wife, he switched from teaching full-time to part-time, claiming "advanced senility" and "a desire to become Grandpa Moses."[22]

Clark's reaction to his wife's death alarmed a number of people. According to Dr. James Hurley, then also a professor at Covenant, Clark told none of his colleagues at Covenant College of his wife's death for several days. Since Clark had strong views against emotion, he tried to avoid showing his sadness. When Clark spoke of his wife's death, tears formed, but Clark quickly wiped them away and apologized.[23] But according to J. C. Keister, a former Covenant College professor and Clark's close friend, Clark did share the news of Ruth's death with him. He recalled:

> Gordon's reaction to his wife's death was very touching. He called me up in the evening of the day she died, wanting to play chess "to get his mind off it." (Up to that point in time, I had been more than holding my own with him in our games over the phone. Not that night!) We played several games, and I lost most of them and drew only one. I was thankful to have been able to minister to him, if only by playing games of chess with him.[24]

THE CHALLENGE OF ART

During his years at Covenant College, Clark applied himself to the artistic disciplines of poetry, drawing, and painting. His interest in writing poetry reached back at least to his early adulthood when he wrote poems, often in French, and mostly to the love of his life, his then-fiancée, Ruth. Clark's softer side included an interest not only in poetry but also in both painting and drawing. This led him to enroll in several art courses at Covenant under

---

21. "Ich weiß sehr wohl was soll es bedeuten dass ich so traurig bin. Es ist nutzlos die Kunde zu mildern: meine liebe Frau starb in Juli, und ich bin allein. Physikalisch gesund, aber allein."—GHC to the Schulze family, December 1977, translated by Douglas Douma, PCA Archives. (The first line of this quote is modified from the famous German song "Die Lorelei.")

22. Zeller, "Departments demonstrate quality," 27.

23. Dr. James Hurley, interview by Douglas Douma, phone, 10 November 2014.

24. J. C. Keister, e-mail to the author, 5 May 2015.

art professor Ed Kellogg, starting in 1975.[25] Years later, in his retirement speech, Kellogg was able to proclaim that the person who took the most classes from him during his career at Covenant was Gordon Clark. Kellogg related that Clark first came to his art class when Kellogg was only in his second year of teaching, and that while Clark was intimidating at first, over time Kellogg grew fond of him.

The nearly unanimous consensus of Clark's friends and family was that he was not a good artist. In fact, Clark admitted as much in a letter to Nick Barker at Covenant College: "Outside professional philosophy I write terrible poems, paint worse pictures, and play mediocre chess."[26] But Clark was not overly concerned about criticism; he painted for the sheer pleasure of the activity and out of love for God's creation.

But art wasn't always enjoyable for Clark. In 1982, the *Chattanooga News—Free Press* interviewed Clark and recorded:

> . . . Dr. Clark, widowed and the grandfather of nine, enjoys chess and painting. Well, chess anyway. The painting is with oils and he "attacks" the canvas with the vigor of a love-hate relationship. "Tell the public that I find the oil painting the most irritating activity I can think (of)," he says, humorously confessing some degree of masochism. He likened the pastime to self-flagellation by "a medieval monk."[27]

Clark was often out of his element when creating art. Kellogg recalled, "Clark was so muscle-bound in his left hemisphere and atrophied in his right hemisphere; my impression was that artwork really frustrated him, that he couldn't master it, that he couldn't rationally figure out what the issues were here."[28] Nevertheless, Clark continued his pursuits. While traveling out West during summers away from Covenant, he drew and painted landscapes, which he brought back to show Kellogg when classes resumed in the fall. Kellogg recalled:

> Clark had gotten a book on the perfect ideal composition in art. He came into my office once before class and almost slapped this book down on my desk and said, "According to this book, this is a perfect composition." He knew that the drawing or painting was just terrible, and it was. He knew it, and was very frustrated

25. "Gordon Clark feels at home on Lookout Mountain," *Covenant Courier* (Lookout Mountain, TN: Covenant College, 1978).

26. GHC to Nick Barker, August 1979, Covenant College faculty file.

27. Brown, "Clark Retains Zest for Life as 81st Year Approaches."

28. Ed Kellogg, interview by Douglas Douma, phone, 27 September 2014.

that he couldn't approach it and do something that came so easy to him with his left-hemisphere approach.[29]

J. C. Keister also recalled a comical story regarding Clark's efforts in art class:

> Regarding his artwork class with Ed Kellogg, I recall seeing him and the rest of the art class outside one day painting the library building on canvas. The contrast was complete between Gordon and the rest of the class. You know what art students (in general) are like—wandering around casually, in various states of very informal dress, while Gordon sat upright in a chair, dressed more formally in a white shirt and slacks, fixing the library building in his gaze and painting laboriously (he always said that he "worked at it!"). I went up to him and examined his painting along with Ed Kellogg. Gordon had painted the roof the color of vermilion. Ed asked (incredulously), "Straight from the tube??" and Gordon responded (forcefully), "Straight from the tube!"[30]

One possible reason for Clark's artistic limitations is closely related to his philosophical system. Clark professed that he did not personally have memory images or mental pictures (a condition now known as aphantasia) and critiqued empiricism for its contention that all men have them. According to Kellogg, "He never advanced beyond kind of an adolescent level of visualization," and, "I remember hearing him say he couldn't remember visual images. I said, 'Dr. Clark, are you telling me that you can't see, in your mind's eye, your wife?' He just sort of looked at me and said, 'No.'" Clearly, for Clark, philosophy was not limited to the classroom; it had practical implications.[31]

Despite the clear challenge that producing art posed to Clark, the aging philosopher continued to study it. This is, perhaps, one of the clearest signs that Clark was a lover of learning, a true philosopher. But study as he might, it wasn't so much a lack of knowledge which held back his artwork, but was rather, perhaps, a lack of sufficient inspiration, passion, or even *emotion*.

29. Ibid.
30. J. C. Keister, e-mail to the author, 5 May 2015.
31. Ed Kellogg, interview by Douglas Douma, phone, 27 September 2014.

BIBLICAL COMMENTARIES

Though Gordon Clark admittedly had a lot to learn when it came to the fine arts, there is no denying that he had an exemplary skill set when it came to prose, philosophy, and Christian thought. His writing career attests to that. The final stage in that writing career consisted primarily of commentaries on New Testament epistles. These commentaries included, in chronological order, *Peter Speaks Today: A Devotional Commentary on First Peter* (1967), *II Peter: A Short Commentary* (1972), *Colossians: Another Commentary on an Inexhaustible Message* (1979), *First John: A Commentary* (1980), *The Pastoral Epistles* (1983), *Ephesians* (1985), *First and Second Thessalonians* (1986), and *Philippians* (1996). Clark's commentaries differed from standard commentaries in a number of ways. They were, for the most part, neither devotional, nor popular, nor technical, but rather expository and philosophical. They were practical commentaries, addressed, as Clark said in his commentary on *Colossians,* to the ordinary Christian.[32]

In the last years of his life he did not slow down in effort but continued writing, completing nearly a dozen more books. His increasing age and the expectation that he was running out of time spurred on his urgency.[33] Writing came to occupy more and more of his time, but the process of writing by hand, then typing what he wrote, then having it published could only move so quickly. He never took to using a computer and did much of his writing by fountain pen and ink. In fact, according to his son-in-law Dwight Zeller, Clark once complained about the high cost of ink; this was surely a sign of a prolific, though perhaps somewhat old-fashioned, writer.[34]

JOHN ROBBINS, CRUSADER FOR CLARK'S PHILOSOPHY

Clark found a publisher for his commentaries and later theological works in John W. Robbins (1948–2008), a young PhD graduate in philosophy from Johns Hopkins University. Robbins first contacted Gordon Clark in the early 1970's. Then in 1973 he wrote Clark a letter asking for help in securing an academic position; Robbins was convinced that his difficulty in doing so was due, not to a lack of credentials, but to the unpopularity of his

---

32. Clark, *Colossians,* 11.

33. "Your letter . . . ends by your saying that you have developed a sense of urgency recently. This I appreciate for I have little time left to do anything."—GHC to John Robbins, 16 February 1981, letter courtesy of The Trinity Foundation.

34. Dwight Zeller, conversation with Douglas Douma, Sangre de Cristo Seminary, 1 June 2015.

philosophical positions as a Christian—positions he shared with Clark.[35] Clark obliged, writing a letter of recommendation for Robbins, a task which he repeated years later when Robbins was again looking for an academic post.[36]

Robbins had read many of Clark's published works while writing his dissertation at Johns Hopkins on *The Political Thought of Sir Robert Filmer,* a seventeenth-century English political theorist.[37] Robbins's widow, Linda, recalled that although he had studied several significant Reformed thinkers extensively, it was not until his discovery of Clark's writings and specifically his reading of Clark's *Religion, Reason, and Revelation* that he was thoroughly convinced that Reformed thinking was in line with the Bible.[38]

Robbins was an intelligent scholar who wrote numerous books influenced significantly by Clark's thought. Prior to earning master's and PhD degrees at Johns Hopkins, he completed an undergraduate degree at Grove City College in Pennsylvania, where he attended with the express goal of studying economics under the *laissez-faire* (and Christian) economist Hans Sennholz. Though Robbins struggled to find a suitable academic post, he did find work in politics, first as a legislative assistant (1976, 1979–1981) and later as chief of staff (1981–1985) to the Libertarian-Republican congressman from Texas, Dr. Ron Paul.

Though Robbins and Clark were in correspondence by the early 1970's, they did not meet in person until 1978 at which time Clark baptized Robbins's daughter.[39] By that time, Robbins had founded a publishing group, The Trinity Foundation (established 1977), utilizing the editing skills he had learned on a previous job he had in Boston.[40] The Trinity Foundation was created with the primary purpose of publishing Clark's books, both new titles and others long out of print. Clark appreciated Robbins's hard work in editing his books and was glad to have a publisher for his books at a time

35. John Robbins to GHC, 17 July 1973, PCA Archives.

36. GHC to John Robbins, 19 August 1974, letter courtesy of The Trinity Foundation. See also: GHC to John Robbins, 3 December 1984, letter courtesy of The Trinity Foundation.; GHC to John Robbins, 5 December 1984, letter courtesy of The Trinity Foundation.; and GHC letter of recommendation for John Robbins, 5 Dec 1984, letter courtesy of The Trinity Foundation.

37. Robbins received his PhD in May of 1973 from Johns Hopkins University. He wrote his dissertation on Sir Robert Filmer, a seventeenth-century English political theorist.—Linda Robbins, interview by Douglas Douma, phone, 1 November 2014.

38. Linda Robbins, interview by Douglas Douma, phone, 1 November 2014.

39. GHC to John Robbins, 1 April 1978, letter courtesy of The Trinity Foundation.

40. John Robbins worked for two years at Western Islands, the publishing arm of the John Birch Society. Linda Robbins, interview by Douglas Douma, in person in Unicoi, TN, 12 December 2015.

when other publishers were uninterested.[41] Robbins was dedicated to getting Clark's views to a larger audience through the foundation; he even refused to take a salary for his work at the foundation until late in the 1990s.[42] Robbins also wanted to write Clark's biography, though he died before he could begin writing it.[43] But even without the biography, Robbins's efforts have proved to be of critical significance; for by publishing Clark's books and his own, Robbins brought Clark's thought to a new generation.[44]

Robbins was fearlessly polemical and through the years alienated many, not only because of his views but also for the uncompromising zeal with which he held to them. An example of Robbins's intractable personality and its results occurred at Sangre de Cristo Seminary. Robbins was hired there in the early 1990s as a visiting professor and taught a course in apologetics, taking over the course Clark had once taught. However, after a dispute in 1999 with the seminary's founder, Dr. Dwight Zeller, Robbins was never invited back to teach.

Dr. Zeller was not the only person to come into conflict with the strong personality of John Robbins. Dr. Greg Bahnsen, a supporter of the apologetics of Cornelius Van Til, engaged in a polemical exchange with Robbins. A number of letters between these two men, in addition to critical reviews of each other's books, were published in the journals *Journey* and *The Trinity Review*.[45] In a sense, the conflict between these two men was a continuation of the Clark-Van Til controversy, but with a younger generation whose polemics exceeded those of their forebears.

41. Dr. Dwight Zeller, son-in-law of Dr. Clark, interview by Douglas Douma, Sangre de Cristo Seminary, 2014; and J. C. Keister, e-mail to the author, 5 May 2015.

42. Linda Robbins, interview by Douglas Douma, phone, 1 November 2014.

43. Robbins, *Gordon H. Clark, Personal Recollections*, 1. See also: John Robbins to Howard Long, 8 April 1986, from the files of Howard and Genevieve Long. Also note: "Shortly before his death he authorized me to write his biography."—John Robbins to the president of Covenant College, 31 May 1985, from the faculty file of Gordon Clark at Covenant College.

44. The author of this biography is a case in point, having first learned of Clark from the final pages of Robbins's *Without a Prayer, The Close of Ayn Rand's System*, a critique of Ayn Rand's philosophy of Objectivism.

45. Greg Bahnsen, letter to the editor in response to John Robbins, *Journey* 3, no. 1 (January–February 1988), 22.; John Robbins, "Contra Bahnsen II," *Journey* 3, no. 3 (May–June, 1988), 14–15.; Greg Bahnsen, letter to the editor in response to John Robbins, *Journey* 3, no. 4–5 (July–October 1988).; John Robbins, "Theonomic Schizophrenia," *The Trinity Review* (February 1992).; Greg Bahnsen, "Cross Examination: In Defense of Theonomy," *The Counsel of Chalcedon* 14, no. 5/6, (July/August 1992): 4–8.; John Robbins, "Will the Real Greg Bahnsen Please Stand up?" *The Trinity Review* (August 1992).

Tragically, the lives of both Bahnsen and and Robbins were cut short. Bahnsen passed away because of complications following heart surgery in 1995 at age forty-seven, and, after fighting cancer for three years, Robbins passed away in 2008 at age fifty-nine. In the continued theological debates since their deaths, neither the Clark camp nor the Van Til camp has had a definitive leader.

THE PRESBYTERIAN CHURCH IN AMERICA: TO JOIN OR NOT TO JOIN

Clark had been through more than his fair share of denominational change: a major denominational separation (the OPC from the PCUSA), another split (the BPC leaving the OPC), a switch on his own to a new denomination (from the OPC to the UPCNA), a transfer of his congregation's allegiance (from the UPCNA to the RPCGS), and a merger (the RPCGS and EPC to form the RPCES). In fact, he was involved in nearly every major denominational struggle in twentieth-century U.S. Presbyterian history. The final struggle Clark had to face in the realm of Presbyterian denominational identity was the question of whether or not the RPCES should join the PCA.

Although the Presbyterian Church in the United States of America (PCUSA) had divided decades earlier in 1936 because of the Fundamentalist–Modernist controversy of the 1920s and 1930s, the next largest Presbyterian denomination—the Presbyterian Church in the United States (PCUS)—had managed to remain united through those unstable decades. Still there existed within the PCUS both fundamentalist and modernist factions which threatened to cause a divide. The modernists in the PCUS sought a union with the UPCUSA. The fundamentalists fought against this plan, and Clark, from a distance, supported their efforts. In the 1950s and 1960s Clark kept abreast of happenings in the PCUS and was a frequent contributor to the church's unofficial publication, *The Southern Presbyterian Journal* (and later *The Presbyterian Journal* when the journal changed names in 1959). In 1955 Clark wrote, "I took on a series of about 30 articles on the Westminster Confession for *The Southern Presbyterian Journal*. These men are winning a tremendous victory against the ecumaniacs. Just this week another Presbytery voted 32–16 against union. I wish I could be down there with them."[46]

The fragile unity in the PCUS came to an end in 1973 when conservatives loyal to the *Westminster Confession of Faith* left the PCUS to form the Presbyterian Church in America (PCA). Although the term

46. GHC to EJC, 14 January 1955, PCA Archives, 309/30.

"fundamentalist" perhaps best applies to an earlier era, most of those who joined the PCA held those basic convictions, especially the doctrine of the inerrancy of Scripture. When the fundamentalists left to form the PCA, the PCUS no longer faced internal opposition to the merger with the UPCUSA, and these latter two groups were able to pursue their long-held plan to merge, forming the PC(USA) in 1983.

Clark's denomination, the RPCES, like the newly-formed PCA, was loyal to the *Westminster Confession of Faith*. As such, many within both churches felt bound to form a single denomination. Clark, however, was in the minority opposed to the merger.

There were a number of reasons why Clark opposed the merger (technically called "joining and receiving") of the RPCES into the PCA. He outlined these reasons in a document (c. 1982) sent to the leaders of the RPCES, cynically called "The Proposal to Abolish the RPCES." In the document Clark summarized his reasons:

> I oppose this merger, first because there is no Scriptural necessi-
> ty for it. Second I oppose these proceedings because they are an
> unmerited insult to the Orthodox Presbyterian Church. Third,
> I believe this merger is reprehensible because it aims to abol-
> ish the Reformed Presbyterian Church. Fourth, the missionary
> methods of the PCA are conclusive evidence that the PCA is not
> loyal to the Westminster Confession and Catechisms.[47]

Regarding the scriptural necessity of a merger (his first reason for op-position), Clark focused on John 17:11, which reads, "Holy Father, protect them by the power of your name—the name you gave me—so that they may be one as we are one." As to what this unity to "be one as we are one" con-sists of, Clark answered "a unitary purpose." He wrote, "The unity for which Jesus prayed was a doctrinal unity, or as Paul called it, 'the mind of Christ.'" Clark felt that although the two bodies were alike in that they subscribed in principle to the WCF, there remained too many inconsistencies of doctrine to form a truly united body, and as such, a merged church would not be unified in the way Christ and Paul meant for churches to be unified.

Clark's second reason for opposing was that he felt it would be an in-sult to the OPC who, only a few years earlier, had themselves approached the RPCES about a merger. A proposed plan of union between the RPCES and OPC had been approved by the OPC but was rejected by the RPCES in 1975. Thus when, in 1981, the PCA voted to receive the RPCES but declined to invite the OPC,[48] Clark saw how easily that action could be interpreted

---

47. Clark, "The Proposal to Abolish the RPCES."

48. Hart, *Between the Times*, 231.

as a slight against the Orthodox Presbyterian Church; such behavior was not in keeping with a spirit of unity. Clark, ever concerned about consistency, wrote, "Those members of the RPCES who voted against the OPC and yet now advocate union with the PCA can hardly base their decision on John 17:11. Nor can the PCA, having rejected the OPC in these new proceedings, appeal to this verse with any degree of consistency." Furthermore, Clark pointed out, "Those of you who know the history you should know will recognize that if there is any man in these three denominations whom the OPC has treated harshly, I am that man. No one has a greater reason to dislike them." However, Clark continued, saying, "Yet so far am I from hating them that one essential condition for my joining the PCA is that the OPC be included."[49] [50]

Clark's desire to keep the RPCES intact was also influenced by his concern for the historical roots of the churches. He warned there was "little enthusiasm for our historic standards in the PCA."[51] He believed that the PCA had distanced itself from the WCF by supporting many missionaries who were "more Arminian than Calvinistic." In support of his claim that the PCA was not loyal to the standards (i.e. the Westminster Confession) Clark argued that the PCA's official publication, *The Presbyterian Journal*, had published an article which identified parts of the Confession with hyper-Calvinism. He had also seen this lack of confessional fidelity a decade earlier in other articles in *The Presbyterian Journal*. Clark was contributing articles to the journal as well, but on one occasion sent a complaint to G. Aiken Taylor, the editor of the paper. Clark complained that one issue "commends Arminians" and an article in that issue "contradicts the Confession."[52] Discord developed between Clark and Taylor when Taylor decided not to publish one of Clark's reviews because he deemed it "too intemperate."[53] Clark pointed out that "the sentences you quote and ascribed to me, and which you thought intemperate, were not my sentences at all" and asked

49. Clark, "The Proposal to Abolish the RPCES."

50. For a time, after the Joining and Receiving occurred, Clark—having refused to attend the PCA church—attended a small OPC church (North River OPC) in the Chattanooga suburb of Hixson, Tennessee. Andrew Zeller, interview by Douglas Douma, Sangre de Cristo Seminary, 6 September 2015. Note that while Clark attended this church, he did not apply for membership. He wrote, "I did not apply for membership in the OPC. There is so much animosity against me there, I could not face a fight to get in."—GHC to Greg Reynolds, 9 December 1984. Provided by Greg Reynolds.

51. Clark, "The Proposal to Abolish the RPCES," 6.

52. GHC to G. Taylor Aiken, 4 March 1970, PCA Archives, 309/57.

53. G. Taylor Aiken to GHC, 30 November 1970, PCA Archives, 309/57.

Taylor twice to acknowledge his fault.[54] When Taylor's responses contained no such acknowledgment, Clark discontinued his work for the journal.[55]

In addition to the reasons written in Clark's "The Proposal to Abolish the RPCES," Clark vocalized an additional reason for his opposition to the merger. On multiple occasions, according to Dwight Zeller, Clark said the PCA's acceptance of secret societies such as the Freemasons was a hurdle to the merger.[56] This is confirmed in a letter Clark wrote to John Robbins saying, "The merger with the PCA is a disaster. By tolerating masons with their ministry they tolerate the worship of Allah, religious exercise from which the name of Christ is banned, and a sort of universalism based on good works."[57]

Clark hoped to continue the RPCES denomination and had support in this mission from Rev. Franklin S. Dyrness, the founder of the Quarryville Presbyterian Retirement Home.[58] Dyrness was heavily involved in the RP-CES. He managed many of their financial assets *pro bono*, including their pension fund.[59] Referring to Clark's "The Proposal to Abolish the RPCES," Dyrness wrote to Clark, "I have received your article regarding J&R. It is superior and we are taking steps to have it duplicated."[60] According to his family, Dyrness fought "tooth and nail" against the merger.[61]

Despite opposition from men such as Dyrness and Clark, the General Synod of the RPCES voted 322 to 90 to approve the merger with the PCA.

54. GHC to G. Aiken Taylor, 12 March 1970, PCA Archives, 309/57.; GHC to G. Aiken Taylor, 21 November 1970, PCA Archives, 309/57.

55. GHC to G. Aiken Taylor, 14 December 1970, PCA Archives, 309/57.

56. Dwight Zeller, interview by Douglas Douma, Sangre de Cristo Seminary, 2015.

57. GHC to John Robbins, 1 February 1983, letter courtesy of The Trinity Foundation.

58. Dyrness, "About the Proposed Union." See also: Dyrness, "'No' to Joining and Receiving."

59. Clark was also a board member of the Quarryville Presbyterian Home during this time. Covenant College, advertisement in *The Tartan* 1980 *Yearbook,* 132, https://archive.org/details/tartan1980unse.

60. F. S. Dyrness to GHC, 1 April 1982, from Gordon Clark's personal papers, in the possession of the Clark family.

61. Dyrness's opposition to the merger can be seen in his church session's opposition. The minutes read: "The session of Faith Reformed Presbyterian Church of Quarryville felt that such a move [joining the PCA] would be ill-advised and detrimental because it would jeopardize the work of the World Presbyterian Missions, compromise the distinctives of the Reformed Presbyterian Church, and insult the brethren of the Orthodox Presbyterian Church. Therefore, all six active ruling elders of our session voted against this proposal."

On June 14, 1982, the RPCES, along with its Covenant Theological Seminary and Covenant College, merged into the PCA.[62]

When the Joining and Receiving of the RPCES and PCA did occur, Dyrness, although aggressively opposed to the merger, felt that it was the correct Presbyterian action to yield to the majority.[63] According to an article in *The Presbyterian Journal*, "For many in the RPCES, the process of bringing the churches together reached its culmination when the Rev. Franklin S. Dyrness of Quarryville, Pa., addressed the combined churches and spoke of his support for the new denomination. In recent months, Dyrness had been a staunch opponent of the proposal."[64] While Dyrness came to accept the merger, Clark did not. Clark felt betrayed and wrote an excoriating letter to Dyrness, effectively ending their friendship. According to Dyrness's family, Franklin was shocked by the letter.[65]

Following the merger, Clark stopped attending presbytery meetings and looked for a new denomination. He ruled out transferring his membership to the OPC because he perceived animosity against him there. He felt theologically comfortable with the RCUS, but he had no contacts there and felt that their center in the Dakotas was too distant. He also ruled out the Covenanters (the RPCNA) because he could not agree with their positions of Psalm-only singing and the exclusion of musical instruments in worship. When he transferred his ministerial credentials it was to the independent Covenant Presbytery. One reason Clark joined the Covenant Presbytery was his friendship with Allan MacRae, whom he had known since the early days of the OPC. MacRae founded Covenant Presbytery in 1971 after leading a group to break away from Carl McIntire's Bible Presbyterian Church, Collingswood Synod.[66] Clark also chose Covenant Presbytery because it was geographically spread out; this meant he was unlikely to play a prominent role or attend many meetings, which was to his liking as he did not enjoy meetings.[67]

---

62. Clements, *Historical Roots*, 235.

63. Nancy Dyrness, Lois (née Dyrness) Mitchell, and Keith Mitchell, interview by Douglas Douma, conference call, 9 November 2014.

64. Taylor, "It Was a New Beginning for the PCA," 4–5.

65. Nancy Dyrness, Lois (née Dyrness) Mitchell, and Keith Mitchell, interview by Douglas Douma, conference call, 9 November 2014.

66. This particular Covenant Presbytery should not be confused with the like-named Covenant Presbytery that became the Reformed Presbyterian Church in the United States (RPCUS), nor should it be confused with the Covenant Presbytery in the PCA.

67. GHC to Greg Reynolds, 9 December 1984, Provided by Greg Reynolds.

"MY GOOD FRIEND"—PERSONAL RECONCILIATION
WITH CORNELIUS VAN TIL

Late in life Clark and Cornelius Van Til crossed paths on at least four occasions. Judging from the two men's actions on these occasions and from words they wrote in those later years, it seems as though any lingering animosity from the days of their controversy was minimal.

The first of these four encounters occurred in the fall of 1977. Clark had been invited by students of Westminster Theological Seminary to visit and give a lecture, and he jumped at the opportunity. Clark's daughter Lois and her husband Dwight Zeller then lived in a nearby suburb, so Clark stayed with them, using his visit to Philadelphia as a chance to spend time with family. Greg Reynolds, a former student of Clark's at Covenant College, then attending Westminster, had the idea of having Clark come to speak. LeRoy Oliver, former chairman of the board of trustees at Westminster (1963–1973) was also keen on the idea. Through Oliver, Reynolds arranged for Clark to speak in the chapel and meet students in Machen Hall. Of this meeting with the students, Reynolds recalled, "I remember marveling at how sharp Dr. Clark was in answering students' questions, some quite challenging."[68] After the lecture Oliver arranged for Clark and Van Til to have a lunch together along with other members of the faculty, including John Frame, Paul Woolley, and Robert Knudsen. According to Dwight Zeller, both Clark and Van Til were glad for the opportunity.[69] The reconciliation between Clark and Van Til was not philosophical, but personal. Both had recently become widowers, and both were advancing in years (Clark was seventy-five and Van Til was eighty-two). Reynolds recalled, "I remember that Clark and Van Til met in the driveway in front of Machen Hall. They warmly embraced one another."[70] Later that year, in an interview for *Christianity Today*, Van Til made a reference to "my good friend Gordon Clark [who] believes in the inerrancy of the Bible."[71]

A second time Clark and Van Til crossed paths later in life was in 1981 when Clark visited Faith Theological Seminary in Philadelphia to give a lecture on apologetics. He was invited by Norris Clark (no relation to himself, but the grandson of Carl McIntire, the president of the seminary). Van Til attended and listened to the lecture. After the lecture, Clark told Dr. Gary L.

68. Rev. Dr. Greg Reynolds (student at Covenant College from 1973–1975 and at WTS from 1976–1979), email to the author, 11 October 2014.

69. Dwight Zeller and Lois Clark Zeller, interview by Douglas Douma, Sangre de Cristo Seminary, 24 April 2014.

70. Rev. Dr. Greg Reynolds, e-mail to the author, 11 October 2014.

71. Kucharsky, "At the Beginning, God: An Interview With Cornelius Van Til," 20.

W. Johnson (then a student at Faith) that Van Til had always been courteous to him and that of all the WTS professors during the controversy in the 1940s it was Ned Stonehouse who had had it out for him [Clark].[72]

Toward the end of his life, Clark's relationship with Van Til, in fact, seems to have been quite positive; far more positive than one might expect considering Van Til's attempt years earlier to nullify Clark's ordination. In a lecture in 1981 Clark said, "I'm on very good terms with all my enemies; I mean my apologetic enemies."[73] In fact, Clark did not think of Van Til as an enemy, but counted him as a friend. According to Clark's grandson, Andrew Zeller, who lived with Clark while attending Covenant College, Clark referred to Van Til as "my good friend Van Til." Zeller recalled, "I heard him say that many times."[74]

Clark and Van Til met again in the fall of 1983 when Clark flew to Philadelphia to give a speech at a dinner in Van Til's honor. According to Frank Walker, a friend of Clark and former student at Covenant College, Van Til was asked who he wanted as the speaker and he chose Clark. Walker also recalled:

> I had an extended conversation one evening with Clark about their relationship, and he said very clearly that he had never held anything against Van Til personally. Their differences were strictly theological. Van Til's followers in the late '40s didn't understand this and began persecuting Clark's supporters and defenders. This was something that both Clark and Van Til regretted. Clark left the OPC only when he realized that nothing would change in the near future. I also spoke to Van Til about his relationship with Clark (probably around 1978) at his home near the campus of Westminster Seminary. Unfortunately, by that time his mind had deteriorated to the point where it was hard to get any meaningful information from him, but I didn't get a sense that he thought of Clark as anything but a dear Christian brother.[75]

A fourth occasion was mentioned by Carl Henry in a lecture given at Westminster Theological Seminary; he said that he, Clark, Van Til, and Alvin Plantinga met in Grand Rapids, Michigan, for an "unpublicized dinner"

72. Gary L. W. Johnson, former Faith Seminary student, interview by Douglas Douma, phone, 5 May 2015.

73. Clark, "A Christian Construction Part 2."

74. Andrew Zeller, conversation with Douglas Douma, Sangre de Cristo Seminary, 2014.

75. Dr. Frank Walker, e-mail to the author, 13 October 2014.

with a "two-or three-hour dialogue." Henry did not provide the date or even the year of this meeting, but judging from his comments about Van Til being "a little past his prime," it was likely sometime in the early 1980s.[76]

Although theological issues still separated the two men, a certain amount of reconciliation and forgiveness must have been shared between them. Two books in the Clark Collection at the Sangre de Cristo Seminary library have notes from Van Til evidencing this fact. The first, Van Til's *The God of Hope: Sermons and Addresses,* with a copyright of 1978, has a note which reads:

> *Gordon H. Clark*
> *Your brother in our*
> *common Savior*
> *Cornelius Van Til*

And a second book of Van Til's, *The Reformed Pastor and The Defense of Christianity & My Credo,* with a copyright of 1980, has a note which reads:

> *to Gordon H. Clark*
> *from Cornelius Van Til*
> *your brother in Christ*
> *Jesus our Lord*

COLORADO AND THE FINAL YEARS

After Clark's wife passed away in July of 1977, Gordon Clark lived alone. His grandson stayed with him for a little over a year (beginning in January of 1982), but by the time Andrew moved out to get married in May of 1983, Clark had put his house on the market. The home had much more space than he needed if he were to live alone, and his frugal disposition motivated him to sell it. When the house sold, late in the summer of the following year, Clark moved into a small apartment (August or September, 1983). Andrew noted that he was sad to see his grandfather move into small, dark quarters that were "well below his dignity." But Clark did not live in the basement-level apartment for long. Less than a year later, at age eighty-one, Clark retired from Covenant College and moved permanently to Sangre de Cristo Seminary, taking the title "scholar in residence."[77]

76. Henry, "New Specter: Postmodernism," minute 3..

77. GHC to John Robbins, 30 August 1984, letter courtesy of The Trinity Foundation.

The seminary, in rural Colorado outside the town of Westcliffe, was founded in 1976 by Clark's son-in-law, Dwight Zeller. When he was a professor at Covenant College, Clark taught in the summers at the seminary as a visiting professor, starting in 1979. Of Sangre de Cristo, Clark wrote:

> There I sleep under several blankets with electric heat in the room, and like the king in Gilbert and Sullivan. Rising early in the morning, first I go and light the fires. It snows there every month except July. Two years ago there was a four inch snow in August. In Jan. they have four foot snows. There are some deer, goats, maybe a bear, and dozens of hummingbirds, who sometimes sit on my finger to drink their sugar-water.[78]

Clark always had a place in his heart for the western states. On road trips he would stop and paint landscapes of the various land formations in New Mexico and of the wildlife in West Texas. While living in Colorado he painted a number of pictures of the area, including some of Horn Peak, the mountain nearest the seminary. A poem, which Clark wrote but submitted anonymously to *The Thorn*, Covenant College's annual literary publication, evidenced his love of the western states:

THE WEST

In the car below the kitchen,
Engine running, packing done,
We our suitcases will pitch in,
Then drive toward the setting sun.

At fifty-five or seventy,
Or even at eleventy,
We cross the Kansas plains,
With windows shut at summer's heat,

The cool air blowing on our feet,
And likewise when it rains,
Down into Carlsbad's caverns deep,
And through Juarez' Mercado creep,

Then north to Santa Fe,
Of course at White Sands' desert place

---

78. GHC to John Robbins, 7 June 1980, letter courtesy of The Trinity Foundation.

And Albuquerque's Spanish base
We stop along the way.

To Mesa Verde toward the west
And Arches at their very best,
We drive to Dinosaurs
Then up the Colorado stream,

Mt. Evans, heavens, like a dream,
We pass our happy hours.
A dream, a dream, say it is not,
Or bury me and let me rot.[79]

When Clark announced his impending retirement from Covenant, Clark's son-in-law prepared a list of reasons to use to convince Clark to move to Colorado, but such a list proved unnecessary. When Zeller invited Clark to relocate, Clark quickly responded, "I'd like to." It was therefore resolved, and in September of 1984 Clark headed to Colorado to teach what would be the final course of his career.[80] Once settled in Colorado he took a driver's test to get his license in the state. He failed the test; it was quite possibly the only test he failed in his entire life. Unwilling to retake the test, he gave up driving and sold his car.

On the morning of April 9, 1985, surrounded by the beautiful landscapes and family he had so loved, Gordon H. Clark passed away. He died in his home at Sangre de Cristo Seminary one week after being released from the hospital with a stomach illness. He had first gone to St. Thomas More Hospital in nearby Cañon City, but because of the severity of his condition, he was transferred to a larger hospital in Colorado Springs. Knowing his death was imminent and that doctors could do nothing for him, Clark convinced them to let him go home. According to family, he was as stoic in death as many believed him to be in life, and he faced the inevitable with whatever grace is possible in such circumstances. The cause of death was cirrhosis of the liver, not from alcohol—which he never drank—but from the effects of the drug Indocin, which he had taken since his forties to treat arthritis. He was eighty-two years old.

At the time of his death, his family included his two daughters and their husbands, twelve grandchildren, and one great-grandchild. A simple gravestone shows the location of his burial at the Ula Cemetery near Westcliffe,

79. Clark, "The West."
80. Andrew Zeller, e-mail to the author, 29 December 2015.

Colorado. According to the bulletin from the funeral service, he had last preached in December of 1984 on the topic of Jesus Christ's incarnation. The funeral service bulletin also records his last words two days before his death: "Dwight, I hope you'll have a good library" (referring to his son-in-law Dwight Zeller and the library at Sangre de Cristo Seminary).[81] This library, quite modest in size, is now the Clark Library, and Clark's portrait hangs on a wall in its center.

CLARK'S LEGACY: A CALL TO CONFORM TO THE CONFESSION

Throughout his career, Clark supported the system of doctrine of the *Westminster Confession of Faith*. His legacy is a call for the church to respect the *Confession* and study its doctrines. For Christians outside of Presbyterianism, in more broadly fundamentalist churches, Clark's emphasis on the *Confession* is a call to expand one's knowledge of doctrines beyond the mere basics of the Christian faith. For Presbyterians, the history of Clark's struggles in the church points to the importance of limiting ordination requirements to the doctrinal system of the Confession, helping to prevent personal opinions or idiosyncrasies from causing animosity within the church.

Yet the value of reading Clark's publications is not limited to just one particular denomination or another. For many, his work provides answers to difficult questions of doctrine and apologetics. For others, his work inspires confidence in the truth of the Christian faith. And for all Christians, regardless of denomination, Clark serves as a champion of the faith. He was a man of great integrity and uncompromising principles. He asked hard questions and wrote prolifically for the benefit of his fellow man and for the furtherance of solid doctrine. His legacy is that of a stalwart defender of Christianity, and his is an example worth following.

81. Dwight Zeller, interview by Douglas Douma, Sangre de Cristo Seminary, 23 November 2014 and other dates.

Appendix A

Life Timeline of Gordon H. Clark

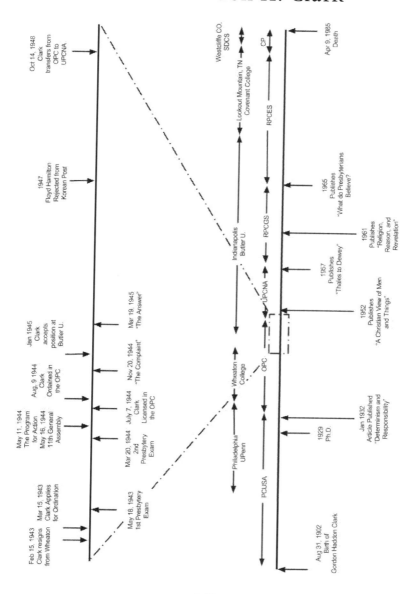

Appendix B

Notes

PROFESSORSHIPS OF GORDON H. CLARK

University of Pennsylvania (instructor 1924–Winter 1936)

Reformed Episcopal Seminary (visiting professor 1930–1936, Fall 1944)

Wheaton College (Fall 1936–Winter 1943)

Butler University (Winter 1945–Winter 1973)

Winona Lake School of Theology (visiting professor, most Summers 1959–1969)

Pensacola Theological Institute (visiting professor, Summers of 1957, 1961, 1970)

Geneva College (visiting professor, Fall 1974)

Covenant College (Fall 1974–Winter 1984)

Sangre de Cristo Seminary (visiting professor, Summers 1979–1984)

GORDON H. CLARK'S AFFILIATIONS AS A MINISTER:

Orthodox Presbyterian Church (1944–1948)

United Presbyterian Church of North America (UPCNA) (1948–1957)

Reformed Presbyterian Church, General Synod (RPC,GS) later to become upon merger the Reformed Presbyterian Church Evangelical Synod (RPCES) (1957–1982)

Covenant Presbytery (1983–1984)

TIMELINE OF THE CONTROVERSY

Date	Event	Location
May 9, 1942	Clark sends letter applying for ordination.	Presbytery
Mar 10, 1943	Clark's article "An Appeal to Fundamentalists."	Guardian
Mar 15, 1943	Clark's letter applying for ordination read.	Presbytery
May 18, 1943	Clark examined by Committee on Candidates and Credentials.	Presbytery
May 1943	Clark's article "On the Primacy of the Intellect."	WTJ
Mar 20, 1944	Clark again examined by Committee and enrolled as candidate.	Presbytery
Mar 30, 1944	Clark's examination in Bible, church history, and Greek.	Presbytery
May 11, 1944	The "Program for Action" sent to select ministers.	N/A
May 16, 1944	Clark's seminary education requirement waiver approved.	11th GA
July 7, 1944	Special Meeting. Clark licensed to preach.	Presbytery
Aug 9, 1944	Clark ordained at Calvary OPC, Willow Grove.	Presbytery
Nov 20, 1944	"The Complaint" Presented on the floor of presbytery on November 20, 1944. (Filed with Stated Clerk of Pres. of Phila. on Oct. 6, 1944)	Presbytery
Jan 10, 1945	Clark's article "Blessed River of Salvation"	Guardian
March 19, 1945	Copies of "The Answer" handed out.	Presbytery
March 29, 1945	Presbytery votes 23–14 and 20–16 against the Complaint.	Presbytery
May 17–23, 1945	Having been defeated at Presbytery the Complaint is made at GA level. A committee of five elected to study doctrines.	12th GA
Oct 9, 1945	Clark's transfer to OPC's Presbytery of Ohio is approved.	Presbytery
May 21, 1946	Report of the committee appointed by 12th GA.	13th GA
Winter 1946/47	"Studies in the Doctrine of the Complaint"—Gordon H. Clark	N/A
Apr 1947	"Whither the Orthodox Presbyterian Church" by Edward Heerema	N/A
Apr-May 1947	7 Letters of Samuel Allen to OPC Ministers	N/A
May 22, 1947	14th GA. Report at 14th GA. Hamilton not sent to Korea.	14th GA
May 13, 1948	Reports at 15th GA	15th GA
Oct 14, 1948	Dr. Clark departs the OPC and joins the United Presbyterian Church	N/A

20th Century American Presbyterian Denominations

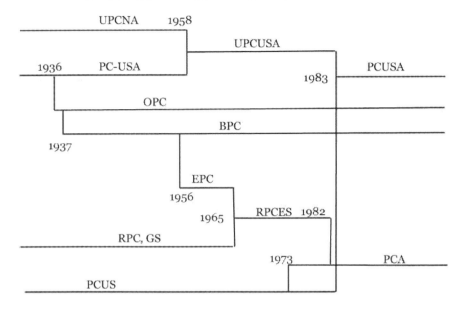

Immediate Family of Gordon H. Clark

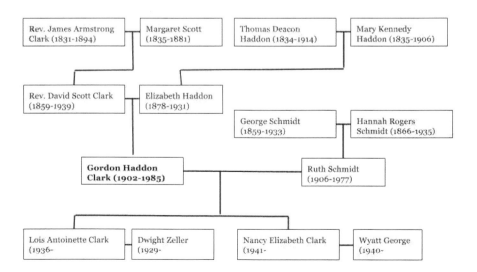

Appendix C

Studies of the Doctrine of
The Complaint

STUDIES OF THE DOCTRINES OF "THE COMPLAINT"

SERIOUS DOCTRINAL ISSUES HAVE been raised in The Orthodox Presbyterian Church during the years 1944–1946. The thirteenth General Assembly elected five ministers to study the four doctrines in question. It is the duty of all ministers and elders of our Church to study these doctrines so as to protect the Church from error. It is the conviction of many of the ministers that the doctrine of *The Complaint* are not the doctrines of the Word of God or of our subordinate standards. We believe that in several respects *The Complaint* goes beyond the Confession and is contrary to the historic position of the Reformed Churches. This paper is one of several, which, appearing during the winter of 1946–1947, aim to preserve the original position of The Orthodox Presbyterian Church.
Gordon H. Clark

THE PHILOSOPHY OF "THE COMPLAINT."

At the General Assembly of May 1946, following a speech by Dr. Van Til, I began a defense of my position. As it took fifty minutes to complete the introduction, wisdom dictated that the Assembly take a recess. The remaining days of the Assembly seemed to me to offer no compelling moment for the main part of my speech. And therefore I take this opportunity to present some of the main material. As an introduction to this paper I should like to indicate my own position on the incomprehensibility of God, and then by way of contrast discuss the theory of the Complaint.

It may be remembered that at the General Assembly I expressed my whole hearted approval of that early portion of Dr. Van Til's address, in which he summarized the doctrines of the incomprehensibility of God. With his explicit remarks in the part of that speech, I agree.

Furthermore, with some of the material in the Complaint contains several columns of quotations from standard reformed writers. These writers are important representatives of Calvinism, and yet they are not infallible. Since, too, the quotations were selected to fit the tenor of the Complaint, it may be that these quotations contain unguarded statements. At least, the quotations may possibly be so made as to alter the intention of the authors.

For example, in *The Complaint*, page 3, column 2, Charnock is quoted as saying, "It is utterly impossible either to behold him or comprehend him." As quoted in the Complaint, this may give a wrong impression. Charnock in the context is talking about literal vision with physical eyes. In this sense it is, as he says, impossible to "behold" a pure Spirit. But the doctrine of the Complaint, as will be show, implies that it is utterly impossible to contemplate or behold God with the mind. This is not the force of Charnock's paragraph; and it is not true. The complainants, by omitting the information that Charnock is speaking of physical sensation, attempt to make it appear that Charnock supports their own, very different, position.

However, if these quotations be detached from the Complaint, the following sentences in particular state nothing else than the truth, as I see it. With these statements I fully agree.

"We cannot have an adequate or suitable conception of God" (Charnock).

"It is utterly impossible to have a notion of God commensurate to the immensity and spirituality of his being" (Charnock).

"When it is said that God can be known, it is not meant that he can be comprehended. To comprehend is to have a complete and exhaustive knowledge of an object. It is to understand its nature and relations . . . God is past finding out. We cannot understand the Almighty to perfection" (Charles Hodge).

In this excellent statement by Charles Hodge attention should be particularly drawn to his definition of *comprehend*. It seems that neither side in the present controversy has always used the term in this exact meaning. Clarity would be more perfectly attained if all of us could limit ourselves to this one meaning. But the force of English usage had led us to think of incomprehensibility as meaning unintelligibility. And it seems to me that the

Complaint teaches rather the unintelligibility or irrationality of God than the incomprehensibility of God in Hodge's sense of the term.

The Answer, which still deserves more thorough study by all those interested in the present matter, was written with the Complaint sharply in view. In opposition to the Complaint's view that incomprehensibility means irrationality or unknowability, the Answer defends the view of Charles Hodge that "to comprehend is to have a *complete* and *exhaustive* knowledge." This meaning does not require the conclusion that God cannot be known at all. It means rather that we cannot know all about God. Therefore, in its account of the doctrine, the Answer puts in the very first place an assertion that incomprehensibility must not be so understood as to deny that God can reveal truth. With this foremost assertion of the possibility of revelation the Answer gives a fair, even if not an "adequate" account of the doctrine. Since I am one of its authors, it obviously represents my views.

The Answer, page 9, says, "Dr. Clark contends that the doctrine of the incomprehensibility of God as set forth in Scripture and in the Confession of Faith includes the following points: 1. The essence of God's being is incomprehensible to man except as God reveals truths concerning his own nature; 2 The manner of God's knowing, an eternal intuition, is impossible for man; 3. Man can never know exhaustively and completely God's knowledge of any truth in all its relationships and implications; because every truth has an infinite number of relationships and implications, these must ever, even in heaven, remain inexhaustible for man. 4. But, Dr. Clark maintains, the doctrine of the incomprehensibility of God does not mean that a proposition, e.g. two times two are four, has one meaning for man and a qualitatively different meaning for God, or that some truth is conceptual and other truth is non-conceptual in nature."

But while these several quotations all reflect sound doctrine, this sound doctrine may be, and in the case of the Complaint part of it has been embedded in a document which by its philosophy and epistemology deviates from the sound doctrine it quotes. Sometimes, as in the case of Dr. Van Til's address in General Assembly, the complainants summarize the doctrine quite acceptably; but when they develop their views, as they have in the Complaint, it is seen that their epistemology so distorts the doctrine that the resultant whole cannot logically be regarded as reformed. The source of the difficulty and the chief issue between the two parties is epistemological. The men who wrote the Answer maintain the position of Warfield, Hodge, Charnock, and Calvin. That the Complaint does not consistently hold this position, but that it alters and vitiates the doctrine by an untenable epistemology, it is the aim of this paper to prove.

To this end the paper discusses first, the Philosophic Background of the Complaint; second the The Philosophy of the Complaint; third, A Subsequent Paper; and fourth, The Biblical Doctrine.

THE PHILOSOPHIC BACKGROUND

The necessity of examining the philosophic background of the Complaint is seen in the fact that certain members of the Assembly openly admitted that they did not understand the issues and accordingly based their votes on their confidence in the ability and scholarship of the complainants. Now, it is not unreasonable for people to follow their trusted leaders when they cannot judge the merits of a case for themselves. But there comes a time to examine the basis of such confidence. A perpetual and blind following of any human leader is not the mark of an educated and conscientious person. The Rev. Robert H. Graham, in a letter dated July 8 1946, speaks of the authors of the Complaint as theological giants. That is his privilege. It is the privilege of all to examine the evidence to see if his estimate is supported by a study of their writings.

Dr. Van Til's views are obviously the philosophic background of the Complaint. Therefore to understand the Complaint, one must examine the philosophy of Dr. Van Til. Now, his views were formed partly by his study of the history of philosophy; and it is also true that his interpretations of history of philosophy is colored by his views. Inasmuch as he has written at length on this history, let us first examine his work in this easily tested field.

To show how Dr. Van Til expounds the views of other men, let us first turn to his Syllabus on Apologetics, page 84, where he is discussing medieval philosophy. He says, "In stating the problem (whether universals are *ante rem*, *in re*, or *post rem*) the scholastics failed to distinguish between God and man. They did not ask first whether the ideas of universals were prior to a thing known in the case of God, in order then in a separate question to ask whether the universals were prior to a thing in the case of man." Now contrast Dr. Van Til's understanding of medieval philosophy with that of Windelband, *History of Philosophy*, page 299: "Even Abelard, however, explains this likeness of character in a multiplicity of individuals upon the hypothesis that God created the world according to archetypes which he carried in his mind. Thus according to his view, the universals exist firstly, *before the things*, as *conceptus mentis* in God; secondly, in *the things*, as likenesses of the essential characteristics of individuals; thirdly, *after the things*, in the human understanding as its concepts and predicates acquired by comparative thought (italics, Windelband's). . . . As regards the real question at issue he had advanced so far that it was essentially his theory that became the ruling doctrine in the formula accepted by the Arabian philosophers—Avicenna—'*universalia ante multiplicitatem, in multiplicitate, et post mutiplicitatem*;' to universals belongs equally a significance *ante rem* as regards the divine mind, *in re* as regards Nature, and *post rem* as regards human knowledge. And since Thomas and Duns Scotus in the main agreed with this view, the problem of universals, which, to be sure, has not yet been solved, came to a preliminary rest, to come again into the foreground when Nominalism was revived."

It is clear that Dr. Van Til says that the scholastics did not do what as a matter of well known fact they did do. It should be specifically noted that this is not just a question of interpretation. Someone might want to defend Dr. Van Til on the ground that every philosopher proposes his own interpretations of the previous philosophers. One man has one view of the scholastics and another man has a different view, and Dr. Van Til is entitled to his. This is not the case at issue. The point is that Dr. Van Til has not correctly represented the views in question. He has said that the scholastics failed to do what as a matter of plain historical fact they did do.

In the next place notice should be taken of Dr. Van Til's account of Descartes. In the mimeographed syllabus on *Christian Theistic Evidences*, page 96, Dr. Van Til says that Descartes "studied the mind as an entity that had nothing to do with the body."

But in *The Principles of Philosophy*, Part Two, Descartes states his second thesis as "How we likewise know that the human body is closely connected with the mind." In Part Four of the same work, section 189, Descartes says, "We must know, therefore, that although the human soul is united to the whole body, it has, nevertheless, its principal seat in the brain . . . " And a few lines below: "the movements which are thus excited in the brain by the nerves variously affect the soul or mind, which is intimately conjoined with the brain . . . " Cf. passim. Again, as in the case of the scholastics, there seems to be a discrepancy between Dr. Van Til's account and the sources.

Dr. Van Til continues, in his *Christian Theistic Evidences*, to say, "Descartes thought of the mind in exclusively intellectual terms. 'L'ame pense toujours' was the principle of his psychology. The emotional and the volitive were disregarded." But it should not be forgotten that Descartes wrote a volume *On the Passions of the Soul*. A brief indication that Descartes did not disregard the volitional and the emotional aspects of man's nature is found in Article 18 of this work: "Our volitions are of two kinds . . . " And then Descartes goes on to distinguish them. Article 41 of the same work says, "The will is so free in its nature that it can never be constrained . . . " Article 45 says, "Our passions cannot be directly excited or removed by the action of the will; but they can be indirectly through the representation (or, imagination) of things which are customarily joined with the passions . . . "

Nor is it necessary to confine the evidence to Descartes work *On the Passions of the Soul. The Meditations* themselves show that Dr. Van Til is not altogether accurate. In Meditation IV Descartes explains error on the ground of a certain relation between the understanding and the will: "I observe that these (errors) depend on the concurrence of the two causes, viz. the faculty of cognition which I possess, and that of election or the power of free choice—in other words, the understanding and the will." Then Descartes continues for a few pages to discuss the will, in spite of the fact that Dr. Van Til asserts that Descartes disregarded the volitional aspect of man's personality. Further evidence will be found in Descartes' *Reply to the Second Objection.*

Then Dr. Van Til continues: "The mind of man was thought of as being independent of God." How could this assertion be made when two thirds the way through Meditation III Descartes writes: "I possess the perception (notion) of the infinite before that of the finite; that is, the perception of God before that of myself, for how could I know that I doubt, desire, or that something is wanting to me, and that I am not wholly perfect, if I possessed no idea of a being more perfect than myself, by comparison of which I knew the deficiencies of my nature?"

A little further on Descartes writes: "I am desirous to inquire further whether I, who possess this idea of God, could exist supposing there were no God . . . " And then he goes on to argue at considerable length that first he could not be dependent on himself; second, that he could not be dependent on his parents; third, that there could not be several causes as the ultimate explanation of his being; and then for some pages Descartes stresses his dependence on God. Finally he says, "And in truth it is not to be wondered at that God at my creation implanted this idea (of God) in me, that it might serve, as it were, for the mark of the workman impressed on his work." And then, "I not only find that I am an incomplete (imperfect), and dependent being, . . . but at the same time I am assured likewise that he upon whom I am dependent possesses in himself all the goods after which I aspire . . . and that he is thus God." But Dr. Van Til asserts that Descartes thought of the mind of man as independent of God!

Dr. Van Til's book, *The New Modernism,* is also faulty in its understanding of philosophy. On page 11 he says, "Leibniz thought it was possible for man, by means of a refined logical apparatus, to learn to distinguish one penguin from another."

Now, Leibniz, in his Discourse on Metaphysics, VIII, (where he is talking about Alexander the Great instead of penguins) says "God, however, seeing the individual concept, or haecceity, of Alexander, sees there at the same time the basis and reason of all the predicates which can be truly uttered regarding him; for instance that he will conquer Darius . . . —facts which *we can learn only through history*." Ibidem XIII: "If anyone were capable of carrying out a complete demonstration by virtue of which he could prove this connection of the subject . . . with the predicate, . . . he *would* bring us to see" etc. Apparently therefore Leibniz teaches that man is not capable of distinguishing one person or one penguin from another by pure logic. Bearing on the same subject, even if not so directly, is *ibidem* V: "To know in particular, however, the reasons which have moved him (God) to choose this order of the universe . . . —this passes the capacity of a finite mind, above all when such a mind has not come into the joy of the vision of God." This passage places limitations on human knowledge which Dr. Van Til apparently misses in Leibniz.

Dr. Van Til continues on page 11 to say, "All knowledge, he contended, that is all true knowledge, is speculative or analytical at bottom. By working up the contents of your mind you may eventually learn all the fields of truth and all they contain."

Now, if the word *analytical* be omitted, the phrase all true knowledge (what would false knowledge be?) and the word, *speculative*, in Dr. Van Til's sentence are sufficiently vague to make the sentence true in some sense or other. But Leibniz never taught that all knowledge was analytical. In the Discourse XIII, Leibniz teaches that some truths are not analytical, but contingent. Some predicates cannot be obtained from their subjects by the law of contradiction; and even in God's perfect knowledge, the "demonstration" of the predicate is not as absolute as are those of numbers or geometry. The contrary does not imply a contradiction, and hence not all truth is analytic. Cf. further, *On the Ultimate Constitution of Things*, of Nov. 23, 1697.

In view of these items that have now been analyzed, it is necessary to conclude that there are historical inaccuracies in Dr. Van Til's treatment of philosophy. Since the items analyzed are not matters of delicate interpretation where one man's opinion is almost as good as another's, but are matters of historical fact, the reader is cautioned not to accept Dr. Van Til's every statement without examination. And if caution is required in the purely historical portion of his work, it would seem reasonable to use even more caution in the study of his constructive argumentation. What it is important to see is that the philosophic background of the Complaint is not to be accepted uncritically. In view of this philosophic background one has prima facie reason to suspect the epistemology and apologetics of the Complaint. It must be clear to anyone who has studied that document that its ideas and accusations are largely based on Dr. Van Til's views, and hence the truth and the accuracy of the philosophic work behind the Complaint are of tremendous importance in estimating its value. Not that the Complaint should be condemned on mere suspicion: the suspicion will be verified by an examination of the document itself.

THE COMPLAINT AND ITS PHILOSOPHY

Of all the documents in the present controversy the Complaint is the most important. It is not the impromptu answers of a single person to a barrage of questions, but it is the result of extended collaboration. Any mistake that one person might have made on the spur of the moment had to pass the inspection of, and would be corrected by, all the other authors. Hence its wording must be considered the most accurate possible; and its presentation must be the most authoritative presentation of the views of those men. It was written, signed, and published by Professor R.B. Kuiper, Professor Paul Woolley, Professor Cornelius Van Til, Professor Edward J. Young—five members of the faculty of Westminster Theological Seminary, and also by Mr. Arthur W. Kuschke and Mr. Leslie W. Sloat, who were at that time connected with the Seminary. (Six other men, not so directly connected with the Seminary, also collaborated.) Hence the Complaint must be considered as the actual position of the large majority of the Westminster faculty. Note in particular that a Complaint against a Presbytery is always a serious matter. And this Complaint speaks of an unblushing humanistic rationalism and vicious independence of God. The awfulness of this charge, and the widespread publicity given to the document, all show that this must have been the most carefully prepared statement that these professors could make. It must accurately express their deepest convictions. Let us then examine this most important document.

The Complaint admits that Dr. Clark distinguishes between what may be called the divine psychology and human psychology in the act of knowing. God's mode of knowing is intuitive, while man's is always temporal and discursive. This distinction, the Complaint claims, is insufficient; a further distinction is needed. It is obvious therefore that the complainants hold to a two-fold theory of something in addition to a two-fold theory of the act of knowing.

Note too that the difference they wish to establish between God's knowledge and man's knowledge is not that God knows and man does not know all the implications of a given truth. This, of course, is true, but it is not the distinction the Complaint insists upon. The Complaint insists on a two-fold theory of something connected with a single truth itself, quite apart from its implications (cf. *The Complaint*, p.6, col. 2).

A little examination will show that this other something, of which the complainants say they are two kinds—one for God and one for man, is the truth itself. The Complaint teaches a two-layer theory of truth. On page 5, col. 1, it says, "Dr. Clark denies that there is any qualitative difference between the contents of the knowledge of God and the contents of the knowledge possible to man." Since they make this as an objection, it must be that they *assert* a qualitative difference between the contents of the knowledge of God and the contents of the knowledge possible to man.

At this point the important question arises, what are the *contents* of one's knowledge? Obviously the *contents* of one's knowledge are the *truths* one knows. The only answer to the question, what does one know? is a list of the truths known. Truth is the object and content of knowledge. The contents of God's knowledge are the truth he knows, and the contents of a man's knowledge are the truth the man knows. The Complaint maintains that these two sets of truths are qualitatively different.

This qualitative difference between the truths God knows and the truths that man knows is further emphasized in *The Complaint*, page 5, col. 2, bottom. Again as an unacceptable conclusion from Dr. Clark's views they state, "a proposition would have to have the same meaning for man as for God." Since this is unacceptable to them, the Complaint must teach that a proposition does not have the same meaning for man as for God. Propositions therefore have two meanings. 'David was king of Israel' means one thing for us; it means something different for God. What is means for God, we cannot know because the meaning God has is qualitatively different from ours, and man can never have God's meanings.

The culmination of this argument in the Complaint is reached in the next column: p.5, col. 3. To make sure that everyone would understand that this is the crux of the matter, to make everyone see that this is the distinction between God's knowledge and man's knowledge that the doctrine of incomprehensibility requires, the complainants have put it in italics. Here is found the main point of the whole discussion. The Complaint says, "we dare not maintain that his knowledge and our knowledge *coincide at any single point*" (italics theirs).

Note well that the complainants are not content to say that God's knowledge differs from man's in certain ways, such as in its extent and in its mode. They insist that there is no point of contact whatever. Not a single point. With this I heartily disagree. Far from denying that there is a *single point* of coincidence, I maintain that there is an area of coincidence. That area includes, "David was king of Israel,' and 'Jesus was born at Bethlehem,' and several other items. These are the points where God's knowledge and man's knowledge coincide. The propositions mean to the man who knows them, to the man who grasps their meaning, exactly what they mean to God, although God, as was said knows implications of these propositions that man does not know; but the truth itself is the same for man as it is for God. If a man does not grasp God's truth, he grasps no truth at all, for there is no other truth than God's truth. God knows all truth. And if a man grasps any truth at all, since it is God's truth, that truth is a point or even an area of coincidence.

The Complaint, on the other hand, makes the truth God has qualitatively different from the 'truth' man has. There is not a single point in common. Whatever meaning God has, man cannot have. And since the Bible teaches that God has all truth, it must follow on the theory of the Complaint that man has no truth. The theory of the Complaint is therefore skepticism.

Another passage in the Complaint serves to make the matter still more clear. A paragraph above has discussed the meaning of the term, *content*. The Complaint itself specifies the sense in which it uses this term. On page 7 col. 3, it states another unacceptable conclusion in propositions these words: "This knowing of propositions cannot, in the nature of the case, reflect or inspire recognition by man of his relation to God, for the simple reason that the propositions have the same content, mean the same, to God and man." Note that these last few words equate *same content* with *mean the same*. Thus it is clear that according to the Complaint the *content* is the *meaning*. And it follows that the Complaint holds that propositions do not mean the same thing for God as they do for men. There is no point of coincidence between the meaning a man has and the meaning God has.

No one therefore can logically avoid the conclusion that the Complaint teaches a skeptical two-layer theory of truth. A proposition is its meaning. A proposition is not the sound waves in the air; a proposition is not the ink marks on paper; a proposition is not the words used. Mens semper cogitate, L'âme pense toujours; the mind always thinks: these are not three propositions—they are one and the same proposition, one and the same truth (or, falsehood), because they are identical in meaning. The Complaint holds that God has one set of meanings, and man has another set (if he have any at all). There is not a single point of coincidence.

The application of this skeptical theory to the practical matter of the preaching of the Gospel is also seen in the last quotation. The Complaint said, "This knowing of propositions cannot, in the nature of the case, reflect or inspire any recognition by man of his relation to God, for the simple reason that the propositions have the same content, mean the same, to God and man."

The Complaint here teaches that if a man had the same meaning God had of a proposition, (such as, Christ died for sin), he could not for that very reason recognize his relation to God. Before a man can be inspired to recognize his relation to God, he must put on propositions a meaning different from God's. Why is this? What use would the Bible be to us, if its words could not mean the same thing to us as they do to God? And what sort of a God is it that could not express, could not reveal, his meaning to man? Or, conversely, how could sentences that mean one thing to God and something else to man reflect or inspire any proper recognition by man of his relation to God? The import of the Complaint in this passage seems to render the preaching of the Gospel futile.

And therefore the Complaint, collaborated upon, signed, and published by a majority of the Westminster faculty, teaches a two-layer theory of truth. And its theory is not in accord with Reformed theology. It is a theory of skepticism that should be attacked and refuted, rather than defended and inculcated, by a faculty subscribing to the Westminster Confession.

A SUBSEQUENT PAPER

Since the publication of the Complaint, some verbal claims have been made that the Complaint is not an accurate presentation of the views of its signers. It has been said that the complainants have changed their views and have moved closer to the Reformed faith. And a paper sent *To the Commissioners to the Thirteenth General Assembly, by a Committee for the Complainants*, is appealed to as evidence. This subsequent paper we must examine, although, in the absence of a retraction by the complainants themselves, such a mimeographed paper can be only of secondary importance. If the complaint no longer represents the position of the complainants, they should, I think, publicly repudiate it and apologize for its skeptical philosophy and baseless accusations. But since this subsequent paper, in its very first paragraph, condemns *The Answer*, one would imagine that it is consistent with *The Complaint.*

An examination of the first part of this paper, the section on The Incomprehensibility of God, will show this to be the case: the complainants have not changed their views. The paper expounds the same objectionable doctrine that is found in the Complaint.

It is true that at one point the papers seems to withdraw from the position of the Complaint. On page 3 it says, "Truth is one. And man may and does know the same truth that is in the divine mind . . . " This statement is entirely acceptable because it flatly contradicts the Complaint. And if the paper as a whole consistently maintained this view, it too would be acceptable. But it is soon seen that this, which seems to be a retraction is but a temporary and superficial lapse from their fixed doctrines. The very same paragraph continues to say that man "cannot possibly have in mind a conception to eternity that is identical or that coincides with God's own thought of his eternity." This is nothing else than the doctrine of the Complaint over again. In the first lines of the paragraph they say that man can have the same truth that is in the divine mind, and immediately below they say that man cannot have the concept of eternity. The conception of eternity that the complainants have—not God's conception of eternity—is the conception of endless years. If this is not God's conception of eternity, it must follow that the complainants have the wrong conception of eternity. Man, according to them, cannot know that God is eternal; he can only know that God has endless duration. Endless duration is an analogy of eternity. God has the truth; man has only an analogy of the truth, and he can be quite sure that he does not have the truth itself.

The committee that wrote this paper attempts to support its contention by pointing out that the Bible frequently speaks of eternity in terms of endless years. The paragraph in question stresses God's condescension or accommodation in revelation. This Scriptural language is well known; God is called the Ancient of Days; he is from everlasting to everlasting; and his years shall not fail. But to argue from these facts to the conclusion that man can have no other concept of eternity except that of endless duration is to argue badly. From the fact that revelation sometimes accommodates itself to man in figures of speech, it does not follow, as this papers says it does, that "*therefore* he cannot possibly have in mind a conception of eternity that is identical or that coincides with God's own thought of his eternity."

The Scriptures also speak of the *arm* of the Lord, the *hand* of God, and the *eyes* of God. Does it follow that we can have no other concept of the being of God expect the concept of a corporeal being? Hand and eyes are figures of speech, and we know that they are figures of speech because the Bible teaches that God is a pure Spirit. Similarly we know that 'endless years' is a figure of speech because in literal language the Bible teaches that God is immutable and eternal.

The conclusion this paper insists upon here is denied in the paragraph itself, for the authors betray the fact that they themselves have a concept of eternity different from that of endless duration. If they had no concept of eternity other than that of an everlasting lapse of time, how would they be able to say, "he is not subject to the passing of time. God's being is without succession." If they did not have the concept of "without succession," they could not have discussed it in this paper.

However, in spite of this testimony from their own material, the committee for the complainants denies that man's concept and God's coincide or are identical. It is true that this paragraph asserts a "correspondence" between God's thought and man's thought. But if man's concept of "correspondence" is no more like God's than man's concept of eternity is said to be, how can one be sure that man means the same thing as God would mean if he says man's thought corresponds to God's? To be sure of a correspondence between two things, it is necessary that both of them be present to consciousness. No one can compare two things if he is acquainted with only one of them. Correspondences and analogies cannot be founded except on some point or area of coincidence. Obviously therefore the complainants have not been converted to the view that truth is *one* and that man may have it. They still hold that man has only an analogy of the truth and not the truth itself.

On page 6 of the same paper their theory of truth is further elaborated. About the middle of the page we read, "The distinction between knowledge of a truth and knowledge of its implications is artificial and atomistic." But if a premise is not distinguishable in meaning from a conclusion, then all truths have been merged into one homogeneous mass and reasoning has become impossible. Consider the distinction between the axioms and theorems of geometry. One of the axioms is that "all right angles are equal." One of the implications or theorems is that "the interior angles of a triangle are equal to two right angles." Is there only an artificial distinction between these two statements? Is it not rather a perfectly natural distinction? The two propositions are essentially, not artificially, different in meaning. And if we extend our view and say that all truths are parts of one system, then the proposition 'Moses spoke to Pharaoh,' could in a sense be called a premise for the proposition 'David was king of Israel.' Why should the distinction between two such propositions be called artificial? What sort of epistemology is it that makes the meaning of one sentence—even though related to every other in the system—only artificially different from the meaning of another?

The authors of this Subsequent paper proceed consistently. At the bottom of this paragraph on page 6 they say, "the human mind likewise cannot know it as a bare proposition, apart from an actual understanding of implications."

While the context refers to one specific proposition, the theory requires this pronouncement to be applied to every proposition. The authors must hold that no proposition can be understood apart from an actual understanding of implications.

The first question that occurs is, why not? Their assertion that it is so, does not make it so. For example, take the proposition 'some books are not interesting.' This is a particular negative, and in the traditional Aristotelian logic a particular negative, while it may be expressed in several forms, does not by itself imply another proposition of different meaning. But if it has no implications, then according to the theory we cannot know what it means. But that is absurd. Have the complainants given sufficient thought to logic to justify their assertion? And quite aside from the technicalities of Aristotelian or non-aristotelian logic, one must ask this second question: when a child is for the first time taught that one plus one are two, does the child have an "*actual understanding of implications?*" According to this theory, before a child can understand the first propositions, he must understand a second proposition—its implications; and of course before he can understand this second proposition, he must understand a third—its implication; and before and so on. The child must know everything before he knows anything. This fits in exactly with the skeptical theory which the Complaint and this Subsequent paper defend.

The authors of the paper may wish to reply that they did not mean to say that the child had to understand all the implications; they meant merely that he has to understand some of the implications.

But look at the sentence again. The world "likewise" seems to indicate that they mean all the implications, for the word "likewise" refers to a comparison between God's knowledge and man's knowledge. Note that they say, "The divine mind cannot know that truth without knowing its implications and the human mind *likewise* cannot know it" etc. The force of the comparison seems to require man to have an actual understanding of all the implications. In other words, a man must be omniscient, if he is to know anything at all, for he cannot know any single truth without an actual understanding of (its) implications.

Although this interpretation is required by their argument, they may have omitted the word 'its' purposely, not noticing that such a purposeful omission ruins their comparison of the divine mind with the human. Now, if they withdraw from their position and try to claim that a man must understand only a few implications before he can understand his first proposition, there is another question that the complainants must answer. They must explain how many implications are needed before a man knows the first proposition. Is it necessary to understand ten theorems of geometry before it is possible to understand an axiom? Or five theorems? Or just one? Then the complainants will have to explain what principle they use to limit the number of five rather than ten, or to one rather than two. When they attempt to make these explanations, it will be clear that they are in utter confusion. If anyone of us will look into his own mind and consider the truths he knows, he will find many propositions there without an actual understanding of their implications.

Before ending this part of the discussion, I wish to draw attention to the following assertions of the paper in question. On page 7, paragraph 1, are these words: "Dr. Clark's fundamental insistence upon *identity* (italics theirs) of divine and human knowledge . . . " On page 8 near the bottom we find, "Dr. Clark insists upon identity of divine and human knowledge of a particular truth . . . "

It is amazing that these men continue to circulate these false statements after I have so many times denied them, I denied them in the examination (cf. Transcript, 31:9–10). I denied them in The Answer (pages 20–21). I denied them in speeches in two Assemblies and in countless conversations. The Report of the committee to the thirteenth General Assembly denied them for me (page 3, next to the bottom paragraph). And in spite of all this, the committee for the complainants has neither seen nor hear these denial, and continue to make the same false statements. Truly, this is incomprehensible.

THE BIBLICAL DOCTRINE

Now let us turn to Reformed doctrine; but instead of examining the Westminster Confession, we may better go directly to the source of authority and examine the Scriptures. It will be highly instructive to contrast the Scriptures with the skeptical theory of the Complaint.

The Gospel of John, which so emphasizes the Godhood of Jesus Christ, has a great deal to say about truth.

John 1:17 Grace and truth came through Jesus Christ.

5:53 Ye have sent unto John, and he hath borne witness unto the truth.

8:32 And ye shall know the truth.

Does anyone now dare to say that there is not even a single point of coincidence between God's knowledge and ours? Is there in this, or in what follows, any hint of a two-layer theory of truth? Are there two qualitatively different truths? Do we possess only an analogy of the truth?

John 8:45 I say the truth.

16:7 I tell you the truth.

16:13 He shall guide you into all truth.

17:17 Sanctify them in thy truth; thy word is truth.

The Word is not something qualitatively different from the truth. The sentences in the Word do not properly bear a meaning different from the meaning God has. The Word is the truth, the truth of God, and we have that truth.

Cf. Also: I Kings 17:24, Psalms 25:5, 43:3, 86:11, 119:43, 142, 151; Rom. 1:18, 3:7; II Cor. 6:7, 7:14, 11:10; Gal. 2:5, 14; Eph. 1:13, Etc.

These verses do not indicate that we cannot grasp God's meaning or that the truth cannot be known, or that God cannot be known.

Since God is truth, this whole matter involves the question of our knowledge of God. Can we know God? It will do us no good, if we can know only something qualitatively different from God; it will not help if there is no point of contact between us and God. The question is, can we know God? If answer be made in terms of negation and analogy alone; if all possibility of God's knowledge and man's coinciding at any point be denied; if no sentence in the bible can possibly have the same meaning for man that it has for God; the logical result is a skepticism that makes revelation impossible and Christianity a vain dream. But if man can know some things that God knows; if man can grasp some of God's meaning; if God's knowledge and man's have some points in common; then true religion will be no delusion, but a glorious reality.

Bibliography

Abrahamson, Adele. "Visiting Philosophers React Against Clark's Epistemology." *The Wheaton Record* (11 November 1965).

Acker, Raymond A. *A History of The Reformed Episcopal Seminary: 1884–1964.* Philadelphia, PA: Theological Seminary of the Reformed Episcopal Church, 1965.

Aldridge, B. L. "Confidential History of the Victor Talking Machine Co." (unpublished manuscript, c. 1928) box 1, folder 5, accession 2069, RCA Corporation Records, Hagley Museum and Library, Wilmington, DE.

Anderson, Owen. *Benjamin B. Warfield and Right Reason.* Lanham, MD: University Press of America, 2005.

The Auburn Affirmation. Auburn, NY: Jacobs, 5 May 1924.

Bahnsen, Greg L. *Van Til's Apologetic: Readings and Analysis.* Phillipsburg, NJ: P&R, 1998.

Beaton, Donald. "The Marrow of Modern Divinity And the Marrow Controversy." *Princeton Theological Review* 4, no. 3 (1906) 317–38.

Betzold, John Wistar, *et al.*, "The Text of a Complaint Against Actions of the Presbytery of Philadelphia In the Matter of the Licensure and Ordination of Dr. Gordon H. Clark" (filed with the Presbytery on 6 October 1944; presented 20 November 1944, Wilmington, DE: Eastlake Church) PCA Archives, 309/10.

Birch, Thomas R. "An American Christian University." *The Presbyterian Guardian* 13, no. 23 (1944): 363–66.

———. "Another Wheaton Teacher Resigns Over Clark Issue." *The Presbyterian Guardian* 12, no. 10 (1943) 160.

———. "The Clark Case." *The Presbyterian Guardian* 13, no. 11 (1944) 171–74.

———. "David S. Clark." *The Presbyterian Guardian* 6, no. 4 (1939) 72.

———. "Dr. Clark Resigns From Wheaton College Faculty." *The Presbyterian Guardian* 12, no. 6 (1943) 86.

———. "Group Looks to Founding of Christian University." *The Presbyterian Guardian* 12, no. 20 (1943) 318–19.

———. "Orthodox Presbyterian Church News." *The Presbyterian Guardian* 13, no. 14 (1944) 219–20.

———. "Phila. Presbytery Hears Complaint in Clark Case." *The Presbyterian Guardian* 13, no. 22 (1944) 354–55.

———. "Presbytery of Philadelphia." *The Presbyterian Guardian* 14, no. 4 (1945) 64.

———. "What's In a Name?" *The Presbyterian Guardian* 6, no. 3 (1939) 49.

———. "With the Standing Committees." *The Presbyterian Guardian* 12, no. 18 (1943) 283–84.

Bouma, Clarence. "That University Project." *The Calvin Forum* (March 1946) 157.

Bradford, Eugene. "The Controversy in the Orthodox Presbyterian Church Regarding the Doctrine of the Universal Offer of the Gospel." (unpublished paper, c. 1948) PCA Archives, 309/37.

Brentano, Franz. *Psychology from an Empirical Standpoint.* Translated by Antos C. Rancurello, D. B. Terrell, and Linda L. McAlister. Routledge, NY: International Library of Philosophy, 1997.

Brown, George B. "Clark Retains Zest for Life as 81st Year Approaches." *Chattanooga News—Free Press* (Sunday, October 17, 1982).

Buswell, J. Oliver. "The Arguments from Nature to God: Presuppositionalism and Thomas Aquinas: A Book Review with Excursions." *The Bible Today* (May 1948) 235–48.

———. "The Fountainhead of Presuppositionalism." *The Bible Today* (November 1948) 41–65.

Carnell, Edward John. "Barth as Inconsistent Evangelical." *Christian Century* (6 June 1962) 713–14.

———. *The Case for Orthodox Theology.* Philadelphia: Westminster, 1959.

Butler University, "Annual Catalogue." (undergraduate course catalogues 1944/1945 to 1972/1973, Butler University, Indianapolis, IN).

Clark, David S. "The Intellectual Defense of Christianity." (unpublished paper, in the possession of the Clark family, c. 1930s).

———. *Protestant Unbelief, or, Rationalism Past and Present.* Reading, PA: Christian Faith and Life, 1937.

———. "The Reality of Me." *The Presbyterian* (25 June 1925).

Clark, F. P., and M. C. Nahm, eds., *Philosophical Essays in Honor of Edgar Arthur Singer, Jr.* Philadelphia: University of Pennsylvania Press, 1942.

Clark, Gordon H. "The Achilles Heel of Humanism." *The Witness* (June–July 1950) 5–6, 19.

———. "Always, Everywhere." Sermon, Bethel Presbyterian, Philadelphia, PA (10 Oct 1922) PCA Archives, 310/64.

———. "Apologetics." In *Encyclopedia of Christianity,* Edwin A. Palmer, ed. (Wilmington, Delaware: National Foundation for Christian Education, 1964).

———. "An Appeal to Fundamentalists." *The Presbyterian Guardian* 12, no. 5 (1943) 65–7.

———. "The Auburn Heresy." (revision of an address delivered February 28, 1935) *The Southern Presbyterian Journal* 5, no. 6, (1946) 7–8.

———. "Augustine's City of God." Audiotape of lecture given at Reformed Presbyterian Theological Seminary, RPTS Library (29 October 1974).

———. *The Biblical Doctrine of Man.* Jefferson, MD: The Trinity Foundation, 1984.

———. "Blest River of Salvation." *The Presbyterian Guardian* 14, no. 1 (1945) 10, 16.

———. "A Christian Construction, Part 1." (from "The Gordon-Conwell Lectures on Apologetics," Gordon Conwell Seminary, South Hamilton, MA, 1981) mp3, http://www.trinitylectures.org/MP3/A_Christian_Construction,_Part_1.mp3.

———. "A Christian Construction Part 2." (from "The Gordon-Conwell Lectures on Apologetics," Gordon Conwell Seminary, South Hamilton, MA, 1981) mp3, http://www.trinitylectures.org/MP3/A_Christian_Construction,_Part_2.mp3

———. *A Christian Philosophy of Education*. Grand Rapids: Eerdmans, 1946.

———. *A Christian View of Men and Things*. Grand Rapids: Eerdmans, 1952.

———. *Colossians: Another Commentary on an Inexhaustible Message*. Phillipsburg, NJ: Presbyterian and Reformed, 1979.

———. "A Contemporary Defense of the Bible." (lecture, Believer's Chapel Tape Ministry, 1977).

———. "The Cosmological Argument." *The Trinity Review* (September 1979).

———. "Criticisms of Christianity Answered." *The Quarryvillian* 1, no. 2 (24 February 1946) 184.

———. "The Decline of Theology in America." (lecture, n.d.) mp3, http://www.trinitylectures.org/MP3/The_Decline_of_Theology_in_America.mp3.

———. "A debate between Gordon H. Clark and David Hoover on epistemology." (Covenant College, 9 April 1983) http://www.trinitylectures.org/MP3/The_Clark-Hoover_Debate.mp3.

———. "Determinism and Responsibility." *The Evangelical Quarterly* 4, no. 1 (1932) 13–23.

———. "Desultory New Testament Curiosities." (unpublished essay, 1984) PCA Archives, 309/123.

———. "Empedocles and Anaxagoras in Aristotle's De Anima." PhD diss., University of Pennsylvania, 1929.

———. "Empiricism." In *Encyclopedia of Christianity*, Edwin A. Palmer, ed. Wilmington, Delaware: National Foundation for Christian Education, 1968.

———. "Empiricism." (lecture from "The Gordon-Conwell Lectures on Apologetics," Gordon Conwell Seminary, South Hamilton, MA, 1981) mp3, http://www.trinitylectures.org/MP3/Empiricism.mp3.

———. *Ephesians*. Jefferson, MD: The Trinity Foundation, 1985.

———. "Ethics and Theology." *The Evangelical Student: The Magazine of the League of Evangelical Students* 6, no. 2 (1932) 29–33.

———. *First John*. Jefferson, MD: The Trinity Foundation, 1980. 2nd ed., 1992.

———. *First Lessons in Theology*. Unpublished systematic theology, c. 1974–1980. Sangre de Cristo Seminary's Clark Library.

———. *God's Hammer, The Bible and Its Critics*, Jefferson, MD: The Trinity Foundation, 1982.

———. "Gordon Clark Remembrances." Handwritten document of Clark's childhood remembrances, courtesy of The Trinity Foundation (c. 1980s).

———. "Heresy Decision Declared Illegal." *The Philadelphia Record* (14 November 1934) PCA Archives, newspaper articles 1934–1935, charges of heresy against presbyterian ministers, 309/81.

———. "Heresy Vote Assailed." *The Philadelphia Inquirer* (22 November 1934) PCA Archives, newspaper articles 1934–1935, charges of heresy against presbyterian ministers, 309/81.

———. "How Does Man Know God?" *The Trinity Review* (July–August 1989).

———. "How Long?" *The Presbyterian* (15 November 1923) 9.

———. *The Incarnation.* Jefferson, MD: The Trinity Foundation, 1988.

———. *In Defense of Theology.* Milford, MI: Mott, 1984.

———. *An Introduction to Christian Philosophy.* Jefferson, MD: Trinity Foundation, 1993.

———. "Irrationalism." (lecture from "The Gordon-Conwell Lectures on Apologetics," Gordon Conwell Seminary, South Hamilton, MA, 1981) mp3, http://www.trinitylectures.org/MP3/Irrationalism.mp3.

———. "Is Christianity a Religion? Part 2." (from "The Gordon-Conwell Lectures on Apologetics," Gordon Conwell Seminary, South Hamilton, MA, 1981) mp3, http://www.trinitylectures.org/MP3/Is_Christianity_a_Religion,_Part_2.mp3.

———. "Is Christianity a Religion? Part 3." (from "The Gordon-Conwell Lectures on Apologetics," Gordon Conwell Seminary, South Hamilton, MA, 1981) mp3, http://www.trinitylectures.org/MP3/Is_Christianity_a_Religion,_Part_3.mp3.

———. *The Johannine Logos.* Nutley, NJ: Presbyterian and Reformed, 1972.

———. *Karl Barth's Theological Method.* Philadelphia: Presbyterian and Reformed, 1963; 2nd ed., Hobbs, NM: The Trinity Foundation, 1997. Citations are to the 1997 edition.

———. "Lecture on Logos. Lecture to the teachers at Chattanooga Christian School." (c. 1984) PCA Archives 310/16.

———. "The Life of a Minister's Son." Sermon (c. 1920s) PCA Archives, 310/107.

———. *Logic.* 3rd ed. 1985; repr., Jefferson, MD: The Trinity Foundation, 1998. Citations are from the 1998 edition.

———. "Logic and Language." *The Gordon Review* 2, no. 1 (1956) 3.

———. *Language and Theology.* Phillipsburg, NJ: Presbyterian and Reformed, 1980.

———. "Language, Truth, and Revelation, Part 1." (lecture from "The Gordon-Conwell Lectures on Apologetics," Gordon Conwell Seminary, South Hamilton, MA, 1981) mp3, http://www.trinitylectures.org/MP3/Language,_Truth,_and_Revelation,_Part_1.mp3.

———. "Language, Truth, and Revelation, Part 3." (lecture from "The Gordon-Conwell Lectures on Apologetics," Gordon Conwell Seminary, South Hamilton, MA, 1981) mp3, http://www.trinitylectures.org/MP3/Language,_Truth,_and_Revelation,_Part_3.mp3.

———. *Logic.* 3rd ed., Unicoi, TN: The Trinity Foundation, 1998.

———. *Lord God of Truth.* 2nd ed., Hobbs, NM: The Trinity Foundation, 1994.

———. *Modern Philosophy.* Jefferson, MD: The Trinity Foundation, 1982.

———. "Miracles and History" (unpublished notes, n.d.) PCA Archives, 310/23.

———. "The Nature of Truth." (unpublished article, c. 1954) PCA Archives, 6/24.

———. "The Next War." *The Presbyterian Guardian* 13, no. 5 (1944) 71–2.

———. "The Order of Justification and Regeneration." *Present Truth Magazine* 27, no. 3 (June 1973).

———. *Philippians.* Hobbs, NM: The Trinity Foundation, 1996.

———. "Predestination in the Old Testament." (lecture, Believer's Chapel Tape Ministry, 1977) mp3, http://www.trinitylectures.org/MP3/Predestination_in_OT_Clark.mp3.

———. "The Primacy of the Intellect." *Westminster Theological Journal* 5, no. 2 (1943) 182–195.

———. "The Proposal to Abolish the RPCES." (c. 1982) PCA Archives, 310/36. Also in draft form in Sangre de Cristo Seminary Library, personal papers of Gordon H. Clark, 1/99.

———. *Religion, Reason, and Revelation,* 2nd ed. Hobbs, NM: The Trinity Foundation, 1995.

———. "Religious Travelogue." *The Witness: A Christian Magazine for the Family,* ed. Richard W. Gray (Willow Grove, PA: Covenant House Church, c. 1954) 19–20. Found amongst Gordon H. Clark's personal papers, folder not numbered.

———. "Reply to Ronald H. Nash." In *Clark and His Critics, The Works of Gordon Haddon Clark.* Unicoi, TN: The Trinity Foundation, 2009.

———. "Resolution on Total Abstinence." (January 1942) PCA Archives, 309/97.

———. "Special Report: Encountering Barth in Chicago." *Christianity Today* (11 May 1962) 35–36.

———. "Studies of the Doctrine of The Complaint." Unpublished paper. (winter 1946–47) SDCS 1/101 and PCA Archives 309/16.

———. "Teaching notes on *Westminster Confession of Faith.*" (12 September 1943) PCA Archives, 312/106.

———. *Thales to Dewey: A History of Philosophy.* Boston: Houghton Mifflin, 1957; repr., Grand Rapids: Baker, 1980. Citations are to the Baker edition.

———. "To Be A Sinner How Bad Must One Be?" transcript of address on *The Midweek Forum Hour* with host Erling C. Olsen, WMCA New York (New York, 11 September 1935) PCA Archives, 309/92.

———. *The Trinity.* Jefferson, MD: The Trinity Foundation, 1985.

———. "The Trinity." *The Trinity Review* 9, (November 1979).

———. "The West" (poem, c. 1980) Sangre de Cristo Seminary Library, personal papers of Gordon H. Clark. Also published anonymously in Covenant College's annual literary magazine, *The Thorn* (1982).

———. "The Wheaton Lectures." In *The Philosophy of Gordon H. Clark, A Festschrift,* edited by Ronald Nash, 25–122. Philadelphia: Presbyterian and Reformed, 1968.

———. *What do Presbyterians Believe?* Philadelphia: Presbyterian and Reformed, 1965.

———. "What is Apologetics?" (from "The Gordon-Conwell Lectures on Apologetics," Gordon Conwell Seminary, South Hamilton, MA, 1981) mp3, http://www.trinitylectures.org/MP3/What_is_Apologetics.mp3.

———. "What Shall We Do?" *The Presbyterian* (16 August 1923) 10–11.

———. "Who Controls our Church?" Memorandum, PCA Archives, 286/15.

———. *William James,* Philadelphia: Presbyterian and Reformed, 1963.

Clark, James Armstrong. "An Account of Life of Rev Jas. A. Clark Written by Himself." Unpublished autobiography in the possession of the Clark family, c. 1860–1880.

Clark, Nancy Elizabeth. "A History of the Reformed Presbyterian Church." (master's thesis, Butler University, 1966).

Clelland, John P. "The Christian University." *The Presbyterian Guardian* 13, no. 14 (1944): 221.

———. "Have We Changed?" *The Presbyterian Guardian* 14, no. 1 (1945) 7–9.

Clements, Don K. *The Historical Roots of the Presbyterian Church in America.* Narrows, VA: Metokos, 2006.

Clowney, Edmund P. "Tichenor to be Ordained." *The Presbyterian Guardian* 15, no. 18 (1946) 281.

Craig, Samuel G. "Reformation Fellowship Incorporated," *Christianity Today* 3, no. 3, (1932) 15.

Crampton, W. Gary. *The Scripturalism of Gordon H. Clark*. Jefferson, MD: The Trinity Foundation, 1999.

Crampton, W. Gary, and Kenneth G. Talbot. "Was Gordon Clark a Nestorian? An Analysis of Gordon H. Clark's book 'The Incarnation,'" copyright 2014 by Whitefield Publishing. http://thegordonhclarkfoundation.com/files/2014/04/The-Incarnation-Review-Edited-2-Completed.pdf.

Crumpacker, Mary M. "Clark's Axiom, Something New?" *Journal of the Evangelical Theological Society* 32, no. 2 (1989) 355–65.

Davis, D. Clair. "John Frame's Pastoral Method for Christian Unity." In *Speaking the Truth in Love: The Theology of John Frame*. 687–709. Phillipsburg, NJ: P&R, 2009.

Deferrari, Roy Joseph and Mary Francis McDonald, introduction to Augustine's "On Faith in Thing Unseen," in *Writings of Saint Augustine Vol. 2*. New York: CMA, 1947.

Dennison, Charles G., Danny E. Olinger, and David K. Thompson. *History for a Pilgrim People: The Historical Writings of Charles G. Dennison*. Willow Grove, PA: Committee for the Historian of the Orthodox Presbyterian Church, 2002.

Dennison, James T. *A Ministerial Register of the Orthodox Presbyterian Church, 1936–1991*. Philadelphia, PA: Committee for the Historian of the Orthodox Presbyterian Church, 1992.

Directory of Bethel Presbyterian Church (Philadelphia, May 1915) Presbyterian Historical Society Archives.

Dorrien, Gary. *The Remaking of Evangelical Theology*. Louisville: Westminster John Knox, 1998.

Dyrness, Enock C. *et al.*, eds., *Bulletin of Wheaton College 1939–1940*, vol. 16, no. 4 (April 1939). http://espace.wheaton.edu/lr/a-sc/archives/publications/catalogs/1939–1940catalog.pdf.

Dyrness, Franklin. "About the Proposed Union." *The Presbyterian Journal* 39, no. 2 (1980).

———. "'No' to Joining and Receiving." *The Presbyterian Journal* 40, no. 49 (1982).

Edgar, William. *Schaeffer on the Christian Life: Countercultural Spirituality*. Wheaton, IL: Crossway, 2013.

Eggenberger, Delbert N. "Clark objects to review." *Journal of the American Scientific Affiliation* 6 (1954) 36–37.

Engelsma, David J. *Hyper-Calvinism and the Call of the Gospel*, 3rd ed. Jenison, MI: Reformed Free Publishing Association, 2014.

———. Review of *The Incarnation*, by Gordon H. Clark, *Standard Bearer* 65, no. 17 (1989).

Ferguson, Sinclair B., and J. I. Packer, *New Dictionary of Theology*. Downers Grove, IL: InterVarsity, 2000.

Frame, John M. *Apologetics to the Glory of God*. Phillipsburg, NJ: P&R, 1994.

———. *Cornelius Van Til: An Analysis of His Thought*. Phillipsburg, NJ: P&R, 1995.

———. *The Doctrine of the Knowledge of God*. Phillipsburg NJ: Presbyterian and Reformed, 1987.

———. *History of Western Philosophy and Theology*. Phillipsburg, NJ: P&R, 2015.

————. "The Problem of Theological Paradox." In *Foundations of Christian Scholarship, Essays in the Van Til Perspective,* edited by Gary North, 295–330. Vallecito, CA: Ross House, 1979.

Fraser, George Macdonald. *The Steel Bonnets, The Story of the Anglo-Scottish Border Reivers.* New York: Skyhorse, 2008.

"Further Study: Westminster." *Wheaton Alumni Magazine* 12, no. 1 (1944) 6.

George, Elizabeth Clark. "Life with Father, Part 1" In *Gordon H. Clark, Personal Recollections,* edited by John W. Robbins, 13–25. Jefferson, MD: The Trinity Foundation, 1989.

Gerstner, John H. "Foreword" In *Hyper-Calvinism and the Call of the Gospel,* 3rd ed., xii–xiii. Jenison, MI: Reformed Free Publishing Association, 2014.

————. *Wrongly Dividing the Word of Truth: A Critique of Dispensationalism* 2nd ed., edited by Don Kistler. Morgan, PA: Soli Deo Gloria, 2000.

Godfrey, W. Robert. "The Westminster School." In *Reformed Theology in America: A History of Its Modern Development.* 89–101. Grand Rapids: Eerdmans, 1985.

Graham, Billy. *Just as I Am: The Autobiography of Billy Graham.* San Francisco, CA: Harper San Francisco, 1997.

Graham, Ruth Bell. *It's My Turn.* Old Tappan, NJ: F. H. Revell, 1982.

Gray, Richard Willer. "The O.P.C. and the University Project," *The Calvin Forum* 14, no. 5 December (1948) 99.

Haddon Charles K. *Memoirs of a Trip Around The World.* Privately printed book, 1923.

————. *Around the World in the Southern Hemisphere.* Privately printed book, 1927.

————. *The Mixer and Server: The Official Journal of the Hotel and Restaurant Employees International Alliance* 26, no. 10 (1917) 35.

Hallock, Joseph Newton, D.D., Ed., "Among the Churches." *Christian Work: Illustrated Family Newspaper* (18 January 1900).

Hanko, Herman. "Chapter 6: The Marrow Controversy." in *The History of the Free Offer* (pamphlet published online by Protestant Reformed Churches in America, 9 March 2013) footnote 46, http://www.prca.org/resources/publications/pamphlets/item/1597-the-history-of-the-free-offer.

Hamilton, Floyd E. "Classification and Mutual Relation of the Mental Faculties." (unpublished paper, c. 1947) PCA Archives, 309/3.

————. "The Teaching of Scripture on The Offer of the Gospel." (unpublished paper, c. 1947) WTS Archives, Stonehouse/Box 6, 1945–1962, folder: Gordon H. Clark controversy.

Hamilton, Michael S. "Fundamentalist Harvard: Wheaton College and the Continuing Vitality of American Evangelicalism." PhD diss., University of Notre Dame, 1994.

Harrison, Everett F. *Baker's Dictionary of Theology.* Grand Rapids: Baker, 1960.

Hart, D. G. *Between the Times: The Orthodox Presbyterian Church in Transition, 1945–1990.* Willow Grove, PA: Committee for the Historian of the Orthodox Presbyterian Church, 2011.

Hart, D. G. and John Muether. *Fighting the Good Fight, A Brief History of the Orthodox Presbyterian Church.* Philadelphia: Committee for the Historian of the Orthodox Presbyterian Church, 1995.

————. "The OPC and the New Evangelicalism," *Fighting the Good Fight, A Brief History of the Orthodox Presbyterian Church.* Philadelphia: Committee for the Historian of the Orthodox Presbyterian Church, 1995.

Heerema, Edward. "The Orthodox Presbyterian Church," *The Calvin Forum* (August–September 1946) 26.

———. "Whither the Orthodox Presbyterian Church." April 1947, PCA Archives, 310/56.

Henry, Carl F. H. *Confessions of a Theologian: An Autobiography.* Waco, TX: World, 1986.

———. *God, Revelation, and Authority.* Waco, TX: Word, 1976.

———. "New Specter: Postmodernism" (lecture, Westminster Theological Seminary, 1996) mp3, https://itunes.apple.com/us/itunes-u/westminster-guests/id535486374?mt=10.

———. "A Wide and Deep Swath," In *The Philosophy of Gordon H. Clark,* edited by Ronald H. Nash, 11–21.Philadelphia: Presbyterian and Reformed, 1968.

Hoeksema, Herman. *The Clark-Van Til Controversy.* Hobbs, NM: The Trinity Foundation, 1995. Originally published in articles in *The Standard Bearer* from 1944–1946.

———. *The Protestant Reformed Churches in America,* 2nd ed. 1936; repr., Grand Rapids, MI: n.p., 1947.

———. *Reformed Dogmatics,* Volume 1. 1966; 2nd ed., Grandville, MI: Reformed Free Publishing Association, 2004.

Hutchinson, George P. *The History Behind the Reformed Presbyterian Church, Evangelical Synod.* Cherry Hill, NJ: Mack, 1974.

Jewett, Paul King. "Biblical authority a crucial issue in Protestantism." *United Evangelical Action* (1 May 1953) 9.

———. *Emil Brunner's Concept of Revelation.* London: James Clarke, 1954.

———. *MAN as Male and Female.* Grand Rapids: Eerdmans, 1975.

Jones, William J. *The Evangelical Student: The Magazine of the League of Evangelical Students* 6 and 7, no. 3 and no. 1, (Oct 1933).

Keiper, Ralph L. Review of *Thales to Dewey* by Gordon Clark, *Eternity* 3, no. 11 (November 1952) 34.

Kelly, J. N. D. *Early Christian Doctrines.* 1960; 5th ed., San Francisco: Harper, 1978. Citations are to the 1978 edition.

Kennedy, Gerry and Rob Churchill. The Voynich Manuscript: The Mysterious Code That Has Defied Interpretation for Centuries. Rochester, VT: Inner Traditions, 2006.

Knudsen, Robert D. "Apologetics and History." In *Life is Religion: Essays in Honor of H. Evan Runner,* edited by Henry Vander Goot. 119–133. St. Catherines, Ontario, Canada: Paideia, 1981.

Kucharsky, David. "At the Beginning, God: An Interview With Cornelius Van Til." *Christianity Today* (30 December 1977) 20.

Kuiper, R. B. *As to Being Reformed.* Grand Rapids: Eerdmans, 1926.

Kuiper, R. B., et al., "The Text of a Complaint Against Actions of the Presbytery of Philadelphia In the Matter of the Licensure and Ordination of Dr. Gordon H. Clark" (filed with the Presbytery on 6 October 1944; presented 20 November 1944, Wilmington, DE: Eastlake Church) PCA Archives, 309/10.

Kuyper, Abraham. *Calvinism: The L. P. Stone Lectures for 1898–1899: Six Lectures Delivered in the Theological Seminary at Princeton.* New York: Fleming H. Revell, n.d.

———. *Common Grace: Noah–Adam.* Grand Rapids: Christian's Library, 2013.

Lachman, David C. *The Marrow Controversy*. Edinburgh: Rutherford House, 1988.

Lightner, Robert. *Neo-Evangelicalism* 4th ed. 1965; repr., Des Plaines, IL: Regular Baptist, 1971. Citations are to the 1971 edition.

Lindsell, Harold. *The Battle for the Bible*. Grand Rapids: Zondervan, 1981.

———. "Carnell on Scripture." letter to the editor in *Christianity Today* 6, no. 18 (1962) 19–20.

Machen, J. Gresham, and Ned Stonehouse, eds., "*The Presbyterian Church in the U.S.A. versus The Presbyterian Church in America*," *The Presbyterian Guardian* 2, no. 11 (1936) 232–35.

MacLeod, A. Donald. *W. Stanford Reid: An Evangelical Calvinist in the Academy*. Montreal: McGill-Queen's UP, 2004.

Marsden, George M. *Reforming Fundamentalism: Fuller Seminary and the New Evangelicalism*. Grand Rapids: Eerdmans, 1987.

Marsden, Robert S. "University Association Holds Stormy Meeting, A Report," *The Presbyterian Guardian* 15 no. 14 (1946) 218–19.

McBee, Basil G. and Reid W. Stewart. *History of the Associate Presbyterian Church of North America*. Apollo, PA: Closson, 1983.

Michener, Albert Oswald. "A History of the Northeast High School, Philadelphia." EdD diss., Temple University, 1937.

Minutes of the Thirty-Seventh General Assembly of the United Presbyterian Church of North America. Pittsburgh: United Presbyterian Board of Publishing, 1895.

Moser, Paul. *Reformed Apologetics and First Principles: An Analysis of the Philosophies of Gordon H. Clark and Cornelius Van Til*. Master's thesis, Western Kentucky University, 1978.

Muether, John. *Cornelius Van Til, Reformed Apologist and Churchman*. Phillipsburg, NJ: P&R, 2008.

Murray, John. "The Weak and the Strong." *The Westminster Theological Journal* 12, no. 2 (1950).

Nash, Ronald H. "Clark and Contemporary Thought." In *Gordon H. Clark, Personal Recollections,* edited by John W. Robbins, 87–91. Jefferson, MD: The Trinity Foundation, 1989.

———. *The New Evangelicalism*. Grand Rapids: Zondervan, 1963.

Naugle, David K. *Worldview: The History of a Concept*. Grand Rapids: Eerdmans, 2002.

Nelson, Rudolph. *The Making and Unmaking of an Evangelical Mind: The Case of Edward Carnell*. New York: Cambridge, 1988.

Newbold, William Romaine and Roland G. Kent. *The Cipher of Roger Bacon*. Philadelphia: University of Pennsylvania, 1928.

Newsome, Mark. "Clark Probes Resultants of Secular Philosophy." *The Wheaton Record*, 11 November 1965.

Nicholas, Robert E. "EP-RP Churches Vote to Unite in 1965." *The Presbyterian Guardian* 33, no. 4 (1964): 61–62.

Noll, Mark A. "The Princeton Theology." In *Reformed Theology in America*, edited by David F. Wells, 15–35. Grand Rapids: Eerdmans, 1985.

O'Donnell, J. J. *The Mystery of the Triune God*. New York: Paulist, 1989.

Oliphint, Scott. *Cornelius Van Til and the Reformation of Christian Apologetics*. Scarsdale, NY: Westminster Discount Book Service, 1980.

Orr, James. *The Christian View of God and the World* 6th ed. (1893; repr., Edinburgh: Andrew Elliot, 1902.

Parkinson, Joel. "The Intellectual Triunity of God." *The Trinity Review*, January 1992.

Patterson, Bob. *Carl F. H. Henry: Makers of the Modern Theological Mind*. Waco, TX: Word, 1983.

Reymond, Robert. *The Justification of Knowledge*. Phillipsburg, NJ: Presbyterian and Reformed, 1979.

———. *A New Systematic Theology of the Christian Faith*. Nashville, TN: Thomas Nelson Publishers, 1998.

Rhoads, Gladys Titzck and Nancy Titzck Anderson. *McIntire: Defender of Faith and Freedom*. Maitland, FL: Xulon, 2012.

Rian, Edwin H. "Needed: An American Christian University." *The Presbyterian Guardian* 12, no. 19 (1943) 289–90, 299–301.

———. *The Presbyterian Conflict*. Grand Rapids: Eerdmans, 1940.

Rian, Edwin, Richard Willer Gray, Robert Strong, and Clifford Smith. "A Program for Action in the Orthodox Presbyterian Church." (May 1944) Ned Stonehouse's collection of papers about the "Clark Case," WTS Archives.

Robbins, John W. "America's Augustine: Gordon Haddon Clark," The Trinity Review, April 1985.

———. *Gordon H. Clark, Personal Recollections*. Jefferson, MD: The Trinity Foundation, 1989.

———. "Foreword." In *Three Types of Religious Philosophy*. Jefferson, MD: The Trinity Foundation, 1989.

———. "Foreword." In *Lord God of Truth*. Hobbs, NM: The Trinity Foundation, 1986.

———. "Introduction." In *Clark Speaks from the Grave*. Jefferson, MD: The Trinity Foundation, 1986.

Roy, Paul L. "Widener Mansion May Become Club." *Gettysburg Times* (3 June 1948) 5.

Rudolph, Robert K. "A Truly Great and Brilliant Friend," In *Gordon H. Clark, Personal Recollections*, edited by John W. Robbins, 99–107. Jefferson, MD: The Trinity Foundation, 1989.

Russell, Bertrand and Hugh MacColl. "The Existential Import of Propositions." *Mind, New Series* 14, no. 55 (July 1905) 398–402.

Schaeffer, Francis. "A Review of a Review." *The Bible Today* (May 1948).

Scorgie, Glen A. *A Call for Continuity, the Theologian Contributions of James Orr*. Macon, GA: Mercer University Press, 1988.

Leslie W. Sloat. "Hamilton to Korea Under Independent Board." *The Presbyterian Guardian* 18, no. 2 (1949) 30.

———. "Orthodox Presbyterian Church News: The Church in 1949." *The Presbyterian Guardian* 19, no. 1 (1950) 8, 16.

———. "Rian Returns to U.S.A. Church." *Presbyterian Guardian* 16, no. 12 (1947) 190.

———. "Testimony Being Circulated." *The Presbyterian Guardian* 17, no. 1 (1948) 14.

———. "University Association Meets, Adjourns to Dec. 12." *The Presbyterian Guardian* 15, no. 20 (1946) 315–317.

———. "Withdrawal of Dr. Rian." *Presbyterian Guardian* 16, no. 10 (1947) 157.

Smith, Morton H. *Reformed Evangelism*. Clinton, MS: Multi-Communication Ministries, 1975.

———. "The Southern Tradition." In *Reformed Theology in America: A History of Its Modern Development*, edited by David F. Wells, 189–207. Grand Rapids: Eerdmans, 1985.

Smylie, James H. *A Brief History of the Presbyterians*. Louisville, KY: Geneva, 1996.

THE STANDARDS of Government Discipline and Worship of The Orthodox Presbyterian Church (Philadelphia: The Committee on the Constitution of The Orthodox Presbyterian Church, 1941).

Stonehouse, Ned B. *J. Gresham Machen, A Biographical Memoir.* Grand Rapids: Eerdmans, 1954.

———. "Dr. Clark Dismissed to U.P. Church." *The Presbyterian Guardian* 17, no. 15 (1948) 260.

———. "Philadelphia Presbytery." *The Presbyterian Guardian* 17, no. 14 (1948) 242.

Storms, Samuel. *Chosen for Life, The Case for Divine Election.* Grand Rapids: Baker, 1987; Revised, Wheaton, IL: Crossway, 2007. Citations refer to the Crossway edition.

Strong, Robert H. "The Gordon Clark Case." Lecture, Reformed Theological Seminary, Jackson, MS, (1977) RTS-Jackson Library, Oversize BX 8999.06 S92, 1977.

———. "Presbytery of Ohio," *The Presbyterian Guardian* 14, no. 21 (1945) 332.

Tartan 1971 Yearbook (Covenant College, 1971) https://archive.org/details/tartan1971unse.

Taylor, G. Aiken. "Clark Elected by RPC." *The Presbyterian Journal* 20, no. 8 (1961) 4.

———. "It Was a New Beginning for the PCA." *The Presbyterian Journal* 41, no. 9 (1982) 4–5.

Tichenor, Alan, *et al.,* "The Answer to a Complaint Against Several Actions and Decisions of the Presbytery of Philadelphia Taken in a Special Meeting Held on July 7, 1944" (presented at Presbytery of Philadelphia in meeting at Mediator OPC, 19 March 1945) PCA Archives, 309/108.

Van Andel, H. J. "The Importance of Common Grace." *Religion and Culture* 6, no. 4 (1924) 50–51.

Van Til, Cornelius. *Christian Apologetics.* Philadelphia: Theological Seminary of the Reformed Episcopal Church, 1939.

———. "Common Grace." In *Proceedings of the Calvinistic Philosophy Club,* edited by Edward Heerema, Autumn 1941.

———. "Common Grace Part I: The Christian Philosophy of History." *Westminster Theological Journal* 8, no. 1 (1945) 39–60.

———. "Common Grace Part II: The Latest Debate about Common Grace." *Westminster Theological Journal* 8, no. 2 (1946) 166–200.

———. "Common Grace Part III." *Westminster Theological Journal* 9, no. 1 (1946) 47–84.

———. *The Defense of the Faith.* Philadelphia: Presbyterian and Reformed, 1955.

———. "Introduction" In *The Inspiration and Authority of the Bible.* 6th ed., Philadelphia: Presbyterian and Reformed, 1970.

———. *An Introduction to Systematic Theology.* Philadelphia, PA: Westminster Theological Seminary, Chestnut Hill, 1949.

———. "Letters to the Editor." *The Reformed Journal* 7, no. 12 (1956) 20–21.

———. "Letter to The Editor," *The Reformed Journal* (December 1957) 20.

———. "Presuppositionalism." *The Bible Today* (April 1949) 218–28.

———. "Presuppositionalism Concluded." *The Bible Today* (June–September 1949) 278–90.

———. "Reflections on Dr. A. Kuyper, Sr." *The Banner* 72, no. 2122 (1937) 1187.

———. "Students and Controversies." *Calvin College Chimes* (March 1922) 87–91.

————. Transcript of interview by Jim Payton, Jack Sawyer, and Peter Lillback, WTS Archives.

Vos, Johannes G. "The Cultic Character of the Toronto Movement." *Blue Banner Faith and Life* 29, no. 2 (1974).

"Waiting to Relocate." *The Reformed Presbyterian Reporter.* (November 1965) 6.

Warfield, Benjamin Breckinridge. *The Plan of Salvation: Five Lectures.* Philadelphia, PA: Presbyterian Board of Publication, 1915.

————. "Introduction to Beattie's Apologetics." In *Benjamin B. Warfield Selected Shorter Writings Volume* 2, edited by John E. Meeter, 93–105. Nutley, NJ: Presbyterian and Reformed, 1973.

Weaver, Gilbert B. "The Concept of Truth in the Apologetic Systems of Gordon Haddon Clark and Cornelius Van Til." Master's thesis, Grace Theological Seminary, 1967.

————. "Man: Analogue of God." In *Jerusalem and Athens,* edited by E. R. Geehan, Phillipsburg, NJ: Presbyterian and Reformed, 1974.

The Wheaton Record. "Chess Enthusiasts Elect Mackenzie in Meet at Clark's." (12 October 1937).

————. "Chessmen Philosophize Future University Meets Possible." (18 October 1938).

————. "Chess Players Must Conquer Dr. Clark." (12 November 1937).

————. "Clark Mentors Pawns, Pupils in Chess Club." (12 October 1937).

————. "Dr. Clark to Address League Next Monday." (5 March 1937).

————. "French Club Hears Clark on Sorbonne." (18 March 1938).

————. "Prof. Clark Returns After Family Death." (28 February 1939).

————. "What Happened to Buswell?" (30 April 1982).

White, William. *Van Til, Defender of the Faith: An Authorized Biography.* Nashville: T. Nelson, 1979.

Wiseman, John. "The Evangelical Theological Society, Yesterday and Today." *Journal of the Evangelical Theological Society* 28, no. 5 (1985) 5.

Woolley, Paul. "Discontent!" *The Presbyterian Guardian* 13, no. 14 (1944) 213–14.

Yeo, John Ji-Won. *Plundering the Egyptians: The Old Testament and Historical Criticism at Westminster Theological Seminary (1929–1998).* Plymouth, U.K.: U of America, 2010.

Zeller, Joel. "Departments demonstrate quality." In *The Thistle* 1977 *Yearbook.* Covenant College, 1977, 27, https://archive.org/details/tartan1977unse.

Name Index

Subject Index

Valparaiso University, 76
Victor, 8
Victor Talking Machine Company, 7
Volker Fund, 180, 224

Weltanschauung, 65, 67
Westcliffe, CO, 243, 244
Western Kentucky University, 225n4
Westminster Confession of Faith, xxi,
        xxiii, 1, 5, 14, 22, 24, 27, 30, 37,
        38, 48, 49, 53, 54, 55, 57, 68,
        78, 82, 90, 119, 127, 137, 144,
        175, 184, 185, 192, 193, 204,
        220, 235–37, 245, 261, 265
Westminster Theological Journal, 94,
        115, 121, 156

Westminster Theological Seminary,
        xxiv, 29, 32, 34, 36, 48, 49, 69,
        74, 76, 79, 82, 83, 85, 93, 99,
        100, 106, 125, 126, 136, 138,
        140, 141, 145, 170, 200, 213,
        240, 241, 258
Winona Lake School of Theology, 179,
        203n15
Wissinoming Presbyterian Church, 5
Witness, The, 154
Worldview, xxi, 58, 64–73, 102, 104,
        105, 139, 171, 192

Zephi, 180

Scripture Index

57188729R00175